Making IT

Making IT

The Rise of Asia in High Tech

EDITED BY HENRY S. ROWEN, MARGUERITE
GONG HANCOCK, AND WILLIAM F. MILLER

STANFORD PROJECT ON REGIONS OF INNOVATION
AND ENTREPRENEURSHIP (SPRIE)

Stanford University Press

Stanford, California 2007

Stanford University Press
Stanford, California

Printed in the United States of America on acid-free, archival-
quality paper

Library of Congress Cataloging-in-Publication Data
Making IT : the rise of Asia in high tech / edited by Henry S.
Rowen, Marguerite Gong Hancock, and William F. Miller.
    p. cm.
Includes bibliographical references and index.
ISBN-13: 978-0-8047-5385-2 (cloth : alk. paper)
ISBN-13: 978-0-8047-5386-9 (pbk. : alk paper)
1. High technology industries—Asia.   2. Information
technology—Economic aspects—Asia.   I. Rowen, Henry S.
II. Hancock, Marguerite Gong.   III. Miller, William F.

    HC415.H53M35 2007
    338.4'7004095—dc22   2006019062

Original Printing 2007

Typeset by G&S Book Services in 10/12.5 Electra Roman

STANFORD PROJECT ON REGIONS OF
INNOVATION AND ENTREPRENEURSHIP
THE WALTER H. SHORENSTEIN ASIA-PACIFIC RESEARCH CENTER

The Walter H. Shorenstein Asia-Pacific Research Center in the Freeman
Spogli Institute for International Studies sponsors interdisciplinary research
on the politics, economies, and societies of contemporary Asia. This monograph series features academic and policy-oriented research by Stanford faculty and other scholars associated with the Center.

Contents

Contents

Preface

This book is the product of an intensive international collaboration among experts from seven countries and regions as part of our program at Stanford University, the Stanford Project on Regions of Innovation and Entrepreneurship (SPRIE).

In the year 2000, in response to many inquiries from around the world, especially from Asia, on how Silicon Valley "works," the Stanford University Press published our book, *The Silicon Valley Edge*. This experience underscored to us the importance of developments on the other side of the Pacific. So beginning in 2002, we held meetings in Kyoto, Seoul, Beijing, Hsinchu, as well as at Stanford, to discuss the progress these regions were making in information technologies.

Out of those meetings and contributions by many authors in Asia comes this book. Its core is a set of chapters on particular regions. We settled on this structure because much of the activity in Asia, as in the United States, takes place in regional clusters. We focused on several regions in Japan, Seoul, Beijing, Hsinchu, Singapore, and Bangalore because they represent the most successful high-technology regions in Asia. There is less on Shanghai, the Multi-Media Corridor in Malaysia and other important regions than we desired, yet, still a wide array is covered.

Our topic is the information technology (IT) industry. As is true of many industries, different analysts use different definitions. For instance, the Organisation of Economic Co-operation and Development (OECD) often refers to the ICT, Information and Telecommunications Technology industry. We also include telecommunications in our definition of "IT." More troubling is software. That sector has two main parts, which are most simply defined as Products (things in boxes) and Services (increasingly supplied on-line). The problem here is with Services. Much human activity can be so classified, so we chose not to spend effort sorting this out. Our contributors adopted their own definitions.

Those looking here for an explicit model that accounts for how Asia rose will be disappointed. For example, one can reasonably maintain that the basic process at work during the period on which we focus, 1970–2004, was one of technology diffusion, principally from the United States and Japan to others. But the paths taken by this process varied greatly, country policies differed, and they changed over time. There are many parameters, some of them fairly well defined (e.g., numbers of "returnees" to Hsinchu in Taiwan) and others not well defined or measured (e.g., "entrepreneurship"). Even getting data on venture capital investment is more difficult than it might seem because of the different definitions in use across regions. Not least as an obstacle to having a unifying theory is the wide range of development of our set of countries from Japan and Singapore at one end to India at the other. The best we have been able to do — or anyone else for that matter — is to array the factors that seem to many industry participants and scholars to have been the most important. The result is some variability among the chapters — along with discussions of many of the same parameters as they were expressed in different regions. We hope this juxtaposition of analysis by Asian scholars who know and study their own regions — combined with cross-cutting consideration of several key institutions — will provide unique insight into the rise of Asia in IT.

Finally, we want to express our gratitude to our many authors who have been thoughtful in considering their own regions, which they know best, as well as entering into a fruitful dialog with colleagues around the Pacific. We owe thanks to many others: to supporters Chong-Moon Lee, Daniel Chen and the Industrial Technology Research Institute (ITRI) of Taiwan; to organizations that hosted meetings — namely, ITRI in Hsinchu, the Stanford Japan Center in Kyoto, the Zhongguancun Science Park; and to the Development Bank of Japan for its survey of high-tech clusters in Japan.

We also acknowledge the members of the SPRIE Advisory Board: John Seely Brown, Carmen Chang, Ta-Lin Hsu, Harry Kellogg, Leonard Liu, Robert Patterson, Chintay Shih, Richard Walker, David Wang, and Kyung Yoon. We are very appreciative of the SPRIE team at Stanford: Jen-Chang Chou, Rowena Rosario, and George Krompacky. And, not least, we are grateful to the faculty and staff of the Shorenstein Asia-Pacific Research Center of the Freeman Spogli Institute for International Studies at Stanford, which kindly provides our home.

Henry S. Rowen
Marguerite Gong Hancock
William F. Miller

Contributors

Jun-Woo Bae is a doctoral student in the KAIST Graduate School of Management. His research interests focus on internationalization and innovation of high-tech start-up companies. His doctoral dissertation is about international entrepreneurship and global start-ups. In addition, he has worked for a high-tech start-up company as a director of product marketing and project management.

Zong-Tae Bae is a professor of innovation and entrepreneurship at the Graduate School of Management in the Korea Advanced Institute of Science and Technology (KAIST). He received a B.S. degree in Industrial Engineering from Seoul National University in 1982, and M.S. and Ph.D. degrees in Management Science from KAIST, respectively, in 1984 and 1987. He was on the faculty of Management at the Asian Institute of Technology (AIT) in Thailand (1989–1991), and worked as a visiting scholar at the Graduate School of Business and Asia-Pacific Research Center at Stanford University (1999–2000). His research interests include various aspects of R&D and technology management and entrepreneurship. He has published articles in the *Journal of Business Venturing, R&D Management, IEEE Transactions on Engineering Management, Science and Public Policy, World Development, Journal of Product Innovation Management, Journal of Engineering and Technology Management, International Journal of Innovation Management,* and *Technovation.*

Rafiq Dossani is a Senior Research Scholar and Executive Director of the South Asia Program at the Asia-Pacific Research Center at Stanford University. He has done research on energy, the IT industry, offshoring, venture capital, and telecommunications in India, and on Asian entrepreneurs in Silicon Valley. He recently edited *Telecommunications Reform in India* (Greenwood, May 2002), reissued in October 2002 in India. Jointly with Henry Rowen, he has edited *The Prospects for Peace in South Asia* (Stanford University Press, 2005). Dr. Dossani is currently Project Director, jointly with Martin Kenney, of a project funded by the Alfred P. Sloan Foundation to study the globalization of business processes. He is also writing a history of the IT industry in India for the Stanford Project on Regions of Innovation and Entrepreneurship (SPRIE).

Kyonghee Han was a visiting scholar at the Department of Human and Community Development at the University of California, Davis. He also held the position of Research Fellow at the Institute for Social Development Studies at Yonsei University in Seoul, Korea.

Marguerite Gong Hancock is the Associate Director of the Stanford Project on Regions of Innovation and Entrepreneurship (SPRIE). She has served as a research director at the Stanford Graduate School of Business, Research Associate at the East Asia Business Program of the University of Michigan, and as a consultant in Boston and Tokyo. Active in linking academia, business, and government, she is a member of the Stanford Entrepreneurship Network, a teacher of executive education at Stanford, and an advisor to Joint Venture Silicon Valley as well as to government leaders on both sides of the Pacific. Co-editor of the *The Silicon Valley Edge* (Stanford, 2000), she is conducting research on greater China's role in the globalization of R&D, the leadership of China's high-technology companies, and a comparative analysis of benchmark indicators for Silicon Valley and high-tech regions in Asia.

Ken-ichi Imai is an expert on the economics and management of the firm, industrial organization, and the economics of technological change and innovation. After receiving his Ph.D. from Hitotsubashi University, Professor Imai became a professor and then Dean of the Graduate School of Business at Hitotsubashi. At the Stanford Japan Center, from 1991 through 2000, he served as the Director of Research as well as the Chairman of the Board from 1991 to 2002. During that period, he was also named a Senior Fellow of Stanford's Institute for International Studies and a Professor, by courtesy, of Stanford's Department of Economics. Professor Imai has been influential in both Japanese and international policymaking. In Japan, he has been one of the key policy advisors to the Prime Minister and the Minister of Economy, Trade, and Industry (METI). He has been an active member of the IT Strategic Council and the Industrial Structure Consultative Council. Abroad, as a member of the drafting committee for the OECD's Technology, Economy, and Policy Project, he has participated in discussions on the rules of conduct for multinational enterprises and global industry.

Martin Kenney is a Professor in the Department of Human and Community Development at the University of California, Davis and a Senior Project Director at the Berkeley Roundtable on the International Economy. His interests are in the history and development of Silicon Valley and venture capital. He is also studying the globalization of high-technology industries and venture capital and the movement of services to India (with Rafiq Dossani). He edited the books *Locating Global Advantage* (Stanford 2004) and *Understanding Silicon Valley* (Stanford 2000). Professor Kenney is the author or editor of five books and has published more than 100 scholarly articles. He has been an invited visiting professor at Hitotsubashi University, Osaka City University, Kobe University, the University of Tokyo, and Copenhagen Business School, and was an Arthur Andersen Distinguished Visitor at Cambridge University.

Jong-Gie Kim is a Professor in the Graduate School of Business and Economics in Information at Myongji University. His research interest includes urban and regional economics. He was a Professor in the Graduate School of Venture at Hoseo University. He was also the President of the Korea Environmental Technology Research Institute in Seoul and a Senior Fellow and Director of Research Coordination at the Korea Development Institute. Dr. Kim has conducted extensive research on regional development policy. He is the editor of *Regional Industrial Development Policy* (1987) and *Regional Development Strategy: A Study of Cheju Island* (1989). Dr. Kim received an M.A. in Urban Planning from the University of Washington and a Ph.D. in regional economics from Cornell University.

Kark Bum Lee is a Professor at the Information and Communications University, School of Management. Professor Lee received his Ph.D. in Sociology in 1983 at the Bielefeld University in Germany. His research interests include networks of venture industries, information and communications policy, comparative policies on B2B e-commerce, and R&D policy.

Noboru Maeda is Professor of Entrepreneurship at Osaka City University's Graduate School of Creative Cities. He graduated from Takasaki City University of Economics and holds an M.A. from Keio University and a Ph.D. from Kochi University of Technology. He worked for IBM and for the SONY Head Office in New York and Tokyo as Product Planner and Vice President in charge of Strategy. He is an Affiliated Fellow of the National Institute of Science and Technology Policy (NISTEP) and was an expert panel member of the Council for Science and Technology Policy of the Japanese Cabinet. In Japanese, he has published many books on start-ups, high-technology clusters, and global business.

William F. Miller is Herbert Hoover Professor of Public and Private Management emeritus, Graduate School of Business, Stanford University. He is also a Professor emeritus of computer science and Senior Fellow emeritus in the Stanford Institute for International Studies. Professor Miller has spent about half of his professional life in business and about half in academia. He is chairman of the board of Sentius Corporation and chairman emeritus of the Borland Software Corporation. From 1979 to 1990 he served as president and CEO of SRI International, as well as Chairman of the Board, CEO, and a founder of the David Sarnoff Research Center (now the Sarnoff Corporation). He was a founding director of the Center for Excellence in Nonprofits. Professor Miller was also vice president and provost, and vice president for research of Stanford. His most recent publication is *The Silicon Valley Edge*, co-edited with Chong-Moon Lee, Marguerite Gong Hancock, and Henry S. Rowen (Stanford, 2000). As both a graduate and an undergraduate, Professor Miller studied at Purdue, where he received the B.S., M.S., Ph.D., and D.Sc., honoris causa.

Sam Ock Park holds a B.A. and an M.A. in Geography, Seoul National University and a Ph.D. in Economic Geography from the University of Georgia. He is Professor of Economic Geography and Dean of the College of Social Sciences at Seoul National University. He served as the President of Korean Geographical Society, President of the Korean Regional Science Association, President of the Pacific Regional Science Conference Organization (PRSCO), and the Chair of the International Geographical Union Commission on the Dynamics of Economic Spaces. He also served as the Pacific Editor of *Papers in Regional Science* and is currently an editorial board member of six international journals. He has published more than 120 articles and 15 books on the locational dynamics of economic activities and regional development, especially on high-tech industries and regional innovation systems. He is the author of *Modern Economic Geography* (1999) and co-editor of *The Asia Pacific Rim and Globalization* (with Richard Le Heron) (1995).

Henry S. Rowen is Co-Director of the Stanford Project on Regions of Innovation and Entrepreneurship (SPRIE) and a senior fellow at the Hoover Institution, former director of the Asia-Pacific Research Center, and a Professor of

Public Policy and Management (emeritus) at Stanford's Graduate School of Business. In U.S. government service, Professor Rowen was Assistant Secretary of Defense, Chairman of the National Intelligence Council, and Assistant Director, U.S. Bureau of the Budget. He also served as President of the RAND Corporation. Professor Rowen's current research focuses on economic growth prospects for the developing world, political and economic change in East Asia, and the tenets of federalism. Among his numerous publications, recent noteworthy writings include "The Growth of Freedoms in China" (APARC, 2001) and "Catch up: Why Poor Countries are Becoming Richer, Democratic, Increasingly Peaceable, and Sometimes More Dangerous" (APARC, 1999). Professor Rowen is the editor of *Behind East Asian Growth: The Political and Social Foundations of Prosperity* (Routledge Press, 1999) and co-editor of *The Silicon Valley Edge: A Habitat for Innovation and Entrepreneurship* (Stanford University Press, 2000).

Jon Sandelin graduated from the University of Washington with a degree in Chemistry (1962), served four years as a Naval Officer on the U.S. Submarine *Ronquil*, and then obtained an M.B.A. from Stanford University. From 1984 to 2003, he worked in Stanford's Office of Technology Licensing (OTL), where he was responsible for licensing all forms of intellectual property, including inventions, computer software, and university trademarks. He also served as a consultant on the licensing of research-related inventions to other universities, nonprofit research organizations, and governments. He served two terms as a Vice President of the Association of University Technology Managers (AUTM) and is past President of the Association of Collegiate Licensing Administrators (ACLA). He is currently serving on the Public Advisory Committee for the U.S. Patent and Trademark Office (USPTO). Granted emeritus status in March 2003, he now devotes most of his time to consulting.

Chintay Shih joined National Tsing-Hua University as Dean of the College of Technology Management in 2004. Previously, Dr. Shih was a Distinguished Visiting Scholar at APARC of Stanford University. He is also a Special Advisor and former President of Taiwan's Industrial Technology Research Institute (ITRI) from 1994 to 2003. He serves as a Member of the Economic Advisory Committee of the President's Office, chairman of the Asia Pacific Intellectual Property Association (APIPA), and managing director of the Taiwan Electrical and Electronics Manufacturer's Association (TEEMA). Dr. Shih is a member of Board of Directors for TSMC and ITRI. Honored as a Fellow of the IEEE in 1992, Dr. Shih also received the Engineering Medal of the Chinese Institute of Engineering in 1995 and the First Medal of the Ministry of Economic

Affairs in 2003. Dr. Shih served as Science and Technology Advisor of Taiwan's Executive Yuan from 1998 to 2004, as President of the Chinese Institute of Engineers between 1998 and 2000, as the Chairman of the Taiwan Semiconductor Industry Association from 1996 to 2000, and as the Chairman of the Chinese Business Incubation Association (CBIA) from 2002 to 2004. He holds a B.S. from National Taiwan University, an M.S. from Stanford University, and a Ph.D. from Princeton University

Sang-Mok Suh is currently a visiting professor at Myongji University in Seoul. He is also Chairman of the Education & Culture Forum 21 and Executive President of the Dosan Memorial Foundation. From 1988 to 2000, Dr. Suh was a member of the Korean National Assembly, where he was active in legislation on economic policy issues, working primarily at the Finance and Economy Committee and the Budget Committee. In Korea, he served as Minister of Health as well as Senior Fellow and then Vice President of the Korea Development Institute (KDI). Dr. Suh also worked for the World Bank as an economist, specializing in the economies of South Asian countries. Dr. Suh received his Ph.D. in economics from Stanford University and a B.A. in economics and mathematics from Amherst College. Dr. Suh has written many articles and has participated in publishing several books on Korean economy and politics, including *To the Brink of Peace: New Challenges in Inter-Korean Economic Cooperation and Integration* (Stanford, 2001). In 2004 he published three books in Korean: *No Government Can Win the Market, From the Age of Politics to the Age of Economics,* and *The Korean Peninsula after Kim Jong-Il.*

Shoko Tanaka has written papers and articles on Japanese political economy and is currently Principal and Consultant with ST Research. She is also an Honorary Associate Fellow at the Institute for Japanese Technology Studies, University of Edinburgh, UK. She received an M.A. in International Relations and Foreign Studies from Sophia University in Tokyo and an M.A. in International Relations and Comparative Politics from Cornell University.

Toru Tanigawa joined the Japan Development Bank (JDB) after he graduated from Kyoto University at the Faculty of Law in 1973. During his nearly three decades at JDB, he worked in credit analysis, planning regional development projects, and international businesses. After he left the bank in 2000, he was a Visiting Scholar in the Asia Pacific Research Center at Stanford University, where he researched regional innovation systems and business incubation and advised start-up firms and entrepreneurs. In 2002, he was appointed as Professor and Deputy Director General of Art, Science and Technology Center for

Cooperative Research at Kyushu University. A leader for university-industry cooperation at Kyushu University, he has also written papers on regional high-tech clusters, business incubation, and university innovation.

Kung Wang is currently the Director and Professor at the Graduate Institution of Industrial Economics at National Central University (NCU) in Taiwan. He was General Director of Industrial Economics and Knowledge Center (IEK) of the Industrial Technology Research Institute (ITRI) from 2000 to 2004, and he established the market analysis and consulting service arm for ITRI. He has held numerous Taiwanese governmental positions, including Advisor for National Science, Director General of Science Based Industrial Park Administration (SIPA), and Commissioner of Fair Trade Commission — The Executive Yuan. In academia, he has served as the Director and Chairman of the Graduate Institution of Industrial Economics, and the Department of Business Administration at National Central University. Other positions have included board director for state-owned enterprises and venture capital funds, advisor to the Taiwanese government, and advisor to industrial and commercial associations. He holds B.S. and M.S. degrees from National Taiwan University and a Ph.D. from the Massachusetts Institute of Technology (MIT).

Yi-Ling Wei is a researcher at the Industrial Economics and Knowledge Center (IEK) in the Industrial Technology Research Institute (ITRI) in Taiwan. Serving as an industrial researcher, she has participated in the program of Industrial Technology Intelligence Service Program between 1996 and 2004, and has composed tens of research reports on the automotive, machinery, and semiconductor equipment industries. At present, she works on the program of "Industrial Cluster and Regional Innovation," which concentrates on analysis of comparisons and connections among Silicon Valley, Hsinchu, Shanghai, and other regions as well as government strategy for domestic industries toward innovative development.

Poh Kam Wong is currently Associate Professor, Business School and Director, Entrepreneurship Centre at the National University of Singapore. He obtained two B.Sc. degrees, an M.Sc., and a Ph.D. from MIT. He has published in numerous international journals on innovation strategy/policy and technology entrepreneurship, including *Organization Science, Journal of Business Venturing, Information Systems Research, IEEE Trans Engineering Management*, and *Small Business Economics and Information Society*. He has also consulted widely for international agencies such as the World Bank and the Asian Development Bank, various government agencies in Singapore, and many high-tech firms in Asia. His current research interests include management of technological innovation, innovation policy, and technology entrepreneurship. He has been a Fulbright Visiting Scholar at U.C. Berkeley and a visiting scholar at Stanford University. He is the founding chairman of Business Angel Network (Southeast Asia) and serves on the board of directors of several high-tech start-ups in Silicon Valley and Singapore. He chairs the NUS Venture Support Fund Investment Committee and is a panel member of the TEC, a public sector innovation fund in Singapore.

Yasuhisa Yamaguchi is the Chief Representative of Oita Office of the Japan Development Bank (JDB). Collaborating with Professor Toru Tanigawa, he has conducted research of eight high-technology regions in Japan. At JDB, he has a long experience in the analysis and financing of regional development in Japan, such as start-ups and urban and regional regeneration projects. His current interests are industrial cluster formation, management of technologies, and IP-based businesses and their financing. His recent writings include "Zero-Emission Manual" (Kaizosha, 2003), "Management Strategy of Kyushu University" (Kyushu University, 2004) and "Oita-gaku, Regeneration of Oita Region" (Akashi-shoten, 2005). Yamaguchi holds a B.A. from Kyushu University and an M.Phil. from Cambridge University.

Mulan Zhao is the Director of the Research Office at the Administrative Committee of Zhongguancun Science Park and has also served as the Commissioner of the Administrative Committee of Zhongguancun Science Park since 1991. She has conducted theoretical and policy research on Zhongguancun Science Park, including *Yearly Report on the Development of Zhongguancun Science Park (1992–2003)*, *Observation and Reflection on the Entrepreneurship in Zhongguancun Science Park (2001)*, *Investigation into the R&D Institutions Established in Beijing by Transnational Companies (1999)*, and *Research on the Regional Innovation Network in Zhongguancun Science Park (1997)*. She also participated in the drafting of *The Regulations on Zhongguancun Science Park*. Previously, she worked at Beijing Municipal Economic Restructuring Commission and the Research Office of the Beijing Municipal Government.

Making IT

1

An Overview

Henry S. Rowen

One of the most dramatic changes in the world economy over the past 30 years has been the rise of Asia in the information technology (IT) industry. The numbers are impressive. In 2003, the value of final consumption of IT goods worldwide, encompassing computers, telecommunications, and components, was about $1,500 billion with Asia (including Japan) comprising about 20 percent of this total. However, Asia produced about 40 percent of these goods, exporting the difference largely to the United States and Europe. The Asian shares of both consumption and production were rising rapidly.

The numbers for China alone are striking. Although still a poor country, it is the world's largest market for cell phones, the largest market for fixed telephone line subscribers, the number two market for cable subscribers, number two for PC ownership, and the number one growth market for broadband direct subscriber lines (DSL). On human capital, China is second only to the United States in terms of number of PhDs produced annually.

This book is about the causes and some major consequences of the rise of Asia in this industry. Geographically, we focus on six regions or countries: (1) Japan, (2) Teheran Valley in Seoul and Daeduk in Korea, (3) Zhongguancun Science Park in Beijing, (4) Hsinchu Science-based Industrial Park in Taiwan, (5) Singapore, and (6) Bangalore in India. In addition, we consider the clustering (or not) of companies within them. Other themes include expressions of innovation and entrepreneurship within this industry. We also discuss the roles of governments, venture capital, and university-business connections.

2   THE QUESTIONS ADDRESSED

In 1970, IT was a far smaller and less global industry. Several European countries and Japan each had national champion computer firms; Asian countries outside of Japan played negligible roles. IBM, the leader throughout the world, was the object of hostile action by the U.S. anti-trust authorities. Today, the scene is radically changed.

We ask these questions:

- Why has Asia emerged so strongly in this industry?
- What were the similarities and the differences in the strategies used among these countries?
- What accounts for their different specializations? How did their firms and governments decide what to make and how to make it?
- Why have companies clustered in particular localities?
- What were the initiating events in each cluster, and what has enabled them to grow?
- What roles have various institutions played — governments (national and local), universities, research institutes, financial institutions, legal professions, and so forth?
- What is changing? In particular, is Asia on the brink of forging ahead in important kinds of technology? If so, what are the implications for the United States?

Today's pattern is not fixed. Companies and governments in all these regions are trying to move up the value chain while others are trying to enter the marketplace and new technologies are emerging. There will be new companies and new industries. But there is also much path dependence; where the leading regions are today depends in good part on where they were yesterday and today's investments will strongly influence where they will be tomorrow. A region with established companies and an environment favorable for creating new ones is not easily displaced.

Although Asian regions are the focus of this book, implications for Silicon Valley and for the United States as a whole are also discussed. This is for several reasons. For one, Silicon Valley is widely seen as the most successful high-tech cluster in the world and a model for comparison and emulation. Another is that the United States, with Silicon Valley as the main hub, has been the principal source of ideas that have led to IT products worldwide, and the Asian nodes in the IT value-added chain are linked in many ways to it. A third is that the rise of Asia poses a challenge to Silicon Valley's eminence.

OPPORTUNITIES SEIZED IN A RAPIDLY
EXPANDING WORLD MARKET

A good place to begin is the vast expansion of the Asian economies and of world trade during the past several decades. World economic growth from 1970 through 2003 averaged 4 percent a year, and world trade growth 6 percent. Growth in much of East and South Asia was much faster. Japan's economy took off right after World War II and grew rapidly for 30 years. Next came the four "Tigers": Korea, Taiwan, Hong Kong, and Singapore, which grew at 8 percent annually for several decades. They have been followed by China's growing at 8–10 percent a year. These countries are having a large impact on the world economy, and so will India if it sustains its recently improved performance.

Essential to these excellent performances were several crucial developments: one was a large reduction in barriers to trade, both tariff and non-tariff, in the developed countries and then widely in Asia. These Asian governments decided to become engaged with the world economy, which is not to say that they thoroughly embraced free trade and investment; only Hong Kong did that. They also invested in training enough scientists and engineers to be able to exploit the excellent opportunities that came their way.

Parallel declines in transportation costs and a huge reduction in telecommunications costs have been major contributors to Asia's rise. For example, the monthly cost of leasing a telecom line between Los Angeles and Bangalore fell from $73,000 to $13,000 between January 2000 and January 2004. India's emergence as a significant player in the software and business processing sectors would not have been possible otherwise. Within China, Voice over Internet Protocol (VoIP) technology is being used. In 2004, domestic long distance calls often cost less than 5 cents per minute and those to North America 25 cents, down from $1 a few years earlier.

There has also been a shift in the composition of trade to lighter-weight goods and to services, with bits of information being the ultimate in low-weight commodities. The industries most affected by these developments—financial services, computers (hardware and software), and many kinds of business services—have created value-added chains that more easily cross national borders than ever before.

The information technology industry, including telecommunications, grew at about 10 percent a year for 25 years to comprise about 4 percent of total world output. It is well known that this growth was driven by advances in computer technology often summarized in Moore's law that states that the number of circuits on a chip doubles every 18 months to two years; it is less well known that even greater advances in storage technologies have occurred.

4   Thirty years ago a memory card stored 2,000 bytes; today a hard disk stores 200 billion bytes. Fiber optics and space technologies have comparably advanced communications capacities.

Although the basic technologies appear to have advanced steadily, from an industrial perspective they have been expressed in epochs—that is, discontinuities in the structures of industries associated with the production of radically new types of products and services, such as the shift from mainframes to workstations and then to PCs. Following came laptops, PDAs, cell phones, and other handheld wireless devices. The advent of the Internet marked a major new epoch resulting in enormous growth in electronic commerce. New business models have also been a striking aspect of this era, including those for search engines, auctions, business services, online games, and more. Major innovations also occurred in the distribution of products, including Dell's direct sales model.

A key change for the industry—with particularly large consequences for Asia—was the emergence of modularized standards in many goods. Modularization entails defining relatively simple interfaces among components of final products. The adoption of such standards meant that vertically integrated computer systems makers had to compete with companies whose products could be more cheaply put together from independent, specialized suppliers of hardware and software within value-added chains. This shift entailed both the dominance of some proprietary ones, especially the adoption of the Windows operating system–Intel microprocessor (Wintel) standard and Qualcom's CDMA telecom technology along with the adoption of open industry standards such as Java and Linux. Market advantages came more through supply-chain management, the creation of new business models, and the exploitation of brand names. Vertically integrated companies such as IBM and DEC disintegrated, and the industry segmented into discrete product categories such as chips, computers, operating systems, and applications software (Grove 1996). New firms entered the industry, many of them in Asia. The large resulting declines in costs and prices fostered a vast expansion in the use of computers.

U.S. government policies also created opportunities for new firms. Important early actions by it were the requirement that AT&T license transistor technology at a low price to all comers and that IBM unbundle its software from its hardware, an action that opened the way to an independent software industry. In addition, the U.S. government step-by-step fostered the development of the Internet, including financing. The ensuing dotcom boom resulted in a host of new online services and firms—many of which have survived the bust.

These developments gave openings to suppliers anywhere in the world, and U.S. firms moved fastest to fill the newly opened spaces. Of 176 semiconductor companies formed in the world between 1977 and 1989, 88 percent were formed in the United States with 55 percent of them in Silicon Valley. During this period, many companies also increased their original equipment manufacturing (OEM) purchases from Asia. The Asian companies had to compete on both cost and quality and many did so with great success. Since then, the roles of Asian firms have expanded greatly in size and in the complexity of their products.

Another factor working to expand the number of participating companies and enabling many of them to be competitive, although located far from the main markets, has been the slowing rate of innovation in some sectors. This has made the trajectory of new products more predictable. In personal computers, it became evident during the 1990s that the Pentium X would be succeeded by the Pentium X + 1, or at least by a chip whose main characteristic would be more circuits within an, at most, incrementally changed architecture. (Intel has recently signaled that this sequence has run its course.) Similarly, in the cell phone industry, independent designers and manufacturers could look ahead a few years and see that 4G will succeed 3G and so on; this enables them to anticipate the kinds of components that will be in demand, even though they can still have the challenge of correctly predicting the particular features that will be demanded by buyers.

The labor cost advantage of Asian workers over those in the developed countries was substantial, but while that advantage was necessary for their firms to enter this market it wasn't sufficient; they also had to meet quality standards. Initially, and to a large extent today, Asian companies worked to specifications set by their customers. Labor cost advantages are fleeting; as the textile and shoe industries show, they can quickly migrate to a yet lower-cost country. Growing competencies were necessary to secure an enduring role.

The IT industry is one of the most international of all. The Asian producers are connected across borders to each other and to consumers throughout the world. Companies in the smaller Asian economies produce largely for export, while those in the larger ones also have substantial or at least rapidly growing and potentially large domestic markets.

In this global marketplace, a de facto and not necessarily long lasting, division of labor emerged: the Americans, and to a lesser extent the Japanese and Europeans, conceived new *products* and offered large *markets* for them while the Asians assembled them. Their assembly/manufacturing, or *process*, function is not as simple as it might seem. Although breakthroughs in processes are less frequent than in products, they can accumulate over time to be properly regarded as revolutionary. A good example is the increase in the size and quality of flat-panel displays that in 30 years went from being digital-watch size to being

6   40 inches or more in size and hung on walls. This occurred largely through improvements within factories in Japan and then in Korea and Taiwan.

This leads to two different ways to view the global character of this industry up to now. One way is by the following sequence. An invention was made in the United States, perhaps in Silicon Valley; product conceptualization was done there; detailed design was also done there or, increasingly, in Taiwan or Korea; complex stages of manufacturing came to be done increasingly in Taiwan (but incorporating high-value components made by U.S. or Japanese firms) and less complex assembly in mainland China; the final product was shipped to users around the world. A similar sequence originated in Japan or Europe with, again, much of the manufacturing occurring in Asia. The software value-added chain was similar, with innovation and architecture being done in Silicon Valley or in another developed country, with application programming or services work performed in Bangalore or some other Indian region. Worldwide marketing and strategy in these sequences were managed by multinational brand-name companies in Silicon Valley, Austin, Tokyo, Helsinki, Seoul, or a few other leading centers.

An alternative representation of these global networks puts the manufacturing skills of Japanese and, increasingly, Korean and Taiwanese companies at the center of the picture. The value they add to final product has grown year by year as they have moved up various value chains for integrated circuits, flat-panel displays, computers, and mobile devices. Their efficiency drives costs down and thereby expands markets. They now outsource assembly operations to China and are reaching out to India for software and design services. Their research and development activities, as well as those of companies in other part of Asia, are advancing. It is safe to predict that Asia will move beyond manufacturing (itself important) to become a significant source of new products, although the timing for major innovations from there is uncertain.

A caution on this point is suggested by the common practice of reporting of gross revenues of production or of exports. Almost always missing in such reporting is the value created domestically associated with these large and growing exports. This is often modest. Thus, in Singapore, 25 percent of the value of its exports of disk drives in the mid-1990s was added domestically and China's domestic value added to its electronics and telecommunications exports in 1995 was also about 25 percent (and might not have grown much since for Singapore, Wong 2000; for China, Chen et al. 2003). These numbers imply that China's exports of $160 billion of high-tech products in 2004 probably required imports of $120 billion in goods and services.

Another caution is the changing nature of supply chains. Increasingly, they are not supplying standard products produced in vast numbers. Rather, more consumer products are being tailored for the often unpredictable changes in consumer tastes. Thus, Dell assembles its computers in the United States, close to the point of sale, in order to minimize the time between a specific customer order and delivery. Of course, as Asian consumers grow in importance its producers will have a locational advantage (Curry and Kenney 2004).

What has determined the different specialties of countries and regions? Historical legacies have been important. Given the combination of India's English-language skills, government policies that blocked the formation of manufacturing skills, and the fact that bits of information did not go through the (dreaded) customs system, it seems inevitable that India would specialize in software services. And Japan's high quality of manufactured goods stems from a long tradition of excellence in crafts.

However, one shouldn't push this line of argument too far. For example, it has often been argued that the near absence of new high-tech companies in Japan is the result of something basic in Japanese culture. We suggest that this view is mistaken. Rather, it is the consequence of actions taken by long ago governments, actions that more recent governments have been trying to change.

NATIONAL STRATEGIES

National technology strategies are the result of the aggregation of the institutions and policies that strongly influence and sometimes determine the role of the country in a range of industries, in our case the information technology ones.[1] These strategies have varied substantially among nations.

The label "national strategies" can be misunderstood. It encompasses not only the policies adopted by governments to promote this industry but also types of behavior that are embedded in society and not quickly changed. An example is the resistance of managers of Chinese companies to accepting control by investors or to merging with other companies.

Here are several key components of these strategies.

Education, Especially of Scientists and Engineers

All our countries did this, although educational opportunities in some were decidedly uneven. In India, education of a small elite to a high level was combined with massive neglect of elementary and secondary education for much of the population. In China, the Cultural Revolution disrupted education for over a decade, and even now many youths in rural areas have poor schooling opportunities. Nevertheless, the absolute numbers of people in these two countries with science and engineering education is large. India has 0.3 scientists

8
and technicians per 1,000 population, 42 out of 62 countries ranked by the World Bank in 1998; it was China at 1.3 per 1,000 (ranked 25th), but that small Indian proportion still came to 300,000 people. Taiwan, with a population of 22 million, graduates 80,000 physical scientists and engineers a year compared with 100,000 in the United States (National Science Foundation 2004, Table 2-36).

In Hsinchu Science-based Industrial Park in Taiwan, the number of returned experts and scholars (as they are called locally), many with advanced degrees, rose from 27 in 1983 to 4300 in 2001, by which time they constituted 4.5 percent of the workforce. In Zhongguancun Science Park in Beijing, in 2002, of 400,000 high tech workers 5,800 had doctorates, 29,000 had master's degrees, and 155,000 had bachelor's degrees.

A pattern that emerged strongly and early in Taiwan was for graduates in science and engineering to go to the United States for advanced degrees, stay to work, and then, for some, to return home, encouraged by government-supplied benefits.[2] (Some "returnees" had not originated in Taiwan but in other parts of Greater China.) This pattern spread to other places, notably India and China. Japan, notably, did not participate strongly in this process. Significantly, not only did the flow of students from Taiwan to U.S. universities peak in the mid-1990s, so did the flow from Korea and China as well (Hicks 2004).

In all of these countries, improvements in the universities are causing more students to stay at home for advanced training. The number of people graduating with PhDs in Korea increased three-fold from 1986 to 1999, in Taiwan it went up four-fold, and in China it increased by forty times (National Science Foundation 2002, Tables 2-29, 2-36).

Acquiring and Developing Technologies

Asian governments had also to decide on technology strategies. Crucial was building the capacity to absorb foreign technologies and, in due course, go beyond them. This entailed acquiring skills in engineering and science including computer science, solid-state physics, integrated circuits, optics, software-related algorithms, robotics, advanced manufacturing, and more. The emphasis was on industrial applications, although Japan invested in a wide swath of sciences, as did China and India on a smaller scale. Korea (centered on the companies) and Taiwan (centered on government research labs) also invested substantially in technology development—investments that have recently produced a remarkable rise in patents registered in the United States.

Governments also had to decide where to have such research done: at universities, research institutes, or companies? The mix varied. Outside of Japan and then Korea in the 1990s, few Asian companies were capable of doing technically advanced research; in all these regions there was a preference for using separate institutes rather than universities because it was easier to focus them on commercially relevant projects. Thus, the Industrial Technology Research Institute (ITRI) in Hsinchu became the major research center of Taiwan, and Korea set up the Korean Institute for Science and Technology (KIST), although much research came to be done in Korea's big companies, notably Samsung and LG. In China, the Chinese Academy of Sciences has been the preeminent institution for scientific and technical research, and major companies have spun out of it after liberalization of the economy began in 1978. Its universities have also assumed commercial roles with, for instance, Tsinghua and Beijing Universities each owning around 200 companies.

In the model in which most research is done in separate institutes, universities focus on teaching. This has been especially true in India. The Indian Institutes of Technology (IITs), the source of many excellent bachelor-level engineers, until very recently have not been research centers; hence, many IIT graduates have come to the United States for advanced degrees.

Trade and Foreign Direct Investment

The main task in Asia was that of catching up. "For most countries, foreign sources of technology account for 90 percent or more of domestic productivity growth." The G-7 countries have carried out 84 percent of world research and development spending (Keller 2004).

Engaging in trade and having foreign companies invest are the two of the most prominent and effective ways to acquire technologies. At one extreme, none of our six countries or regions has come close to adopting a laissez-faire strategy on trade and investment. At the other extreme, until the early 1980s, China's trade was modest and until the mid-1980s, India was almost economically autarkic. Singapore was unusual in adopting a policy of free trade and relative openness to foreign investment — although being selective in the companies it allowed in. In general, in Asia as widely elsewhere, domestic products were widely substituted for imports, a preference that was only gradually reduced over time. Exports were promoted with success but this policy meant having a large flow of imports to enable the exports to occur. (Recall the previous observation on low domestic values-added.) Much learning accompanied trade, especially from importing (Keller 2004).

There was a trade-off. Some industries were seen as strategic for reasons of national security, or because their technologies were advancing rapidly and there might be opportunities to jump in, or because there were perceived export opportunities. The computer industry in the latter part of the 20th century was the quintessential example; it met all of these criteria. Recently, the biotechnology industry is widely seen as strategic, as is the nascent nanotechnology industry. The perceived disadvantage of openness was that foreign competition would keep local industries from developing and cause loss of control to outsiders of industries deemed strategic. The policy response was sometimes to protect them at the price of forgoing learning advantages by restricting imports and, even more, by restricting direct investment.

All our Asian governments favored electronics early. Consumer electronics products were good fits because they involved labor-intensive manufacturing in which they had a cost advantage and, being light in weight, they were cheap to transport. Computers had similar advantages. Demand was growing rapidly in the advanced countries, transport costs were low, and the modularization of supply chains enabled their companies to find segments in which to compete.

Governments found many ways to promote chosen industries: supporting research, favoring local producers in their purchases, erecting tariff and non-tariff barriers against imports, directing banks to lend to designated firms, excluding investments by foreign companies, supplying land at cheap rates, financing companies spun out of government laboratories, and more.

Faced with the choice of protection versus allowing foreign direct investment, Singapore made inviting multinational companies (MNCs) central to its strategy. Taiwan encouraged them early (but then became less inviting), with some early arrivals from Japan and the United States plus Philips from Europe. India was long hostile to all foreign firms. Notably, in the 1960s it drove IBM out of the country. However, Texas Instruments got established in Bangalore in the 1970s and helped seed that high tech cluster. Japan and Korea remained hostile to MNC investment well into the 1990s; they favored the alternative of licensing foreign technology. During the 1990s, China allowed MNCs in on a large scale, usually on condition that they bring technology. Acquiring technology and business know-how from abroad via direct investment has become a key part of its strategy. This pattern shows the error of any assertion that MNC investment is necessary for high-tech development — but it surely helps.

Telecommunications Investments

As mentioned previously, advances in telecommunications technologies have greatly helped the geographical diffusion of the IT industry. It is hard to imagine India's software services sector progressing so much without the large decline in international telecommunications prices. The adoption of cell phone technology in China, now with 350 million users, is having profound economic and social consequences; there are corresponding large investments in fixed lines. Korea is the most broadband "wired" country in the world, and Japan is fast catching up.

This surge in telecommunications positions some Asian countries to lead in new services and technologies. Korea and Japan lead in online gaming. China has been trying to establish its own Internet security standard — a move that has been deferred because of objections by foreign firms and governments — but this story is not over. With growth in its markets and, especially, if China brings new technologies to the table, its influence will grow in the setting of global standards.

Finance and Industry Structure

In Chapter 10 (on venture capital in Asia), Kenney, Han, and Tanaka assert that this institution as known in the United States has barely existed in Asia outside of Taiwan. Asian financial institutions, predominantly banks, have favored well-connected and established companies. Thus, Japan created the keiretsu, the main banking system; Korea the chaebol conglomerates; under government instruction, banks in China supported companies spun out of the Academy of Sciences and leading universities; Taiwanese banks supported companies with links to government research institutes; and in Singapore, government-linked companies received preferential treatment.

There wasn't much room in these systems for young, high tech firms whose founders lacked personal connections. Risk capital of the type needed by such companies — equity — was in short supply. Some companies got started when established ones invested in the new field of computers. Others started in a traditional way by using entrepreneurs' savings and support by family and friends. Governments, national and local, often met this need through directing that banks make loans on favorable terms or by supplying real estate. Taiwan was an early mover in recognizing the need for organized risk capital and others followed during the 1990s, but even now the venture capital sector is widely under-developed. Its most developed part consists of venture capital arms of established companies that make strategic investments in start-ups.

Different financial policies and institutions were associated with — and reinforced — different industrial structures. Japan already had large and medium-sized companies, some of which moved into IT, and its financial system was oriented toward supporting them. (Sony was unusual in being a new entrant after World War II.) Korea's path was similar. In contrast, Taiwan's IT industry was long dominated by small, agile firms, and it developed the most advanced venture capital system in Asia. With the main exception of Tata Consulting

12   Services (TCS), India's software industry consists mostly of companies created during the past 20 years. Not coincidentally, India had a relatively advanced stock market.

Creating High-Tech Regional Clusters

Regional clusters are a ubiquitous economic phenomenon. They are driven by agglomeration economics, a term that denotes the several kinds of benefits that firms in similar lines of work can derive from proximity. The pioneer economist on this topic, Alfred Marshall, and more recent scholars, Paul Krugman and Michael Porter among them, have examined this phenomenon (Porter 1990; Krugman 1991). Broadly, there are effects external to a given firm such that actions by one firm spill over to the benefit of others. There can be learning benefits when specialists move from one firm to another or even talk informally. Having common suppliers is another mechanism, and having a local venture capital industry helps with the financing of new companies. (Venture capitalists, who supply expertise along with their money, tend not to be in the advance guard for they arrive when there is business, but their arrival strengthens a region.)

Whether or not companies in a given industry segment locate closely together depends on the net effects of several factors. Kenney and Florida identify five main ones: (1) transportation and communications technologies and networks; (2) time and speed demands in specific markets; (3) pricing pressures; (4) knowledge capabilities; and (5) proximity to customers (Kenney and Florida 2004). The resulting patterns among parts of the IT industry vary greatly and have changed over time. The enormous growth of the IT industry and changes in its technology, including the aforementioned modularization, fostered much specialization at the level of the firm. For many products, the logistic supply chain from R&D and design at one end to sales and after-market services at the other became distributed globally among specialist firms. At the same time, many firms at similar stages in these supply chains became concentrated geographically. Silicon Valley is the outstanding example. Although it began by doing everything from innovating, designing, manufacturing, marketing, and managing globally, its scope has narrowed to doing research, global marketing, and other headquarters functions, as manufacturing and much design work moved elsewhere. This has led to the saying (only a little exaggerated): "There is no more silicon in Silicon Valley."

In Asia, Taiwan has created a major cluster of computer manufacturing and design companies; Shanghai is developing a silicon foundry and design complex, and Beijing (in Zhongguancun Science Park) a software cluster. Singapore has become the center of a Southeast Asia hard disk drive production complex, most of whose companies are U.S. based and do their design work in Silicon Valley (McKendrick 2004).

A cluster has workers with the right skills and a supporting infrastructure of suppliers; upstream and downstream companies locate there; and specialists in finance and accounting arrive. The local government learns the needs of its companies, creates favorable conditions for them, and lobbies for support from the central government. Such interactions entail feedback processes in which strength begets more strength, with the result that products are brought to market more quickly and more cheaply than otherwise would happen.

Sometimes universities or major research institutes are foci for a knowledge cluster (as distinct from a production cluster) and help create and sustain it, as MIT and Harvard have done in Boston, Stanford and UC Berkeley in Silicon Valley, KAIST in Daeduk in Korea, ITRI in Hsinchu, and the Academy of Sciences and major universities in Beijing. Universities benefit from the clusters they foster by placing graduates in local companies and getting feedback of technology and gifts from them.

After asserting the distinction between knowledge and production clusters, a qualification is needed. Technical progress in the flat-panel display industry has been driven substantially by learning by doing in factories with major contributions by equipment makers and material suppliers; the result has been a huge increase in the size and quality of products. In this case, knowledge was accumulated through production (Murtha et al. 2001).

With varying degrees of success, most of our Asian governments tried to promote their IT industries by offering incentives to companies to locate or start up in them, incentives that include real estate and tax benefits and consulting services. They often establish formal incubators. Motivating them was the marked success of several U.S. companies, notably around Boston and in Silicon Valley. Hsinchu Science-based Industrial Park in Taiwan, created by the government, was an Asian pioneer and remains the most successful in nurturing home-grown companies, some now large. It began with original equipment manufacturing (OEM) for foreign firms, progressed to doing original design manufacturing (ODM), and was the origin of Taiwan's highly successful semiconductor fabrication industry. Korea set up a science research park in Daeduk, south of Seoul. China has many such parks, both national and local; its national "Torch Program" has 53 parks throughout the country, the most famous of which is Zhongguancun Science Park (ZGC) in Beijing (a cluster already developing before it was so designated).

14   Incubators can be especially useful when the wider economy poses obstacles for start-ups, which is why they are so prominent in mainland China. They are favorable microenvironments, and experiments can sometimes be tried in them. In Chapter 7 on Zhongguancun Science Park, Zhao points out that it was originally named the "Beijing Experimental Zone for Development of High and New Technological Industries." New rules could be tried that, if successful, might be applied nationwide.

It is far from true that governments are responsible for the formation of all regional clusters. The Boston and Silicon Valley instances were market, not government created and among our set in Asia, the Teheran Valley software cluster in Seoul (in a district named after a sister city) is a case of spontaneous creation. The main Indian regions—Bangalore, Mumbai, Hyderabad, New Delhi, Chennai, major cities where educated workers were in ample supply— were also basically formed by the market, not by government. However, as Dossani notes in Chapter 8, it was only after the Indian government created the first software park with satellite communications that Bangalore took off.

With the exception of a group of semiconductor companies in Kyushu and media companies in Tokyo, high-tech clusters are not prominent features of the Japanese landscape. This is probably a consequence of Japan's having few young companies.

Clusters can last a long time, but there is no good reason to assume that they are eternal. Growth eventually slows as empty space is filled, land prices increase, congestion worsens, and—sometimes—changes in technology and the marketplace disfavor a region's companies. (The fate of Detroit in the auto industry is such a case.) New clusters can then arise. Dossani reports in Chapter 8 that infrastructure limitations are holding back—but clearly not yet stopping—the further growth of Bangalore. A shortage of land is limiting the growth of Hsinchu so the Taiwanese government is developing science parks elsewhere. Silicon Valley faces inherent constraints—notably high housing prices—as well as competition from increasingly skilled companies is Asia.

One might reasonably ask if the arrival of low-cost, digitized information is making clusters obsolete. Is the future likely to see companies spread out more geographically? Activities that do not have to be in high-cost localities, such as Silicon Valley, have been moving elsewhere for a long time, and no doubt this migration is aided by low-cost telecommunications. Many production activities are widely dispersed today. Perhaps the arrival of technology that virtually erases distance will change this pattern, but there is reason to doubt that clustering will soon end, especially at the high end of value chains where the creation of ideas and the making of key business decisions entails much face-to-face interaction.

These factors have led to very different patterns in our countries.

Japan entered the IT era already industrialized and with a rapidly growing economy. It had a major consumer electronics industry and went on to create formidable positions in integrated circuits, computers, flat-panel displays, and capital equipment. It spends one of the world's largest shares of GDP on R&D, about 3 percent. After a short period of new company formation after World War II, during which Sony was one of the few successful new high-tech firms, it accomplished this largely by renewing its existing companies, such as Toshiba, Fujitsu, NEC, and Hitachi. Foreign firms were largely excluded. (However, IBM was "grandfathered.") Instead, it licensed much technology from abroad. Its national universities and research institutes were of high quality, but the professors were civil servants and the universities were kept distant from industries. As Maeda points out in Chapter 3, Japan had found the right solution for catching up. However, the difficult decade of the 1990s has produced a change in strategy to one of greater openness. In addition, new companies are beginning to be formed, mostly by sponsored spin-offs from established ones.

Korea's strategy emulated that of Japan. So did its types of IT products. Its now successful companies were not as well established at the outset as the Japanese ones, but government support together with prodigious efforts, high savings, and a mercantilist impulse to export created an array of strong ones. It, too, kept foreign firms out and relied heavily on licensing. It is a remarkable fact that in the early 1990s Korean companies paid U.S. companies almost as much for technology in fees and royalties than the rest of the non-OECD (Organisation for Economic Co-operation and Development) world combined. And it was also spending an increasing share of GDP on research, an investment reflected in a sharp increase in U.S. patents. After an initial spate of company formation, Korea, too, had few start-ups. Today, however, its strategy is also shifting as a result of the traumatic financial crisis of 1997–1998. It is more open to foreign firms, has invested heavily in broadband communications, and is trying to create a more entrepreneurial system, a topic discussed by Bae et al. in Chapter 6.

Taiwan's strategy was to create a strong export-oriented manufacturing industry, initially with technology and direct investment from the United States and Japan, and with a focus on improving manufacturing processes. Its strength had long been in electronics and came to be concentrated in computers, integrated circuits, and, recently, wireless technologies and flat-panel displays. By the 1990s, foreign MNCs were switching to buying from domestic Taiwanese firms. Still later, after 2000, Taiwan has encouraged foreign firms to set up R&D operations there, with some success. Over time, there has been a large increase

16   in R&D, also, as in Korea, reflected in a marked increase in U.S. patents making Taiwan fourth in the world after the United States, Japan, and Germany.
The industrial base had initially consisted of many small firms, some of which
have become large, along with companies spun off from its Industrial Technology Research Institute (ITRI). This highly entrepreneurial system created the
most advanced venture capital industry in Asia. Recently, its companies have
become increasingly engaged in triangular trade with, on one side the OECD
countries, and, on the other, assembly operations on the mainland.

Singapore's strategy was to have foreign firms bring technology and market
know-how to make goods for export. Having succeeded, its strategy has shifted
to a more home-based innovation and entrepreneurial one. This change, undertaken in characteristically thorough Singaporean fashion, entails promoting entrepreneurship and attracting entrepreneurial talents from overseas,
reducing government red tape, fostering a venture capital industry, and encouraging small enterprises.

China's high-tech strategy has been, as noted previously, to train many technologists, to help scientists and engineers in research institutes and universities to form companies, to make state-owned companies more market focused,
and to encourage foreign firms to bring technology and management skills
through direct investments. Foreign MNCs and Taiwanese companies are responsible for a large proportion of China's IT exports. Large investments in
telecommunications have been a core part of the strategy. The Zhongguancun cluster in Beijing has made a remarkable transition from a set of government research institutes, state companies, and universities in a non-market
system to a more dynamic, market-driven place with many new companies.

India has not had much of an IT strategy—which, given its bureaucracy, is
probably a good thing. Only when liberalization gathered momentum, and
with small investments in satellite communications, did the software industry
take off. The opening of the telecom sector is having beneficial effects as is reform of the financial sector that has boosted the venture capital industry.

THE SIX REGIONS EXAMINED MORE CLOSELY

Hsinchu, Zhongguancun, Bangalore, Singapore, Teheran Valley, and
Fukuoka illustrate the large differences among Asian high-tech clusters.

Hsinchu Science-based Industrial Park (HSIP)

The preeminent example of a successful, government-created cluster, one with
little direct foreign involvement, is HSIP in Taiwan. It was set up in 1980 in a
place with established universities, and since then the government has invested

about $1 billion in it. As Shih, Wang, and Wei point out in Chapter 4, almost all Taiwanese IT manufacturers came to be located in the 88-kilometer-long belt from Taipei to Hsinchu.

HSIP was a key part of an economic development strategy from the 1960s centered on Taiwan's becoming engaged with the world economy (as were those of the other small Asian "Tigers"). In Taiwan, it combined government support for industries deemed to fit its potential along with reliance on markets.

The Industrial Technology Research Institute, ITRI, had been set up earlier, in 1973, as Shih et al. put it "after referring to the experience of Korea and recommendations of European and U.S. experts." It acquired CMOS technology from RCA in 1976, established a demonstration IC factory in 1977, and spun off the UMC company in 1980, the first of ITRI's spin-offs. It was followed by the Taiwan Semiconductor Manufacturing Company (TSMC) in 1987, the Taiwan Mask Corporation in 1988, and the Vanguard International Semiconductor Corporation in 1994. By the end of 2000, 31 companies had come out of ITRI.

Benefits to companies in HSIP included import duty and tax exemptions, rent subsidies, bilingual schools, preferential credit, and research support. The government supported the financing of start-ups by supplying seed money. HSIP companies paid-in capital went from NT $43 billion at the beginning of park operations (1979) to NT $910 billion in 2002.

Graduates from Hsinchu's universities became the core of the local workforce, while the government offered inducements to former students who had gone abroad for graduate studies and to work, to return. By 2003, there were 4,318 returned students and scholars; 119 companies had been founded by them.

In 1996, ITRI set up the Open Laboratories for collaborative research and incubation services. Its Incubation Center, set up in 1996, by 1999 had 33 young firms and had spun out 7. Altogether, from 1973 to May 2002, 5,000 ITRI staff had moved to the private sector in HSIP.

At the end of 2002, HSIP had 335 companies (282 domestic and 53 foreign) with total sales of NT $70 billion (U.S. $2 billion) in the IC, PC and peripherals, communications, optoelectronic, precision-machinery, and biotechnology industries. The supporting infrastructure for the IC industry in 2000 had 140 design houses, 8 wafer material suppliers, 4 mask manufacturers, 16 wafer foundries, 48 sealing enterprises, and 37 testing organizations.

Taiwan now faces, as do other countries in Asia and elsewhere (including Silicon Valley) a challenge from a mainland China that today has a modest level of industrial technology but is determined to move up the value chain and has the requisite assets for doing so. It has major assets in being Chinese and having a good knowledge of global markets. Its largest challenge is in creating more valuable intellectual property.

Zhongguancun Science Park

Zhongguancun in Beijing (ZGC for short) has the largest concentration of high-tech companies in China. It had 12,000 of them in 2002 with more than 400,000 workers and revenues of $29 billion. Sixty-four percent were in the information technology industry with the rest in advanced manufacturing, biomedical, materials, and energy sectors.

Shortly after China's reform movement started, in 1980, a researcher, Chen Chunxian, left the nuclear laboratory of the Academy of Sciences to set up the first privately funded research and technology institute in Beijing. He was followed by other entrepreneurial scientists and technicians. A striking fact is that from 1950 to 1978 the Chinese Academy of Sciences "which owned the all the technology . . . in all that time did not sell one product. Since the reforms, 40,000 products have been passed to companies and have been put on the market" (Segal 2002; Zucker and Darby 1995).

By the end of 1987, the Academy had spun out several dozen high-tech enterprises, including the computer companies Legend (now called the Lenovo Group) and China Daheng Information Technology. Most were PC related. By the end of 1987, hundreds of enterprises were crowded along a ten-kilometer long street called Zhongguancun Electronics Street.

During this period, Tsinghua University and Peking University also established their own high-tech enterprises. There were two main motives: one was to supplement low salaries and enable them to keep the best people; the other was to move technology from laboratories to the market. University-funded enterprises have played an important role in Zhongguancun's development.

In 1988, the Beijing Experimental Zone for Development of High and New Technological Industries was set up with the power to try new rules and institutions on a small scale before moving them nationwide. It became known as the Zhongguancun Science Park. It was small, with only 10,000 workers in 1989, but about to take off. Waves of start-ups in ZGC coincided with, and depended on, the rapid growth of China's IT industry. The domestic market was greatly aided by large government investments in telecommunications; paralleling this was China's rapidly growing participation in the global IT market. Essential to this strategy has been an openness to foreign goods and direct investments.

At the beginning the region had important assets and daunting liabilities. The main assets were many scientific and academic institutions, a well-educated and talented group of scientists, a willingness to experiment, and supportive governments, both at the national level and locally. The liabilities, also substantial, included poorly defined laws, including those for intellectual property rights; an array of state-owned companies; bureaucrats micromanaging state-owned enterprises; weak managerial skills; isolation from world markets; and an underdeveloped financial system, especially for risk capital.

Essential to the successes that followed were networks of relations that connected families, the new entrepreneurs, the institutes from which they had come, universities, local governments, and national ministries. The institutes supported their spun-off entrepreneurs in several ways, including financially; local officials for the most part worked to reduce regulations, arranged for finance usually in the form of loans, and did not interfere excessively in the inner workings of many enterprises; universities set up enterprises and maintained close ties to their graduates; and national ministries kept research money flowing to institutes and universities.[3]

As a result, ZGC has become the largest high-tech R&D center in China. From 1988 to 2002, the number of its companies grew from 527 to over 12,000 (of which perhaps 4,000 are not really viable) with total employment going from 10,000 to 420,000. In 2002, 55 of these companies were listed on an exchange and 33 had sales of over U.S. $12 million per year. ZGC firms have 40 percent of the market for software applications and 50 percent of the PC hardware market. It has the No.1 Chinese portal, Sina.com, and the top online game firm in China, ourgame.com. It is the leading place in biotechnology, new medicines, and new materials, but these industries are still small.

At the lower end of company sizes, 4,300 had sales of less than $120,000. This is far from an equilibrium situation. For example, 82 percent of the 4,300 small companies lost money in 2002. The number of firms in ZGC is likely soon to shrink.

Today, China gets most of its technology from overseas with multinational companies as the main source. In ZGC, they account for 43 percent of the Park's total revenues and 78 percent of its exports. Actually, what is being transferred is not only technology in a narrow sense but also design techniques, know-how, and managerial skills, including knowledge about how to solve problems and how technologies are related to each other. Investments made by multinationals are a kind of package that combines money, products, technology, talent, managerial skill, and ideas. Many are establishing research centers; for example, Intel, Microsoft, and Novozymes (a Danish enzyme company) have set up such centers there. China's poor protection of intellectual property discourages the transfer of advanced technologies, but it has not prevented a large and sustained flow of direct investment by foreign firms.

Another major source of "capital" is the human kind, embodied in returnees from overseas. It is remarkable that the total of 4,900 such people (3,500 since 1999) had started 1,800 companies in ZGC by 2002. In two years they had started two companies each working day on the average.

20   ZGC has both advantages from being in the capital city and disadvantages. The advantages include a large flow of money from government ministries both directly for procurement and indirectly through support of institutes and universities, and it benefits from the idea incorporated in the Beijing Experimental Technology Zone, "What is not forbidden by the law is not against the law." Two examples: one is that a venture capital limited partnership can be established, and the other is that the scope of a business need not be clearly defined. The disadvantages lie in the notion that from the vantage point of "Silicon Valley—or Shanghai or Shenzhen—there are benefits in being far from the emperor, whether he is seen as being in Washington or Beijing."

Regarding ZGC's human resources, about half the workforce has at least bachelors degrees. There are over 30 online job service web sites, and 42 percent of workers find jobs through them. The job market is a classical free market one: employment at will by both the employee and the employer. Those who don't measure up are dismissed, an especially effective measure in the early development stage when other enterprises offered lifetime employment. Worker mobility is high; two-thirds of employees working for less than three years have changed jobs. (A rate this high may be dysfunctional.)

The ZGC system has changed. Tax advantages were reduced in 1993 and the Academy of Sciences ended its support for many successful firms in order to support new ones. Competition has been encouraged among domestic firms and has intensified with the arrival of foreign ones. Corporate forms were adopted with ownership being expressed through stock issuance, appointment of general managers, and boards of directors.

Close university links to business are also under pressure for change. Universities and research institutes within ZGC run their own ventures, often holding 100 percent of their equity. Problems inherent in these connections have become evident. Lack of clarity in ownership law has been a barrier to raising capital. Efforts are underway to clear up enterprise ownership, to enable university-founded enterprises to operate independently, and to set rules so that teaching, research, and operation of university-founded enterprises can be mutually beneficial and not in conflict. This requires a separation of the teaching and research missions of universities from commercial activities that may be socially useful but that can detract from their core missions.

China's financial system, especially for risk capital, remains underdeveloped. Despite the fact that the Beijing Municipal People's Congress enacted the first local law allowing limited partnership venture capital firms, this organizational form has yet to be adopted, and a mergers and acquisition market has just begun to emerge. High-tech companies are listed in Hong Kong or, ideally, on NASDAQ. (A recently established NASDAQ-like second board at the Shenzhen exchange might provide a domestic market listing for young firms in a few years.) In 2002, 21 ZGC start-ups received RMB 830 million (U.S. $100 million) of venture investments. Foreign investors are still dominant; 12 local institutions supplied 29 percent and 7 foreign ones supplied 71 percent.

In little over 20 years ZGC has come a long way. Its future depends on that of China, which faces challenges in building institutions, including those of law and finance and those for the creation of technology. Given its record, it will overcome them.

Bangalore

Dossani reports in Chapter 8 that, contrary to a widespread belief, the Indian software industry did not originate in Bangalore. Companies in Mumbai, which had advantages in finance, labor, communications, legal, and accounting services, and marketing and sales skills, began it.

However, Bangalore's importance has grown while that of Mumbai has declined. By 2000, firms in Bangalore were responsible for 25 percent of the country's software exports. Several factors were responsible for its rise, including an agreeable climate (it is called the "Garden City"); the presence of the Indian Institute of Science, defense companies strong in electronics, aeronautics and machine tools; access to a large supply of educated engineers; few labor troubles; and, not least, being the site chosen in 1985 by Texas Instruments (TI).

The central government was long a huge obstacle to Indian modernization, notably including its near economic isolation from the world. Policies began to improve in the mid-1980s and, especially, after 1991. Contributing to Bangalore's being a late entry in the software industry was poor government planning and "an endless bureaucracy" that produced inadequate infrastructure. That began to improve only after 1999.

Despite these local deficiencies, TI was influenced by the central government's decision to undertake the Software Technology Park (STP) system, beginning in Bangalore, in 1985. It supplied satellite bandwidth to software exporters, mainly to overcome the country's poor telecommunications. In the mid-1980s Bangalore's superior telecommunications helped to attract Infosys and Wipro, now leading firms, from their original locations in Pune and Mumbai.

TI's decision not only demonstrated an MNC voting for Bangalore, it also showed the industry a new and more profitable way of doing business by pioneering offsite software development. Its satellite links to the United States

22   allowed programmers to work in India real-time for the first time, a method quickly copied by Indian firms that moved in.

Although it necessarily competes with other regions, in a recent survey of software firms in Bangalore, almost half cited the availability of high-technology professionals and the presence of research institutes as the most important reason for their being there. It appears that agglomeration economics are finally at work.

Singapore

As described by Wong in Chapter 5, Singapore's strategy was based on the rule of law, good government services, free trade, stable macroeconomics, and attracting foreign investments in industries that would export. The government has played an active role in many sectors, both through direct ownership and through quasi-state enterprises. Its compulsory savings system (the Provident Fund) is a major source of finance. It has a strong educational system and a highly competent and honest government. It is a story of great success.

Wong portrays Singapore's high tech industry as having undergone several transformations. First, there was an industrial take-off in the early 1960s, originally based on technology transfer from MNCs. The mid-1970s brought the rapid growth of process technologies within the MNCs and the growth of local suppliers. In the late 1980s came more applied R&D on the part of MNCs, public R&D institutions, and local firms. The fourth phase starting in the late 1990s entailed a shift to high-tech entrepreneurship, deeper R&D, and the creation of technology.

As part of the effort, as Wong puts it, "to re-make Singapore into a competitive knowledge-based, entrepreneurially driven economy," in 1999 the government created a U.S. $1 billion fund to boost the venture capital industry (much of which has been invested abroad), allowed entrepreneurs to start ventures in their homes, relaxed listing requirements on the stock exchange, and changed the bankruptcy law. The government is also encouraging professionals to learn about entrepreneurship, attracting talent from abroad, reducing government regulations, and improving start-ups' access to capital.

What has been accomplished? It is too early for definitive results, but there is more spending on R&D and measures of innovation have increased. The role of MNCs remains strong as they sustain strong export growth. A remaining obstacle is the paucity of mechanisms like the small business support schemes in the United States in which government funds match private funds or an organization like ITRI in Taiwan to help bridge the gap between R&D and seed investment by venture capitalists or angel investors. In addition, the scarcity of aggressive leading users of new technologies makes it difficult for Singaporean start-ups to have their first customers at home; they need to go abroad from the beginning.

There is now the view, beginning to be acted upon, that changing the mindset of Singaporeans toward entrepreneurship might require fundamental changes in the educational system, social security, and the public sector recruitment system, all politically sensitive matters.

Teheran Valley and Daeduk

In Chapter 6 Bae et al. report that the first attempt in Korea to develop clusters was to build industrial complexes in the early 1970s to house heavy and chemical industries. These parks did not include such functions as education and R&D.

The first science and technology park, Daeduk Science Town, was started in the early 1980s by moving existing government-sponsored research institutes from Seoul. At first it had only R&D institutions but "Daeduk Valley" (by analogy with Silicon Valley) emerged in the mid-1980s when researchers created new companies.

The other principal high-tech "valley," Teheran Valley, developed in the southern part of Seoul from the mid-1980s. Although the government helped by building physical infrastructure, Teheran Valley is essentially a market phenomenon. In the mid-1990s, about 100 IT-related companies located along Teheran Road, and by 2002, many IT firms, start-ups, venture capital firms, and corporate HQs were set up. About 2000 IT, Internet-related, mobile communications, and foreign IT companies are located there, and many financial institutions, banks, and trading companies have moved in. It is becoming the center for innovation and incubation in Korea. About half of all the software and IT ventures in Korea are there. The proportion of venture capital–funded companies there is relatively high. Its companies specialize in culturally related products such as content, multimedia, design, fashion, and service industries such as venture capital, banking, IT services, and consulting. Teheran Valley has the image of a highly innovative and knowledge-generating region and being the center of entrepreneurship in Korea.

Bae et al. list several problems:

- Entrepreneurs' poor knowledge and experience with markets, management, law, and finance. Founders are usually engineers weak in marketing.
- A small domestic market requires them to look abroad; this is a barrier but one that can have long-term advantages.

- Poor support habitats, networks and social and financial infrastructure with high costs, traffic congestion, and no major universities or R&D institutions.
- Poor understanding of the nature of ventures and entrepreneurship. These are risky ventures with high rewards for the successful. The prevailing social attitude still punishes failure, a deterrent to taking risks.
- Inefficient or heavy-handed government policies. The government has played a positive role by developing technology, transferring technology from government research institutes to small and medium-sized enterprises (SMEs) and supporting joint R&D between SMEs and institutes. However, it should abandon its system of "authenticating" venture firms, the market can handle this function.

Bae et al. conclude that the key needs are more successful entrepreneurs as role models, more education on entrepreneurship, a higher quality of ideas generated (with links to government helping), internationalization, more skillful venture capitalists, and the expansion of infrastructure.

Japan (Fukuoka and Other Clusters)

Japan is different. Its companies have a remarkable capacity for renewal and for absorbing and advancing new technologies, in contrast to the model (Taiwan and India) in which new firms have done much of this. However, Japan's success in catching up with the most advanced nations together with its economic stagnation during the 1990s has caused many people to question the appropriateness of the Japanese model for the future.

Imai describes four regional clusters in Chapter 2.

One is the Aichi-Toyota Cluster, a combination of integral type innovation and strong entrepreneurial leadership, based on just-in-time production. Toyota aggressively outsources and fosters start-ups in its group.

A second, Fukuoka's New Semiconductor Cluster, has engineers who have spun off from large companies, Sony's engineers who concentrate on "post PC" technology, and Kyushu University professors who are creating new linkages for the "Silicon Sea-Belt Project," which links the island to Taiwan and Northeast China.

A third is the Sendai cluster around Tohoku University, which is strong in material development.

Tokyo is also a major cluster, the center of a cultural phenomenon captured in the phrase "Japanese Cool," which includes pop music, electronic appliances, architecture, fashion, animation, and cooking. Exports of such products have tripled during the past decade to over $12 billion. He sees the Tama area northwest of Tokyo as the first planned industry cluster in Japan and as a guideline for clusters nationwide. Companies there, unlike many in Japan, focus on product innovation instead of process innovation. Sixty percent of their leaders have created spin-offs from larger companies. Many of these companies are in such "cool" industries as manga comics, animation, and games. It is only natural that workers for these companies tend to be in Tokyo, in the same way that lawyers, accountants, patent attorneys, programmers, and consultants have also migrated there.

Tanigawa, based on a survey by the Development Bank of Japan, puts Japanese clusters into three categories:

- The Silicon Valley model—Sapporo, Yonezawa, and Fukuoka
- The traditional Japanese cluster model—Aichi and Hiroshima
- The maverick or unique cluster model—Sendai, Kyoto, and Tokushima

He sees the key concepts in Silicon Valley–type clusters as "entrepreneurship," "organic horizontal collaboration beyond business connections," "open environment," and "international linkages." Aichi, the home of Toyota and the world's leading auto cluster, represents the traditional Japanese model with historical continuity, distinctive craftsmanship, and vertical relationships. The companies have a commitment to each other that has sustained the cluster's vitality. Its future depends on Toyota's performance. The mavericks, Kyoto, Sendai, and Tokushima, each differ. Some Kyoto start-ups, Kyocera, Omron and Rohm, became global companies within one generation. Local horizontal collaborations are rare, and the region seems closed-minded. The core of Sendai is Tohoku University, whose resources have attracted public and private research organizations. Start-ups from the university have begun to appear, but their business volume is low and networking is weak. The Tokushima region has two large companies: Otsuka Pharmaceutical (chemical products manufacturer) and Nichia (electrical manufacturer) and not many others.

Yamaguchi reports on a study of the Fukuoka area carried out by the Development Bank of Japan (DBJ) and the Fukuoka Industry, Science, and Technology Foundation (IST) with the cooperation of Kyushu University (KU). Its focus was its semiconductor cluster that now accounts for 35 percent of Japan's domestic semiconductor production. This concentration has been fostered by local universities, foundations, and research centers. It is attracting large semiconductor manufacturers and R&D and design centers. Ninety percent of these firms are local, and many are spin-offs from larger firms. They engage in much horizontal collaboration on R&D and market development. Yamaguchi reports that decision-making within the large companies is moving from Tokyo headquarters to regional branches, such as those in Fukuoka, in order to speed decisions. He asserts that Fukuoka is becoming more like Silicon Valley.

Running through this book are the themes of innovation and entrepreneurship.

Innovation

Innovation — being first to market with a new product, process or business model — is the source of gains in productivity, sustains existing firms and leads to the formation of new ones and sometimes new industries. At their root, innovations are based on wholly new physical or conceptual discoveries — for example, inventions, such as the discovery of the transistor effect by scientists at Bell Labs in 1947. The modification of desktop computers into laptops making them smaller and portable was an innovation, again an important one. Both inventions and innovations involve ideas but not all ideas are equal. Some, called "basic," such as the transistor effect, open up wholly novel, at first poorly understood, paths for development, while others, called innovations, such as the shift from desktops to laptops, are steps along more-or-less defined paths. Another type of innovation involves a different class of ideas — new business models (such as Internet auctions) or enterprise resource planning software.

Inventions and innovations are ideas, and ideas have a dual character. One aspect is that they are public goods in that one person's use of an idea does not mean less of it is left for others to use, and potential users can't be excluded, unless it is kept secret or potential users are legally prevented from doing so. Their other aspect is that ideas with potential commercial value need work to enable them to reach the market; their creators or others familiar with the idea often have an advantage in carrying this work forward. Here geography enters. For example, biotech clusters form close to where leading biologists work, usually in major universities. This is because the biotechnology industry is close to its scientific roots. In the early 21st century this is less true of the IT industry but it still holds.

Broadly, Asia has not been the source of information technology inventions (although Japan has made some). The story is very different regarding innovations in products, process, and business models. Much of the most influential process innovation has been the just-in-time production system, pioneered by the Toyota Motor Corporation, which has transformed manufacturing worldwide. Indeed, a major strength of high-tech Japanese companies, and increasingly of Korean and Taiwanese ones, is manufacturing process innovations. Japanese companies have also made important consumer electronics product and service innovations such as the Sony Walkman and NTT DoCoMo's cell phone service. The visual arts, including anime and computer games, are successfully exported innovations. An important business model innovation is TSMC's IC foundry service, in which the maker of chips is not tied to any particular design.

It is a mistake to think only in terms of breakthroughs in technology. Consider advances in manufacturing processes. The flat-panel display industry illustrates this point (Murtha et al. 2001). All the technologies in use were invented in the United States, but the industry developed in Japan (with some U.S. companies participating). Most of the innovating U.S. firms were also looking for commercial breakthroughs; they failed to discern them, and so didn't invest in manufacturing. The Japanese firms settled for incremental advances and did invest. The result was a large cumulative advance over 30 years in the size of flat-panel displays from digital watches and calculators to laptops to wall-mounted TVs. This was done largely through the accumulation of know-how in factories by skilled engineers. Rapidly growing demand and large investments by Korean and then by Taiwanese companies enabled them to break into this market in the 1990s. Murtha et al., conclude that this rapid progress was made possible through continuity of effort with incremental improvements, learning on the job, and speed of response as prices kept falling rapidly.

Imai also discusses the Japanese system of innovation in Chapter 2. It has been described as "incremental" in manufacturing with a focus on high quality. However, he sees the distinction between "product" and "information" as becoming blurred. Both express "patterns," and the difference is that when one is "expressed" on steel you get a car, but when one is expressed on a computer disk or a paper you get software. The former involves a material on which it is difficult to "write," and therefore requires complementary materials, expertise, and trained skills. Not only digital architecture and design are needed but also continuous, incremental manufacturing innovation.

The architecture for automobiles, cameras, printers and other consumer electronic products is of the "integral type," which differs from the "module type" architecture of Silicon Valley. "Integral" architecture requires a delicate coordination among interdependent parts and devices whereas in the modular type, as described previously, the parts work independently. The modular system leads to an open industrial network, while the integral system, dominant in Japan, is found in closed networks among a few companies. Both types coexist, depending on the degree of industrial maturity and the prevailing technological and market structures. Japan is moving toward modular systems and is opening its markets, but the integral system core will remain because it

28   is vital for Japan's ability to innovate. Integral systems do not quickly respond to rapid change, but have an advantage in sectors where the rate of change is moderate.

Japan's strategy has been to invest heavily in R&D, develop excellent technologists, become a master of manufacturing, and learn how to market successfully to the world. Its mercantilist drive to export and to keep most foreign firms out led it instead to license technologies that its good engineers then improved. Its brands acquired worldwide reputations. Its large domestic market, second in the world to that of the United States, makes it unique in Asia — although China's market is catching up fast. However, government efforts to make breakthroughs in technology, including creating a distinctive computer operating system, did not go well. Altogether, it was a successful strategy for rapidly catching up; Japan became dominant in consumer electronics, but not in computers. This was — and is — an effective system for industries whose technologies are changing at a moderate rate, not too fast and not too slow, not a characteristic of the IT industry between 1970 and 2000. Now, with the rapid spread of broadband and with the convergence of consumer electronics and computers, Japan has forged ahead in some sectors.

Its main challenge, similar to that facing the United States, is how to respond to rapidly growing China (and India) and one of its responses is also similar: offshoring of manufacturing to Taiwan, Southeast Asia, and, increasingly, China. Japan's so far unmatched competency in manufacturing is being challenged by the rapid rise of manufacturing competency at low costs in other Asian nations, notably in Korea and Taiwan and, recently, in China. There is a wide under-appreciation (at least in the United States) of the importance of such competencies. They are less visible than those in products that consumers can inspect, but they determine their cost and quality.

Almost all non-Japanese Asian companies have been technology and business followers. The development patterns of the software industry in Ireland and India clearly show both the "advantages and disadvantages of being a follower" (Arora et al. 2000). One can grow without a broad set of technical abilities and many markets, and technical and business model uncertainties are reduced. The negatives can include many followers competing with consumers reaping most of the benefits while leading firms can block the way up the value chain. Nonetheless, followers can create a basis for moving up the value chain to creating innovations.

As Dossani writes in Chapter 8, "From its origins and until about 1990, India's software firms played the role of a follower of the U.S. software industry, competing for the same work that similar U.S. firms were doing — though they mostly obtained work lower down in the value chain relative to comparably sized U.S. firms and moved up the chain more slowly than U.S. firms. When compared across a time scale, it appears that there is a follower-leader relationship between American and Indian software services firms, with a lag of about a decade."

An important measure of innovative capacity is patenting, especially in the United States, the global patenting standard. Japan has been consistently second only to the United States in the number of total patents and is among the top countries in IT ones. It leads the world in R&D spending as a share of GDP; this ratio has consistently been higher than in the United States or Germany.

The rise in patents from Taiwan and Korea is striking. In 2001, Taiwan was fourth in the world, ahead of Britain and France, and South Korea was eighth. According to Fuller, "three Taiwanese firms have ranked among the top 30 worldwide holders of U.S. high technology utility patents in recent years" (Fuller 2005). [However, patents vary in importance, and a recent ranking of countries by "influential" patents puts Taiwan at 11th and Korea at 12th (Narin 2003).] Hu and Jaffe conclude, "Korea and Taiwan are graduating from imitation to innovation. The number of patents granted in the U.S. to these two economies has been growing rapidly. On per capita patent count terms, Korea and Taiwan are catching up with the lower-tier developed economies. Anecdotal evidence suggests that knowledge diffusion from the advanced economies, particularly U.S. and Japan, played an important role in this catching up process" (Hu and Jaffe 2001). Using patent citation data, they found that Korea is closer to Japan while Taiwan draws for ideas about equally between Japan and the United States. This difference correlates with the high incidence of direct investment and capital goods flow from Japan to Korea and the high incidence of people flows between Taiwan and the United States.

Another indicator is the output of scientific publications. This is growing rapidly in Asia. In Chapter 5 Wong shows growth rates for Korea, Singapore, and Taiwan during the 1990s ranging from 12 to 20 percent annually. Citations of scientific papers originating in non-Japanese Asia have also been growing rapidly. The starting point was low, but they grew by six times between 1995 and 2002 (National Science Foundation 2004, Table 5-52).

Another innovation indicator is the flow of money for technologies as measured by fees paid for licenses and royalties among unaffiliated entities. In 2001, Japanese firms paid American firms $1.8 billion, and the reverse flow was $400 million. In that year, Koreans paid Americans $740 million while receiving from them $18 million; Taiwanese firms paid U.S. firms $230 million while receiving $2 million in return (National Science Foundation 2004). However, the pattern of net payments is shifting markedly in the direction of a more equal balance.

30   The main strategic challenge faced by companies in non-Japanese Asia, especially Taiwanese and Korean companies, is becoming more innovative. They are being squeezed from below in costs and increasingly in skills by China and above by the United States and Japan in technology. Their strengths are substantial: for Taiwan, being ethnically Chinese gives them an edge in the world's lowest-cost manufacturing place and its largest future market; its firms are adaptable, and they have close links with their Japanese and U.S. counterparts. Companies are doing more research, and ITRI is doing more advanced work. There may be a larger role for its universities in the overall innovation system. As for Korea, its large firms already support high levels of R&D.

According to Wong, in the early 1990s the Singapore government began shifting from promoting the acquisition of technology to supporting its diffusion and innovation. It also increased public spending on research and development, especially on the life sciences, and increased tax incentives for MNCs to do R&D in Singapore. There are several indicators of results from these efforts. Singapore's ratio of R&D spending to GDP went from 0.2 percent in 1978 to 2.2 percent in 2002, a ratio higher than shown by the U.K. and the Netherlands. The number of research scientists and engineers per 10,000 workers went from less than 30 in 1990 to 74 in 2002. Its publications per capita in 1998 exceeded those of Japan and came close to those of France and Germany. By 2001, Singapore's level of patents per capita was higher than those of France and the U.K., although behind Taiwan, Germany, Japan, and the United States. Although foreign firms received over half of Singapore-origin patents during the 1990s, the share of those held by individuals and domestic firms had grown.

A major technology decision was to make Singapore into a life science hub. A U.S. $1 billion fund was created for several new life science research institutes, to co-fund R&D projects by global pharmaceutical firms, and the building of a new life science park, Biopolis. This move implies reduced dependence on the IT industry, in part because of the rise of China and India in that sector.

Wong writes: "The key challenges to sustaining the development of the innovation system appear to be finding ways to augment the small absolute size of the talent base, greater investment in basic research capabilities of local universities, and improving policy support for technology commercialization activities through new programs such as the SBIR and STTR program in the United States. The need to intensify investment in precompetitive basic research and infrastructures is especially important for the biotech cluster as well as certain ICT subsectors, such as wireless and broadband applications."

Entrepreneurship

Entrepreneurship is an elusive topic. It can be defined broadly to encompass people who take initiatives within companies, but we prefer to identify it with those who create new companies. In Joseph Schumpeter's view, innovations always involve the building of new plants and equipment and are introduced by new firms and by new men (Schumpeter 1939).

Not all companies start in the proverbial garage as Bill Hewlett and David Packard did. Some of today's large IT firms, such as Tata Consulting Services (TCS) in India and Hynix and Samsung Electronics in Korea, were founded by established companies. Others have come out of government laboratories, such as Legend computer (now Lenovo), which came from the Chinese Academy of Sciences and the Taiwan Semiconductor Manufacturing Company (TSMC) which came from Taiwan's ITRI.

Entrepreneurship is found in all societies and business sectors. This is how a large part of the world's peoples — farmers, shopkeepers, artisans, peddlers — earn a living. So if entrepreneurship is ubiquitous, how can one explain the fact that in high-tech industries there are wide variations in its incidence among regions? In Asia, Taiwan led the high-tech entrepreneurial procession. and then, with a lag, followed China and India. Japan and Korea were different; they did not create many high-tech companies. Nor has Singapore yet created many successful ones.

The best answer seems to be that these large differences come from established institutions being reinforced by government policies. Thus, in Japan the overarching goal of its postwar leaders was catching up with the United States, and it chose to guide its enterprises "administratively" to this end by preserving in modified form the economic control system introduced during World War II. Finance, labor laws and practices, foreign trade, and investment were all oriented to their support. The result was an internally consistent system of education, finance, labor, trade, foreign investment policy, and tax laws that enabled its established companies to renew themselves. There was little room in this system for new companies.

Korea also established a successful system of large firms that the financial sector, labor system, policies on trade and foreign investment, and an array of regulations sustained. Taiwan's small to medium-sized firm structure is also relatively stable. Successful systems tend not to change; why should they?

But some countries have undergone large systemic changes. China's has been most dramatic, from state/collective ownership and extreme autarky to a system with rapidly growing private ownership and huge foreign direct investment. This shift came from the dramatic failure of the original model along

32   with a compulsion to develop quickly. India, less dramatically, is also undergoing large changes — partly motivated by the example of China. Poor performance during the 1990s and the financial crisis of 1997–1998 brought significant policy changes in Japan and Korea, respectively. Singapore's shift toward
promoting home-grown entrepreneurship is less derived from a crisis than
from a concern about long-term dependence on MNCs.

One can reasonably ask how much difference it makes that a country does
or does not have many new high-tech firms. The effects are hard to estimate.
Acknowledging the limits to our understanding, we can identify three mechanisms by which entrepreneurship provides social benefits. One is that new
firms reallocate resources, especially human resources, from old sectors to
new ones. A competitive market causes the shrinkage and disappearance of
existing firms and the creation and growth of new ones. (For example, there
has been high turnover in the leading U.S. companies, including those in the
Fortune 500, during the past 50 years.) Of course, established companies can
reinvent themselves, as they have in Japan.

Start-ups also speed the entry of new technologies to the market. This is especially important in rapidly changing industries — "high-tech" ones — where
there can be large first-mover advantages. While large firms are the wellsprings
of technological advance, they are often faced with more opportunities than
they can or want to exploit. Established firms have older physical and human
capital, and their workers may lack the skills to take quick advantage of a new
technology. Since their managements are often focused on meeting the expressed needs of current customers, they usually select opportunities that fit
those needs (Christensen 2003). Many start-ups have their beginnings in exploiting large firms' unused ideas, sometimes sponsored or founded by the
originating firm but often by people who leave to build new ones — with occasional disputes over the ownership of intellectual capital. Because there is
always uncertainty about which ideas will be winners, the best way to select
them is for many firms to be started and for the market to choose.

Viewed broadly, there is a two-way interaction between large and small
firms; not only do small firms emerge from large ones, through sponsorship,
through people with the relevant know-how leaving large firms for smaller
ones, or through ideas getting into the air (Brown and Duguid 2000). A famous
example of the last of these mechanisms is the set of innovations made at
Xerox Park that ended up being exploited by others, such as the young Apple
Computer Corporation. Things also work the other way, with large companies
buying small ones to get their technology and talent.

A third function of new firms is motivational. They give entrepreneurs opportunities to demonstrate their skills as well as opportunities to make more money than as employees of large firms. This motivation helps to account for the high incidence of new company formation by scholars who returned to ZGC. There are, of course, risks. They can be reduced if a person can return to the firm she has left, or readily join another one; in short, an open labor market supports entrepreneurship.

Indian IT Entrepreneurship

As noted in Chapter 8, the environment for entrepreneurship for many years was unfavorable. The government favored state-owned enterprises (SOEs) and it was unwilling to give out downstream contracts to the private sector. By design it stifled the private sector. For example, CMC's legally sanctioned monopoly on the maintenance of all IBM's machines in India after IBM's withdrawal in 1978 meant that private firms could not obtain this business.

The pioneering software firms were branches of existing companies. Tata Consulting Services (TCS), long the leader, was part of the Tata empire. IT firms that have grown large dominate the Indian market (the top 10 have a 70 percent market share), and they inhabit their own domains: TCS in Mumbai, HCL in Delhi, Satyam in Hyderabad, Infosys and Wipro in Bangalore. Small firms and the diaspora were not important initially and so were unable to help in the flow of information.

Bangalore was not a uniquely friendly place for entrepreneurs but it had a large pool of engineers and the legacy of the learning derived from the early presence of Texas Instruments. Returning nonresidents prefer Bangalore, and they have become conveyors of new ideas and capital. Foreign firms also prefer it, partly because they do not need local venture capital and partly for its climate and its labor pool.

India's system of finance had positives and negatives. Positive was the ease with which small firms could get listed on the Bombay exchange. Negative was the existence of restrictive rules on venture capital until 1999; the firms that became leaders were financed by their parents. After the 1999 reforms and along with their increasing wealth during the Internet boom, nonresident Indians (NRIs) in the United States began to invest in start-ups. Dossani reports that a high proportion of the founders of the eight largest IT firms received some of their education in the United States. He argues that the importance of NRIs is likely to grow — although it is unlikely to be as important as that of the overseas Chinese to China.

Before the 1990s, after several decades of excellent performance by the Japanese industry, any observer noting that Japan had few new high-tech companies would probably have met with indifference. Success spoke for itself. (Rowen and Toyoda 2003). Large firms had thrived under the keiretsu system of inter-locking relationships among suppliers, manufacturers, distributors, and financiers, along with associated phenomena of low labor mobility and an em-phasis on bank rather than equity financing. This system's strengths include lower transaction costs and more company investment in training from stable relationships. Its virtues are strongest in industries where technical change oc-curs at a moderate rate and there is a long development time horizon, as in au-tomobile manufacturing. This has not been characteristic of the IT industry.

As Maeda writes in Chapter 3, "For the past three decades, almost no technology-oriented start-ups, like Sony, Honda and Kyocera, have succeeded. The reason is clear: high-tech start-ups were not needed in the catch-up phase. It was better not having them for the total effectiveness of the economy. Even if some start-ups were born, they died." He goes on to say: " 'What to make' is be-coming more important than 'how to make' and start-ups are needed for this."

Financial and legal barriers have impeded start-ups that could help un-leash the economic gains from innovation. In particular, small businesses have had difficulty in securing funds. Firms that rely on such intangibles as intellectual property—as necessarily do most high-tech firms—are handi-capped by banks' biases toward firms with more employees, fixed assets, and loyal main bank relationships.

Telecommunications policies, reflecting the Japanese preference for es-tablished institutions, were long an obstacle. NTT used its monopoly power to charge high access fees, thus discouraging demand for networked comput-ers and use of the Internet. With less regulation, increased competition had a galvanizing effect, including the introduction of broadband capacity and In-ternet usage. NTT's DoCoMo's i-mode, introduced in 1999, gave rise to sev-eral successful new ventures, such as Rakuten and Access, which provide con-tent, applications, and services through cell phones. In 2000, nearly half of all people using the Internet in Japan (a total of 47 million) did so through cell phones. In short, when the rules changed, so did behavior.

Kenney et al. report in Chapter 10 that several initiatives over the years to cre-ate a venture capital industry failed to fund many new companies. The govern-ment tried to help. In 1995, small and medium-sized enterprises became eligi-ble for money as well as data from the government; it was made easier to form venture capital firms, regional banks and corporations set up venture capital affiliates, and some independent venture capital firms also were formed. At that time, Softbank attracted much attention. It had made a lot of money from investments in U.S. start-ups and then invested heavily in more than 600 Japanese start-ups. In response to the arrival of the Internet, two new stock markets were founded: Mothers, in 1999, and NASDAQ Japan in June 2000. Both attracted more high tech-related companies as a percentage of listings, but the numbers were small and NASDAQ Japan stopped operating in August 2002. As Kenney et al. report in Chapter 10, "In the collapse of the tech bubble, Japanese venture capitalists such as Softbank experienced enormous losses. Since then, there has been little investment in start-ups." Potential entrepreneurs in big firms are unwilling to risk resigning to establish smaller firms. "The difficulties venture capital has had in taking root in both Korea and, especially, Japan seem to be intimately linked to the overall configuration of those societies and their political economies." They conclude that the start-up firms lacked deep technical expertise and did not attract the best young engineers; that few Japanese venture capitalists were technically savvy former entrepreneurs or experienced managers; that other needed parts of an entrepreneurial habitat, such as experienced lawyers, accountants, and other network constituents, never existed in Japan. As a result, "when the downturn came, few start-ups were able to survive and like the New York phenomenon of 'Silicon Alley,' the 'Bit Valley' habitat simply disbanded."

How deeply embedded is this low incidence of entrepreneurship? Imai writes that the people who led the industrialization during the Meiji Restoration became known as the zaibatsu entrepreneurs. They read the state of the world, foresaw the path to capitalist industrial development. and ensured that information and capital flowed to the necessary places. "Entrepreneurs riding the wave of change can reap huge profits, and these 'hero entrepreneurs' have indeed existed in Japan . . . the inflation-adjusted income of the zaibatsu leader Yataro Iwasaki is thought to be greater than that of Bill Gates today."

After World War II, the new, young business leaders aggressively exchanged information among companies. Lacking experience, they found that obtaining information on other companies allowed them to anticipate developments, decrease uncertainty, and ward off dangers. There was also a surge of company listings on the Tokyo Stock Exchange. There were many people in established companies alert to Schumpeter's "new combinations." They enabled Japan to catch up to the more advanced countries in a few decades.

Imai contests the customary definition of entrepreneurship (that used by the editors of this book) that holds it to mean the creation of new organizations, by reference to a Neo-Shumpeterian school that defines it to be alert-

36 ness to new opportunities — that is, discovering new combination of goods and services — and argues that this takes place within established Japanese companies. Indeed, it is evident that this happens to an impressive extent. He writes that the middle-ranks of large Japanese companies have many people with an entrepreneurial spirit that serve as reserves for spin-off ventures. A major reason that so few such ventures have been created is that Japanese human capital had high opportunity costs in alternative uses. Elite engineers and managers became embedded in the traditional system and helped make the Japanese system rigid. However, he sees Japan's hierarchical system, centered on politicians and bureaucrats, as losing its hold on power. The traditional system centering on "Nagata-cho" (politicians) and "Kasumigaseki" (bureaucrats) is weakening. Networks of experts, including young politicians and knowledgeable bureaucrats, have begun to operate at the intersection of public and private domains. Imai asserts that "Japanese entrepreneurship is now ready for the next stage."

With MITI (now METI) in the lead, there have been many actions since the mid-1990s to remove the obstacles to entrepreneurship inadvertently created in earlier years, including making it easier to start firms, increasing labor mobility, deregulating capital markets, creating stock markets with less restrictive listing requirements, being more open to foreign firms, and reducing barriers to university-business connections.

Maeda reports that "something new and important is happening. In the so-called lost decade, tens of spin-off companies grew fast, with some going to IPO." This is a corporate "spin-off" phenomenon rather than a new, independent, "start-up" one. He writes that in Sony, for example, if an outstanding performer wants to spin-off, the management will support him and seek to ally with him. Of course, spin-offs occur in all clusters, but in Japan it appears that they are more likely to be sponsored by the originating company than elsewhere. The new high-tech entrepreneurs are elite engineers who are good at strategic collaboration with big companies. They are producing profits from the first year and use government funds cleverly. They aim at early stage IPOs, have close relations with professors, and seek global collaborations from an early stage.

There are still less than 50 of these companies, not enough to change the structure of industry. Maeda finds that that their founders' primary interest is not getting rich via stock options but to be specialists free from lay-offs. Some of their employees may leave in five years to set up their own companies. Moreover, young professionals with MBA degrees, many with experience in the United States, are starting to leave big corporations and government offices like METI. In Maeda's simulation, by the year 2010, about 450 R&D-focused start-ups will have had IPOs and about 80,000 engineers will be working in them. This number of new firms would be about 10 percent of the total listed, which Maeda asserts would be a critical mass.

In sum, although it is evident that Japan has found it difficult to move from a successful catch-up strategy to a moving-out-in-front strategy in the IT industry, it is undergoing significant changes, which, if sustained, might restore Japanese entrepreneurship to the heights reached in the Meiji era.

Entrepreneurship in Taiwan

Taiwan has arguably demonstrated the most successful entrepreneurial activity among our regions. Until the 1990s its IT industry was dominated by a large number of small firms. For instance, in the Hsinchu Science-based Industrial Park the average number of workers per company was 37 in 1991. They were fast followers of technology, making components and assembling products for foreign companies on an OEM basis. They developed close relations with Japanese and U.S. companies, in which the U.S. companies would supply product specifications and some technologies and would take the resulting products. This sector developed a flexible, adaptable structure with a fine division of tasks among companies.

Taiwan got into the electronics business in the 1950s by making radios, TV sets, and calculators. Many of these companies were financed from profits made in traditional industries (textiles, chemicals, hotels, lumber), and many failed. However, skills developed in producing calculators were valuable in making the transition to computer making, often done by new firms.

The movement of skilled professionals has long been an important part of Taiwan's rise. It led the way in inviting engineers with work experience in the United States to help build its computer industry. That phenomenon peaked in the mid-1990s, and since then the number of students going to the United States for study and work experience has declined sharply — so much so that the Taiwanese government is introducing a scholarship program to increase the number. There has also been a large-scale movement of business people between Taiwan and mainland China. An often-cited number is about 300,000 Taiwanese working in the Yangzte River Delta region alone, largely for Taiwanese companies.

Although the electronics industry got well underway without benefit of a venture capital industry, as noted in Chapter 10, the IT industry received a boost from 1983 legislation providing a tax rebate of up to 20 percent for individuals who maintained an approved venture capital investment for at least two years (an advantage that ended in 2000).

The dynamism of the Taiwanese electronics industry is shown by the

38   turnover in companies. The annual entry rate of electronics firms averaged
1,100 and an exit rate of 300 from 1986 to 1991, with entries of 900 and exits of
450 per year from 1991 to 1996 (Amsden and Chu 2003).

In the 1980s, the IT industrial structure changed with the spinning off of integrated circuit companies from ITRI as reported previously. TSMC went on
to develop the world's most successful pure foundry model. The success of
foundries led to the creation of an IC design industry, including such design
houses as MediaTek and NovaTek that spun out from UMC. An industry that
consisted of 51 companies in 1991 grew to 225 companies in 2002, thus making
it one of the three biggest IC design industries in the world, together with the
United States and Israel, with sales of the largest 10 IC design firms totaling
U.S. $3 billion in 2003.

According to Kenney et al., Taiwan is the Asian leader in funding new high-tech companies. It "is a textbook case for the ways in which the government
can alter the risk-reward calculation. The 20 percent tax rebate created a powerful incentive, but it did not eliminate risk. Moreover, the government created relatively simple and transparent rules that aligned the incentives for the
fledgling venture capitalists with the government's objectives."

THE IMPORTANCE OF CROSS-BORDER LINKAGES

It is hard to miss the high proportion of scientific and technical papers published in the leading scientific and technical journals that have Chinese- and
Indian-born authors, many of them at U.S. universities. Increasing numbers
are returning home. This was a major source of talent for Taiwan in the 1980s
and 1990s, and now there is a growing flow back to China and India. They return not only with scientific and technical skills but also with know-how about
organizing and conducting research projects and building companies. The
contributions of returnees to Hsinchu and ZGC have been described above.
Foreign nationalities constituted over one-fourth of Singapore's professional
IT manpower in 1995–1997 and is likely to have increased since then.

Whether among Silicon Valley, Hsinchu, ZGC, or Bangalore, linkages
have been critical. Some of these places have become hubs, such as Silicon
Valley, linked through flows of goods, people, capital, and technology into a
global network.

Kenney et al. describe three types of people links between Silicon Valley and
Asia. The first was the human linkage provided by Asian students who stayed in
the United States and worked in Valley firms and elsewhere in the United
States, such as at Bell Labs. They soon began launching their own start-ups
while they kept close relationships with friends and families in Asia. The second

link consisted of Asian students and seasoned managers who returned to their various nations, either joining the Asian operations of Silicon Valley firms or setting up companies that contracted with Silicon Valley ones. The third link was Asians trained at home who then joined the overseas operations of Silicon Valley firms. Each link was a conduit for information transfer and learning. The repeated interactions that occurred on many levels created awareness of what was occurring in Silicon Valley, not only in terms of the technical and managerial skills but also of its entrepreneurial character.

A recent international network example is the Semiconductor Manufacturing International Corporation (SMIC), a silicon foundry whose headquarters are in Shanghai. It has three chip fabrication plants (fabs) in Shanghai, one in Tianjin, and three being built in Beijing. Ninety percent of its output is exported. Almost all of its early management team were veterans of the semiconductor industry and had spent most of their professional careers in leading semiconductor companies worldwide before they joined SMIC. Chief operating officer Marco Mora, for example, had more than 18 years of management experience at STMicroelectronics N.V., Texas Instrument Italia S.p.A, Micron Technology Italia S.p.A., and WSMC (a Taiwanese foundry). Of its 4,400 workers, 500 came from Taiwan, 300 from the United States, and 200 from other places outside of China. Significantly, all but one of its initial management team started out in Shanghai. Its funding was also global: from H&Q Asia Pacific, Walden International, New Enterprise Associates, Oak Investment Partners, Vertex, Goldman Sachs, and four Chinese state banks.

In sum, it is hard to imagine anything like the present global IT industry without these many kinds of connections. In the present post-bubble era, it is common, almost a rule enforced by venture capitalists, that Silicon Valley start-ups establish a part of their operations from the outset in some place in Asia. Costs are lower, and able people can be recruited.

This process is a win-win-win one in that the individuals who have moved have benefited from good educations and valuable work experiences. Silicon Valley firms have gained from having superior talent, and the places from which these people have come are gaining from returnees bearing valuable human capital. However, this system is in jeopardy. The number of students from (at least) China, South Korea, and Taiwan who have come to the United States for doctoral studies peaked in the mid-1990s and has markedly declined thereafter. Worse, since the disaster of September 11, 2001, the U.S. government's restrictions on issuing visas has discouraged many students and scholars from going there for study and work while, at the same time, non-U.S. countries are vigorously marketing their universities. By late 2005, many of

40   these restrictions were eased. Unless this happens decisively there will be a large deterioration in this beneficial set of linkages.

MAIN THEMES OF THE BOOK

This book shows that there were several paths to developing a significant place in the global IT industry. By the 1990s, all six countries or regions had adopted some strategies — or exhibited patterns of behavior — that were similar, even though they differed markedly in others.

Similarities

Eventually all adopted growth-positive development policies. This was crucial. No country that failed to adopt at least a minimum set of policies to promote development — including substantial reliance on the private sector, some degrees of openness to the outside world, encouragement to capital formation, and investment in education — has succeeded in the IT industry. India and China were late entrants, but by the 1990s they had both done so and have flourished thereafter.

All these regions invested in educating enough scientists and engineers to be able to participate significantly in this sector. This does not mean that all had good general educational policies. That of India has been notoriously inadequate, and the distribution of education in China has been very uneven.

All had to acquire these technologies. At the beginning of the period examined in this book (circa 1970), only Japan among the six had a substantial technological base, and in the following decades even it had to acquire many technologies from abroad (while also advancing them). The need for technology from abroad was much stronger for the other five.

All these governments actively promoted their IT industries. They all saw this as a key set of industries. Telecommunications has widely been seen as "strategic" throughout the world, and computers came to be seen as a leading-edge sector in which they could establish market positions. The products were light and hence cheap to move; the adoption of universal standards enabled new firms to enter; demand for products was growing rapidly; and the largest market, the United States, was relatively open.

All had some kinds of openness to the outside world. No successful country or region can be isolated. Our six were engaged with the world, not only through trade but also through other mechanisms as well. These mechanisms — licensing, investments by MNCs, flows of people to and from other countries — enabled them to acquire foreign technology and know-how.

In particular, all had linkages with the United States. These were of several
kinds and the mix of them varied among countries.

In none were universities important sources of technology. The role of universities was to produce trained people; for most of this period this was especially true at the undergraduate level.

The financial systems of all changed. These changes affected their IT industries. The role of banks diminished and that of stock markets increased. All
sought to develop venture capital industries, but the results were mixed.

Differences

Legal rules were established and reasonably effective in all the regions except
for China.

Openness was expressed in different ways:

- Japan, Korea, and India long held off foreign direct investment while
  Singapore, Taiwan, and China welcomed it—but selectively.
- Japan, Korea, and Taiwan became major acquirers of technology through
  licensing.
- Flows abroad of students (many of whom stayed to work) and the in-
  migration of people skilled in technology and management were important for Taiwan, India, Singapore, and China but much less so for Japan
  and Korea.

Promotion of their IT industries. This was done in different ways, some effectively and some less so. A wide array of instruments was used. These included
the training of computer scientists and engineers; trade protection; inviting
MNCs or, on the contrary, denying direct investment by foreign firms (preferring other instruments such as licensing) ; incentives for private R&D; government spending on R&D; creation of dedicated research institutes; recruiting
of experts with foreign experience; supplying cheap real estate, tax breaks;
and more.

Linkages with the United States. Although all had strong links with the
United States, the mixture of ways differed in regard to trade, foreign direct investment, licensing, and movements of people. There were also widespread
connections between Japan and East Asia. Dense business connections have
been established between Taiwan and mainland China.

Entrepreneurship. Some regions had active entrepreneurship expressed
through the formation of new firms (Taiwan, India, China) while there was
little in others. Singapore, Japan, and Korea have been making legal and policy changes to encourage it.

Innovation. Only Japan among the six displayed technical innovativeness

42 throughout the period. Taiwan, Korea, and Singapore, especially, began to develop it during the 1990s (measured, for example, by U.S. patents).

Regional clusters. These became prominent in all these countries except
Japan. They were mostly government-created except for Teheran Valley in
Korea, the Indian clusters, and the nascent IC one in Fukuoka, Japan.

Mobility of labor. All had mobile labor markets except Japan and Korea.
Their governments recently have taken actions to encourage it.

Financial systems. These evolved during this period, but only Taiwan had
a well-developed venture capital system by 2000.

Research institutes. Research institutes specializing in IT became ubiquitous, but their significance varied. In particular, they were significant sources
of new companies in Taiwan and mainland China but not in the others.

A LOOK AHEAD

There is a growing belief in scientific and technical circles worldwide that
Asia is becoming not only a place for making things but also — perhaps soon —
a creator of technology. All our countries or regions that have not already done
so are establishing a base for being innovators. They have able, well-trained
people, have or are developing needed institutions, and are connected to the
world of ideas.

Previously we discussed important indicators of progress. One is the large
and growing numbers of well-educated scientists and engineers. The number
of PhDs granted in Korea from 1986 to 1999 increased four times, in Taiwan
five times, and in China about 50 times (from 100 to 200 to more than 7,000)
(Hicks 2004). Others are increased spending on research and development;
the high and rising level of patents of Japan, Korea, and Taiwan; growth in scientific publications and in their quality measured by citations; and the shift
toward neutrality in the balance of royalty and license fees with the United
States. Still others are the stellar group of biologists Singapore has recruited
and the setting up by foreign firms of R&D centers in China — about 150 in
number. Today, these centers seem to be doing much more "D" than "R," but
that mix will surely shift toward doing more research.

China has great ambitions in science and technology, and, given its accomplishments, they are likely to be realized, although the timing is uncertain. Between 1995 and 2000 China's spending on R&D more than doubled.
It was still only 1 percent of GDP, but it was growing at 10 percent a year and
the government says it want to increase that share (Walsh 2003). By the year
2000 China ranked eighth in the world in scientific papers contributed by

Chinese authors (3 percent of the world total) compared with its being 15th in the world five years earlier. This is not to assert that China's capacities are up to those of the industrialized countries. This will not likely happen soon, but China is on the move.

The rise of Asia in innovativeness will have mixed impacts on others. The generation of new ideas can benefit everyone. It also gives their creator an advantage — as Silicon Valley has demonstrated. What should not be in doubt is that the United States and every other country will face a large challenge coping with the rise of an innovative Asia.

NOTES

1. There is a connection between the justly popular topic of national systems of innovation and this label of national technology strategies. The difference is that, Japan excepted, for most of the period covered in this book the focus of governments and companies was less on innovation and more on acquiring already developed technologies. A seminal publication on innovation systems is Nelson and Rosenberg (1993).

2. This flow diminished during the 1990s as better employment and educational opportunities emerged in Taiwan. The Taiwanese government is now undertaking a scholarship program to reinvigorate the flow of students to the United States.

3. These and some of the following points are emphasized by Segal.

REFERENCES

Abernathy, F. H., J. T. Dunlop, J. H. Hammond , and D. Weil. 2002. "Globalization in the Apparel and Textile Industries: What Is New and What Is Not?" In M. Kenney and R. Florida, eds. *Locating Global Advantage: Industry Dynamics in the International Economy*. Stanford, CA: Stanford University Press.

Amsden, A. H., and W.-W. Chu. 2003. *Beyond Late Development: Taiwan's Upgrading Policies*. Cambridge, MA: MIT Press.

Arora, A., A. Gambardello, and S. Torrisi. 2000. "In the Footsteps of Silicon Valley? Indian and Irish Software in the International Division of Labour." Discussion Paper 00-041, Stanford Institute for Economic Policy Research (SIEPR).

Brown, J. S., and P. Duguid. 2000. In C. M. Lee, W. F. Miller, M. G. Hancock, and H. Rowen, eds. *The Silicon Valley Edge: A Habitat for Innovation and Entrepreneurship*. Stanford, CA: Stanford University Press.

Chen, X., L. K. Cheng, K. C. Fung, and L. J. Lau. 2003. "The Estimation of Domestic Value-Added and Employment Induced by Exports: An Application to Chinese Exports to the United States." Unpublished manuscript.

Christensen, C. 2003. *The Innovator's Dilemma*. Boston: Harvard Business School Press.

Curry, J., and M. Kenney. 2004. "The Organization and Geographic Configuration of the Personal Computer Value Chain." In M. Kenney and R. Florida, eds. *Locating Global Advantage*. Stanford, CA: Stanford University Press.

44   Fuller, D. B. 2005. "The Changing Limits and the Limits of Change: The State, Private Firms, China and Global Industry in the Evolution of Taiwan's Electronics Industry." *Journal of Contemporary China* 14(45).

Grove, A. S. 1996. *Only the Paranoid Survive: How to Exploit the Crisis Points That Challenge Every Company*. New York: Doubleday.

Hicks, D. 2004. "Benchmarking Growth: Are We Looking in the Wrong Direction?" Presentation, Tokyo.

Hu, A. G. Z., and A. Jaffe. 2001. "Patent Citations and International Knowledge Flow: The Cases of Korea and Taiwan," Working Paper 8528, National Bureau of Economic Research.

Keller, W. 2004. "International Technology Diffusion" *Journal of Economic Literature* 42(3):752.

Kenney, M., and R. Florida. 2004. *Locating Global Advantage*. Stanford, CA: Stanford University Press.

Krugman, P. 1991. *Geography and Trade*. Cambridge, MA: MIT Press.

McKendrick, D. 2004. "Leveraging Locations: Hard Disk Drive Producers in International Competition." In M. Kenney and R. Florida, eds. *Locating Global Advantage*. Stanford, CA: Stanford University Press.

Murtha, T. P., S. A. Lenway, and J. Hart. 2001. *Managing New Industry Creation: Global Knowledge Formation and Entrepreneurship in High Technology*. Stanford, CA: Stanford University Press.

Narin, F. 2003. Presentation, CHI Research, NAS Sackler Colloquium, Irvine CA. May 11.

National Science Foundation. 2002. Science and Engineering Indicators. Appendix Tables 2-29, 2-36, 2-41, 5-52.

———. 2004. Appendix Tables 2-36, 5-52.

Nelson, R., and N. Rosenberg. 1993. "Technical Innovation and National Systems." In R. Nelson, ed. *National Innovation Systems*. New York: Oxford University Press.

Porter, M. E. 1990. *The Competitive Advantage of Nations*. New York: Free Press.

Rowen, H. S., and A. M. Toyoda. 2003. "Japan Has Few High-Tech Startups: Can It Be Changed? Does It Matter?" Asia/Pacific Research Center, Stanford University.

Schumpeter, J. A. 1939. *Business Cycles*. New York: McGraw-Hill.

Segal, A. 2002. *Digital Dragon: High Technology Enterprises in China*. Ithaca, NY: Cornell University Press, p. 71.

Walsh, K. 2003. "Foreign High-Tech R&D in China: Risks, Rewards and Implications for U.S.-China Relations." Monograph, Henry L. Stimson Center.

Wong, P. K. 2000. In D. G. McKendrick, R. F. Doner, and S. Haggard, eds. *From Silicon Valley to Singapore: Location and Competitive Advantage in the Hard Disk Drive Industry*. Stanford, CA: Stanford University Press.

Zucker, L. G., and M. R. Darby. 1995. "Virtuous Circles of Productivity: Star Bioscientists and the Institutional Transformation of Industry." Working Paper 5342, National Bureau of Economic Research.

I   THE EARLY DEVELOPER: JAPAN

2

STABILITY AND CHANGE IN THE JAPANESE SYSTEM

Ken-ichi Imai

The central theme of this book is how the intersection of entrepreneurship and innovation has been expressed in Asia in the information technology industry. Both of these are about creating something new, and our premise is that the two in combination are superior in creating value — for example, speeding new combinations of goods and services, or swift restructuring of high-tech clusters.

To many observers, the pace of change in Japan's industries appears extremely slow in comparison with the United States. This leads to the questions, "Is there no entrepreneurship in Japan's industrial circles; is there no intersection of entrepreneurship and innovation in Japan"?

Our answer is that we need to reconsider the definition of entrepreneurship and to understand the evolutionary nature of Japanese innovations. The central concepts discussed in this chapter are a "process-oriented definition of entrepreneurship," "an integral type of innovation system," and "path-dependence (or embeddedness)" for both entrepreneurship and innovation.

We then examine the status and the prospects for five high-tech clusters in Japan.

OVERVIEW OF HIGH-TECH CLUSTERS AROUND THE WORLD

Cloning Silicon Valley

Journalist David Rosenberg illustrates in his controversially titled book, "Cloning Silicon Valley,"[1] the areas of the world currently acknowledged as high-tech clusters, along with areas that are gaining attention as potential high-tech clusters. Of the 13 high-tech clusters he shows, none are in South

48   America, Africa, Eastern Europe, China, or Japan. There are several explanations for this. Perhaps the author lacks knowledge about Japan, or had difficulty identifying a single key area. Even a Japanese person would have difficulty answering the question, "Where are the high-tech clusters in Japan?" Or
perhaps the statistical data that the author needed were not available. Also, a
Japanese reader might react to the title "Cloning Silicon Valley," by saying
"We are grateful to be excluded, as we wouldn't stand to be labeled as clones."

However, the author uses the word "cloning" simply to draw the reader's attention, and the subtitle of the book defines his focus: "The Next Generation
High-Tech Hotspots." In fact, the author, who describes clusters in Europe, Israel, and Asia, is clearly not advocating the American model nor is he preju-
diced against Asia.

I believe that in Japan there are several candidate high-tech clusters; in fact,
five will be discussed here. But there are some conceptual problems to be addressed first.

What Are Clusters?

Innovation is not evenly distributed around the world, even in the developed
countries, but rather is concentrated in small regions. These are referred to as
"high-tech clusters," "industrial clusters," "industrial milieu," and so on; they
are best represented by Silicon Valley.

Our focus here is on where the *next* Silicon Valley will emerge. More specifically, the question is whether Silicon Valley will embrace biotechnology and
nanotechnology and continue to develop dynamically, or will there be clusters
with differing characteristics such as Cambridge, Austin, and Helsinki, or, further, will areas with close ties to Silicon Valley, such as Israeli's Tel Aviv, India's
Bangalore, and Hsinchu in Taiwan, strengthen their roles in the Silicon Valley
network.[2]

In connection with these questions, this chapter asks whether Japan can
form competitive technical/industrial clusters and how Japanese corporations, consumers, and government must change their "mindset" in order to be
successful.

Why Clustering?

In the past, a phenomenon called "industrial agglomeration"[3] occurred from
the presence of natural resources in certain areas or from the spillover benefits among firms in an industry being close together. For today's fast-moving
technologies there are three main explanations.

First, modern technology has a complex, dynamic character. In some cases, it can be disassembled into discrete, component parts, but a large part of these systems requires know-how and tacit knowledge. With today's information technology, where designs are clear, information can be transmitted around the world and the parties involved need not gather in one place and debate. This is not so, however, for systems with an inexact architecture. Discussing issues face to face is vital. Furthermore, these systems are constantly evolving, and opinions can be divided concerning the best path of development and the possibility of future lock-ins. When this occurs, if groups doing similar work are in close proximity the exchange of information allows different ideas to be tested in parallel and new directions can result. This typically does not occur in the case of development by isolated, independent firms. Intense interaction among the parties is a primary force for the creation of clusters.

Second, knowledge about economic activity is "restricted in time and place," and close proximity is needed to avoid damaging time lags. Often, the entrepreneur and the experts must work together in the same area at the same time. With today's complex technical systems, the smooth execution of plans is not easy. Therefore, this analysis makes a distinction between "Modular" types of products and "Integral" ones (discussed later on).[4] The success of Silicon Valley is largely owed to "Architecture" laying out the structure of the whole and specifying relations among the parts. "Modularization" is the defining of independent subsystems that are connected to the whole via simple interfaces. With this structure, the first architecture and modularization to be formed for each type of system often becomes the standard, and there is considerable competition among companies to be the first to develop the standard. However, as discussed later, the times when such pioneering yields power depend on the maturity of the industry and its industrial characteristics. For example, in mobile telephones with built-in digital cameras, as miniaturization and multifunctionality advances, "integral" connections, or what Takahiro Fujimoto refers to as "Suriawase" (which can be roughly translated as "subtle combination") among the parts is crucial and a system different from the Silicon Valley model is needed, This suggests the possibility for new types of clusters, which is a key focus of our research.

Third, and most importantly, the economic mechanism underlying the kind of cluster suggested here is not a structured "organization" or a "pure competitive marketplace," but what Imai and Kaneko[5] define as a "network." However, a network solely of "connections" among people or enterprises is inadequate. The emergence of a dominating leader or strong backing from the government would cause a reversion to a conventional and rigid type of organization. Currently, the only viable system contains specialist groups of venture capitalists,

50   technical consultants, accountants, and attorneys who assist entrepreneurs. As discussed subsequently, the way in which such a system is created in Japan will influence the efficacy of its technical clusters.

DEFINING ENTREPRENEURSHIP

Entrepreneurship warrants close examination. How the entrepreneur conceives and develops innovation are essential points of examination.

It is an ambiguous concept. Rosenberg used the large-scale surveys and interviews conducted by the Global Entrepreneurship Monitor (GEM).[6] He also used "the ratio of adults in the entire population who have recently started or are actively engaged in starting a new business." According to GEM, the highest-ranking nations are South Korea (14.3%), the United States (12.7%), Brazil (12.3%), and Austria (11.1%). Middle-ranked nations include Norway and Canada (7.9%) and Singapore (2.1%). Japan and Ireland are among the lowest ranked with only 1.3 percent. In other words, entrepreneurial activity in Japan is merely one tenth of that in the United States. If taken at face value, this is evidence that Japan will not have innovation clusters in the future.

The low rate of new business formation in Japan has been a problem for some time, but a comparison that focuses only on the ratio of adults who are considering starting a new business places too much importance on the cultural mentality. Also, the GEM data are questionable. Professor Wong Poh Kam of Singapore University makes an important distinction between entrepreneurship out of necessity (as in Brazil and other poor countries) and entrepreneurship out of opportunities (as in the developed countries). According to survey data on entrepreneurship performed by Japan Small and Medium Enterprise Corporation,[7] the ratio of people who are starting businesses and who want to do it if opportunity comes is 45.2 percent in the United States, 39.0 percent in France, 36.4 percent in Japan, 31.6 percent in Germany, and 30.2 percent in England. These are much smaller differences than in those in the GEM findings.

Recently, in Japan the number of people considering starting a business has been increasing, but will they actually spin off from big companies or succeed in an IPO? This chapter focuses on the actual behavior of businesspeople. For example, Shin Yasunobe's observation[8] on recent Japanese initial public offerings is impressive: The number of IPOs in 2002 exceeded that of those in the United States, especially in the IT sector. The number of Japanese IPOs (57) was more than double the number in the United States (21). Moreover, Japanese entrepreneurship has changed, and focusing only on start-ups misses an important part of the picture. Here we should consider the several dimensions of entrepreneurship. According to the Gartner survey[9] of entrepreneurship research, there are two different concepts of entrepreneurship; the first considers the "characteristics of entrepreneurship" and the second group considers "the outcomes of entrepreneurship." We need to capture both aspects.

Here we address some basics. It is appropriate to start from Joseph Schumpeter's conception of entrepreneurship, since not only was his contribution first and quite original but he also includes both aspects of entrepreneurship.

His key words were a "new combination" of goods and services, and he maintained that the outcome of entrepreneurship is "creative destruction." He did not, however, explicitly discuss just how these economic functions are performed. Schumpeter's successors, the so-called Neo-Schumpeterian school, corrected this deficiency: First, Israel Kirzner redefined entrepreneurship as "alertness" to new opportunities—that is, discovering a new combination of goods and services. If this discovery is genuine, alertness leads to implementation in the market. Alertness is especially effective in a market disequilibrium. Therefore, this conception of entrepreneurship is highly process oriented. Second, learning and knowledge play an important role. Alertness is the result of learning and knowledge. Entrepreneurship is embedded in a specific environment and depends on past processes of economic change.[10]

The text that follows addresses why "spin-offs" are important in Japan's transformation.

Path Dependence of Japanese Entrepreneurship[11]

The Japanese economic system, pre— and post–World War II, centered on big businesses, which used technology imported from Europe and America. Because this process continues, Japan is often viewed as lacking in entrepreneurship. However, this was not always so.

Immediately after the Meiji Restoration, Japan invested nearly 20 percent of its national income in constructing roads, harbors, and railroads, and with this infrastructure as a basis and learning from the experience of Europe and America, quickly developed an industrial system. The leaders who drew up blueprints for industrial development and implemented them became known as the zaibatsu entrepreneurs. Whether it be Hikojirou Nakamigawa of Mitsui, or Heigoro Shoda of Mitsubishi, the zaibatsu organizations were created by entrepreneurs who read the state of the world and foresaw the path to capitalist industrial development. In developing economies, information needed for investment decisions is scarce, with only a few people having access. At that stage, the zaibatsu entrepreneurs ensured that information and capital flowed to the necessary places. Such people can reap huge profits and these "hero

52   entrepreneurs" have indeed existed in Japan. (On a side note, the inflation-adjusted income of the zaibatsu leader Yataro Iwasaki is thought to be greater than that of Bill Gates today.)

However, as the zaibatsu grew, they gained control of much of the economy through stock holdings and monopolistic practices, eventually connected with the military, and transformed themselves into a mechanism for monopolistic control of the nation.

Their disassembly by U.S. occupation forces and banishment from the business world left the remaining business elite to run the show. In the beginning there was apprehension as to whether the reconstruction of Japanese companies was possible.[12] However, the first graduates of the University of Tokyo's Department of Economics, Hitotsubashi University, and Keio University were then businessmen in their 40s, and the banishing of the older leaders led to reviving management. This shift was a hidden but key factor in postwar economic growth.

After the war, these businessmen aggressively exchanged information on key topics such as investments. Given their lack of experience, obtaining information about other companies allowed them to anticipate developments, decrease uncertainty, and ward off threats to their own companies. The fact that they were not individualistic business starters but elite white-collar businessmen allowed the smooth flow of information. There was also a surge of company listings on the Tokyo Stock Exchange during this period. As they learned that only mutual growth could meliorate conflicts, incentives for growth became stronger, and growth came to be measured by sales rather than profits. Formerly loosely connected corporate groups were motivated to grow. Growth reconciled conflicts of interests and supported the forming of networks. With rapid growth, expectations of that growth being mutual strengthened relationships among companies and promoted trust, thereby creating a positive growth cycle.

However, such behavior can lead to a pattern where growth is the only thing in sight. Indeed, if it were to stop, this positive cycle could turn into a vicious downward spiral. Moreover, information exchange in corporate networks risks being corrupted by group politics. New directions and innovation are not easily born in this situation; they tend to become protective networks, like cartels. In the period after the rapid growth era it is not surprising that cartels became a large social problem, one that still remains.

Change Ignited by Crisis

The turning point was the oil crisis of the 1970s. Crises prompt a rearrangement of relationships between companies, and the oil crisis prompted a shift to a looser network model, just as the dismantling of the zaibatsu moved the solid monopolistic system into the keiretsu system, which was at least more flexible than the zaibatsu. Japanese companies began using electronic technologies in all areas of manufacturing to conserve energy. Leading small and medium-sized enterprises needed to rationalize, and they concentrated on their core technologies; in turn, big businesses swiftly improved their systems. This network system crossed corporate and industrial borders and led to horizontal connections. Its success attracted global attention.[13]

The technical innovation, called "mechatronics," a fusion of microelectronics and machine technology, was a "new combination" as outlined by Schumpeter; those who promoted it also fit Schumpeter's definition of an entrepreneur as "an innovator who implements change within markets through the carrying out of new combinations of productive means."[14] Hence, it is not only company presidents who are entrepreneurs but rather the technical leaders alert to new combinations. Viewed this way, in the mid-ranks of Japanese large companies there were many entrepreneurs. They also serve as reserves for new ventures, as discussed further along.

Professor Ronald Dore, who deeply understands the industrial scene in Japan, applies the phrase "flexible rigidity."[15] The transformation ignited by the oil crisis produced "flexibility" in product manufacturing, but relations among companies and financial institutions remained "rigid." It is true that most subsidiaries of large companies have people dispatched from financial institutions; most venture capital (VC) in Japan comes from financial institutions, and independent VC sources make up a very small portion of the whole.

As Kenney, Han, and Tanaka note in Chapter 10, what is called venture capital in the United States is risk capital for the financing of young firms. It involves control over them by the venture capitalists who sit on their boards, give advice, and sometimes replace founders. Such a system has scarcely existed in Japan until recently. "Venture capital" in Japan is called private equity in the United States and covers many kinds of investments in established companies.

It is important to identify which parts of the Japanese system are flexible and which parts are rigid, and to discern how even the rigid parts may change.

Japanese Entrepreneurs Viewed Broadly

In recent studies on entrepreneurship, for example as published in the Handbook of Entrepreneurship Research,[16] the focus is on small companies with entrepreneurs who are the driving force. Given this view, it is only natural that nowhere in Japan is a candidate for Rosenberg's next-generation Silicon Valley.

However, there is a strong argument against this view. It is the opinion of scholars, such as William Baumol[17] of Princeton University and Timothy Bresnahan[18] of Stanford University, that much research emphasizes small

54   companies and venture businesses too much, and puts too little importance on the contributions of large corporations to innovation. Many successful entrepreneurs come from big businesses. That is common in Silicon Valley but it has not been in Japan until recently. Even Microsoft might not exist today without the early support of IBM. The IBM managers did not understand the longer-term consequences of their adopting the DOS operating system and Intel chip combination for the IBM personal computer. If they had, Microsoft would not now exist nor perhaps Intel.

Among the various arguments, Clayton Christensen[19] of Harvard University has submitted the sharpest analysis. The distinction between "sustaining technology" and "disruptive technology" and the behavior that they bring about reflects the essence of the problem. Most new technology improves the performance of an existing product, and Christensen calls this "sustaining technology." On the other hand, although "disruptive technology" may initially have a lower performance, some customers are attracted by low price, small size, and better user-friendliness and can eventually bring about a value standard entirely different from the former market. Some well-known examples include the desktop personal computer as disrupting the mainframe computer, the transistor displacing the vacuum tube, and Honda's small off-road motorbike competing with the long-distance motorbike by BMW.

The important point is that when a successful company faces a disruptive technology, to try even harder, to form a more detailed plan, to respect the wishes of the customer, and to take a long-term view only makes things worse. Japanese companies, faced with disruptive technologies, threw all of their efforts into manufacturing, and no one stopped to think that this would worsen the situation. It was not necessary to improve in fields that were already flexible but rather to change organizations and structures that could not adapt to the disruptive technology where changes were needed.

Rigidity in the Japanese System

Of course, Japanese companies and the government noticed these problems, and companies reformed their organizations, employment systems, research systems, and relations with other companies. Central and local governments aggressively pushed the development of venture businesses. However, as the phrase "Japan's lost decade" indicates, these attempts were not wholly successful. Here is some corroborative evidence.

First, according to Yasunobe "the high turnover of top U.S. IT companies versus the low turnover of Japanese ones" indicates clearly how slow Japan's structural change has been. Whereas in the United States from 1982 to 2002 among the top 15 IT companies, 12 were replaced, in Japan from 1981 to 2000 just 8 companies were replaced. (Furthermore, the newly listed companies include NTT, NTT-DoCoMo, and KDDI, which were created by privatizing public corporations.)

Moreover, telecommunications should have been at the core, but the government could not agree on regulations and there was a long-standing, mutually unprofitable, conflict between the Ministry of Post and Telecommunications and NTT that resulted in high-cost telecommunications. In the meantime, NTT was also hindered by the Telecommunications Business Law and NTT Law, which made organizational reforms difficult and entrepreneurship virtually impossible. The largest hurdle to market entry, the "supply and demand adjustment regulation," was eventually lifted, but by that time the only way to compete was by lowering costs. Even Koichi Suzuki, the charismatic entrepreneur who led the newly formed IIJ to challenge NTT, conceded that he could not overturn the advantages possessed by "established companies with deep pockets."

Moreover, the making and using of computer software and hardware, which should have been at the heart of innovation, did not meet global standards, let alone excel. Japan's IT governance is still ruled by the "legacy system," with the newer outsourcing system simply added on, which has caused the two systems to squeeze each other with no room for maneuvering, leaving them "stuck-in-the-middle." With a few exceptions, Japanese companies did not restructure their IT systems.[20]

Fields That Thrived in the Rigid System

This is not to say that there was no entrepreneurship in the IT sector. Led by Oboshi Kouji and Keizo Tachikawa, NTT DoCoMo branched from NTT and created the i-mode, unique to Japan. Untypically, the two top players were not IT engineers, but Keiichi Enoki and Mari Matsunaga, who came from the world of advertising and who emphasized usability. Usually, such a success would be evaluated from a marketing standpoint, but looking back, this innovation showed that it was possible to do creative deconstruction even in Japan's rigid system. If those alert to new combinations are in the key part of an organization and have influence, a rigid organization can move forward and innovation is possible.

An example of "flexible rigidity" is the automobile industry. Toyota and Honda have long had their own network strategies, assigning certain design, development, and production work within the company, while also flexibly outsourcing work. This allows them to absorb the latest information tech-

56   nology. This flexibility is based on the philosophy of founder Kiichiro Toyota and his just-in-time idea to create products customers want, when they want them. This tradition has been rigid in a good sense.

In Honda's case, a hidden organizational innovation has become a tradition. The presidents of Honda retire young, unthinkable in other Japanese companies, and this symbolic reorganization allows Honda to stay youthful in its technology strategy. This might seem to be a small thing, but without the pressure of outside forces the rejuvenation of leaders has been difficult, and in the aging corporate environment of Japan the decision of Soichiro Honda to create a rule of rejuvenation within the company is a prime example of entrepreneurship and leadership.

In infrastructure, which is greatly affected by technological innovation, the parcel delivery service by logistics operators such as Seven-Eleven and Yamato Transport deserve special mention. They used information technology and labor management to create a highly successful system of small convenience stores. Toshifumi Suzuki used IT and trial and error adoption of employee suggestions in anticipation of the new economy.

These are all network-type companies that have done well in the long period of economic stagnation. None used destructive technologies or was a venture company that used the latest scientific knowledge to create a new market. They refined available technologies using entrepreneurial "alertness." They suggest that the world map of candidate sites for a next-generation Silicon Valley should possibly include the Toyota cluster, for example.

CHARACTERISTICS OF JAPANESE INNOVATION AND CLUSTERS

Japanese innovation does not supply much digital information itself but competes in the combination of IT and physical products such as automobiles, cameras, mobile phones, appliances, or "cool" products such as games or animation-related items. Even services, such as convenience stores, come from these combinations. Until recently, Japan was thought to be competitive in "product manufacturing," but as information technology takes center stage, the distinction between "products" and "information" is becoming blurred. Both are expressions of certain "patterns" and the difference is that when a specific pattern is "expressed" on to steel you get a car and when a pattern is expressed on to a computer disk you get software.

Takahiro Fujimoto, a professor at the University of Tokyo and expert on the automobile industry, focuses on distinctions among what he calls 'material[s] to be expressed'" and classifies them as shown in Figure 2.1.[21] Fujimoto holds that the Japanese innovation system has achieved international acclaim in

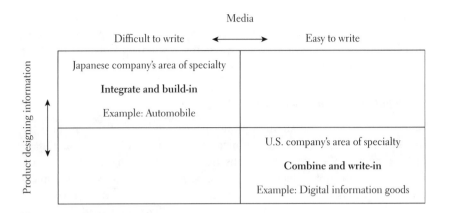

FIGURE 2.1   Areas of Specialty in the United States and Japan
SOURCE: Fujimoto, 2003, p. 95.

fields where great efforts are made to shift "difficult to write but difficult to de-
teriorate" design information on to materials and to ship the completed product to the customer or "built-in" type industries. It follows that sheet steel is
hard to manipulate and specialized technical skills are required to design a
mold suitable for the high pressures needed to transform the material into, say,
a car. In-depth know-how, accumulated over the years, relating to pressing
methods is essential. In contrast, digital information such as software on a disk
is easy to store, carry, and revise, and hardly deteriorates.

Essential Differences between the United States and Japan

An essential difference is implied between the two types of product architecture. Quantitative devices and software are based on logical thinking that contains design information in a series of blocks with specific functions dealing
with specific demands. These are "module" type products. In contrast, a car is
made of many parts—engine, body, suspension, and transmission—that not
only each have a required function but are dependent on one another to perform. All of the parts working together smoothly is a necessary condition for a
comfortable driving experience. This is an "integral" type product.

The difference is clear. In module systems, so long as the interface adheres
to given standards, parts made by different companies in different parts of the
world can be used interchangeably. This is an "open" industrial network.
Quite different are "integral" products made in industries with "closed" networks among a small number of companies with mutual understanding of the
environment, which lies behind the explicit information.

58   As is evident from the foregoing, Japanese clusters tend to be closed networks among a small number of companies. So long as Japanese industry sticks to products that require integral systems, it will have difficulty breaking away from closed production networks.

All but the Automobile Industry

Although there are many automobiles available on the market, they are built using the same principles with similar components. Although there have been several significant breakthroughs, the technology remains relatively uniform, and no disruptive technology has emerged. Secure long-term employment, complex manufacturing techniques, and development of organizational structure — all cornerstones of Japanese industry — have flourished. This situation will not last forever. Already, not all car parts are of the integral type. On the other hand, in computers, modular systems such as Wintel's interface are not adequate for real-time signal processing, and linkages with a variety of household appliances will require new types of integral systems. Both modular and integral systems are necessary, depending on technology and market conditions.

Although it is easy to understand Japan's competitive advantage in an integral type of industrial system, what about such industries as household appliances? Appliance manufacturers such as Hitachi, Fujitsu, NEC, and Mitsubishi have faced disruptive technologies and competition from module systems based on American standards. They have also had to switch from vertical to horizontal organizations. However, a "horizontal labor market" has barely formed, and with companies nearby which had kept their old employment structure it was close to impossible for needed changes to be implemented. In addition, company directors, who should have behaved entrepreneurially, did not realize how critical the situation was.

Additionally, why has the Japanese IT industry stagnated after expanding initially to the point where it threatened the superiority of the United States? [22] In 1995, when the Ministry of International Trade and Industry proposed an emergency report (which I chaired) to sound the alarm on the need for the computer industry to change into a horizontal structure, the participating presidents of appliance manufacturers were not at all enthusiastic. Similarly, at a conference called "The Future of the Japanese Computer Industry" [23] at the Stanford Japan Center, almost all the Japanese speakers spoke positively about their management systems, failing to address questions from the Americans on how Japan was going to adjust to structural changes in computer-related industries. In retrospect, this shows how difficult it is to let go of past successes.

At the same time, the Japanese corporate system had three inherent problems that could not be solved by entrepreneurship.

First, for corporations and the government to change, labor and financial markets needed to help carry them out. However, they lacked flexibility. For example, bank loans were based not on potential profits but on land and fixed capital of the company, and the labor market could not move excess workers into places that lacked them. The kinds of entrepreneurial markets that exist in the United States were nonexistent. Workers must be able to move not only within a company, but to different ones, to different industries, to different regions, as in a "horizontal labor market." Of course, MITI (later METI) set about making many changes, beginning in the late 1990s. Especially, the so-called Hiranuma Plan, led by then METI's Minister, "Plan for the Creation of New Markets and New Jobs" (May 2001) targeted new skill-developing systems and greater labor mobility (abolishing employment mismatches through private-sector activity, enhancing pension portability). The plan also proposed creating 1,000 new firms originating in universities and regional industrial clusters. However, the concept of lifetime employment was still strong due to a historical reason that qualified engineers and managers have a tendency to identify more strongly with their companies than with their technical specialties or performances (Rowen and Toyoda 2002).

Second, when technological innovation occurred in a social infrastructure—namely, in communications, energy, and logistics—there was a tendency to make light of its social impact. Too much attention was given to the "creation" side of creative disruption, and with too little attention to the disruptive side, thereby creating a confrontation between the reformers and the Old Guard. Even economists failed to give a persuasive theory, only trotting out old-fashioned ideas about the perceived benefits of increased competition brought about by cost cutting.

Third, simply put, the macroeconomic environment was excessively bad. When the economy's growth rate fell from 3 percent to 1 percent, the margin for reform in the private sector was drastically reduced. Japanese entrepreneurs had built networks on the prerequisite of growth and when growth stopped, a fall into a downward spiral was inevitable.

POTENTIAL FOR CHANGE

Such a situation cannot be solved like a mathematical simultaneous equation. This is because "Social Embeddedness" is powerful, as sociologist Mark Granovetter puts it, and the social economic system cannot be reset easily. There are many reasons for this, and it is important to find out the way to move away

60 from this "embeddedness." Reforms over the past ten years have lowered the presence of vested interests among companies and businessmen. Although some critics claim regulatory reform in Japan has not made great advances, at the very least, expectations for vested interests will have less importance in the future. If this is the case, the main obstacle noted by Timothy Bresnahan has been gradually taken away. He put it aptly: "The stories of emerging regions we have studied in our project have also shown that one driver of entrepreneurship in these areas has been the low costs of local human capital. When human capital has high opportunity, costs of alternative productive uses (employment in large established firms in leading industries like ITC itself, automobile, chemicals, etc.), this is hardly an issue for public policy. The question is far more serious when the opportunity costs for local human capital comes from artificially high wages in relatively unproductive jobs — e.g., excessive levels of employment in public administration, or in intermediaries of various sort, which is typical for instance of countries like Italy or Japan."[24]

In reality, the rigid core of Japan's inefficient public sector and intermediaries between public and private sectors has been melting. In this climate, it is highly likely that corporate spin-offs, discussed in Maeda's contribution, will continue to gather momentum.

The companies named in Figure 2.2 that went public have continued to grow. They are innovative. For example, Megachips created the first fabless company (which consolidated with Megafusion); more than 10 percent of Samco's International Lab's activities are foreign (which is not remarkable in much of the world but is in Japan), and it has research labs in Silicon Valley and Cambridge; and Yozan employs many Chinese engineers, some of whom have gone home to set up their own companies.

It is important to examine the concept of a "spin-off" more broadly. One definition is that a spin-off is created when a division becomes independent from the parent company. This usually comes from an organizational change in the parent with little consideration given to the division's "identity." However, the core operations of the company can be identified, and the departments that should be spun off — or spun in from other companies — become apparent. According to Maeda,[25] spin-ins include, among other things, an Internet car sales company and a mobile phone software company bought by Softbank two years ago.

There is another definition of spin-off in which teams leave one company and form another. The most famous example is the so-called "Traitorous Eight" who left Shockley Laboratories to form National Semiconductor. That was "unfriendly," but there are "friendly" or "sponsored" spin-offs in which the parent firm helps the new one, and perhaps has an equity stake in it. The most

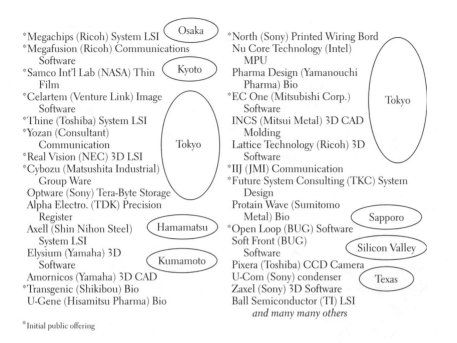

*Megachips (Ricoh) System LSI — Osaka
*Megafusion (Ricoh) Communications
    Software
*Samco Int'l Lab (NASA) Thin — Kyoto
    Film
*Celartem (Venture Link) Image
    Software
*Thine (Toshiba) System LSI
*Yozan (Consultant)
    Communication — Tokyo
*Real Vision (NEC) 3D LSI
*Cybozu (Matsushita Industrial)
    Group Ware
Optware (Sony) Tera-Byte Storage
Alpha Electro. (TDK) Precision
    Register
Axell (Shin Nihon Steel) — Hamamatsu
    System LSI
Elysium (Yamaha) 3D
    Software — Kumamoto
Amornicos (Yamaha) 3D CAD
*Transgenic (Shikibou) Bio
U-Gene (Hisamitsu Pharma) Bio

*North (Sony) Printed Wiring Bord
Nu Core Technology (Intel)
    MPU
Pharma Design (Yamanouchi
    Pharma) Bio
*EC One (Mitsubishi Corp.) — Tokyo
    Software
INCS (Mitsui Metal) 3D CAD
    Molding
Lattice Technology (Ricoh) 3D
    Software
*IIJ (JMI) Communication
*Future System Consulting (TKC) System
    Design
Protain Wave (Sumitomo
    Metal) Bio — Sapporo
*Open Loop (BUG) Software
Soft Front (BUG)
    Software — Silicon Valley
Pixera (Toshiba) CCD Camera
U-Com (Sony) condenser — Texas
Zaxel (Sony) 3D Software
Ball Semiconductor (TI) LSI
    and many many others

*Initial public offering

FIGURE 2.2   Emerging Spin-off Start-ups in Japan
SOURCE: Maeda, 2003.

common case is where engineers and others simply leave a firm to start a new one. We can place Japanese spin-offs in the "sponsored" category.

Signs of Change

There are some signs of change in the Japanese system. While working for Toshiba, Fujio Masuoka pioneered "flash memory" technology, now used widely for mobile and digital phones. At the time, the company was focusing on DRAM technology and failed to see the potential in flash memory. It sold the technology license to Intel, allowing it to corner the market. Masuoka has since moved to Tohoku University to develop a technology that surpasses flash memory.[26] This move from a company to a university shows how a new seed was successfully re-embedded.

Another case, discussed later, is the semiconductor cluster in Fukuoka Prefecture. All the key individuals moved from other cities, such as Mr. Ueki who moved his fabless semiconductor company from Osaka, and Mr. Shigeoka who moved from a major national manufacturer and now works for a venture

62   business creating testing devices for semiconductors. These individuals have moved out of the closed corporate environment and have demonstrated "re-embeddedness" in their new starting places (Fukuoka[27]).

Yasunobe Shin, former manager of the IT policy division in the Ministry of Trade and Industry, left to become president of Woodland Co., a mid-size software company. He had to weigh the opportunity loss arising from leaving his prestigious position against the opportunity to re-embed new knowledge into the Japanese software industry and invigorate it. The Japanese system is showing signs of fundamental change.

The Cool Innovation

Innovations may be gathering momentum in areas other than those initially assumed. Foreign journalists refer to this as "Japanese Cool." In his popular paper titled "Gross National Cool,"[28] Douglas McGray argues that Japan has become a cultural superpower through pop music, electronic appliances, architecture, fashion, animation, and cooking, to the point of excelling its economic power of the 1980s. McGray coined "Gross National Cool" as a play on the phrase "Gross National Product."

In English slang, "cool" can mean anything stylish, trendy, and smart as opposed to swanky or garish. Japanese products such as animation, pop music, and even design and lifestyle magazines are being thus defined. In a lead article in the Asian edition of *Time* magazine entitled "What's Right with Japan," foreign observers argued that Japan's Gross National Cool should be taken into account as a key economic engine.

The *Time* article reports that the export value of "cool" Japanese cultural products in such fields as media, entertainment, and licensing has tripled during the past ten years to $12.5 billion. In comparison, the value of manufacturing exports rose only 20 percent. The article reads: "Forget about salary men, gridlocked politics and zombie corporations. Japan is transforming itself into Asia's cultural dynamo — and might be reinventing its economy in the process."

At present, I evaluate GNC as one element in the "re-embedding" of the Japanese innovation system. The scale is quite small compared with the $4 trillion GNP. It is significant only as an example of Japan escaping the belief that it is inferior to Hollywood or Europe in the cultural arts.

PROSPECTS FOR REGIONAL CLUSTERS

Here we address the sorts of innovation clusters that will emerge in Japan during the coming decade.

All activities in Japan, social to cultural, are centered around Tokyo, which makes it easy to gather knowledge and information from neighboring businesses rather than running costly in-house research and development projects. This, in economics, is an "externality." In addition, the intermingling, which occurs in metropolitan areas, produces economic gains, according to Jane Jacobs. For example, if a cool design lab is located down the street from a local manufacturer, a new combination is likely to arise naturally. Tokyo clearly meets this first criteria for a cluster laid out previously.

Second, Tokyo has thousands of similar organizations, making it easy to pair up for innovative projects. Also on the demand side, there is a large pool of middle-class consumers. Looking at the intermingling clusters in the Tokyo area from this viewpoint, Tokyo has the potential for becoming a multifaceted innovation site. However, the Tokyo metropolitan area is not a single cluster. It is a mosaic of different clusters. Here we focus on the Tama area northwest of Tokyo because it is known as the first "planned industry cluster" and is a guideline case for cluster creation projects nationwide.

Most companies in the Tama area are of medium size with a focus on "product innovation," not the "process innovation" that has long been a Japanese specialty. Most are independent, without a parent or subsidiaries. In comparison with others of similar size, they spend more on research and development and hold more patents. Most noteworthy, however, is that their technological potential is tied to bringing new products to the market. They get support from organizations such as the Tama Association, and 60 percent of the product innovation companies are led by people who have created spin-offs from larger companies and know the Tokyo market. Tama also has many companies engaged in the "cool" industries such as manga comics, animation, and games. It is only natural that workers for these companies typically are in Tokyo, in the same way that lawyers, accountants, patent attorneys, programmers, and consultants have also migrated there. These specialists can live in the countryside, but when a problem arises, the more complex the problem the more specialists are required to solve it.

These changes encourage urban concentration in much the same way as the traditional system, where, for instance, politicians and government officials work in close contact. As a result, corporate headquarters are in Tokyo. Of course there are merits and demerits in every cluster; there is a size threshold for every cluster, and crossing it can lead to loss of advantages.[29]

There are two possible scenarios. In one, all specialists gather in Tokyo and all other regional clusters fail to reach a minimum threshold. Tokyo may be-

64   come a globally attractive prospect but the losses throughout Japan as a whole would be too great. For example, the auto-industry cluster would merely become a production base for manufacturing high-quality cars, and Tohoku University's cutting-edge technology may simply receive funds from foreign users.

In the other scenario, at least four areas have the capacity to become an innovation cluster.

The Aichi Automobile Cluster

The Aichi automobile industry cluster, more accurately the Toyota cluster, is a key Japanese innovation cluster. Its integral architecture could easily have become a closed network system, but efforts are being made to create a modular system with as much openness as possible. For example, module groups have already been created as follows:

- Cockpit module: instrument panel, air conditioner, audio equipment
- Front-end module: bumper, headlamp, condenser
- Door module: automatic windows and the like

Toyota is changing into a "software first" type of[30] product manufacturing company. Its network is one of the leaders in both product manufacturing and IT utilization, with strong research and development for its next-generation automobiles. It will certainly become an innovation cluster with the power to draw exceptional specialists from around the world.

Independent Clusters in Kyoto

Kyoto is known for corporations that have their own specialized technologies, such as Kyocera, Rohm, Omron, Murata, Horiba, and Nidec. There are questions about how such differing companies could form a single cluster. There are no systematic work links among them.

But there are similarities: (1) corporate governance with clear ownership; (2) no big bank ownership and a corporate policy to have no debt; (3) the political talk of Kasumigaseki does not reach them — as is also true (or used to be) in Silicon Valley; (4) multiproduct and small-lot production systems. These characteristics are markedly different from the battered traditional production system in Japan. We can say that these companies share similar entrepreneurial spirit. Also, the cluster's corporations, from big to small, produce products globally recognized for their quality. The fact that the second generation of entrepreneurs who spun off from Kyocera or Omron are developing their new companies may strengthen the concept of Kyoto clustering.[31]

However, in this information society, a shared spirit needs to be defined
more definitely. Kyoto needs to become an attractive destination for travel and
a desirable environment to work and live in for people around the world. Larry
Ellison of Oracle Corp. loves Kyoto and dreams of living near the picturesque
Nanzen temple, and many European artists and designers also want to work
there. There is a view that places where creative people live are places where
creativity is born, and Kyoto qualifies as such a location.

University-Business Cooperation Cluster in Sendai

A new arena for global competition known as NBI Converging Technology
combines N (Nanotechnology), B (Biotechnology), and I (Information Tech-
nology. It has already begun, centered in the United States. In fact, Silicon
Valley is looking to NBI Converging Technology to drive the "next generation
Silicon Valley" to rival other centers such as Austin, Boston, Washington, and
Oxford.

If Japan fails to join this race, it might fall behind other industrialized nations. In Japan, the Sendai Cluster can realistically compete on a global scale
by combining the acumen of local businesses with the academic research of
Tohoku University. The university leads the world in material development using nanotechnology, the key to NBI development. (See Figure 2.3.) It established The New Industry Creation Hatchery Center (NICHe) in April 1998
with the aim of vitalizing domestic industry through university collaboration

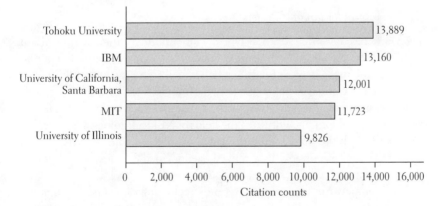

FIGURE 2.3   Citation Rankings: Institution Rankings in Materials Science
SOURCE: ISI Essential Science Indicators, 1991–2001.

66   with industry. When the Law for Promoting University-Industry Technology Transfer was passed in May 1998, the university quickly created Tohoku Technoarch Co., Ltd.

Fukuoka's New Semiconductor Cluster

This is a next-generation semiconductor cluster, mapped out by the leader, Professor Hiroto Yasuura from Kyushu University. As microfabrication technology advances, integration of the design and production process is again necessary. Following the example of the automobile industry, this reintegration will not move to an old-style closed vertical integration type of organization, but rather is likely to take be an advanced "virtual vertical integration" system.

Many companies in this cluster are working on "post-PC" technologies, with Sony Nagasaki producing processors for the computer entertainment sector, with Sony Semiconductor Kyushu making CDs for digital cameras and Mitsubishi Fukuoka producing power semiconductors for use in automobiles.

The "Silicon Sea-Belt Project" is a cross-border project for the design and production of semiconductors spanning Kyushu, South Korea, Taiwan, China, and India. Around 40 percent of global semiconductor production occurs in this area. This region is likely to become the biggest market in the world within the next five years, with more than 500 million workers earning over five million yen annually. This area will emerge as a far richer market than Europe or even North America. IT products will be able to move in a loop from the formation of technical standards, to design, to production, and on to consumption.

The Prospect for Japan's Clusters

The world has now entered a new type of competition for innovations. Much of this will center on NBI converging technology. Japan must participate in this game and make it to the finals. If it fails, it will take a second- or third-class position in the world. It will lose the benefits from NBI technology in Japanese daily life, such as highly advanced medical treatment. Considering Japan's research and development abilities in the fields of NBI technology, I believe that Japan can reach the finals. Although Japan was ranked 26th in IMD's World Competitiveness Yearbook, it is ranked second in the index of technology competitiveness. Japan is entitled to the silver medal.

This competitiveness includes not only technologies owned by large enterprises or universities but those developed by small and middle-sized enterprises. For example, SiXON Ltd. is introducing SiC into distributed power supplies, electric cars, and a wide range of other industries. What makes this possible is the skill of a small Kyoto company called ACT. Mr. Okamoto of ACT, not a specialist in nanotechnology, was aware of the importance of this business opportunity. Now he pursues atomic/molecule-level polishing using an atomic force microscope in Kyoto University. Such innovative manufacturing by SMEs and their clustering in Tokyo, Osaka, and Kyoto had created a unique competitive advantage in Japanese manufacturing, but it has now deteriorated, due to the shift of production to other Asian countries. It is a time for such capabilities to born again.

Despite this, Japan lacks active discussion about to make all this happen. I assume this is because the country lacks established locations to achieve such progress. If so, why doesn't Japan use the so-called "special economic zone," a concept recently discussed in political circles, to create such places. These would be more than places where business rules would be relaxed; they would be "entrepreneurial special zones" as proposed by Professor Edward Feigenbaum in *The Japanese Entrepreneur: Making the Desert Bloom*.[32]

We have proposed five candidates for the next-generation of high-tech regional clusters, each focused on a separate technology but connected through networks that intermediate with the demand side. Initial demand comes from big cities like Tokyo (especially the inner city), a part of Osaka, Nagoya, and Fukuoka.

SUMMARY AND CONCLUSION

1. Japan's economic system can be analyzed as a dynamic set of industrial networks. Entrepreneurship and innovation have played a key role in its transformation. We have adopted "network" analysis as a tool to investigate this phenomenon. We have explored the prospect of creating the next generation of high-tech clusters in Japan.

2. We started with Schumpeter's concept of the entrepreneur as a person who creates "new combinations." However, Schumpeter did not explicitly discuss the process of transformation. We viewed it as a process of entrepreneurial alertness with sequential actions to create new economic opportunities. We pointed out that the middle-ranks of large Japanese companies have many entrepreneurs that served as reserves for spin-off ventures.

However, actual changes in this area have not been rapid; in fact, the number of spin-offs has been rather small during the past ten years. A main reason was that Japanese human capital had high opportunity costs of alternative uses. Elite engineers and managers have become embedded in the traditional system.

68   This embeddedness made the core of Japan's system rigid, but there are signs of change. This system can't change entirely, but new economic and social relationships can be introduced sporadically and sequentially. It is certain that Japanese entrepreneurship is readying for the next stage.

3. We also need a new definition of innovation. Japan's innovation system has been characterized as "incremental" in manufacturing with a focus on high quality. However, today excellent manufacturing is based on digital design and intensively uses digital devices. The distinction between "product" and "information" is becoming blurred. Both express certain "patterns" and the difference is that when one is "expressed" on steel you get a car, but when one is expressed on a computer disk or a paper you get software. The former involves a material on which it is difficult to "write" and therefore requires complementary materials, expertise, and trained skills. Not only digital architecture and design are needed but also continuous, incremental manufacturing innovation.

The architecture for automobiles, cameras, printers, and other consumer electronic products is of the "integral type," which is different from the "module-type" architecture prevalent in Silicon Valley. "Integral" architecture requires a delicate coordination among different parts and devices *interdependently*, while the module type allows the parts to work independently. Naturally, the module system leads to an open industrial network, while the integral system leads to closed networks among a few companies.

This difference in architecture cannot continue for long. Both types coexist, depending on the degree of industrial maturity and technological and market structures. Actually, Japan is adopting module systems and is opening its markets. Yet, the core of integral systems will remain, because they are vital for Japan's innovation. Integral systems do not quickly respond to rapid change, but have an advantage in an environment where the rate of change falls in the middle.[33]

4. A cluster is created at the intersection of entrepreneurship and innovation. Without entrepreneurial alertness, innovation does not materialize and clusters do not form. Without innovation, entrepreneurship alone leads to a simple expansion of traditional economic activities and fails to produce an innovation cluster.

Three cases exemplify our proposed next-generation clusters.

First is the Aichi-Toyota Cluster, a combination of integral type innovation and strong entrepreneurial leadership, based on just-in-time products. Toyota aggressively outsources and fosters start-ups in its group. It has created a unique innovative cluster.

Fukuoka's New Semiconductor Cluster, re-embedding new relationships into old industrial networks, centered on automobile factories. Key people are engineers who spun off from large companies, Sony's engineers who concentrate on "post PC" technology, and Kyushu University professors who are now re-embedding new linkages for the "Silicon Sea-Belt Project."

Finally, Japanese universities, who were firmly embedded in the old European-style system, have begun to mobilize their human and knowledge resources. According to the Nikkei Venture Business Survey, more than 100 new businesses have come them during the past three years. Among them, we place high hopes on the Sendai cluster around Tohoku University. It is world class in material development, which is key to Nano-Bio-Info convergence. However, the supporting infrastructure, such as middle-level staff and technology licensing offices, is still weak and needs bolstering. Concrete infrastructure policies are needed rather than simple calls for structural reforms within political circles.

5. In the information economy, the quality of innovation depends on efficient coordination and integration of knowledge. Japan's traditional hierarchical system centering on "Nagata-cho" (politicians) and "Kasumigaseki" (bureaucrats) is now losing its stronghold on power. Networks of expert groups, including young politicians and knowledgeable bureaucrats, have begun to demonstrate their capacity to operate at the intersection of public and private domains.

However, there is a unique problem associated with the over-concentration in Tokyo. There is a natural tendency for expert groups to gather there, especially in its center. Even if they prefer living in the countryside, the numbers of experts are limited, so having an office in Tokyo is necessary for efficiency. In fact, in recent years many lawyers, accountants, patent attorneys, programmers, and consultants have migrated to Tokyo. Whether this is a transitory or a more long-term phenomenon is difficult to know.

I predict that the Tokyo concentration will continue for a while, but there is another possibility, as discussed previously. Central to this outcome is the location of key knowledge. Usually new ideas are created through interactions in big cities like Tokyo; town architectures, home design, apparel and foods, or new types of journalism and lifestyles are constantly being created and recreated. The accumulation of such incremental innovations has been an engine of Japanese economic development. But now, a more profound knowledge that is deeply rooted in academic research or anchored in history and culture is critically needed. Such knowledge might come to be located in a cluster other than Tokyo. From this perspective, we have emphasized the Kyoto cluster. Of course, its future is unknown, but it is certain that history matters.

NOTES

This chapter summarizes several research projects by the Japanese team of the Asia/Pacific Research Center (APARC) of Stanford University for SPRIE (Stanford Project on Regions of Innovation and Entrepreneurship) and is written by Kenichi Imai, the Japanese team project leader. Though we are still debating publication, this report was first presented at a conference at Stanford University on October 27–28, 2003. The Japanese team consists of scholars and DBJ (Development Bank of Japan) groups. Full reports were originally written in Japanese with summaries in English posted on the Internet at the URL indicated at the end of this chapter. The term "this project" refers to all reports as a whole, but we will try to cross-reference all sources.

1. David Rosenberg, *Cloning Silicon Valley*, Prentice-Hall, 2002.

2. This discussion essentially relates to the boundaries of a cluster. In fact, Silicon Valley, if its boundaries are widened to include the other side of San Francisco Bay, is already a large biotech cluster with the largest biotech market capitalization of any cluster.

3. Hiroyuki Itami, Shigeru Matsushima, and Takeo Kikkawa, *The Essentials of Industrial Agglomeration* (in Japanese), Yuhikaku, 1998.

4. Masahiko Aoki and Haruhiko Ando, eds., *Modularization—The Essentials of the New Industrial Architecture* (in Japanese), Toyo Keizai Shimposha, 2003. Another excellent source is Takahiro Fujimoto, Akira Takeishi, and Yaichi Aoshima, *Business Architecture*, Yuhikaku, 2001.

5. Kenichi Imai and Ikuyo Kaneko, *Network Organization Theory*, Iwanami Shoten, 1988.

6. GEM. http://www.gemconsortium.org.

7. Japan Small and Medium Enterprise Corporation (Chusho-kigyo Sogo Jigyo-dan), "International and Regional Comparisons of Entrepreneurship" (in Japanese), mimeograph, 2001.

8. Shin Yasunobe, "Social and Economic Stickiness Surrounding Entrepreneurs and Evolving Changes in Japan," mimeograph, Stanford Japan Center, 2003.

9. W. Gartner, "What Are We Talking about When We Talk about Entrepreneurship?" *Academy of Management Review* 5(1), 1990.

10. Mark Granovetter, 2001.

11. Much of the following is taken from Kenichi Imai and Ikuyo Kaneko, *Network Organization Theory* (in Japanese).

12. Testimony in that period by the late Professor Yoshitaro Wakimura of the University of Tokyo in an interview with the author.

13. Though this improved system flourished for a time, when the new architectural concepts emerged (architecture and modular types, mentioned previously), further additions to this "patchwork-type" system could not be made, thus hindering the change of systems and locking-in the old system. This is discussed in detail in the following section.

14. Yuichi Shionoya, Nakayama Ichiro, and Tobata Seiichi, *Theory of Economic Development*, Iwanami Shoten, 1977, Vol. 1, pp. 198–199.

15. Ronald Dore, *Flexible Rigidities*, Stanford University Press, 1986.

16. Zoltan J. Acs and David B. Audretsch, eds., *Handbook of Entrepreneurship Research*, Kluwer Academic Publishers, 2003.

17. William Baumol and James Tobin, *Growth, Industrial Organization and Economic Growth*, Edward Elgar, forthcoming.

18. Timothy Bresnahan et al., "'Old Economy' Inputs for 'New Economy' Outcomes: Cluster Formation in the New Silicon Valleys," *Industrial and Corporate Change* 10(4), 2001.

19. Clayton Christensen, *The Innovator's Dilemma*, Harvard Business School Press, 2001.

20. Tsutomu Harada, Stanford Japan Center Discussion Paper, forthcoming.

21. Takahiro Fujimoto, *Competence Construction Competition* (in Japanese), Chuokonron-Shinsho, 2003.

22. According to Henry Rowen, Robert Noyce, a founder of Intel and co-inventor of the integrated circuit, in the mid-1980s told one of Rowen's classes that in the 1970s and 1980s the pattern in the computer industry had been that the U.S. industry would make a big advance and then Japanese companies would overtake them; following that, the cycle would repeat. He said he was worried because he didn't see what the next breakthrough would be that would save the U.S. industry. It turned out to be the Internet.

23. "Study of International Cooperation in Global Policy: Research into Future Trends in the Computer Industry," mimeograph, Stanford Japan Center, 1995.

24. T. Bresnahan et al., op. cit., p. 858.

25. Based on Maeda's rejoinder to Henry Rowen's comments to Maeda's presentation (July 16, 2003).

26. Reference to "Hidden Giants: Flash Memory Creator Seeks Japanese Lead," Nihon Keizai Shimbun (evening edition), September 1, 2003.

27. "There is a high density of companies in similar fields in the Fukuoka area, making horizontal cooperation easy; in this open environment, relations beyond company walls are born easily. In Tokyo and Osaka it is difficult for us to meet presidents of large corporations. In Fukuoka, it's possible" (remarks by JM Net President Ueki, in an interview with the Weekly Toyo Keizai, April 2, 2003).

28. Douglas McGray, "Japan's Gross National Cool" *Foreign Policy*, June 2002.

29. Peter Maskell, "Future Challenge and Institutional Preconditions for Regional Development Policy," in M. P. Feldman and N. Massard, eds., *Institutions and Systems in the Geography of Innovation*, Kluwer Academic Publishers, 2002. The cluster analysis by Hayashi and Bunno in this project provides a clear analysis of the overwhelming concentration of companies in Tokyo.

30. "Software first" is a term created by Edward Feigenbaum. It implies that "we need to change our hardware-first mind set now" and move to "software-first technology." Lecture memorandum, which was delivered at the K-S Venture Forum meeting in 1998.

31. Among the second-generation companies, the followings are noted:

- CCS Inc., which was created by Mr. Yoneda, who spun off from Kyocera; http://elux-inc.com/gaiyo/index.html
- ASYEK, which is a spin-off company from Rohm; http://web.kyoto-inet .or.jp/people/asyck

- A company called Faith which is famous for its downloadable ringer tone melody and is extremely profitable; http://www.faith.co.jp/nshp/pages/topset.ht

32. Edward Feigenbaum and David Brunner, *The Japanese Entrepreneur: Making the Desert Bloom*, Nikkei Shimbun, 2003.

33. According to Rowen and Toyoda (2002), Masa Aoki suggested the following perspective in the course of their personal communications: "One might consider different industries along a spectrum of technological innovation. At one end, there is great stability. In the middle, changes occur in a moderate rate. At the other end, changes are rapid. Japanese firms generally do poorly at the stable, commoditized end, where competition takes place over prices. At the opposite end, they do not respond quickly to rapid change. They excel, however, in the middle" (p. 15).

REFERENCES

Acs, Z. J., ed. 2000. *Regional Innovation, Knowledge, and Global Change*. London: Pinter.

———. 2002. *Innovation and the Growth of Cities*. London: Edward Elgar.

Acs, Z. J., and D. B. Audretsch, eds. 2003. *Handbook of Entrepreneurship Research: An Interdisciplinary Survey and Introduction*. Dordrecht: Kluwer Academic Publishers.

Acs, Z. J., H. L. F. de Groot, and P. Nijkamp, eds. 2002. *The Emergence of the Knowledge Economy: A Regional Perspective*. New York: Springer.

Barabasi, A.-L. 2002. *Linked: The New Science of Networks*. Japan Broadcast Publishing Co.

Bresnahan, T., et al. 2001. "'Old Economy' Inputs for 'New Economy' Outcomes: Cluster Formation in the New Silicon Valleys." *Industrial and Corporate Change* 10(4).

Castells, M. 1989. *The Informational City: Information Technology, Economic Restructuring, and the Urban-Regional Process*. London: Blackwell Publishers.

Christensen, C. M. 2001. *The Innovator's Dilemma: When New Technologies Cause Great Firms to Fail*. Boston: Harvard Business School Press.

Dore, R. 1986. *Flexible Rigidities: Industrial Policy and Structural Adjustment in the Japanese Economy 1970–80*. Stanford, CA: Stanford University Press.

Feldman, P. M. 1994. *The Geography of Innovation*. Dordrecht: Kluwer Academic Publishers.

Fischer, M. M. 2001. *Knowledge, Complexity and Innovation Systems*. New York: Springer.

Fujimoto, T. 2003. *Competition in Creating Core Competence* (in Japanese). Chuoko-ron-sha.

Fujimoto, T., A. Takeishi, and Y. Aoshima, eds. 2001. *Business Architecture: Strategic Design of Products, Organizations, and Processes* (in Japanese). Yuhikaku.

Granovetter, M., and R. Swedberg, eds. 2001. *The Sociology of Economic Life*. Boulder, CO: Westview Press.

Hayashi, T., and T. Bunno. 2003. "Venture Business Growth and the Cluster Factors" (in Japanese). SJC Discussion Paper DP-2003-004-J. http://www.stanford-jc.or.jp/research/publication/DP/DP_e.html.

Imai, K. 1992. "Japan's Corporate Networks." In S. Kumon and H. Rosovsky, eds. *The Political Economy of Japan: Cultural and Social Dynamics.* Stanford, CA: Stanford University Press.

Imai, K., and I. Kaneko. 1988. *Network Organization Theory* (in Japanese). Iwanami Shoten.

Itami, H., S. Matsushima, and T. Kikkawa. 1998. *The Essentials of Industrial Agglomeration* (in Japanese). Tokyo: Yuhikaku.

Jacobs, J. 1961. *The Death and Life of Great American Cities.* Kajima Institute Publishing.

Johnson, S. 2001. *Emergence: The Connected Lives of Ants, Brains, Cities, and Software.* New York: Scribner.

Kodama, T. 2003. "TAMA Initiative as a Leading Example of Cluster Formation in Japan" (in Japanese). Unpublished manuscript.

Lee, C.-M., W. Miller, M. G. Hancock, and H. Rowen, eds. 2000. *The Silicon Valley Edge: A Habitat for Innovation and Entrepreneurship.* Stanford, CA: Stanford University Press.

Maeda, N. 2003. "Restructuring of Japanese Innovation System with High-Tech Start-ups: Creative Destruction of Catch-up Model, in Micro, Macro and Regional Levels" (in Japanese). SJC Discussion Paper DP-2003-003-J. http://www.stanford-jc.or.jp/research/publication/DP/DP_e.html.

Ministry of Economy, Trade and Industry (METI). 2001. *The Creative Transformation of Japanese Organizations* (in Japanese). Marui Press.

Rosenberg, D. 2002. *Cloning Silicon Valley: The Next Generation High-Tech Hotspots.* New York: Prentice-Hall.

Schumpeter, J. A. 1926. *Theorie der Wirtschaftlichen Entwicklung.* Iwanami Shoten.

Yasunobe, S. 2003. "Social and Economic Stickiness Surrounding Entrepreneurs and Evolving Changes in Japan" (in Japanese). Unpublished manuscript.

3

Japan Actually Has Start-Ups

Noboru Maeda

The industrial restructuring of Japan is behind that of the United States and the European Union (EU). "The lost decade," a phrase often used in Japan, could become the lost two decades unless Japan makes a quantum leap forward in the process.

Many reasons are given, such as financial policy and delay in implementing deregulation. The key reason, however, may be at the micro level. The Japanese closed business model, which generated value in the catch-up age, no longer creates value in the IT age. It is no longer able to create innovations.

The current situation is similar to that in the United States from the mid-1970s to the 1980s. Experts have pointed to the lack of innovative efforts on the part of corporations while they were focusing instead on finance and taxes. It is time for Japan to learn from the United States of 20 years ago.

For the past three decades, almost no technology-oriented start-ups, like Sony, Honda, or Kyocera, have succeeded. The reason is clear: High-tech start-ups were not needed in the catch-up phase. It was better not having them for the total effectiveness of the economy. Even if some start-ups were born, they died.

Now, as the world changes to an information society, "what to make" is becoming more important than "how to make," and start-ups are needed for this. The absence of them is the key reason for the delay in changes in Japan's industrial structure. To our surprise, however, something new and important is happening. During the so-called lost decade, tens of spin-off companies grew fast, with some going to IPO. Some achieved over $500 million in annual sales within 10 years. By 2010, the number of spin-off start-ups should exceed 450; that would be more than 10 percent of the total number of companies on the stock market.

After World War II, all Japanese resources were aligned for efficiency of mass production. The war changed a starving nation to one of the richest nations in 30 years. Probably this business model will be treated in business administration textbooks as one of the most successful in the 20th century.

However, Michael Porter of Harvard University asserts[1] that Japan's economic slump came from continuing to apply the 30-year-old successful strategy in the new world. The "do things better" strategy matches Japanese nationality, culture, and history. Japan is good at homogeneous group activities needed for improvement of mass production. Unique activities are obstacles. Company-supplied dormitories, uniforms, mass employment of recent graduates, in-house education, an improvement suggestion system, morning meetings, a seniority wage system, and so on were very useful in the "how to improve" world.

When we look back to the sixth century, Shoutoku-Taishi, the prime minister of the age, expressed the famous slogan, "Consensus and peace are the most valuable." A 1,300-year history of agriculture on a tiny island created DNA oriented to operational improvement.

Porter and Clayton Christensen, also of Harvard University, offer two examples[2] of Japanese enterprise weakness. One is the semiconductor industry, and the other is entrepreneurship.

Japanese semiconductor companies such as Toshiba, NEC, Hitachi, and Mitsubishi produce about 20 kinds of semiconductors. In contrast, U.S. and European companies like Intel, TI, Motorola, and Philips concentrate on three or four kinds of semiconductors such as flash memory, digital signal processors, microprocessors, and application-specific integrated circuits (ASICs). They make higher profits.

On entrepreneurship, Porter and Christensen observe that in the United States, top executives of big corporations leave to become CEOs of tiny start-ups. In Japan, this never happens. Elite engineers in big corporations never risk starting their own businesses.

WHY THERE HAVE BEEN ONLY A FEW JAPANESE START-UPS

It is often said that Japanese culture is not suitable for start-ups. However, history shows this view to be wrong. Many were born right after World War II and some after the dotcom bubble. Table 3.1 shows their history.

The problem is that few high-tech start-ups were created during the past 20 years. R&D-oriented start-ups, like Incs, Thein, Samco, and Megachips,

TABLE 3.1

History of Japanese Start-ups

Generation	Year	Group Name	Industry	Start-up Company
First	1945–	Postwar start-up	Manufacturing	Sony, Honda, Kyocera, Casio, Rohm
Second	1970–	Guts start-up	Service	Pasona, NOVA, Doutor, HIS, Takefuji
Third	1990–	Internet start-up	E-business	Softbank, Rakuten, Askul, Monex
Fourth	2000–	High-tech start-up	Real + E-business	Incs, Thinem Samco, Megachips

are considered exceptions. The reasons given are a poor culture for entrepreneurs, no risk money allotted for R&D and manufacturing, and no first customers for new firms. Actually, these are not the basic reasons. Here are two of the real reasons.

One is that high-tech start-ups were not needed in Japan when it was catching up. The best engineers were needed to make operational improvements. Even if some unique technology-oriented start-ups were born, they had no room to develop their businesses.

The second reason is that most high-level engineers did not want to start their own businesses. This is why even when high-tech start-ups are needed, few R&D start-ups are developed at first.

Some people[3] are starting to say that these high-level engineers, especially in big corporations, are like slaves who blindly follow their managers' orders and should be released for the progress of Japanese industry. Actually, their numbers are few,[4] and they have few successful entrepreneurs as role models.

THE EMERGING SPIN-OFF REVOLUTION

As shown in Table 3.2, something is happening to promote high-tech start-ups. Several are emerging, some have gone public, and others are going to IPO in a year or so. Two are listed in the No. 1 Tokyo Stock Market.

The founders are elite engineers, spinning out from big companies. They are good at strategic collaboration with big companies; are producing profits from the first year; use government funds cleverly; aim at early stage IPOs; have close relations with professors; and seek global collaborations from an early stage.

There are still less than 50 of these start-ups, not enough to change an entire industry. However, young engineers of leading corporations and doctoral

TABLE 3.2

The New Wave–Emerging High-Tech Start-ups in Japan

Company	Founder	Ex-company	Founded	Application
Incs	Shinjiro Yamada	Mitsui Metal	1990	3D CAD Die Molding
Thine	Tetsuya Iizuka	Toshiba	1992	LCD System LSI Design
Megachips	Masahiro Shindo	Mitsubishi Elec.	1990	Digital Image LSI Design
SAMCO	Osamu Tsuji	NASA	1979	Thin Film Technology
Yozan	Sunao Takatori	Consultant	1990	Cell Phone System LSI
Optware	Hideyoshi Horimai	Sony	1998	Tera-byte Optical Storage
Lattice Tech	Hiroshi Toriya	Ricoh	1997	Ultra Super Light 3D Software
EC-One	Yukihiro Kayama	Mitsubishi Corp.	1998	Software Parts
North	Asao Iijima	Sony	1990	Print Circuit Board
Cybozu	Toru Takasuka	Matsushita	1997	Group Ware
Adtex	Fusahiko Hasegawa	IBM-Japan	1993	Hard Disk
Celartem	Jiro Shindo	Venture Link	1996	Image Processing

students from leading universities are going to work for them. For some, it is more difficult to join than to join Sony, Honda, or Kyocera.

Through interviews, we found that the primary interest of these engineers is not acquiring company stock but development as business specialists who would be free from layoffs. They may leave in five years to set up their own companies. In this way, the number of start-ups will increase year by year. Young non-engineers with MBA degrees are starting to leave big corporations and government offices such as the Ministry of Economy, Trade and Industry (METI).

High-level people are starting to become mobile for the first time in 50 years. METI and cabinet offices are setting up committees[5] to develop policies to support spin-offs. According to my simulation,[6] in the year 2010, about 450 R&D start-ups will have IPOs and about 80,000 engineers will be working in these companies. This number of IPOs would be about 10 percent of the total in the open market. It would be a critical mass.

THE NEED FOR MICRO-LEVEL TRANSFORMATION OF ENTERPRISES

The current Japanese situation reminds me of "managing our way to economic decline," the 1980 *Harvard Business Review* paper of Hayes and Abernathy. They emphasized the unwillingness of corporations to innovate as the real culprit rather than poor government financial and tax policies. It is time for Japan to learn from the United States of 20 years ago.

CORPORATE VENTURING

The principal catchphrase of technology management has changed every 10 years.[7] In the 1960s, it was "managing R&D"'; in the 1970s, it was "technology transfer"; in the 1980s, it was "technology innovation"; in the 1990s, it was "technology strategy"; and in the 2000s it will be "corporate venturing."

Corporate venturing addresses big corporations' "innovators dilemma," by using start-ups' entrepreneurship. Tools of corporate venturing are in-house start-ups, risk money investment as a corporate venture capital company, collaboration with start-ups, joint development with start-ups, incubation of start-ups, and so on.

Among these, collaboration with spin-offs is the most important one for Japan. In many Japanese companies, often a person who leaves is regarded as practically a criminal.[8] Sony, Fujitsu, NEC, Ricoh, Recruit, and Mitsui Corp. are among the few exceptions. These companies are trying to help spin-offs. In Sony, for example, if an outstanding performer shows an inclination to spin off, members of senior management, even the CEO or COO, congratulate that person, and the top management will seek to ally with the resulting spin-off entity.

Toyota, for example, helped a new 3D image software development start-up called Lattice Technology in 1999. Its founders were Ricoh spin-offs in 1997. Toyota is using its technology as a first customer, powerful support indeed for a tiny start-up.

NEC had a patent on which it had spent U.S. $10 million that was not being well used. The inventor wanted to use it outside NEC to expand the market. NEC agreed and helped to establish a start-up, offering its monopoly use with a license fee and two years of free support in administration and laboratory equipment use. NEC also secured the right to acquire stock in the start-up as an option. (This is the first case of taking advantage of a change in regulation.) NEC has no equity in the start-up, so the start-up has a free hand. Knowing it was supported by NEC, some venture capitals invested in it.

Koji Nishigaki, the president of NEC, is quoted as follows: "In Japan, too many high-level graduates are gathering to big corporations. It is not easy in one corporation for tens of thousands of high-level persons to all show their capability. NEC is starting to put some high-level persons outside of NEC with IPR as start-up founder, and support them with risk money as their equity."[9]

Interest in spin-offs is in contrast to in-house start-ups. The latter are not showing much success, except a few, such as Sony's PlayStation, Mitsubishi's Net-One, and Plus Stationaries' Askul. Corporate staffs are averse to risk, so often it is better to spin operations off.

MACRO-LEVEL TRANSFORMATION: THE NATIONAL BUSINESS MODEL

The research and development investment ratio to GDP in Japan has long been the highest in the world, at about 3.2 percent in 2001. It is often said that the return on these investments, however, has been low. A key reason could be that it has been spent following the "old" national business model.

The keyword for Japan used to be "catch-up." In the United States, the keyword is the Silicon Valley model (or e-business model) based on entrepreneurship. Despite the excesses of the dotcom bubble, the IT industry is transforming and creating connections among various industries—financial services, retail, life sciences, and others. These combinations are generating many start-ups with new jobs being created, as opposed to the massive layoffs by big corporations. In Europe, there have been many changes: pan-European product development; mergers and acquisitions (M&As) among European companies; mix of managers' nationalities within a company; restructuring of warehouse, plant, and logistics; unification of product quality and safety regulations; and so on. With the new business model, the market is innovating through creative destruction.

THE FIVE-CIRCLE MODEL

What is the business model that can keep Japanese industry dynamic for the coming 30 years? The author has proposed a combination of an e-business model and the Japanese manufacturing model into a five-circle model that links together five industries: devices, mini operating systems, information electronics, communication networks, and digital content and services. The first three circles comprise Japan's long-time strength in manufacturing. In particular, Japanese industry is strong in key devices such as flat-panel displays, storage, system LSI (large-scale integration) microdevices, and so forth. The United States has traditionally been strong in the two remaining two circles: communication networks and digital content and services. However, in the evolving e-business era, the most important factors are security and ease of use (i.e., the man-machine interface), which may give Japan an opportunity to leverage its extensive expertise in manufacturing. During the PC age, Intel and Microsoft controlled e-business. However, in the coming mobile age, Japanese tiny and complex nonmodular hardware and software technology will be strong. The key issue for Japan is whether combinations of these areas of expertise are possible.[10] Here, high-tech start-ups will be mandatory. Big corporations and universities alone are not good at these niche and high-response business areas.

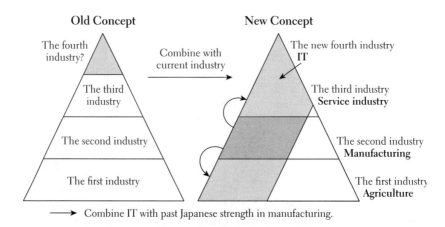

FIGURE 3.1   New Concept of Japanese IT Business

Risk-taking start-ups can promote these combination businesses, with the co-operation of big corporations and universities.

These combinations are illustrated in Figure 3.1 in a generic way.

The fourth industry is a cross section of IT and the other. Because of Japan's strength in devices, it can take advantage of the second industry, the manufacturing area, and the IT industry. The combination of the manufacturing and service industries would create new values.

REGIONAL-LEVEL TRANSFORMATION: MEGA-CLUSTER NETWORKS

Clusters could change Japan's industrial structure and its regions. METI started an industrial cluster policy with 19 regions in 2000, and MEXT started its knowledge-cluster policy with 15 regions in 2001.

This cluster strategy is very different from the 1980s industry agglomeration policy. The key factors are not plants controlled from headquarters in Tokyo or Osaka but rather local companies, including start-ups and collaborations with local universities and local government institutions. The results depend on regional leadership.

It is interesting to compare this approach with those in different localities. Silicon Valley was created by the market, not by government at any level. Austin in Texas and Research Triangle Park in North Carolina had some local government support. Michael Porter showed the success factors of five sample regions in the United States.[11]

In Germany, cluster development has been an important issue. The federal government has promoted the BioRegio.[12] Three regions were selected among 16 candidates for concentrated support; in five years Germany developed three active bio clusters and exceeded the UK in bio start-up activities.

Cluster development should be bottom-up, as Porter shows with the examples of California's wine cluster and Italy's shoe making. However, in countries like Germany and Japan, where bottom up clusters have not developed, central government can help.

A COMPARISON OF U.S., EU, AND JAPANESE REGIONS

In the past three years, the author and his colleagues studied various overseas regions. Clusters where low-technology industries were successfully transformed to high-technology ones were selected. In the United States, Austin in Texas, Research Triangle Park in North Carolina, San Diego in California, and Silicon Valley were selected. In Europe, Dortmond, the old coal and steel town, and Munich were selected from Germany. Sofia Antipolis, often called a French Tsukuba, and Oulu, a tiny town with a population of only 120,000 were selected in Finland.

Through on-site interviews and document research we identified key success factors. They included the presence of research institutes, venture capitalists, university-industry connections, an anchor company, good quality of life, among other things. If a given element is fully achieved or matches the evaluation standard, 5 points are given; but if the element is not achieved, 0 points are given. The maximum number of points is 100 as a total. (See Figure 3.2.)

Silicon Valley scored 90 points; San Diego, Dortmond, and Munich each received 70; and Sophia Antipolis tallied 60 points. A score of more than 70 points looks to be an indicator of a successful cluster. Japanese regions trying to become clusters currently score about 30 points.

SPIN-OFF TREE

In U.S. and European successful clusters, spin-off start-ups almost always play important roles. From the local anchor companies, many spin-offs were born 20 to 30 years ago. And from them came others.

In the San Diego bio cluster, 40 start-ups were born in the 20 years from the creation of the anchor company, Hybritech, which was set up in 1978. There are many varieties of spin-offs: from bankruptcy, from management conflicts, or for new business development. Similar catalysts for new firm creation exist in Silicon Valley and in Research Triangle Park.

20 Elements	Austin		Oulu		Sapporo	
Enabler						
1 Specific area	In a city	5	In a city	5	In a city	5
2 Specific industry	IT, software	5	IT? communications	5	IT? software	5
3 Local resources	University students	2	University students	1	University students	2
4 Reactive	Number of jobs for students	3	Population decline	4	Economic recession	3
5 Anchor company	Dell '84	2	Farmos '60	3	BUG '77	2
6 R&D institute	MCC '83	4	VTT-Electronics '70	3	Hokkaido University	2
7 Public institute	Drawing	5	Collaboration	3	Collaboration	2
8 Visionary accelerator	Prof. Koznetsky	5	Prof. Oksman	5	Prof. Aoki	2
9 Industry-university fusion	SEMATECH	5	VTT, Ouli University	5	Hokkaidou University	2
10 Connect function	IC ≤ '77	5	Techno Polis '82	5	Business café	4
11 Local competition		3		3		1
12 VC, angel		5		2		2
13 Business support	ATI	5	Oulu Tech	3		2
14 Other industry fusion	Nanotechnology	1	Biotechnology	3	Biotechnology	3
15 Global		5		3		2
16 Spin-off		4		3		3
17 Big corporation collaboration		5		2		1
18 IPO		5		2	Soft front, open loop	2
19 Country recognition		5		5		3
20 Quality of life		4		1		3
Total		83		64		51

5 points × 20 = 100 points

FIGURE 3.2   Cluster Self-Evaluation Chart

The quality of the original institution is important. In Austin, many spin-offs came from public laboratories such as MCC and SEMATEC, and from big corporations such as IBM, TI, Motorola, and Dell. In Oulu, Finland, VTT-Electronics, the national research laboratory, created over 200 spin-off start-ups during the past 30 years; this number is more than the total of 200 researchers at the VTT-Electronics laboratory.

In Japan, Sapporo Valley is the only cluster where we can show a genealogy tree of multiple generations of spin-offs. However, it is very small.

CLUSTER AS A NATIONAL INNOVATION SYSTEM

Porter has criticized Japan's Tokyo and Osaka concentrations as ineffective agglomerations.[13] "More than 50 percent of manufacturing industry shipments are concentrated in Tokyo and Osaka. This kind of economic geography is damaging the efficiency of the nation. How to change it should be the key policy issue of Japan. In a global economy, the merit of huge agglomeration in one place no longer applies. Continuous competitive advantages can be obtained from local advantages

We have named potential world-class clusters in Japan as mega clusters. Mega clusters would combine high-tech technology with Japanese strength in manufacturing. Examples include IT mega clusters in Tokyo, bio mega clusters in Osaka/Kobe/Kyoto, nanotechnology mega clusters in Sendai, and environment technology mega clusters in Northern Kyushu. Each mega cluster contains IT, bio, nano, and environmental components, and they compete and collaborate with each other. This mega cluster network will act as a national innovation system for Japan.

IMPLICATIONS FOR JAPANESE SCIENCE
AND TECHNOLOGY POLICY

The Small Business Innovation Research (SBIR) program in the United States encourages R&D start-ups with decentralized government help.

In Germany, BioRegio, the bio model cluster development project, created collaborations with MPG, the public basic research institute located all over Germany.[14] BioRegio also created a close collaboration with big pharmaceutical companies.

Japanese public laboratories and big corporations need to have experiences working with high-tech start-ups. It is time to involve them in the Japanese national innovation systems.

84

CONCLUSION

The lost 10 years did not pass in vain. Hundreds of elite engineers of big corporations started their own companies as spin-offs. They have outstanding technologies. We can say the second and third Sony, Honda, and Kyoceras have been born.

At the micro level, big companies need to solve the innovators' dilemma. They can use the power of high-tech start-up in corporate venturing.

At the macro level, Japan needs a new business model. Thanks to the high-tech start-ups, we can develop the five-circle model, a combination of the e-business and Japanese manufacturing models.

At the regional level, Japan needs to implement a mega cluster concept as a key part of the Japanese national innovation system.

NOTES

This chapter was originally written for a workshop co-sponsored by the Stanford Project on Regions of Innovation and Entrepreneurship (SPRIE) and the Stanford Japan Center–Research (SJC-R). The author wishes to thank Professor Henry S. Rowen, Shorenstein Asia-Pacific Research Center, Stanford University, for provocative conversations and written comments that led to refinements of the text. Any remaining errors are the author's.

1. Michael Porter and Hirotaka Takeuchi, *Can Japan Compete?* Diamond, 2000, pp. 6–7.

2. Porter and Takeuchi, op. cit., pp. 126–131. Clayton Christensen, *The Innovator's Dilemma* (in Japanese), Shoeisha, 2000, p. 8.

3. Shuji Nakamura, *Break through with Anger*, Shueisha, 2001. Tetsuya Iizuka, "Top Niche Company," *Nikkei Business*, January 1, 2000. "Techno Garden," *Nikkei Business*, September 23, 2002.

4. Noboru Maeda, "From Collaboration to Combination of University, Industry and Government," *Organizational Science* 34(1), 2000.

5. METI: "Spin-off Study Committee," headed by Professor Takeru Ohe, Waseda University, started at the end of 2002. The author is one of the committee members. In April 2003, the recommendation report "Unchain from the Big Corporation's Closed Culture" was published. Cabinet Office: "R&D Oriented Start-up Development Project Committee" started October 2002 assigned by Prime Minister Koizumi and headed by Professor Shuichi Matsuda, Waseda University. The author is one of the committee members.

6. Noboru Maeda, *Spin-off Revolution*, Toyokeizai, 2002, pp. 253–261.

7. Presentation by David Weber, director of MIT's Management of Technology (MOT) program, at MOT MO International Conference at Keidanren Hall, March 2003.

8. Ian MacMillan, professor of management at The Wharton School, University of Pennsylvania, defined spin-off and spin-out at the METI spin-off committee in March 2003. Spin-out means wishing to keep no relationship with the parent company after the split. Spin-off means wishing to keep some kind of relationship after the split.

9. "Can Japan Build Up a Knowledge-Oriented Country?" interviews with top management and professors and with NEC president Koji Nishigaki, *Asahi Newspaper*, July 9, 2002.

10. Takahiro Fujimoto, professor of economics at Tokyo University, describes the ability of firms to integrate a vast number of individual parts and components to make a fine-tuned whole as "suriawase" (literally "grinding" but better translated as "integration").

11. Five regional cluster study reports are available on the Council on Competitiveness websites: http://www.compete.org/nri/clusters_innovation.asp and http://www.compete.org/publications/clusters_reports.asp

12. BioRegio is one of the federal government policies of selecting cities to support through competition. Selection and concentration define the basic policy. Masayuki Kondo and Noboru Maeda, "A Study of European Start-up Supporting Policies," Economic Research Center/Kochi University of Technology, 2000, pp. 24–27, 54–63. Noboru Maeda, *Spin-off Revolution*, Toyokeizai, 2002, pp. 124–131.

13. Michael Porter, *On Competition*, Diamond, 1999, p. 119.

14. Max-Planck-Gesellschaft.

REFERENCES

Chabbal, R., and N. Maeda. 2000. "The Development of Research Related Start-ups — A France-Japan Comparison." National Institute of Science and Technology Policy (NISTEP) Discussion Paper 16.

Christensen, C. M. 1997. *The Innovator's Dilemma: When New Technologies Cause Great Firms to Fail*. Boston: Harvard Business School Press.

Feigenbaum, E. 2002. *The Japanese Entrepreneur: Making the Desert Bloom*. Nikkei.

Florida, R. 2002. *The Rise of the Creative Class*. New York: Basic Books.

Gibson, D., G. Kozmetsky, and R. Smilor. 1992. *The Technopolis Phenomenon*. Lanham, MD: Rowman & Littlefield.

Goto, A. 2000. *Innovation and Japanese Economy*. Iwanami Shinsho.

High Tech Austin Annual LLC. 2002. "High Tech Austin: The Ultimate Who's Who of the Austin High-Tech Community." 4th ed.

High Tech Austin Annual OECD. 1999. "Boosting Innovation: The Cluster Approach."

———. 2001. "Innovative Clusters: Drivers of National Innovation System."

Hokkaido History of IT Industry. 2000. "The Birth of Sapporo Valley." Yellow Page.

Iizuka, T. 2003. "Challenge of Spin-off Start-up." PHP.

Ishihara Y., N. Maeda, et al. 2003. *Strategy for Cluster Initiatives in Japan*. Yuhikaku.

Kondo, M., and N. Maeda. 2002. "A Study of European Start-up Supporting Policies." Unpublished manuscript, Economic Research Center/Kochi University of Technology.

86   Maeda, N. 1999. "Japanese New Business Model." NISTEP Policy Study 3.
———. 1999. *The Transnational Strategy by Autonomous New Combination* (in Japanese). Tokyo: Doyukan.
———. 2002. *Spin-off Revolution*. Toyo Keizai Publishing.
Maeda, N., et al. 2003. "Success Factors and Policy of Regional Cluster." NISTEP Discussion Paper 29.
Porter, M. 1998. *On Competition*. Boston: Harvard Business School Press.
———. 2001. "Cluster of Innovation." Regional Foundations of U.S. Competitiveness, Council on Competitiveness.
Porter, M., and H. Takeuchi. 2000. *Can Japan Compete?* Diamond.
Sakakibara, K. 1999. "Entrepreneur Business — Japanese Issue." NISTEP Policy Study 2.
Sapporo Valley. 2002. "Spirits of Sapporo Valley." Sapporo Industry Development.
Smilor, R. W., G. Kozmetsky, and D. V. Gibson. 1988. *Creating the Technopolis: Linking Technology Commercialization and Economic Development*. New York: Ballinger.
Yamazaki, A. 2002. *Cluster Strategy*. Tokyo: Yuhikaku.

Appendix 1

Japanese Clusters

Toru Tanigawa

The Development Bank of Japan (DBJ) and Stanford University have jointly examined the characteristics of eight Japanese regions. The survey was done by DBJ headquarters and seven of its branches in collaboration with Kyushu University; the Research Institute of Economy, Trade, and Industry (RIETI); Stanford Japan Center–Research; and other universities.

Individual DBJ branches selected the regions and did the survey of 2,738 companies. Professor Toru Tanigawa of Kyushu University supervised the research.

The characteristics deemed of particular importance were innovation, the climate for entrepreneurship, and international linkages. The report also identifies similarities to the model of Silicon Valley, the "home of high-tech ventures."

The last part contemplates the potentials and directions of Japanese cluster development in the future.

ENTREPRENEURSHIP AND INTERNATIONAL LINKAGES

The survey revealed that business start-ups seldom are company spin-offs (13% overall, but 34% in Sapporo) or supported by a university or research institution. Also, that risk capital from venture capitalists is rare; start-up money typically comes from bank loans. The clusters display little entrepreneurial activity. However, recently there has been more business-academia collaboration and an increase in regional venture funds. This could create more start-up activity, but Japan's cultural and social atmosphere still discourages risky start-ups, and most top-class university graduates want to join large organizations.

88   International linkages are also weak. Three-fourths of the surveyed companies are not involved in international trade and have no or few interests overseas, and even their domestic linkages are weak. Employment of foreigners is
also rare, although three areas — Hiroshima, Tokushima, and Fukuoka — were
relatively open to it.

Japan's clusters appear to be self-contained agglomerations of companies
with high degrees of role segmentation. Their procurement and sales functions are mostly domestically focused, which limits stimulation, internation-
alism, and their capability to innovate and compete internationally.

INNOVATION: SOME HISTORIES

Aichi is known for its inventions in the automatic loom industry dating from
over a century ago as well as more recent innovations in mass-production
technology, forging technology, and quality-control systems that comprise the
foundation of its automobile cluster today.

Yonezawa, Yamagata's electrical and machinery cluster, developed out of
an integration of traditional textiles and machinery industries with the aerospace engineering industry, which located there during World War II.

Fukuoka managed a transition from its longtime strength in the steel industry (machinery and metal processing) to its current semiconductor industry
cluster.

Such regions have fostered distinctive technologies over long periods. They
are not only survivors, they flourish. The presence of supporting industries
and people with a strong sense of belonging to a region reinforces an autonomous capability to make progress. This includes an ability to adapt to environmental change that suggests a good potential for competitiveness.

TRADITION OF CRAFTSMANSHIP

The Japanese craft tradition is focused on production technology rather than
products. More than half of them chose "production process technology and
combination of technology" to a question regarding their most advanced technology. Only one fourth replied affirmatively to the choice "development of
an innovative product is the first priority," although it was selected by relatively
high percentages in Kyoto (48%) and Fukuoka (47%).

Only in Sapporo, Sendai, Kyoto, and Fukuoka did 50 percent or more of
the companies' presidents hold bachelor's or higher degrees. In Aichi's automobile cluster, over 80 percent of the presidents had two-year college degrees

or less. This contrasts with typical foreign, technology-based companies, in which most managers have master's or doctorate degrees.

This difference in education may be related to the emphasis on production technology or learned craftsmanship, and that accumulation of know-how is more highly prized than academic achievement. That is, production-process technology innovation ("how to make") is ranked above product innovation ("what to make").

Japanese culture stresses the production of high-quality products using extremely sophisticated craftsmanship accumulated over years rather than the creation of novel products that match the market trend. At one time a distinctive competitiveness was present among Japanese industry clusters in manufacturing, but recently other Asian countries have achieved rapid growth through this strategy — severely affecting the prosperity of Japanese industries. This may indicate that the future strategies of Japanese industries may focus more on product innovation than craftsmanship.

VERTICAL COLLABORATION

Companies in most regions had a "vertical collaboration model," and many — particularly in Aichi, Hiroshima, and Fukuoka — still do. This keiretsu relationship included the core enterprise's intervention in its affiliates' business, including capital, management, production, and sales. However, currently the affiliates often have more autonomy in terms of capital and management.

The cluster of Toyota and its group companies in Aichi Prefecture is representative of the vertical collaboration model. Information as well as outputs are shared within the group and build on each other — they cannot be easily transferred outside by spin-offs. Thus, at a time when modularization has become a standard industrial tool, Toyota's vertical collaborations seems to be a major factor in its sustained successes.

However, much depends on the core enterprise's performance. If the core company has a downturn or shifts its stronghold overseas, then the whole cluster would be affected.

SURVEYED CLUSTERS' CURRENT SITUATIONS
AND CHARACTERISTICS

Finding an appropriate platform with which to compare the clusters is difficult because their core industries differ. However, we assigned them to three categories: (1) Silicon Valley model — Sapporo, Yonezawa, and Fukuoka, (2)

90   traditional Japanese cluster model—Aichi and Hiroshima, and (3) maverick or unique cluster model—Sendai, Kyoto, and Tokushima.

Silicon Valley Cluster Model (Common in Sapporo, Yonezawa, and Fukuoka)

Key concepts in Silicon Valley–type clusters are "entrepreneurship," "organic horizontal collaboration beyond the business connection," "open environment," and "international linkages."

The surveyed Sapporo cluster has several software ventures from Hokkaido University and spin-offs from private companies. However, the cluster lacks international linkages, which seems to be a barrier to its further development.

The presence of successful IT companies with distinctive business strategies and multi-layered and horizontal collaborations characterizes the Yonezawa cluster. The area has business-academia collaborations involving Yamagata University in organic electroluminescence ("organic E").

Clusters in Fukuoka are probably the closest to the Silicon Valley model. There are many spin-offs; companies are engaged in innovative product development; and there are horizontal collaborations. Many companies have strong international linkages. The semiconductor cluster stresses R&D, such as integrated circuit (IC) design, and takes advantage of its proximity to an automobile cluster in Kyushu and to IT clusters in other parts of Asia.

Traditional Japanese Cluster Model (Common in Aichi and Hiroshima)

The Aichi cluster represents the traditional Japanese model with historical continuity, distinctive craftsmanship, and vertical collaboration. The companies around the core, Toyota, constitute the leading automobile cluster in the world. The cluster does not meet SPRIE's benchmarks of "entrepreneurship" in the sense of creating new companies (but it does fit Ken-ichi Imai's definition in his chapter), but the individual companies have a commitment to each other that has sustained the cluster's regions vitality. However, its future depends on Toyota's performance.

The other cluster in this group is in Hiroshima. It once served as a national military stronghold, home to Kure Naval Base, because of its advanced steel and iron processing and shipbuilding industries and its competencies in placer iron processing. Its present machinery cluster derived from the munitions industry of World War II. Toyo Kogyo Co. (presently Mazda Motor Co.) in automobiles, and Mitsubishi Heavy Industries Co. in shipbuilding have been its mainstays. They are still core companies but the region has suffered from the decline in their business performances. Companies are now diversifying and entering new markets in order to survive.

Maverick or Unique Model (Kyoto, Sendai, and Tokushima)

Kyoto, Sendai, and Tokushima do not fit either of the preceding models. Kyoto has some start-ups that became global companies within one generation, such as Kyocera, Omron, and Rohm. Kyoto has an exclusive social environment that might have caused local entrepreneurs to seek overseas know-how and technologies. Although the number of its entrepreneurs has grown, local horizontal collaborations are rare and the region seems closed-minded. However, some universities have recently been encouraging technology transfers to business.

The core of Sendai is Tohoku University, whose resources have attracted public and private research organizations. Government and industry are fostering a support network for start-ups, and enterprises from the university have begun to appear. However, the business volume is low, and networking is weak.

The surveyed Tokushima region has two large companies — Otsuka Pharmaceutical (chemical products manufacturer) and Nichia (electrical manufacturer) — but not many others. Tokushima University is fostering technology seeds and human resources. One of its graduates, Prof. Shuji Nakamura (University of California, Santa Barbara), is the inventor of the blue light-emitting diode.

CONCLUSION

Japan naturally exhibits industrial clustering. The DBJ survey documents the character of several, some of which have remarkable vitality, such as Aichi, and some of which are newly formed, such as Fukuoka in semiconductors.

Japan shows that there is more than one way to international success. There is much to be said in favor of the Silicon Valley model, but there is also much to be said in support of the traditional Japanese one. A task facing Japan is to choose where each is appropriate.

Appendix 2

SEMICONDUCTOR CLUSTER FORMATION
IN FUKUOKA

Yasuhisa Yamaguchi

A study of the Fukuoka area[1] was carried out by a joint team of the Development Bank of Japan (DBJ), and the Fukuoka Industry, Science and Technology Foundation (IST) with the cooperation of Kyushu University (KU). Its purpose was to understand how the semiconductor cluster has formed there and to clarify its characteristics.

The Kyushu area accounts for 35 percent of Japan's domestic semiconductor production. During the past few years, the area has been in a transitional stage of forming a new semiconductor industry focused on logic rather than memory microchips.

In Fukuoka Prefecture, there is an accumulation of expertise in large-scale integration (LSI) technologies by Kyushu University, Kyushu Institute of Technology, Waseda University, and the System LSI College.[2] For example, Kyushu University founded the "Kyushu University System LSI Research Center" under the leadership of Prof. Hiroto Yasuura, and is planning an incubation center; Kita-Kyushu City has invited the Information Technology Faculty of Waseda University and GMD[3]-Japan to the Kita-Kyushu Science and Research Park; and Fukuoka City has established the Fukuoka Soft Research Park and a foundation named the Institute of Systems and Information Technology (ISIT) to develop LSI systems. As a result, large semiconductor manufacturers are locating design centers and R&D centers in this area.

The enterprises in this cluster are of three types: (1) large semiconductor device companies, (2) parts suppliers and hardware manufacturers (such as assembly and packaging), and (3) system design companies (or hybrid companies involved in both software and hardware). Among these, the assembly and packaging companies are distinctive, there being 151[4] in Fukuoka Prefecture alone (366 throughout all of Kyushu). They produce lead frames, metallic moldings, and semiconductor fabrication equipment for the large companies.

Ninety percent of these firms are locally based, and many are spin-off companies.

For example, Mitsui High-Tech, Inc. was spun off from Yasukawa Electric Corporation, and Ishii Tool and Engineering Co. Ltd. from Mitsui High-Tech. A third characteristic is their horizontal collaboration on R&D and market development.

System design and software companies are also moving into Fukuoka because of the talent there and to be close to the semiconductor companies. Following the completion of Fukuoka Soft Research Park in 1996, NEC, Fujitsu, Matsushita, Sony, and Hitachi established design divisions. Sony moved its area headquarters there in 2001. Fabless venture companies such as Logic Research Co. Ltd., JM-Net, Inc., and Thine Electronics Kyushu Co. Ltd., also located in the same Momochi area.

INTERACTION AND DIVERSIFICATION

In the past there has been neither active interaction nor business cooperation between the assembling and packaging companies and the design companies, because most were in the keiretsu of the big companies. However, the Sony group has begun to open its doors to the assembling and packaging industry. The presence of the Microelectronics Assembly & Packaging (MAP) workshop has had a great impact. It began in the Assembling and Packaging Device Council (consisting of 200 companies and chaired by Prof. Hajime Tomokage, Fukuoka University) a part of Fukuoka IST Prefecture's foundation. Its aim is to strengthen the collaboration among companies. It was also motivated by the companies' desire to move to higher value-added products.

Many semiconductor-related companies have now recognized the so-called *common platform* movement — multilayer integration of system development, design, production, packaging, inspection, marketing, and customer service. The Fukuoka cluster's platform is trying to fulfill these functions.

PUBLIC SUPPORT

The public sector supplies not only the facilities (e.g., the Kita-Kyushu Science and Research Park and Fukuoka Soft Research Park) but also R&D, human resource development services, and marketing (e.g., holding forums to promote companies in sales).

TABLE 1
Location of Semiconductor-Related Factories in Kyushu

Location	Total (C)	Local Factories (D)	(D/C)	Semiconductor Makers			Manufacturing Equipment Makers	Parts/ Submaterials Makers	Materials Makers	Other
				Integration	Wafer Process	Assembly Process				
Fukuoka (A)	170	153	90.0%	1	2	12	36	102	10	9
(A/B)	38.9%	44.9%	—	12.5%	0.0%	17.6%	39.6%	51.3%	23.8%	34.6%
Saga	24	12	50.0%	0	0	1	3	10	10	0
Nagasaki	9	6	66.7%	0	2	5	0	1	1	0
Kumamoto	92	64	69.6%	2	1	17	28	29	8	7
Oita	57	43	75.4%	1	0	12	15	22	3	4
Miyazaki	30	19	63.3%	2	0	3	2	13	5	5
Kagoshima	55	44	80.0%	2	0	18	7	22	5	1
Total (B)	437	341	78.0%	8	3	68	91	199	42	26

SOURCE: Kyushu Economic Research Center.

NOTE: Unit number of factories and plants.

The prefecture government has formulated the "Silicon Sea Belt Plan" to make Fukuoka an LSI development center in Asia. System LSI College has been evaluated highly by the private companies. Fukuoka Venture Market (FVM) supports fundraising and company matching, and as of May 2002, 580 companies were participants, and an investment of 8 billion yen had been raised.

COMPETITIVENESS THROUGH INNOVATION

Logic and system LSI developments require state-of-the-art microfabrication technologies, and coordination between design and production activities is increasing in importance. As accuracy standards have risen, microfabrication is reaching technological limits. The system LSI technology to build multiple modules on one chip is called *system on chip* (SOC). Sony and Toshiba, for instance, jointly developed a 90 nm process chip by integrating a CPU for the new PlayStation and the animation processor "graphics synthesizer."

System-in-package (SIP) technology has been growing rapidly in Kyushu. Advantages of SIP are (1) smaller dimensions through the adoption of three-dimensional modules, (2) shorter development times, (3) low mask cost, (4) easy-to-change designs because of module-based production systems, and (5) faster processing speeds via shortened wiring systems. On the other hand, SIP is unsuitable for mass production, thus making production costs relatively high.

Based on replies to a questionnaire, the competitiveness of the Fukuoka packaging industry is sustained by microfabrication technology, local technologies, and instrumentation technology and by applying them to higher value-added products. In addition, most of these companies are locally based and are not affected by strategizing in distant headquarters.

Saga Electronics Co. Ltd. has strengths in (1) microfabrication, (2) local production, (3) sophistication of packaging technology (from SOC to SIP), and (4) flexibility. These have enabled shortening of the delivery time from 21 days (in 1996) to 5 days (in 2002).

Ueno Seiki, Inc. has world-class technology in (1) trimming and forming devices, (2) BGA ball mounts, and (3) test handlers. More than half of its sales volume is overseas.

DECISION MAKING ON THE MANUFACTURING SITE

Among large companies, such as Sony and Mitsubishi Electronics, decision making is moving from the Tokyo headquarters to the regional branches. This helps to promote rapid response to changes in the business environment and the flexibility that accelerates development.

In 2001, Sony founded a semiconductor design and management company, *Sony Semiconductor Kyushu, Inc.*, (SSK) that (1) integrates its branch factories in Kyushu, (2) brings closer to the production site some functions that had been handled at headquarters, (3) develops new trading partners, (4) redeploys people, and (5) participates in industry-academia-administration collaborations. The main aim is quick decision making for business in Asia and Kyushu. The Sony parent company's headquarters is still in charge of developing special devices such as system LSI for its new PlayStation, but SSK makes most decisions on production and design for key devices such as CCD, LCD, MOS, Mixed Signal, and so on.

In 2003, *Mitsubishi Electric, Inc.* moved authority for all of its automotive-related semiconductor business from its Tokyo headquarters to Fukuoka.

ELECTRONIC MANUFACTURING SYSTEM (EMS) DEVELOPMENTS

The Fukuoka area has a locality advantage in EMS for the Asian market or Asian foundries. That is why fabless venture companies such as Logic Research Co. Ltd., JM-Net, Inc., and Thine Electronics Kyushu Co. Ltd. are there.

Logic Research, Inc. was established in 1992 by Tadaaki Tsuchiya. He was a sales engineer at Fujitsu for 10 years, but quit in 1990, because he realized the limits of promotion in a big company and wished to go back to Kyushu. His company does LSI designs and uses Taiwanese foundries.

ENTREPRENEURSHIP AND ITS LINKAGE IN FUKUOKA

Fukuoka has traditionally been an international trade city open to unfamiliar things from the world outside. Horizontal collaboration (interactions among companies beyond keiretsu frameworks) is easy, and the open-mindedness there provides opportunities to build credibility. Kazuo Ueki, CEO of JM-Net, Inc., made the following comment. "It is almost impossible to have a chance to meet the president of a large company in Tokyo or Osaka, but not in Fukuoka."[5]

PEOPLE SKILLS AND INFORMAL COMMUNITIES

Key factors for success these days are not so much the devices and technologies but rather people with special skills — not only in semiconductors but in all industry. From the interviews, Fukuoka, as compared to Tokyo, has higher numbers in terms of its ratio of talented people — the "settlements ratio," meaning the sense of belonging to a community more than to an organization. Such communities act as informal networks and reduce transaction costs.

According to the survey, system design companies are particularly enthusiastic about information exchange activities within Fukuoka. As an example, the MAP workshop enables one-to-one exchange of intelligence. In this sense, Fukuoka is similar to Silicon Valley.

NOTES

Chief Representative, Oita Representative Office, Development Bank of Japan.

1. The Japanese full report was written by Professor Koichi Sakaguchi (KU), Toru Nabeyama (DBJ), Yasuhisa Yamaguchi (DBJ), Yoshihiro Kubo (IST), and Professor Toru Tanigawa (KU).

2. This college is managed by Fukuoka IST.

3. The German Research Institution of Information Technology, which recently merged with Fraunhofer Gesellschaft.

4. Of the 170 total firms in Kyushu's semiconductor industry in 1999, 151 were in microelectronics assembly and packaging, while the remaining were in materials (10 firms) and others (9 firms).

5. As interviewed by Toyo-Keizai, April 2, 2003.

REFERENCES

Aoki, M., and A. Haruhiko, eds. 2002. *Modularity* (in Japanese). Toyokeizaishinposha.

Fujimoto, T., T. Akira, and A. Yaichi, eds. 2001. *Business Architecture* (in Japanese). Yuhikaku.

Kyushu Industrial Advancement Center. 2000. *An Approach to the Strategic Industries in Kyushu Area* (in Japanese).

MAP2003 Organization Committee. 2003. Database of Semiconductor Companies in Kyushu and Asian Countries, Kyushu Economic Research Center.

Porter, M. E. 2001. "Monitor Group: On the Frontier." In *Clusters of Innovation: Regional Foundations of U.S. Competitiveness*. Council on Competitiveness.

Tomokage, H., ed. 2003. *Innovation: Spirits of Technology* (in Japanese). Kyushu Semiconductor Industries Technology Innovation Association.

Yamazaki, A., and H. Tomokage, eds. 2001. *A Scenario for Creating Semiconductor Clusters* (in Japanese). Nishinihon-shinbunsha.

11   THREE ASIAN IT TIGERS

4

HSINCHU, TAIWAN

Asia's Pioneering High-Tech Park

Chintay Shih, Kung Wang, and Yi-Ling Wei

At the beginning of the 1980s, the total output value of the information hardware industry in Taiwan was less than U.S. $100 million. By 2001, this total exceeded U.S. $20 billion, fourth highest in the world. This industry has played a large part in Taiwan's economic development and in the global development of the industry.

There has been much curiosity about how this was done. The rise of the Hsinchu Science-based Industrial Park (HSIP), sometimes called the Silicon Valley of the East (Mathews 1997), has attracted much attention from around the world as a model.

During the past three decades, Taiwan's high-tech industry structure changed from being characterized by labor-intensive PC assembly to one that was an increasingly knowledge centered, with the rise of the integrated circuit (IC) and thin-film-transistor liquid crystal display (TFT-LCD) industries. Furthermore, its competitive advantage between the 1960s and 1980s in low-cost manufacturing began being lost to mainland China, India, and other developing countries during the mid-1990s.

This chapter reviews the key institutions of technology, human resources, financial capital, and government policy for Hsinchu's development during the past two decades; the evolution of connections between Silicon Valley and Hsinchu; and growing links with mainland China. Despite political obstacles, Taiwan's high-tech industry increasingly relies on this latter connection because of China's fast-growing market and low costs of manufacturing. Encouraging greater innovation and entrepreneurship in Hsinchu is essential for the sustained growth of Taiwan's high-tech industry.

This development came in four stages, as described in the following subsections.

The Labor-Intensive Period (1952–1969)

The government put out its first four-year economic construction plan in 1953 with the goal of developing low-tech, labor-intensive industries such as textiles, plywood, home appliance assembly, and the like for domestic use and import substitution.

In 1960, the government passed the Investment Encouragement Statutes, which reduced land taxes and other levies to promote local economic development and attract foreign investment, including investments in electronics factories. With commitments from foreign investors, including General Instruments, Texas Instruments, RCA, Sanyo Electric, Matsushita Electric, and some local consumer electronics makers, Taiwan developed a substantial components industry that paved the way for an information electronics one.

The 1960s was a period of transformation from an agricultural economy to an industrial one. The currency was depreciated to promote exports, and high interest rates were adopted to suppress inflation. As a result, exports, as well as the economy, grew rapidly. In the 1960s major legislation was enacted that helped promote an industrial economy. It marked the first economic transformation of Taiwan (Kuo-ding Lee 1999).

The Capital-Intensive Industry Period (1969–1980)

As the domestic market became saturated, it was necessary to expand exports. The government was already offering tax benefits and low interest rate loans for exports. Then, in 1966, it set up export processing zones (EPZs) to encourage foreign investments and expand overseas markets.

In the 1970s a rapid growth occurred in sales of home appliances such as televisions, refrigerators, and videocassette recorders. Government policies then were (1) to localize electronic parts and components for color TV sets through technological cooperation with Japanese companies that invested in Taiwan; (2) to develop cathode ray tubes (CRTs) and assemble black-and-white TV sets under original equipment manufacturing (OEM) contracts for U.S. companies (Chunghwa Picture Tubes of Taiwan acquired CRT technology from RCA and become one of the world's leading display manufacturers as a result of the policy); and (3) to allow Philips to set up a factory in 1970 to support production of black-and-white CRTs.

By taking advantage of standardized technology, imported equipment and lower labor costs in Taiwan, foreign companies supported the rapid growth of the consumer electronics industry. Building on those achievements, it began to produce terminals, monitors, and other products associated with TV sets in the beginning of the 1980s.

However, Taiwan recognized the need to build more technology-intensive industries with higher value added and to rely less on low-cost labor.

The Technology-Intensive Period (1980–1995)

Taking advantage of the rapid worldwide growth of the IT industry, local semi-conductor and other IT products were developed quickly, replacing tradi-tional industries to become Taiwan's top industries. The pattern was one of OEM and original design and manufacturing (ODM) production, based on vertical disintegration of value chains as companies in the United States and Japan began to move their manufacturing abroad.

In 1980, the Taiwanese government established the HSIP. It chose Hsinchu partly because it was near academic and research institutions such as National Tsing Hua University (NTHU), National Chao Tung University (NCTU), and the Industrial Technology Research Institute (ITRI), all of which provided excellent human resources.

The government issued a regulation in 1990 aimed at encouraging more in-vestment in R&D, automated assembly lines, and pollution-prevention mea-sures. In 1991, the Six-Year National Construction Plan began in earnest. Telecommunications, information, consumer electronics, precision machin-ery and automation, high-performance materials, semiconductors, pharma-ceuticals, aviation, medical and health care, and pollution-prevention prod-ucts were designated as focal industries.

The High-Tech-Oriented Industry Period (1995–present)

This move toward a knowledge-based economy is marked by higher R&D spending and technology upgrades. The total value of production of electron-ics, machinery, chemicals, and transportation vehicles reached NT $4.77 tril-lion in 2003 from NT $2.97 trillion in 1996 and NT $960 billion in 1986; this brought the manufacturing sector's share from 26 percent in 1986 and 45 per-cent in 1996 to 55 percent in 2003. (The electronics industry has a 60 percent share of this total, mainly in components and semiconductor products.)

By 1995, Taiwan had become the third-leading information products pro-ducer in the world behind the United States and Japan. Its products, includ-ing notebook and desktop computers, monitors, scanners, mouses, computer

104   motherboards, CD-ROMs, and the like have grown severalfold during the past decade. In 2003, the top 20 international procurement offices in Taiwan, such as HP, Apple, and Dell, bought U.S. $45 billion information technology (IT) products up from only U.S. $11.3 billion in 1997.

Taiwan's high-tech electronics industry had taken the front seat in the island's drive for development. The strengths of the high-tech industry came from the increasing value that was being added domestically to its products. Its firms were increasing their investments in research and development.

Looking back, one sees that trade policies shaped industries differently during different periods. Today's high-tech electronics industry did not come from nowhere. Government policies played a key role in this development.

THE IT INDUSTRY IN THE HSINCHU SCIENCE-BASED INDUSTRIAL PARK

Porter (2001) describes industrial clustering as a widespread feature in the world economy. Some clusters, including Silicon Valley, are formed under the combined influence of enterprises, capitalists, joint ventures, academic institutions, and private investors (Williams 2000). In contrast, HSIP — the Silicon Valley of the East — was established by government to speed the transfer to the private sectors of existing technologies. The abundant human resources from nearby universities and research institutions played a major role in its the development (Chang and Yao 2001).

The growth rate of Taiwan's information technology industry was at its highest from the 1980s to the 1990s. The northern Taiwan area, including Taipei, Taoyuan, and Hsinchu, is more industrialized than elsewhere. Taipei County led in 2001 in output value and the number of IT firms; however, the annual growth rates of production between 1991 and 2001 of both Hsinchu City and Hsinchu County were the highest at 51 percent and 44 percent, respectively. Revenue in HSIP during the 1990s expanded by nine times. By 1976, the government had decided to establish a science-based industrial park. A government delegation visited science-based industrial parks in Silicon Valley and Boston in 1977, selected Silicon Valley as the model, and established the Hsinchu Science-based Industrial Park (HSIP) in 1980. (Although both are very successful high-tech clusters, there is a large difference between Silicon Valley and Hsinchu, notably in the direct role of government and in the creation of technology.)

The science park supports high-tech start-ups through comprehensive and generous subsidies, including tax and import duty exemptions, grants and subsidized credits, reduced rents in high-quality factory buildings or sites, living amenities for high-level researchers, and access to government and university research facilities (Amsden and Chu 2003). Over time, the government has increasingly supported advanced technology research, and, since, 1983, a venture capital industry.

The securities market has also played an important role. For one thing, equities have become a popular investment for the public; for another means to encourage people to invest in the stock market, the government exempted capital gains from taxation and introduced stock transaction tax discounts.

The annual revenue of HSIP reached U.S. $24.97 billion in 2003, and its average growth rate from 1983 was 32 percent. Taiwan's share of the world's IC foundry capacity was over 70 percent in 2003, accounted for primarily by TSMC and UMC, the two largest foundries in the world. HSIP companies invested NT $48.3 billion in R&D in 2001, 7.3 percent of sales (compared to the average of 1.3% in Taiwan overall). In the IC industry, the investment in R&D at NT $34.3 billion was the highest among all industries, while the ratio of R&D investment to revenue of the biotechnology industry at 20 percent was the highest in the Park.

LINKAGES BETWEEN HSINCHU AND THE UNITED STATES, ESPECIALLY SILICON VALLEY

According to the Science Industry Park Administration (SIPA), by July 2003 there were 4,318 returnees working at HSIP, and they had established 119 enterprises inside the Park. Senior Chinese engineers with overseas experience have long played an important role. Technology transfer often accompanies the movement of people; this is a highly effective way to acquire technology. Furthermore, the management concepts brought back by these experienced and skilled returnees have become rooted in the park and have helped its overall development. Returnees promote interaction between companies in HSIP and overseas multinational enterprises through their business and social networks.

In 1917, the Chinese Institute of Engineers (CIE) was founded in the United States by a group of far-sighted Chinese engineers. With the advice of Yun-Shun Sun and K.T. Lee, the CIE-ROC (founded in 1950) and the CIE-NY (founded in 1953) came together in 1966 to found the Modern Engineering and Technology Seminar (METS). Cooperation between engineers in Taiwan and the United States helped Taiwan to create the infrastructure for industrialization and to promote industrial research and development. Over the years, the METS, held every two years in Taiwan, set the stage for Taiwan's great microelectronics advances by introducing many new technologies. During the 1960s and 1970s, before networks with foreign experts were fully developed, the

106   METS was the main channel for science and technology talents to move between the United States and Taiwan.

Dr. Wen-Yuan Pan, director of the RCA research lab, was a key figure. He
served as the second METS convener and was invited to draw up the "draft
plan for integrated circuits" in July 1974, which became the master plan for IC
industry development. Dr. Pan persuaded several foreign technical experts to
join the Technical Advisory Committee (TAC) to work out a detailed plan for
implementation by ITRI. Eventually, among 14 firms, RCA was chosen as the
partner with its CMOS design and manufacturing technology.

The overseas members of TAC still provide suggestions for R&D directions
to ITRI, while some of its members have returned to work in Taiwan, including Dr. Eric G. Lean, who left IBM USA in 1992; he is chairman of International United Technology and former general director of OES/ITRI. Another
is Dr. Genda Hu, vice president of TSMC and former general director of
ERSO/ITRI, who came from Silicon Valley in 1996. Dr. Steve Cheng, the first
general director of Computer and Communication Research Laboratories
(CCL) of ITRI, left Bell Labs in 1990. Among venture capitalists is Dr. Paul
Wang, chairman of Taiwan Venture Capital Association, who has worked for
IBM since 1970, served as the advisory for government and ITRI in the 1980s,
and established the Pacific Venture Partners in Taiwan in 1990.

The METS and TAC are industry organizations. The government also set
up an advisory apparatus. An Advisory Board of Science and Technology was
formed in the Office of the Premier that included prominent foreign experts
in various fields of science and technology. The Science & Technology Advisory Group (STAG) was set up in 1979 as its staff. From 1979 to 1988, the convener of the STAG was Mr. K.T. Lee, the Minister of State.

The background of returnees has changed over time. Because of the scarcity of high-tech job opportunities in Taiwan and more attractive opportunities in the United States in the early days, most students studying science and
engineering abroad between the 1960s and 1970s then went to work in the labs
of large companies, such as IBM, AT&T, and RCA. During the 1980s, the entrepreneurial opportunities of the San Francisco Bay area attracted more students from Asia including Taiwan. At the same time, the Taiwanese government was planning to establish a science park with an environment similar to
that of Silicon Valley. HSIP, established in 1980, was the first high-tech startup
designed to appeal to returnees from the United States.

Their number has increased dramatically. HSIP had only 39 returnees in
1985, but it had 4,340 by 2003. By July 2003, the 4,300 had established 119 firms
out of the total of 370 firms in the Park. Along with bringing their technical
and management knowledge, returnees of Chinese origin from Silicon Valley

also brought a spirit of innovation and entrepreneurship and have played important roles in founding new companies.

In the early 1980s, few companies had been established inside the Park, in- cluding Microtek International, Inc. (MII), an image scanner maker, and Wang Computer and United Microelectronics Company (UMC), a spin-off IC company from the government research institute, ERSO/ITRI. In 1979, Bobo Wang, a former engineer at Xerox USA, established MII with Benny Hsu, an entrepreneur in Southern California; it made cheap desk-type scan- ners for the consumer market; it had its initial public offering (IPO) in 1988. After the success of Microtek International, several scanner suppliers, includ- ing Umax Data Systems and Mustek System, followed in quick succession. HSIP became the world's leading scanner industry cluster during the 1980s. The world market share of Taiwan's scanners peaked at 91 percent in 1998 with production output of U.S. $829 million.

Returnees from Silicon Valley also brought management skills. Mr. Patrick Wang, who received an MBA degree from Stanford University, established Microelectronics Technology, Inc. (MTI) in 1983, Taiwan's first company for microwave and satellite communication technology. Its global positioning sys- tem (GPS) products, mobile satellite phones, were much used during the 1990 Gulf War.

ITRI has had many returnees including Dr. Ding-Hua Hu, Dr. Chintay Shih, Dr. Ding-Yuan Yang, and Dr. Ching-Chu Chang, all of whom gradu- ated from Stanford's Sloan Program in the 1980s. In 1991, Dr. Nicky Lu, who received his PhD degree from Stanford University, founded Etron Technology with four other returnees in HSIP, Inc. Led by Dr. Lu, Etron, together with ITRI and sponsored by the Ministry of Economic Affairs, developed Taiwan's first submicron technology for producing DRAMs. The two co-founders of Etron, Dr. Hu Chao and Dr. Shu Mao, former IBM technical experts, estab- lished TM Technology, Inc. in 1994 and set up Elite Semiconductor Memory Technology, Inc. in 1998. In 2003, Etron and Elite Semiconductor were ranked in the top 10 IC fabless companies in Taiwan.

Not all such companies have succeeded. Most failures happened in the early years of HSIP. In 1981, Dr. Wei-Kuo Wu, who received his PhD degree from UC Berkeley and had five years of experience at Fairchild Semiconductor, founded a semiconductor manufacturing company, Advanced Device Technology, Inc. It was never profitable. In 1989, Dr. Wu went to mainland China to establish Nanker Electronics Group in Guangdong for IC manufacturing.

Another well-known case of a returnee starting a business is Dr. Richard Chang. He had worked for 20 years for Texas Instruments and joined World- wide Semiconductor Manufacturing Corp. (WSMC) between 1998 and 1999,

108   a wafer foundry business established in Taiwan in 1996. Dr. Chang left Taiwan when WSMC was taken over by TSMC; in 2000 he established the foundry SMIC in Shanghai to compete with TSMC and UNC.

Qusel Electronics was another returnee failure. Founded in 1984 by several returnees from Silicon Valley, it was the first 64K and 256K DRAM company in Taiwan. Investors included the Development Fund of Executive Yuan, Chiao-Tung Bank, Multiventure Investment Inc., and Qusel USA Company. It closed down in 1987 due to inadequate technology and the failure to respond quickly enough to the shorter life cycle of memory products. Some of its managers went on to important jobs in Taiwan's IC industry, including S. J. Paul Chien, current Chairman of Vanguard International Semiconductor Corporation (VIS), and Dr. Chin Wu, former President of ALi Corporation.

All of this activity has been helped by a set of networking organizations. Important ones in the Chinese-American community are the Monte Jade Association, the Chinese-American Semiconductor Professional Association (CASPA), Silicon Valley Chinese-American Computer Association (SV-CACA), and venture capitalists that invest in high-tech start-ups in Taiwan and Silicon Valley, including H&Q Asia, Pacific Venture Group, and Acorn Campus. However, most companies in the Hsinchu Science-based Industrial Park are homegrown and locally financed; foreign capital accounted for only 8 percent of invested capital in the Park in 2003.

The flow of students to the United States peaked in the mid-1990s and then declined. The number going there for PhDs reached 1,300 in 1994 and then fell to less than 800 by 1998 (NSF Science and Engineering Indicators 2002, appendix table 2-41). This change was due to a strong demand for graduates with bachelor degrees in Taiwan and improvements in Taiwan's graduate programs.

VERTICAL DISINTEGRATION OF THE IT INDUSTRIES

During the past 20 years, PCs and PC-related products became the largest industry in Taiwan in terms of revenues. Numerous vendors of PC-related parts and components grew into globally competitive suppliers of monitors, scanners, discs, motherboards, hubs, keyboards, mouses, cases, audio boards, video cards, power supplies, and optical and disc drives. Together these Taiwanese firms constituted a key cluster activity and expertise in the vertically disintegrated supply chain for IT. Taiwan's production value for all IT hardware products ranked third in the world from 1995 to 2000, then declined to fourth position as mainland China moved ahead. However, the contribution of Taiwanese IT companies to mainland China's output value is more than 70 percent of its hardware production.

As a result of vertical disintegration, OEM-focused exports, and dependence on imported automation equipment and key components (such as CPUs and hard disks), the ratio of input value of primary factors to production value in the information industry is 20 percent today in Taiwan. In response to government incentives, since the 1960s, many foreign electronics companies have set up large-scale, highly automated television and electronics plants for export. In the initial stage of the electronics industry, Japanese companies arrived early and became the leading and long-standing vendors of parts and components. To meet the Taiwanese government's "local content" requirement, Japanese firms transferred technology to their local parts suppliers as well as their joint-venture partners.

Taiwanese firms have established efficient supply chains to serve OEM customers with experienced engineers and managers, using technologies transferred from MNCs. They have low costs, flexibility, speed, and quality, inspired by keen competition and the severe demands of foreign customers. Although some Taiwanese companies have moved assembly plants abroad, their headquarters are still the hubs of global logistics. Consequently, the majority of OEM customers, including HP, Dell, and Apple, have set up international purchasing offices in Taiwan rather than production plants.

THE KEY ROLE OF THE INDUSTRIAL TECHNOLOGY RESEARCH INSTITUTE (ITRI)

ITRI was established in 1973 by the Taiwanese government. Its mission is to raise the level of Taiwan's industrial technology, to help upgrade existing industries, to build new ones, and to make technological advances.

ITRI is the most prominent research institution in Taiwan. It holds more than 5,300 patents and produces an average of 2.4 patents daily. Since the 1990s, ITRI has had a budget financed by the government (Ministry of Economic Affairs) and by industry. Over time, it has moved to doing more advanced research.

ITRI has had five presidents. Between 1978 and 1985, President Hsien-chi Fang took developing industries seen as strategic as his management priority. From 1985 to 1989, President Morris Chang promoted technology dissemination and the spin-off of semiconductor companies. From 1989 to 1994, President Otto C. C. Lin increased technology services and expanded corporate participation and industrial benefits. Between 1994 and 2003, President Chin-tay Shih introduced the concept of total resources management (TRM), which involved integrating ITRI's tangible resources (machine instruments and equipment and real estate), and intangible ones (intellectual property,

110   prestige, industrial relationships, experienced research manpower, management knowledge, and international networking).

ITRI's most important contributions have been developing an IC industry, developing talent, and distributing that talent throughout the industry as a means of technology transfer, along with commercializing activities through spin-offs and its open lab.

Anchor of Taiwan Semiconductor Industry

ITRI has played the role of development planner and research center for this industry. Creating an IC industry was among ITRI's high priorities.

This effort began around 1966 as foreign companies such as GI, TI, and Philips set up semiconductor assembly factories. Their assembly and testing technologies and quality management processes established the foundation for Taiwan's semiconductor industry.

In 1974, the government founded the Electronics Industry Research Center (ERIC, the predecessor of ERSO) in ITRI to introduce IC technology from abroad. ERIC acquired complementary metal-oxide semiconductor (CMOS) technology from RCA in 1976, based on a recommendation by the Technical Advisory Committee (TAC). In 1976, ITRI recruited several domestic young engineers and a few young returnees and sent them to RCA. With RCA's help, in 1977 an IC manufacturing demonstration plant was set up on ITRI's campus.

This led to ITRI's spinning off UMC in 1980. ITRI transferred design-ready and preliminarily marketed products to UMC, including musical ICs and ICs for phone keyboards, digital watches, memories, and calculators. UMC went on to raise the wafer yield rate, lowered production costs, and quickly reached the break-even point.

Then, in 1987, ITRI spun off Taiwan Semiconductor Manufacturing Corporation (TSMC) with Philips as a partner. This was the first six-inch wafer foundry using VLSI technology. Because TSMC's innovative business model, that of a pure foundry, separated design from manufacturing, it fostered design companies such as Silicon Integrated Systems Corp. (SiS), Realtek, Weltrend, Sunplus, ICSI, and Etron. The number of IC design companies went from 56 in 1990 to over 240 in 2003. In 1988, ITRI spun off the mask laboratory of ERSO as the Taiwan Mask Company (TMC). By 1990, Taiwan's semiconductor industry was almost fully developed, with upstream (design), midstream (manufacturing), and downstream (packaging and testing). By 1995, it was the fourth largest IC industry in the world. Taiwan was in the top five countries with cutting edge 0.5-micron (500 nm) production technology. That year, its revenues were U.S. $3.3 billion and its world market share 2.2 percent. In 2003,

IC revenues were U.S. $23.8 billion, with U.S. $5.5 billion in design, U.S. $13.7 billion in manufacturing, and U.S. $4.6 billion in packaging and testing. IC industry revenues were in fourth position, behind the United States, Japan, and South Korea.

In 1991, the Ministry of Economic Affairs funded an IC submicron technology development project at ERSO. In 1994, it spun off Vanguard International Semiconductor (VIS), the first own-brand DRAM manufacturing company in Taiwan. At that time, the private sector was not happy to see another potential competitor established by government. In addition, there was a heated debate as to whether the government's role should be one of supporting existing companies. Therefore, since 1995, the strength of the semiconductor industry has led to the government's no longer using spin-offs as a technology transfer mode.

Developing and Spreading Talent

High-quality talent is the main source of competitiveness in the cluster, and developing it has been one of ITRI's missions. An example is the cultivation of IC design talent in universities. In 1983, the NSC (Executive Yuan), Ministry of Education, and ITRI jointly undertook an IC chip design and manufacturing project. ITRI suggested having teachers and students participate and provided a basic logic circuit component database and some CAD tools to each university. The project annually trained 150 to 200 professionals to acquire IC design and CAD skills. A customer-design IC company, Syntek Semiconductor Corp., was established by a design manager of ERSO in 1983. In 1987, to promote a domestic design industry, ITRI spun off its VLSI lab to set up TSMC, the first wafer foundry in the world.

Moves by people from ITRI to companies have been an important channel for diffusing technology. Over 16,000 employees have graduated from ITRI since 1973, 81 percent to private industry; among them more than 5,000 are in HSIP, especially in the semiconductor and computer peripheral industries. Prominent graduates of ITRI include Morris Chang (chairman of TSMC), Robert Tsao (chairman of UMC), and Ming-Kai Tsai (chairman of MediaTek, the premier semiconductor fabless company in Taiwan).

Moving Industrial Technology from Lab to Commerce

During the past 30 years, ITRI has nurtured many new industries such as monitors, special chemicals, semiconductors, photoelectric, precision instruments, telecommunications, microelectronics, biotechnology, along with many others. Its strategies can be divided into three stages: (1) A focus on manufacturing

112   technologies and establishing pilot-runs for mass production. (2) In the 1980s, spinning off companies, notably UMC and TSMC. This spin-off strategy involved close relationships among capital, technology, and talent. (3) During the 1990s, focusing on open laboratories, incubation centers, multi-industry cooperation, patents, and intellectual property rights.

The Spin-Off Model for Technology Transfer

Davenport et al. (2002) and Ziemeski and Warda (1999) argue that spin-offs are particularly suitable when there are limitations in the local environment. It is very difficult for private companies that need a quick market response to acquire technologies that require large investments in plant and equipment and involve significant commercial uncertainties. Consequently, in the 1980s ITRI used the spin-off company model to introduce new technology into the industry.

Rush et al. (1996) found only one institute in their study, ITRI in Taiwan, which had made significant use of the spin-off option to seed new firms in the integrated circuit and related industries.

Spin-offs kept ITRI from becoming a mass-production factory and allowed it to focus on R&D. It is up to ITRI to initiate transfer of a complete production technology along with key personnel. In order to help this process, in 1990 it published "The ITRI Spin-off Company Planning and Founding Guidelines." The strategy considers several factors, such as the ability of industry to receive the technology, operating strategy and policy, and organizational factors. The evolution of Taiwan's industry is reflected in changes in ITRI's strategy. From fostering the IC industry in the 1970s and 1980s, by the late 1990s its spin-offs focused on key materials and components industries, such as the DVD read-write head, which helped the optical storage industry.

Today, the biotechnology industry is being encouraged by government; hence, the Biomedical Engineering Center (BMEC) was established in 1999. The characteristics of this industry include long periods of research, clinical trials, and capital intensiveness, factors that cause it to be especially risky for small and medium-sized enterprises, the main entities of Taiwan's industry. This sector may require use of the spin-off model.

ESTABLISHING THE OPEN LAB

Before the 1990s, ITRI had not only promoted industrial technology by way of technology transfers and spin-offs, but it had also accumulated abundant know-how relating to technology management; it became a consulting service for new technology-based ventures. Since 1996, the ITRI Open Laboratory has provided an "on-site" environment for knowledge interaction, one that brings together professionals from many disciplines to promote high-tech industries and serve the R&D Park.

The Open Laboratory includes provision for technology collaboration and a business incubator. Under technology collaboration, a company is set up in which the parties work together on developing state-of-the-art technology, while the business incubation center nurtures new, high-tech start-ups.

The Open Laboratory's benefits to companies include savings on costs of various kinds—R&D personnel, infrastructure, purchase of facilities and instruments, acquisition of information, along with a variety of technology supports. Other benefits include use of ITRI's R&D experience, whereby the company enhances its image. The philosophy of the Open Laboratory is total resources management, which has two main components: (1) the entrepreneurial spirit combined with ITRI's R&D capabilities and (2) the strengthening of ITRI's concept of service to business.

There are three kinds of targeted customers for the laboratory: The first is an existing large company. The laboratory is an innovative environment in which such companies can incubate their new ideas and set up new teams as internal entrepreneurs and innovators. The second kind is small to medium-sized enterprises (SMEs) that typically are unable to do much R&D and benefit from being in the lab. To keep new talent flowing through, tenants can stay no longer than three years. The third kind is start-up firms (defined as less than 18 months old and technology based). Their founders can get comprehensive support. They also are encouraged to collaborate with other firms and research labs in ITRI.

Up to March 2004, there have been 205 firms with more than 5,300 people associated with ITRI's Open Lab, including 113 start-ups with $1.3 billion of paid-in capital.

THE CREATION OF TECHNOLOGY

In 2002, national R&D expenditures were 2.3 percent of the GDP, up from 1.7 percent in 1990. In 1990, the government was responsible for 54 percent of R&D expenditures; by 2002 this figure had decreased to 38 percent as companies invested more. However, compared to other major nations, such spending is still low. Encouraging such spending is one of the government's urgent priorities.

In 1997, Taiwan was ranked seventh among countries in the number of patents granted in the United States. As of the year 2000, Taiwan's rank had risen to fourth place. It was ranked second overall in the number of patents per million

114　people with new ones dominated by Taiwan's burgeoning semiconductor industry. From 1993 to 2003, the number of Taiwan's patents granted in the United States on semiconductor components ranked third place, behind the United States and Japan. As for the quality of patents, measured by patent citations, in 1995 Taiwan was ranked seventh and had moved up to third place in 2003. However, the weakness of Taiwan's position in patents is the connection between scientific research and technology. The Science Linkage Index (SLI) measures the number of science and technology documents cited by a certain patent. Taiwan's SLI rating was 0.24 in 2003 with the United States at 4.62, England at 3.59, and Israel at 4.51. It is increasingly important for industry to gain scientific knowledge from the academic community. The relationship between industry and academia in Taiwan needs to be improved.

In the Global Competitiveness Report 2002–2003, distributed by the World Economic Forum (WEF), Harvard University professor Michael E. Porter described a National Innovation Competitiveness Index. Taiwan ranked eighth on the overall index. In component indices "innovative policy" and "innovative clusters," Taiwan was ranked fourth and fifth, respectively. This shows that intellectual property protection and governmental promotion of industrial competitiveness are effective. Taiwan has world-class enterprises, efficient supply chains, competition among firms, and relatively strong industrial clusters.

THE ROLE OF TAIWAN'S IT COMPANIES IN MAINLAND CHINA

Increases in costs for land and labor combined with mainland China's rapid growth—with the prospect of a vast market—have led Taiwanese companies to invest there. By the end of 2002, there were 56,000 Taiwanese investors in mainland China. Contracted investment reached U.S. $61 billion (7.4% of total investment). Due to governmental restrictions, many Taiwanese investments are transferred to the mainland through a third location. For example, a large amount of investment from Hong Kong actually originates in Taiwan.

In 2003, Taiwan's electronic and electric appliance industries invested U.S. $1.4 billion in mainland China, which made up 30 percent of all Taiwan's investments there. These industries have moved labor-intensive activities to China, including much electronic component assembly work, with the result of an across-the-straits division of labor in these industries.

As of the year 2001, the total revenue of Taiwan's information industry was U.S. $43 billion. Production in Taiwan accounted for 47 percent, while production in mainland China made up 37 percent. Only two years later, in 2003, global revenues of this industry amounted to U.S. $57 billion, with production in Taiwan making up 21 percent, production in mainland China making up

63 percent, and that in other locations 16 percent. Over 60 percent of total revenues from information products produced in mainland China are generated by Taiwanese companies.

INTERNATIONAL BRANDS

A challenge faced by Taiwan's IT industry is a lack of global brand names. Its products that rank number one in the world include notebook computers, LCD monitors, ADSL, and cable modems, while those ranked number two include digital cameras and Ethernet switches. However, most are OEM products. Products bearing indigenous-brand names account for only 7 percent of notebook computers, 15 percent of LCD monitors, 13 percent of ADSL, 15 percent of cable modems, 19 percent of digital signal cameras (DSCs) and 28 percent of Ethernet switches. According to Interbrand's survey, Taiwan's top 10 brands in 2004, included Trend Micro, Asus, Acer, Kang Shih-fu, Cheng Shin Tire, Ben Q, Giant, ZyXEL, D-Link, and Advantech. Among them, the value of brand of BenQ and Acer increased the most, 35 percent and 24.4 percent, respectively. Although the market value of Taiwan's top 10 companies had grown in 2003, *Business Week's* list of the world's top 100 companies does not include any from Taiwan.

Most of Taiwan's information and electronics companies work to keep relationships with OEM customers rather than developing branded products. They have fewer channels to access end users, and creating an international brand name requires high product quality, a long-term strategy, and a huge marketing investment. Acer, for example, during the past 20 years, invested over one hundred billion NT dollars on international brand marketing. Due to this investment, as of the second quarter of 2004 its notebook computers were the top sellers in Western European countries. For the first time, Acer overtook Hewlett-Packard and other leading brands there.

THE VENTURE CAPITAL INDUSTRY

During the 1960s and 1970s, the government encouraged multinational companies (MNC), including Philips, Philco, RCA, Zenith, General Instruments, Sanyo, and Matsushita, to invest in the consumer electronics, calculator, and TV monitor industries. However, the MNCs moved away gradually after the early 1980s because of rising labor costs and appreciation of the New Taiwan dollar.

This shift supplied an incentive to create new firms and venture capital is a common institution of financial support for entrepreneurs. The institution

116   was seen as helping innovative ideas or technologies to be commercialized. Following the model of the United States, several other developing and newly developed countries also established venture capital firms in the private and/or public sector. In general, companies in high-tech clusters that have access to active venture capital funds are more competitive than those that do not. The result, according to the *Asian Venture Capital Journal*, was that the Asian venture capital pool increased from U.S. $21.9 billion in 1991 to U.S. $94.1 billion in the first half of 2003.

In 1973, the Executive Yuan established a Development Fund as the first stage of venture capital in Taiwan. The Fund makes investments with the aims of industrial upgrading and improving the structure of industry. For example, it acquired a 48 percent share of TSMC (a highly successful investment) in 1987. Nonetheless, through the early 1980s the supply of risk capital for new, high tech firms was scarce because of rigidities in the financial system and the absence of successful cases to serve as examples. The government wanted to develop a high-tech industry rather than build state-owned companies. Creating a private venture capital industry was viewed as an essential step.

In 1983 the government passed a regulation that specified the requirements for venture capital firms, the scope of investments, and incentives for venture capital firms that invest over 70 percent of their capital in new high-tech businesses. In 1984, the first venture capital firm, Multiventure Investment, Inc., a joint venture between Acer, Inc. and Continental Engineering Corporation, was set up.

The growth of this industry contributed greatly to the expansion of Taiwan's high-technology industries. Through the end of 2002, 217 funds had been approved, and today there are 194 funds with total paid-in capital of NT $150 billion, with an average fund size of NT $780 million. Following a slump in 2001, 18 new funds were established in 2002, although fundraising activities are still down overall. Some of 2002's new funds were set up by financial holding companies or large conglomerates seeking to diversify their investments. The majority of other new funds were established by government participants. The accumulated amount of venture capital investments since 1984 to 2003 was NT $162 billion in over 300 domestic high-tech companies, the majority of which have gone public in domestic and foreign markets or have been acquired. The distribution was semiconductors (17%), other information technologies (16%), electronics (15%), and telecommunications (14%). Most of this money went to finance expansion stages, followed by start-up and mezzanine stages. (In 2002, about one-third of the capital was invested in seed and start-up stages.) This led to the emergence of a high-technology industry of over NT $1.5 trillion. To help SMEs raise capital, barriers for them to be listed on the

Taiwan Stock Exchange or the GreTai Securities Market (the over-the-counter securities exchange, OTC) were lowered.

Previously, to encourage the formation of the venture capital industry, the government had provided a 20 percent income tax deduction to individuals and corporations holding shares in venture funds (to be received after a two-year vesting period). However, this measure was repealed in December 1999.

In the United States, pension funds are the largest sources for venture capital operation (Sagari and Guidotti 1991). In contrast, pension funds in Taiwan cannot currently invest in venture capital because of less flexible exit mechanisms under the corporate law in Taiwan compared with the limited partnership format in the United States. However, the Taiwanese government is considering removing this prohibition.

Money comes from a variety of sources, including companies, banks, insurance companies, securities firms, and individuals. To inspire the venture capital industry, the government is assessing the deregulation of pension funds investing in venture capital.

TECHNOLOGY TRADE

Taiwan has strong international positions in the personal computer and semiconductor industries. In a short time its IC industry grabbed a significant market share. An IC design industry has developed. A network of product packaging and testing businesses has emerged that can swiftly manufacture and ship products, an important attribute given the short life cycle of IT products.

Major MNCs have adopted a build-to-order (BTO) strategy to reduce costs of inventory. OEM and component suppliers now have to bear inventory costs and the risks of fluctuations in component prices. Most MNCs focus on new technology and products and marketing; meanwhile, Taiwanese OEM manufacturers must put at risk large sums of capital to expand production. In the short term the shift of Taiwanese businesses to mainland China mitigates these problems; however, average product prices continue to fall. This has decreased profits as percent of sales of Taiwan's top 20 major manufacturing companies (semiconductor companies excluded) from 8.6 percent in 1998 to 4.8 percent in 2003. A trap of low costs and low profitability is a major challenge faced by these industries.

In an effort to lower production costs, in advanced countries only high value-added, core technologies are pursued, with manufacturing being transferred to Asia. About 68 percent of companies in the world use outsourcing strategies, with an average of 26 percent reduction in costs. Mainland China, India, and Taiwan have been the main beneficiaries. Total purchases by the 20 leading IT

118   companies dealing with Taiwan increased from U.S. $11.3 billion in 1997 to U.S. $45 billion in 2003, of which the top five were HP, Dell, Sony, Apple, and IBM.

Due to the rapid investment in advanced technology and mass production, the Taiwanese IT industry spends a considerable sum every year to acquire technologies from abroad. This amount went from NT $7 billion in 1990 to NT $35 billion in 2002. In contrast, the value of technology exported by this industry is relatively small. In 1990, this figure reached NT $401 million. As of 2002, due to the overseas investment in the printed circuit board (PCB) industry along with technology transfer income, the value of technology exports was NT $10.5 billion. However, the trade technology trade deficit reached NT $24.7 billion in 2002 compared with NT $6.6 billion in 1990.

The increasing technology trade deficit comes from reliance on technology from advanced nations given that most companies are OEM suppliers. The Taiwanese companies owning R&D activities were relatively small and unable to satisfy market needs, thus, the industry had a profound need for foreign technology. The success of the OEM business model has made foreign customers rely on Taiwanese companies more, but these companies have to pay more in royalties to keep up with new product development.

The recent expansion of TFT-LCD production capacity is one factor causing the increasing technology deficit. Since the 1990s, several companies have engaged in TFT-LCD panel manufacturing by licensing technology from Japanese companies, such as Sharp, Matsushita, and Toshiba. In 2004, Taiwan held first place in production capacity of TFT-LCD panels. Taiwan is not yet exporting knowledge-intensive products (such as innovative technology and its own intellectual property). This is a major challenge faced in the upgrading of the high-tech industry.

CONCLUSIONS AND CHALLENGES

During the past 20 years, high-tech industries have become the backbone of Taiwan's economy. They not only filled the gap left by out-migration of traditional industries but also increased value to exports. The role of the government was crucial. It funded research institutions, mainly ITRI, to upgrade technologies through the Technology Development Program (TDP), and to create the IC industry through the spin-off model in the 1980s. Subsidies of science and technology projects have reduced the risks of developing technology development to SMEs.

The government selection of the Hsinchu area, with its talents in National Tsing Hua University, the National Chiao Tung University, and the Industrial

Technology Research Institute was enormously successful. The Silicon Valley–like environment of HSIP attracted many returnees to invest in start-ups.

In addition to returnees, S&T experts in such professional groups as METS, TCA, and STAG were invited to transfer their experiences. Chinese-origin social societies formed by entrepreneurs, scientists, and engineers living abroad, such as the Chinese Institute of Engineers (CIE), Monte Jade Science and Technology Association, along other associations have played important networking roles.

In 1983, the Taiwanese government began to encourage venture capital and to liberate capital markets. Over 200 venture capital funds and a couple of investment banks have invested in technology-based start-ups. The government continues to modify laws and regulations including deregulating the scope of venture capital investments and encouraging private equity in emerging industries.

To keep up with the 21st century's trends toward knowledge-based economics and the rapid development of mainland China's economy, Taiwan's IT industry has begun a new wave of transformation, featuring an innovation-based approach to strategic development.

Several challenges have been identified, including strengthening ties between industries and universities, the challenge from mainland China, and the need to move to higher value-added activities. These challenges are addressed in "Challenge 2008: National Development Plan" published by the Taiwanese government in 2002. This plan includes 10 key components, such as the e-generation manpower cultivation plan, the cultural and creative industry development plan, the international innovation and R&D base plan, the industrial value heightening plan, the e-Taiwan construction plan, and the operations headquarters development plan.

For Taiwan to be a global innovation center, annual R&D expenditures are targeted to be 3 percent of Taiwan's GDP. The main directions of R&D will be Systems on a Chip, broadband Internet, and wireless communications. Already, around 70 domestic companies have R&D centers, including Acer, Quanta, Foxconn, Tatung, VIA, Chi Mei, Ben Q, Lite-On Electronics, Wistron, and D-Link. Nearly 20 multinational companies have set up R&D centers, including HP, Dell, IBM, Intel, Microsoft, Sony, Pericom, Aixtron, Becker, Butone, and Ericsson. ITRI will play an important role in global R&D networking.

Due to the rising tide of globalization, the rapid development of mainland China, and trends favoring knowledge-based economics, Taiwan has reached a turning point. To become a center for value-added industry and innovative

120   R&D, the government must improve its basic infrastructure and environment for investment. The mechanisms of cooperation among industry, university, and research institute that make up a national innovative system need to be strengthened for the next stage of industrial transformation.

REFERENCES

Amsden, A. H., and W. Chu. 2003. *Beyond Late Development: Taiwan's Upgrading Policies.* Cambridge, MA: MIT Press.

Asian Venture Capital Journal (AVCJ). 2004. *The 2004 Guide to Venture Capital in Asia.* Hong Kong: Author.

Bahrml, H., and S. Evans. 1995. "Flexible Recycle and High-Technology Entrepreneurship." *California Management Review.*

Bureau of Statistics. http://140.111.1.192/statistics/service/sts4-5.htm.

Cabral, R. 1998. "The Cabral-Dahab Science Park Management Paradigm: An Introduction." *International Journal of Technology Management* 16(8):721–722.

Chang, B. L., and C. W. Hsu. 2002. "Government Policy's Influences on Science-Based Industrial Park Development in Taiwan." *Made in Taiwan: Booming in the Technology Era.* Singapore: World Scientific Publishing.

Chen, T.-J., and Y.-H. Ku. 2002. "The Development of Taiwan's Personal Computer Industry." International Centre for the Study of East Asian Development (ICSEAD), Kitakyushu.

Davenport, S., A. Carr, and D. Bibby. 2002. "Leveraging Talent: Spin-off Strategy at Industrial Research." *R&D Management* 32:241–254.

Hong, C. Y. 2001. "Capital Investment and Industrial Takeoff." *Energy: How to Create Miracles for Semiconductor and PC Industries.* Chinatimes.

Hong, Y. E. 2003. "Innovation Engine—ITRI: The Hand That Rocks the Success of Industry in Taiwan." Common Wealth.

Hsinchu Science-based Industrial Park. http://www.sipa.gov.tw/index_apis.php.

Hsu, C. W., and H. C. Chiang. 2001. "The Government Strategy for the Upgrading of Industrial Technology in Taiwan." *Technovation* 21:123–132.

Hsu, J. Y. 1997. "Development of Semiconductor Technology in Taiwan—Government Intervention, Cross-Boundary Social Network and High-Tech Development." *Geography Journal* 23. Department of Geography, College of Natural Sciences, National Taiwan University.

———. 1999. "A Flowing Mount: Labor Market and High-Tech Development in HSIP." *Taiwan: A Radical Quarterly in Social Studies* 35.

———. 2001. "Time Strategy and Dynamic Learning of Enterprises: An Example of IC Industry in HSIP." *Cities and Design* (11/12):67–96.

Hsu, T. S., C. Y. Tong, and M. H. Chuang. 1998. "National Innovation System and Innovation Policy Analysis—Empirical Study on IC Industry in Taiwan." *Science and Technology Management Journal* 3(2):127–154.

Huang, C. C., and R. I. Wu. 2003. "Entrepreneurship in Taiwan: Turning Point to Restart." CELCEE Publications, c20031276.

Huang, T. H. 2001. "The Legend of Notebook Computer." *Energy: How to Create Miracles for Semiconductor and PC Industries.* Chinatimes.

Huang, W. C. 1998. "Make the Dreams Come True — The Incubator." *ST-Pioneer* 4.

Industrial Technology Research Institute (ITRI). 2003. "Industrial Technology and ITRI — The Seeing Brain." Industrial Technology Research Institute, Hsinchu, Taiwan.

Lin, H.-Y., and Y. Lin. 1990. "Industrial R&D Trends and Related Policy in Taiwan." Industrial Technology Research Institute, Hsinchu, Taiwan.

Lin, T. I., and Y. Lin. 1990. "The Study of Industrial R&D Development and Policy in Taiwan." Industrial Technology Research Institute, Hsinchu, Taiwan.

Meyer-Krahmer, F. 1997. "Science-Based Technologies and Interdisciplinarity: Challenges for Firms and Policy." In C. Edquist, ed. *Systems of Innovation: Technologies, Institutions, and Organizations.* London: Pinter, pp. 298–317.

Ministry of Information and Communication (MIC). 1991. "Review on PC Industry in Taiwan."

National Science Foundation. 2002. S&E Indicators. Appendix Table 2-41.

Oakey, R., and S. Cooper. 1989. "High Technology Industry, Agglomeration, and the Potential for Peripherally Sited Small Firms." *Regional Studies* 23:347–360.

Pandey, I. M., and A. Jang. 1996. "Venture Capital for Financing Technology in Taiwan." *Technovation* 16(9):499–514.

Porter, M. E. 1998. "Clusters and the New Economics of Competition." *Harvard Business Review* (November–December): 77–90.

———. 2000. "Location, Competition, and Economic Development: Local Clusters in a Global Economy." *Economic Development Quarterly* 14(1):15–34.

Sagari, S. B., and G. Guidotti. 1991. "Venture Capital: Lessons from the Developed World for the Developing Markets." Discussion Paper 13, International Finance Corporation.

San, G. 2001. "The Returnee's Influence to High-Tech Industry — The Case of HSIP." *Human Resource and High-Tech Industrial Development in Taiwan.* Research Center for Taiwan Economic Development, National Central University.

Saperstein, J., and D. Rouach. 2002. *Creating Regional Wealth in the Innovation Economy: Models, Perspectives, and Best Practices.* Upper Saddle River, NJ: Pearson Education, p. 235.

Saxenian, A. 1994. *Regional Advantage: Culture and Competition in Silicon Valley and Route 128.* Cambridge, MA: Harvard University Press.

———. 2004. "Taiwan's Hsinchu Region: Imitator and Partner for Silicon Valley." In *Building High-Tech Clusters: Silicon Valley and Beyond.* Cambridge, UK: Cambridge University Press, pp. 190–228.

Schumpeter, J. A. 1934. *The Theory of Economic Development.* Cambridge, MA: Harvard Business Press.

Shih, C. T. 2001. "History and Prospects of IC Industry Development in Taiwan."

———. 2001. "Innovation and Entrepreneurship — High Technology Development in Taiwan." SPRIE Research Workshop.

———. "R&D and Innovation Trends of Industry-Research Institution Cooperation." Science and Technology Policy Development Report SR9001.

122   SME White Book. 2002.

STAG. http://www.stag.gov.tw/content/application/stag/about/index-english.php?ico =1&selname=about.

Taiwan Stock Exchange Corporation. http://www.tse.com.tw/home.htm.

Taiwan Venture Capital Association (TVCA). 2003. *Taiwan Venture Capital Association Yearbook.*

Tsay, C. L., and Dai, P.-F. 2001. "Trends and Impacts of Returned Talents in Taiwan: An Example of High-Tech." In G. San and M.-C. Chang, eds. *Human Resources and the Development of High-Tech Industries in Taiwan.* Research Center for Taiwan Economic Development, National Central University.

Wang, E. C. 2002. "Public Infrastructure and Economic Growth: A New Approach Applied to East Asian Economics." *Journal of Policy Modeling* 24(5):411–435.

Wang, K. 2001. "The Comparison of Innovation Strategy to IC Industrial Clusters of Taiwan and China." The Technological Policy Forum of Taiwan and China in 2001, Kuo Ding Li's Technological Development Fund.

———. 2002. "Report of Technology Talent Requirement Survey." ITRI-IEK.

Wang, K., et al. 2003. "Hsinchu Science-based Industrial Park: Past, Present and Future." Anthology of papers presented at the First ITRI Symposium on Science Cluster Development—Silicon Valley, Hsinchu, and Shanghai.

Wang, W. C. 2002. "Analysis on Development of Advanced Level Science and Technology Labor in HSIP." *Guidepost for Science and Technology Development Quarterly* 2(2).

Wong, P. K. 2002. "Benchmarking the Regional Nexus of Innovation and Entrepreneurship." SPRIE Research Workshop, February 25–27.

Wu, S. H., and R. C. Shen. 1999. "Formation and Development of IC Industry in Taiwan." *Taiwan Industry Studies*, 1:57–150.

Wu, T. Y., et al. 1980. "How the Foreign Investment Influences Taiwan's Economy." Unpublished manuscript, Central Research Institute.

5

THE RE-MAKING OF SINGAPORE'S HIGH-TECH
ENTERPRISE ECOSYSTEM

Poh Kam Wong

Among developing economies, Singapore has achieved one of the most impressive economic growth records during the past four decades, averaging 8.1 percent gross domestic product (GDP) growth per annum from 1960 to 2000 (Wong 2003a). Despite a significant economic slowdown during the past several years, Singapore's per capita gross national product (GNP) of U.S. $23,000 in 2002 [on a purchasing power parity (PPP) basis] still stands as the third highest in Asia and approached 70 percent of the U.S. level (World Bank 2003). In 1965, Singapore's PPP-adjusted per capita income was less than 16 percent of that of the United States; as recently as 1980, it was still less than 50 percent (Wong 2001a).

The rapid economic growth of Singapore has been achieved through a consistent public policy focus on attracting and "leveraging" direct foreign investment by global multinational corporations (MNCs) to achieve continuous industrial restructuring and upgrading (Wong 2003a). From being a regional entrepot trade and shipping hub in Southeast Asia, Singapore has evolved into a global transport and communications hub, as well as a leading Asian petroleum refining, electronics/IT manufacturing and financial/business services center, all the while pushing toward higher value-added products and services. Many MNCs have chosen Singapore to be their regional headquarters, with some (for example, the United States's Mobil and Denmark's EAC) even relocating their global headquarters to the city-state. Even as the city-state economy has increasingly diversified into services, it nonetheless retains a strong advanced manufacturing base. Unlike Hong Kong, where most manufacturing activities have hollowed out, Singapore was able to maintain the share of GDP in manufacturing over 25 percent, despite rising labor and land costs. By

124 leveraging the high concentration of electronics, information and communications technology (ICT), and chemical manufacturing activities in Singapore, the Singaporean government has succeeded in attracting a significant and growing base of R&D activities by the leading global MNCs in these industries (Wong 2002a).

The high reliance on investment by global MNCs is part of a larger economic development strategy that seeks to position Singapore as a major business node in the global system of trade and capital flows (Wong 1998). Like Hong Kong, Singapore was among the first developing economies to adopt an open economy policy emphasizing free trade and movement of capital and welcoming foreign investment in export-oriented manufacturing. The government of Singapore also adopted policies similar to those of Hong Kong in providing a "business-friendly" environment through emphasizing the rule of law, relatively clean and efficient government services, and stable macroeconomic policies. Despite these similarities, however, the state played a much more important role in the island economy of Singapore as compared with the laissez faire of Hong Kong. Besides a virtual monopoly role in providing various "traditional" social and physical infrastructural services (such as public education and health-care, sea-ports and airports, telecommunications and public utilities), the Singaporean state had extensive direct business involvement in many sectors of the economy normally deemed private, through a web of quasi-state enterprises ("government-linked corporations" or GLCs in local parlance) that are effectively owned or controlled by a number of government investment holding companies. The business involvement of the state through these GLCs covers not only "strategic" industries such as airlines, aerospace and defense manufacturing, and telecommunications, but also banking, logistics services, shipbuilding, construction, and even food manufacturing. Besides such direct business involvement, the state's control over the financial system also goes significantly beyond the normal monetary and fiscal policy instruments, through institutions such as Central Provident Fund (CPF) (a compulsory wage savings scheme) and licensing control over domestic consumer banks. In addition, the state exerts significant influence over the functioning of the labor market, through highly selective policy instruments such as permanent residency and employment control, foreign workers' levy, and an extensive public scholarship system that creams off the best students to eventually staff the upper echelons of public services and GLCs. Finally, through its significant ownership of land and active participation in the provision of public housing and social community facilities, the state's influence weighs heavily on the property markets and extends deep into the social fabric of the society. Through these control levers, the state in Singapore has been able to exercise significant industrial policy intervention over its domestic economy, despite having a very open economy that is highly dependent on foreign investments and external trades, because these policies have been primarily of the "market-enhancing" varieties (Wong 2001). Indeed, Singapore has been consistently ranked as among the freest economies in the world (Heritage Foundation 2004).

While this unique economic development model combining an open-economy framework with a strong state involvement in leveraging MNCs to pursue targeted industrial policy objectives has produced remarkable success in the past, enabling the country to move from the Third to the First World in the short period of 35 years since political independence, concerns have been growing among the city-state's political leaders that this prevailing development model needs to be changed now that the economy has to compete "close to the frontier" of the global knowledge economy, as opposed to the earlier, easier task of technological catch-up. Not only is it harder now for Singapore to compete for global MNC investment as a result of its high cost structure and the growing reluctance of the world's technological leaders to shift their core innovation assets to Singapore. More significantly, new economic growth and innovations in the global marketplace are increasingly coming from young, dynamic firms clustering in a small number of high-tech "hotspots" in the world that provide the critical mass of advanced knowledge sources (universities, advanced public and corporate research labs), venture capital, entrepreneurial talents, knowledge workers, specialized professional services, sophisticated end-users, and enabling institutions like intellectual property protection, public exit markets, among other factors. In a field long dominated by the Silicon Valley, new competing high-tech regions have emerged around the world, including Israel in the Middle East, Ireland in Europe, Shanghai and Beijing in China, Seoul in Korea, and Bangalore in India (Rosenberg 2002). There is thus a perceived danger that the traditional policy incentives for attracting and supporting large, global MNCs not only may not work for attracting young, entrepreneurial firms, but that this very strategy of relying on large established MNCs for job creation and technology transfer may stifle the development of indigenous entrepreneurship and technological innovation.

Despite the bursting of the dotcom bubble and the global meltdown of the technology stock markets in 2000–2002, which may have blunted somewhat the appeal of the Silicon Valley model for high-tech development, the concern for policy change in Singapore actually escalated in the light of the weak performance of the Singaporean economy during the past several years. This occurred in the wake of the 1997 Asian financial crisis and the global economic

126   slowdown exacerbated by the events of September 11, 2001, and the recent Asian
SARS scare. Indeed, a high-level committee was formed in 2002 to study how
to "fundamentally re-make" the Singaporean economy to better compete in
the global knowledge economy, where advanced knowledge, technological innovation, artistic creativity, and entrepreneurial dynamism are becoming the
decisive sources of competitive advantage (ERC 2002).

This chapter examines the emerging structural shifts of Singapore toward a
more entrepreneurial and innovative regional high-tech hub during the past
decade, highlighting the key changes that have occurred in the underlying "enterprise ecosystem" for the Singaporean economy as a whole as well as for two
key high-tech clusters — the larger, more established electronics manufacturing
cluster, and the information and communications technology (ICT) services
cluster. The emergence of a fledgling biotech cluster is also briefly discussed.
The policy changes that have been instituted by the government to facilitate
this structural shift are briefly reviewed, and their likely impacts are discussed.

STRUCTURAL SHIFTS TOWARD AN ENTREPRENEURIAL
HIGH-TECH ECOSYSTEM: A CONCEPTUAL OVERVIEW

Historical Development of Singapore's Economy:
The Technology Capability Development Perspective

The Singaporean economy has undergone a series of structural transformation since the 1960s. Wong (2003a) identified four phases in the economic development of Singapore from the technological development perspective:

1. *Industrial take-off.* The period from the early 1960s to the mid-1970s, characterized by high dependence on technology transfer from foreign MNCs.
2. *Local technological deepening.* The period from the mid-1970s to the late 1980s,
   characterized by rapid growth of local process technological development
   within MNCs and the development of local supporting industries.
3. *Applied R&D expansion.* The period of the late 1980s to the late 1990s, characterized by the rapid expansion of applied R&D on the part of MNCs, public
   R&D institutions, and, later, local firms.
4. *High-tech entrepreneurship and R&D intensification.* The period from the late
   1990s to the present, characterized by the emerging emphasis on high-tech
   start-ups and the shift toward technology creation capabilities.

As highlighted by Wong (2003a), Singapore has in essence shifted over the
past four decades from emphasizing *using* technology to *creating* it. Each successive phase has built upon the resources accumulated earlier. The momentum has continued as new forms of growth were introduced, involving new actors and new forms of linkage among existing actors. In particular, there was a

phased build-up of MNCs, local manufacturing enterprises (particularly in the electronics supporting industries), public research institutes and centers (PRICs) and university R&D, and, in the last phase, local high-tech start-ups pioneering new products. In terms of technology capability development, there was a sustained shift from learning to use (with high reliance on internal transfer by MNCs) to learning to adapt and improve (via "learning by doing" within MNCs as well as "learning by transacting" in local firms acquiring external technology), learning to innovate (mainly applied R&D in product or process), and finally, learning to pioneer (creating indigenous intellectual property and commercializing it in the marketplace through new ventures).

While the foregoing perspective on how Singapore shifted from using to creating technology provides useful insights on the economic development history of Singapore, it is incomplete in that it does not explicitly take into account the dynamic interaction between the structure of enterprises and the nature of technological capability development. To do so we need to examine the economy from an *enterprise ecosystem* perspective.

The High-Tech Enterprise Ecosystem Perspective

Using the conceptual framework of Wong (2003b), we characterize a high-technology enterprise ecosystem as driven by three sets of factors: the structural composition and dynamics of competition and cooperation among existing enterprises, the rate and pattern of technological innovations, and the rate and pattern of new entrepreneurial firm formation. New technological innovations can be diffused into the existing enterprise ecosystem from outside the system (international technology transfer, entry of foreign firms via direct foreign investment, DFI) or from within (through indigenous R&D by existing firms or public research institutes) and commercialized through existing firms or new start-ups. Together, the output of the innovation and entrepreneurship system represent the two key drivers for change to the existing enterprise ecosystem, especially if they take the form of "disruptive innovation" through new firm formation (Christensen 1997). Such innovation-driven start-ups are not only more likely to lead to the creation of new industrial clusters, but often also cause Schumpeterian "creative destruction" of incumbent enterprises in existing clusters. Fueled by technological and/or market innovation, some of these dynamic new firms ("gazelles") can grow rapidly to become the dominant firms in the enterprise ecosystem in the future, contributing most of the new economic growth and job creation in the process (Birch and Haggerty 1997). The three key measures of the dynamism of the high-tech enterprise ecosystem are therefore (1) the overall rate of output or value-added growth of the aggregate

128   cluster; (2) its structural compositional change (new sectors vs. established ones), and (3) the extent of "churn" among the firms competing in the cluster, especially among the largest firms.

The pattern and intensity of technological innovation and entrepreneurial start-ups not only strongly influence the dynamism of the key high-tech clusters of the economy, but also affect the co-evolution and co-development of a set of specialized resources that in turn become the input to fuel future innovation and entrepreneurial activities, in a virtuous cycle of cumulative causation. These specialized resources — trained technical manpower; entrepreneurial talents; experienced venture capitalists and business angel investors; highly knowledge-intensive professional services providers and institutions such as venture law firms, investment banks, and intellectual property management services — may initially be imported from outside the economy (through in-migration of foreign talents, licensing of foreign technology and DFI), but for a self-sustained virtuous cycle to develop, a substantial degree of local "learning by doing" must occur for these resources and institutions to be rooted in the local clusters and to achieve a distinctive sophistication not available in other regions.

In this ecosystem framework, the Silicon Valley model experiences a constant "churning," with new, high-growth firms representing a significant part of the ecosystem versus old, established incumbents. The constant threats of new rivals put pressure on the incumbents to invest significantly in R&D, while the strong presence of world-class universities and public research institutes further adds to the high volume of new innovations generated in the local economy. Although many of these innovation flows are commercialized by the incumbent firms that are financing the R&D investment, a significant part is channelled into new innovative start-ups by university professors and students or experienced staff leaving incumbent firms. To sustain this constant stream of entrepreneurial entries, a significant pool of specialized resources such as risk capital (in the form of venture capital and angel investors) and professional services firms (such as venture law firms, IPO underwriting firms, IP management services firms) is needed. Further feeding the entrepreneurial subsystem is a high degree of mobility of experienced people who leave the incumbent enterprises and the public R&D sector to become entrepreneurs or employees of young firms. Finally, the openness of Silicon Valley to foreign talents and ideas means that there is a constant flow of innovations and people into the system, as they are either absorbed into existing firms and university or public R&D institutes or directly into entrepreneurial start-ups.

In contrast to the "Silicon Valley" model, Singapore's enterprise ecosystem in the 1980s and early 1990s had a strong dominance of economic output by large, foreign MNCs. While openness to global competition forced these foreign MNC subsidiaries to continuously upgrade the technological base of their operations in Singapore, this primarily took the form of diffusing product technological innovations transferred from parent/affiliate firms and incremental local process engineering and improvement, with little significant R&D activities conducted in Singapore itself (Amsden and Tschang 2003). Local R&D by indigenous enterprises and public research institutes (PRIs) and universities was also relatively weak, while the flow of innovations to industry through commercialization of public R&D was minimal, whether through technology licensing to existing firms or through high-tech start-ups (Wong 1999). New entrepreneurial firm formation primarily took the form of ex-employees of MNCs leaving to start new firms to supply components or provide subcontract manufacturing and logistics support services to the existing MNCs (Wong 1992, 2002a).

How much progress has Singapore made in shifting toward the stylized Silicon Valley model? To examine the structural shifts achieved so far, we used the preceding framework to present in the next section the available empirical evidence on how the various components of the high-tech enterprise ecosystem of Singapore have evolved over the past decade or so.

THE CHANGING HIGH-TECH ENTERPRISE ECOSYSTEM
OF SINGAPORE

Development of the Innovation System

The size and characteristics of the innovation subsystem of Singapore can be measured through a number of well-established indicators—R&D intensities, scientific publications, patenting, product/process innovation intensities in firms, and university/PRI-industry linkages.

R&D Intensities

Table 5.1a shows the changing intensities of R&D investment in Singapore over the period 1978–2002 as measured by the Gross Expenditure on R&D (GERD) to GDP ratio. Singapore's R&D intensity was only around .2 percent in 1978, and was still less than 1 percent in 1990, but by 2002, it had risen to 2.2 percent, exceeding the level of the UK and the Netherlands, although still behind the more advanced Scandinavian countries (Table 5.1b). Another indicator of R&D investment intensity, as measured by the number of research scientists and engineers (RSEs) per 10,000 persons in the labor force, also shows that Singapore has made significant progress, rising from less than 30 in 1990

TABLE 5.1A

Growth Trend of R&D in Singapore, 1978–2002

Year	GERD (S $ million)	GERD/GDP (%)	RSEs	RSE/10,000 Labor Force
1978	37.80	0.21	818	8.4
1981	81.00	0.26	1,193	10.6
1984	214.30	0.54	2,401	18.4
1987	374.70	0.86	3,361	25.3
1990	571.70	0.84	4,329	27.7
1991	756.80	1.00	5,218	33.6
1992	949.50	1.17	6,454	39.8
1993	998.20	1.06	6,629	40.5
1994	1,174.98	1.10	7,086	41.9
1995	1,366.55	1.13	8,340	47.7
1996	1,792.14	1.39	10,153	56.3
1997	2,104.56	1.49	11,302	60.2
1998	2,492.26	1.76	12,655	65.5
1999	2,656.29	1.84	13,817	69.9
2000	3,009.5	1.89	14,483	66.1
2001	3,232.7	2.11	15,366	72.5
2002	3,404.7	2.19	15,654	73.5

SOURCE: National Survey of R&D in Singapore, various years, Agency for Science, Technology and Research (previously National Science & Technology Board).

TABLE 5.1B

Comparative R&D Indicators: Singapore and Selected OECD/Asian NIEs

Grouping	Country	Year	R&D/ GDP (%)	Researchers per 10,000 Labor Force
G-5	Japan	2001	3.1	100
	Germany	2001	2.5	65
	United States	2001	2.8	90[a]
	United Kingdom	2001	1.9	55[b]
	France	2000	2.2	65
Industrialized small countries	Finland	2001	3.4	140
	Switzerland	2000	2.6	64
	Sweden	2001	4.3	103
	Ireland	2000	1.2	49
	Netherlands	2000	1.9	52
	Denmark	1999	2.2	66
	Norway	1999	1.7	78
	Australia	2000	1.5	68
	New Zealand	1999	1.0	46
Asian NIEs	Korea	2001	3.0	61
	Taiwan	2001	2.2	61
	Hong Kong	1996	0.3	n.a.
	Singapore	**2002**	**2.2**	**74**[c]

SOURCE: Main Science and Technology indicators 2003–2001, downloaded from www.sourceoecd.org, and various national sources.

[a] 1999 figure.
[b] 1998 figure.
[c] RSEs per 10,000 labor force.

TABLE 5.2

Output of Scientific Publications: Singapore Versus Selected Countries

Grouping	Country	Number of Articles in 1998 (per million inhabitants)	Growth Rate of Number of Publications, 1990–1999 (%)
Small	Austria	449.36	3.84
industrialized	Belgium	475.49	2.60
countries	Denmark	770.27	1.61
	Finland	737.43	3.63
	Netherlands	684.75	0.95
	Norway	588.20	1.25
	Sweden	945.44	0.72
	Switzerland	973.40	2.60
NIEs	Hong Kong	89.73	9.14
	South Korea	119.58	21.96
	Singapore	**433.44**	**12.96**
	Taiwan	244.71	12.29
	Ireland	343.59	4.18
	Israel	873.87	0.63
G-7	Canada	640.87	−1.03
	France	465.97	2.68
	Germany	463.69	2.14
	Italy	296.60	3.77
	Japan	371.42	3.15
	United Kingdom	665.77	0.89
	United States	612.04	−1.06

SOURCE: *Science & Engineering Indicators 2002*, National Science Board.

NOTE: Article counts (on a per capita basis) are based on fractional assignments; for example, an article with two authors from different countries is counted as one-half of an article for each country.

to 74 by 2002, with the latter figure being above the OECD mean as well. As another indicator of the deepening of Singapore's R&D system, the proportion of total R&D expenditures classified as "Basic Research" had increased from less than 12 percent in 1996 to over 15 percent by 2001 (calculated from ASTAR various years).

Scientific Publication Intensities

Table 5.2 shows the growth rate of international scientific publications by Singapore-based institutions between 1990 and 1999 versus major countries. As can be seen, with the exception of Korea, Singapore achieved the highest annual growth rate of about 13 percent compared with an average of less than 3 percent for all advanced countries. Measured in terms of publications per capita of population, Singapore had achieved a level in 1998 that approached those of France and Germany and exceeded Japan's. While it is true that the

TABLE 5.3A

Growth Trend of US Patents Awarded to Singapore Inventors, 1976–2002

Countries	1976–1980	%	1981–1985	%	1986–1990	%	1991–1995	%	1996–2000	%	2001–2002	%	Cumulative Total 1976–2002	%
					Patents by Singapore Inventors[a]									
Singapore assignee	6	35.3	24	68.6	40	48.8	108	36.9	480	50.9	529	57.5	1,187	51.8
Individuals[b]	4	22.2	14	22.2	23	22.2	30	22.2	61	22.2	61	22.2	193	22.2
Companies	2	11.1	10	11.1	16	11.1	64	11.1	353	11.1	396	11.1	841	11.1
Universities and PRICs	0	0.0	0	0.0	1	1.2	14	4.8	66	7.0	72	7.8	153	6.7
Foreign assignee	11	64.7	11	31.4	42	51.2	185	63.1	463	49.1	391	42.5	1,103	48.2
Individuals	0	0.0	1	2.9	1	1.2	2	0.7	5	0.5	0	0.0	9	0.4
Companies	11	64.7	9	25.7	40	48.8	182	62.1	436	46.2	377	41.0	1,055	46.1
Universities and PRICs	0	0.0	1	2.9	1	1.2	1	0.3	22	2.3	14	1.5	39	1.7
Total[a]	17	100	35	100	82	100	293	100	943	100	920	100	2,290	100

SOURCE: Database of the U.S. Patent and Trademark Office (USPTO) (various years).

[a] Patents where at least one inventor is a Singaporean.

[b] In the U.S. patent database, some patents are not given specific assignees. These patents are included with those assigned to a Singaporean individual as long as at least one inventor is a Singaporean.

impact of Singapore's scientific publications (as measured by citations per paper) still remains low when compared with the more advanced countries, this may be largely due to the recentness of Singapore's publications.

Patenting Intensities

Table 5.3a summarizes Singapore's patenting trend over the period 1976–2002, as measured by the number of U.S. patents granted to Singapore-based inventors. Growth in patenting was relatively slow before the 1990s, but it has accelerated significantly since, especially since the mid-1990s, when the number of patents granted more than doubled. For the period 1996–2001, Singapore's utility patent growth rate was the highest among all OECD countries and Asian NIEs. In terms of patenting per capita, by 2001 Singapore achieved a level that exceeded some OECD countries like France, the UK, and Norway, although still significantly behind Taiwan, Germany, Japan, and the United States (Table 5.3b).

Firm Innovation Intensities

Last, but not least, Table 5.4 shows indicators of the innovation intensities of Singaporean manufacturing and business services firms in 1999 compared with selected European firms in 1996. As measured by the proportion of firms engaging in innovation activities, Singaporean manufacturing firms still scored relatively poorly, although their business services counterparts appear to fare better. However, for manufacturing firms that engaged in innovating activities, Singapore firms appear to exhibit relatively high innovation performance as measured by the proportion of sales derived from new products introduced during the past three years.

Role of University and Public Research Institutes (PRIs) in Innovation

From the late 1980s to the early 1990s, public sector R&D [conducted by government agencies, universities, and public research institutes (PRIs)] accounted for 40 to 50 percent of total R&D spending in Singapore. However, since the early 1990s, the share of public sector R&D spending had declined to around 37 percent and had remained relatively stable over the last seven to eight years. The public sector accounted for the bulk of basic R&D spending, while private sector primarily pursued applied R&D and experimental development, with only 4 percent devoted to basic research in 2002 (ASTAR 2002). However, in terms of U.S. patent output, local PRIs and universities accounted for a

TABLE 5.3B

Patent Indicators: Singapore Versus Selected Countries

Country	All Patents[a] per 1,000 Population 2001	Utility Patents[b] Growth Rate 1996–2001	Utility Patents[c] / GERD (number per U.S. $ million) 1990	Utility Patents[c] / GERD (number per U.S. $ million) 2000
Singapore	**0.90**	**27.5**	**0.07**	**0.13**
G-7 Nations				
G-7 average	1.61	8.70	0.19	0.21
Canada	1.41	10.1	0.24	0.27
United Kingdom	0.85	10.1	0.15	0.14
United States	3.46	7.5	0.31	0.32
Japan	2.79	7.6	0.23	0.21
Germany	1.56	10.6	0.18	0.22
Italy	0.38	7.3	0.09	0.14
France	0.83	7.7	0.10	0.14
Asian NIEs				
Hong Kong	0.82	21.9	n.a.	0.24
South Korea	0.81	18.8	0.07	0.27
Taiwan	3.00	23.1	0.35	0.74
Selected European OECDs				
Finland	1.65	10.5	0.12	0.15
Denmark	1.21	14.7	0.10	0.12
Netherlands	1.09	10.8	0.20	0.15
Norway	0.72	13.9	0.06	0.10
Sweden	2.36	15.3	0.15	0.17
Switzerland	2.63	5.0	0.25	0.16

SOURCE: U.S. Patent and Trademark Office.

[a]All patents include utility, plant, and design patents and SIRs. Nationality of patent is determined using the "at least one inventor resides in specified country" convention.

[b]Nationality of patent is determined by residence of first-named inventor at time of grant.

[c]Nationality of patent is determined by residence of first-named inventor.

proportionately much lower share of the total number of U.S. patents granted to Singapore-based inventors, despite an increasing trend (4.5% over 1991–1995, 6.6% over 1996–2000, and 7.5% over 2001–2002). The extent of university-industry collaboration in R&D also appeared to remain relatively weak; in 2002, private sector funding accounted for only 2.7 percent of total university R&D spending. In a survey of manufacturing firms at the end of 1999, the importance of collaboration with local universities/PRIs was ranked behind collaboration with customers and suppliers (Wong and He 2003a), although some improvements appeared to have occurred compared with the findings of another survey taken two years earlier (Wong 1999). The picture appears to be brighter in terms of the extent of university technology commercialization through licensing;

TABLE 5.4

*Proportion of Enterprises Engaging in Innovation Activities
in Singapore 1999 Versus in Selected European Countries, 1996*

| Country | Manufacturing Sector | | Knowledge-Intensive Business Services Sector |
	Percentage of Enterprises Engaging in Innovation Activities	Percentage of Product Innovators' Turnover due to New or Improved Products in Last 3 years[a]	Percentage of Firms Engaging in Innovating Activities[b]
Ireland	73	32	75
Germany[c]	69	43	63
Austria	67	31	41
Netherlands	62	25	58
United Kingdom	59	23	56
Sweden	54	31	50
Norway	48	20	42
France	43	21	46
Luxembourg	42	n.a.	83
Finland	36	25	44
Singapore	**32**	**29**	**57**
Spain	29	27	n.a.
Belgium	27	14	42

SOURCE FOR SINGAPORE DATA:
Wong, P.K., M. Kiese, A. Singh, and F. Wong (2003). "The Pattern of Innovation in Singapore's Manufacturing Sector," *Singapore Management Review*, 25(1).
Wong, P.K., and A. Singh (2004). "The Pattern of Innovation in the Knowledge-Intensive Services Sector of Singapore," *Singapore Management Review*, 26(1) (forthcoming).
SOURCE FOR EUROPEAN DATA:
Eurostat. (1999). *Memo: Community Innovation Survey*. Memo No. 6/99, 21 May 1999.
European Communities. (1999). *Innovat*. Eurostat database, CD-ROM.
Foyn, F. (1999). "Community Innovation Survey 1997/1998." *Statistics in Focus: Research and Development*, 2/1999, Eurostat.
NOTE: European figures are for 1996 except for Norway, which are for 1997.
[a] Singapore value for proportion of turnover is derived from midpoint estimate of categorized variable.
[b] European figures are for NACE 72 (computer and related services) and 742 (architectural and engineering activities and related technical consultancy) only. As such, they are not wholly comparable with the Singapore results.
[c] Including ex-GDR from 1991.

based on data for the National University of Singapore (NUS), the largest and oldest university in Singapore, the cumulative number of external technology licenses issued had increased to 107 as of 2003, with about one-quarter issued since 2002.

Collectively, these indicators suggest that Singapore had made significant

136   improvement in increasing the intensity of innovation efforts, and this had translated into rapid gains in innovation outputs as measured by patenting and scientific publications. However, a gestation period seems to occur between the new knowledge-generation activities and observable product and process innovation by enterprises. Indeed, more detailed analysis suggests that innovation at the firm level still appears to be highly concentrated in a small number of large firms, even though much progress had been made in terms of broader diffusion. As of the end of 2002, the top 20 patenting organizations in Singapore accounted for 57 percent of the total cumulative number of patents awarded to Singapore-based organizations, and of these, 14 (70%) were foreign MNCs, with another 2 (10%) being a public R&D institution and a university, and only 4 (20%) were local firms (Wong and Ho 2003). Nevertheless, local firms had over the years increased their share of both U.S. patents granted as well as R&D performed versus foreign MNCs; by the early 2000s, local firms had accounted for over 40 percent of total private-sector R&D performed in Singapore (calculated from ASTAR various years), and received more than half of all U.S. patents granted to private organizations (see Table 5.3a).

    While there are thus encouraging signs of progress on the innovation front, to gain a more complete picture of how the growing innovation output is transmitted into the enterprise ecosystem, we need to examine how the entrepreneurial subsystem has been performing as a carrier of innovation. This is done in the following section.

Development of the Technology Entrepreneurship System

Entrepreneurial Propensities Indicators

A useful source of data on the entrepreneurial propensities of the people of Singapore is the Global Entrepreneurship Monitor (GEM) study, which has the advantage of providing international comparison (Reynolds et al. 2002). Table 5.5 summarizes several measures of Singapore's entrepreneurial propensities as derived from GEM for the years 2000–2002, and the relative international ranking of Singapore based on these measures. Overall, as measured by the total entrepreneurial activities (TEA), just less than 6 percent of Singapore's adult population between ages 18 and 64 was found to be engaged in new entrepreneurial pursuit versus 6.6 percent in 2001 and 4.2 percent in 2000. About five out of six of these new entrepreneurs in Singapore in 2002 indicated they were doing so to pursue opportunities rather than out of necessity. In terms of business sectors, the majority of the new entrepreneurs were in the services sector, with manufacturing representing less than 12 percent. Based on a compos-

TABLE 5.5

Entrepreneurial Propensity of Singapore Adult Population, 2000–2002

	2000	2001	2002
Singapore			
Total Entrepreneurial Activity Rate (TEA)	4.2	6.6	5.9
Opportunity Entrepreneurial Activity Rate	–	5.1	4.9
Necessity Entrepreneurial Activity Rate	–	1.2	0.9
High Growth Potential Entrepreneurial Activity Rate	–	–	1.3
United States			
Total Entrepreneurial Activity Rate (TEA)	16.6	11.6	10.5
Opportunity Entrepreneurial Activity Rate	–	10.3	9.1
Necessity Entrepreneurial Activity Rate	–	1.3	1.1
High Growth Potential Entrepreneurial Activity Rate	–	–	0.8
Ranking of Singapore's Entrepreneurial Propensity in GEM Study			
Total Entrepreneurial Activity Rate (TEA)	20 of 21	25 of 29	21 of 37
Opportunity Entrepreneurial Activity Rate	–	21 of 29	19 of 37
Necessity Entrepreneurial Activity Rate	–	21 of 29	24 of 37
High Growth Potential Entrepreneurial Activity Rate	–	–	10 of 37

SOURCE: Autio, Wong, and Reynolds (2003); Global Entrepreneurship Monitor (GEM) Project Database.

ite measure developed by Autio (Wong and Reynolds 2003), over one-fifth of all entrepreneurial ventures covered by the survey (or 1.3% of all respondents) could be considered as "high growth potential" ventures.

From an international comparative perspective, Singapore ranked relatively poorly in terms of (TEA) in 2000 (19th out of 21 countries) and 2001 (27th out of 29), although there was a visible improvement in 2002 (21st out of 37). However, Singapore appears to rank better in terms of opportunity entrepreneurial rate (19th out of 37 countries in 2002 vs. 24th out of 29 in 2001), and more so in terms of "high growth potential" entrepreneurial rate (10th out of 37 countries in 2002).

Overall, the GEM study certainly confirmed that Singapore has lower entrepreneurial propensities compared with most advanced OECD countries (except Japan, France, and Belgium), although the picture is actually not as bad as painted by some impressionistic journalistic accounts. Singapore certainly ranks higher than the reported 35th-place ranking by the World Competitiveness Yearbook (WCY) based on the response of surveyed executives to the question "entrepreneurship is common in your country" (IMD 2003). More importantly, Singapore appears to perform much better in terms of opportunity-driven and high growth potential start-up propensities.

New Firm Formation in High-Tech Clusters

As an alternative measure of entrepreneurial activities in Singapore, Table 5.6 shows the trend in new enterprise formation in Singapore from 1996 to mid-2003, based on the actual records of the Registrar of Companies and Businesses (RCB). These records cover all incorporated companies and sole proprietorships and partnerships, although they exclude many forms of self-employment. As can be seen, while the overall new firm formation rate fluctuated between 30,800 and over 37,000 per year over the period, new venture formation in the high-tech sectors fluctuated more, exhibiting much higher growth (over 40% per year) during the dotcom boom years of 1999 and 2000, followed by a sharper collapse (33% vs. 5% for non-high-tech firms) in 2001 and a slower recovery (4% vs. 10%) in 2002. Over the entire period, start-ups in high tech sectors accounted for less than 10 percent of total new firm formation. A closer examination of the breakdown of new firm formation by high-tech subsectors reveals that five clusters — IT services, telecommunications (including the Internet), business and engineering services, manufacturing of machinery (including precision engineering and contract manufacturing) and electronics manufacturing — accounted for the bulk (91%) of all high-tech start-ups.

Sources of High-Tech Entrepreneurs

While there is no comprehensive study of where the high-tech entrepreneurs come from, a number of recent studies suggest that a major source appears to be staff leaving existing high-tech enterprises, typically MNCs. For example, Wong, Lee, and He (forthcoming) found that there was a higher propensity for employees of enterprises engaging in product innovation to leave and start their own firms. Zhang, Wong, and Soh (2003) found from a survey of 128 high-tech entrepreneurs in Singapore that a significant proportion of these high-tech founders had prior work experience in the corporate sector. In addition, the local universities as a source of high-tech spin-offs, although still relatively small, has grown significantly in recent years: The cumulative number of technology spin-off by NUS professors has increased to over 40 by 2003, more than double the number just three years ago. Finally, start-ups by fresh university graduates also appeared to be another emerging source: a survey of alumni of NUS who graduated in 2002 found more than 2 percent had started their own businesses within six months of graduation, double the rate of the graduating cohort four years ago (NUS Consulting 2003).

TABLE 5.6

Number of Start-up Registrations, 1996–2003

Year of Registration	1996	1997	1998	1999	2000	2001	2002	2003 (up to June)
			Number					
All industries	33,753	33,122	30,791	35,747	37,368	33,972	37,138	18,667
Non-high-tech	31,151	30,434	28,335	32,111	32,256	30,557	33,591	17,087
High-tech	2,602	2,688	2,456	3,636	5,112	3,415	3,547	1,580
			Percentage Change					
All Industries	5.3	−1.9	−7.0	16.1	4.5	−9.1	9.3	
Non-high-tech	4.6	−2.3	−6.9	13.3	0.5	−5.3	9.9	
High-tech	13.8	3.3	−8.6	48.0	40.6	−33.2	3.9	

SOURCE: Unpublished data compiled from Singapore Department of Statistics based on records of Registrar of Companies & Business.

TABLE 5.7A

Growth of Singapore's Venture Capital Industry, 1985–2002

Year	Cumulative Funds under Management (S $ billion)	Government Initiatives to Promote VC Industry or Major Developments in VC Industry
1985	0.16	Launch of EDB VC Program
1986	0.26	Launch of first major local VC Fund; first Pioneer VC awarded
1988	0.4	Promoted first USVC to set up in Singapore
1989	0.6	—
1990	1.2	Initiated first Seed Fund
1991	2.1	—
1992	2.4	—
1993	2.6	Initiated Singapore Venture Capital Association; EDB as patron
1994	3.5	Initiated second Seed Fund and set up Regional Investment Fund
1995	5.3	Initiated first Specialized Comms and Media Fund
1996	6.2	—
1997	7.4	Initiated first Specialized Info Tech Fund and Pharm Bio Growth Fund
1998	7.7	Set up Life Science Investments
1999	8.8	Initiated third Seed Fund. Set up PLE Investments. Launched U.S. $1 billion Technopreneurship Fund
2000	10.2	Launched M-Commerce Fund and launched U.S. $1 billion fund for life sciences
2001	13.7	—
2002	15.2	Total number of funds under management in Singapore increased to 144

SOURCE: EDB Yearbook 1999/2000; Tan, A. (2003). "Singapore's Venture Capital Sector Alive and Kicking," *Straits Times*, October 13, 2003; EDB Year 2001–In_Review, Press Release, January 22, 2002, http://www.sedb .com/edbcorp/sg/en_uk/index/in_the_news/press_releases/2002/edb_year_2001-in-review.html.

NOTE: Number in brackets is the number of VC fund management companies.

Development of Specialized Resources

As emphasized previously, the development of the innovation and entrepreneurial subsystems is dependent on, and co-evolves with, the development of specialized resources. These resources not only serve as crucial inputs to the two systems, but are in turn enhanced through the process of "learning by doing." In this section, we examine the development trend of several of these key specialized resources.

Venture Capital and Business Angel Investment

Table 5.7a shows the trend of growth of venture capital funds managed in Singapore over the period 1985–2002, while Table 5.7b shows the trend of ac-

TABLE 5.7B

Venture Capital Investment in Singapore-Based Ventures, 1999–2002

	1999	2000	2001	2002
Venture capital (VC) investments in Singapore companies	S $413 million	S $601.3 million	S $384.4 million	S $155.0 million
Gross domestic product (GDP)	S $140.7 billion	S $159.9 billion	S $153.5 billion	S $155.7 million
VC investment/GDP ratio	0.30%	0.38%	0.25%	99.6%
Average VC per investment	S $3.17 million	S $3.3 million	S $5.4 million	S $2.4 million
Number of companies	130	182	73	65

SOURCE: Singapore Economic Development Board. Cited in Wong, P. K., Wong, F., Ho, Y. P., Singh, A., and Lee, L. (2002). *Global Entrepreneurship Monitor 2002: Special Seminar and Press Release Global Entrepreneurship Monitor 2003*.

tual venture capital (VC) investment in Singapore-based companies over the more recent period of 1999–2002. As can be seen, the number and amount of VC funds managed out of Singapore has grown dramatically during the past 10 years, spurred in part by a significant injection of co-funding by a number of government holding companies as institutional investors (Temasek Holdings, TIF Ventures) as well as the establishment of a number of VC funds directly managed by government agencies or government-linked companies (for example, EDB Investment, Vertex Management, EDB Life Science Investment). However, in terms of actual investment in Singapore-based ventures, the record appears to be less positive: Over the four-year period of 1999–2002, a total of less than S $1.6 billion were invested in 450 Singapore-based firms, or just over 10 percent of the total VC funds managed out of Singapore in 2002. A sizable portion of the VC funds managed in Singapore thus appears to have been invested overseas instead, using Singapore only as a regional hub for fund management.

As VCs fund only a very small proportion of start-ups, and in the context of Singapore typically not at the seed stage, a critical concern is the availability and sophistication of business angel investors to provide the crucial seed funding at the early stage of new ventures. It has been estimated by the GEM 2002 study that the aggregate amount of angel investment in the 37 countries covered by the study to be five times more than the amount of VC investment in these countries (Reynolds et al. 2002).

From the GEM study in Singapore, the proportion of adults in Singapore who had engaged in angel investing activities appears to have been increasing from 2000 to 2002, rising from about 1.6 percent in 2000 to 3.9 percent in 2002 (see Table 5.7c). While this is still significantly below the 4.9 percent recorded

TABLE 5.7C

Business Angel Investment Propensities of Adult Population:
Singapore Versus United States, 2000–2002

	2000	2001	2002
Singapore	1.3	2.0	3.6
United States	7.0	6.0	4.9
Ranking of Singapore in GEM countries covered	18 of 21	19 of 29	12 of 37

SOURCE: Global Entrepreneurship Monitor (GEM) Project Database.

by the United States, business angel investment propensity in Singapore appears to rank higher than its entrepreneurial propensity ranking among the 37 countries covered by GEM in 2002 (12th vs. 21st). Moreover, the average amount of investment per angel investor in Singapore also appears to be above the average of the 37 countries covered by GEM 2002. What is not clear, however, is the level of sophistication of the angel investors in Singapore, particularly with respect to high-technology, innovation-driven start-ups; available evidence based on a recent informal survey of Singaporean angel investors (Wong 2004) suggests that the level of sophistication is significantly lower than is found in the Silicon Valley; in particular, they invest less time in post-investment mentoring and monitoring.

Technical Manpower Resources

A critical mass of qualified technical manpower is necessary to support sustained R&D efforts in key technology fields, and an adequate pool of experienced technical project managers and business-savvy technical professionals is needed for their subsequent commercialization through incumbent or new firms. In terms of aggregate numbers, Singapore appears to have done well in increasing the supply of graduates trained in technical disciplines during the past two decades (see Table 5.8). From an output of about 2,200 per year in the 1970s and 5,200 per year in the 1980s, the annual flow has increased to 11,600 in the 1990s and over 17,000 by the early 2000s. The proportion of university graduates (vs. polytechnic graduates) also increased from about 30 percent to more than 40 percent in the same period. In addition, Singapore had been able to attract a steady influx of foreign scientists and engineers over the past 10 years. While precise statistics on the in-migration of qualified technical manpower are not available, the annual R&D surveys indicated that foreigners typically accounted for more than a quarter of the total pool of RSEs in Singapore in recent years (ASTAR various years). Similarly, more than one-

TABLE 5.8

Average Output of Technical Manpower from Tertiary Education
Institutions in Singapore, 1970–2001 (number of graduates per year)

	1970–1979	1980–1984	1985–1989	1990–1994	1995–1999	2000–2001
University level[a]	680	1,040	2,162	3,198	4,863	7,045
Polytechnic level[b]	1,516	2,463	4,836	6,639	8,493	10,341
Total	2,197	3,504	6,998	9,837	13,356	17,386
University graduates as percentage of total						
	31.0	29.7	30.9	32.5	36.4	40.5

SOURCE: Calculated from *Singapore Yearbook of Labour Statistics* (various years), and *Singapore Yearbook of Manpower Statistics* (various years).

[a] Includes degree courses from SIM.

[b] Includes diploma courses from ISS.

third of Singapore's IT manpower in recent years consisted of foreigners (Wong 2002b). The proportion is even higher in the emerging life science fields; for example, two-thirds of the RSEs in the new Institute of Nano-Biology (INB) in 2003 were foreigners.

In terms of quality, however, Singapore's technical manpower resource development may still have some way to go to catch up with the advanced countries. Among RSEs engaged in R&D activities in Singapore, the proportion with master's degrees or PhDs remained relatively low at around 40 to 44 percent from the early 1990s to 2001, although there was a noticeable jump to 48 percent in 2002 (calculated from ASTAR various years). The annual World Competitiveness Report also rated the availability of technical manpower in Singapore as behind most of the advanced OECD countries (see Table 5.19), even though the quality of its general workforce as a whole was rated among the best in the world (IMD 2003).

Knowledge-Intensive Business Services (KIBS)

Besides technical manpower and risk capital, several other specialized professional services have been identified as important in facilitating the growth of high-tech entrepreneurial clusters, including law firms specializing in intellectual property (IP) and new ventures, head-hunting and human resources, consulting, market research and PR firms specializing in start-ups, investment banking services for mergers and acquisitions (M&As), and IPO underwriting (Lee et al. 2001). More generally, the availability of a sophisticated base of knowledge-intensive professional services firms to which new start-ups can outsource their non-core work can facilitate the formation of new firms.

144   While there are no comprehensive data available on KIBS firms specializing in providing services to high-tech start-ups and innovating companies, a survey of three major subgroups of KIBS firms (IT services, business/management consulting, technical and engineering services) in Singapore in 2000 shows that more than one-third of these firms were engaging in providing services that support the innovation activities of their manufacturing customers (Wong and Singh 2004). The numbers of industrial design firms, patent engineers and licensing agents, IP management services firms, and business incubators have also been reported to show significant growth over the past few years (EDB 2003), albeit from rather low bases. For example, the number of registered patent agent increased to 77 by mid-2003, more than double that of the previous year, while the number of business incubators had increased to more than 40.

Social Networks

Although less tangible, various studies of Silicon Valley (see, for example, Lee et al. 2001; Saxenian 1997) have emphasized the importance of a dense social network in facilitating the exchange of ideas and the acquisition of critical resources (capital, key founding team members, early customers, among other things) by high-tech entrepreneurs. While there are no well-accepted measures of such social network characteristics that can be used to compare across regions, the recent study by Zhang, Wong, and Soh (2003) emphasized that social network ties, both direct and indirect, were indeed widely used by high-tech entrepreneurs in Singapore in acquiring their first investor, first key management team members, and first customer. Moreover, they found that the use of social networks (vs. other methods such as attending exhibitions or cold calls) has a significant positive impact on the likelihood of acquiring resources, after controlling for the level of prior knowledge of the resource owners or referrals. Thus, it appears that the entrepreneurial social networks are of importance in Singapore, even if their networks of specialized resources are less dense than in Silicon Valley.

Dynamism of High-Tech Clusters

How have the above-chronicled developments in the technological innovation and entrepreneurship systems in Singapore affected the overall growth and dynamism of its key high-tech industrial sectors? In this section, we examine the available empirical evidence on how the enterprise ecosystem of the key manufacturing and services clusters in Singapore has changed over the past decade or so. Three related questions need to be addressed:

- How has the economic performance of Singapore's key high-tech manufacturing and services clusters changed over the period?
- Has there been a healthy "churn" among the leading players?
- Has there been a shift from dependence on foreign firms to local entrepreneurial firms?

Dynamism of the Overall Economy

Although the average GDP growth rate of Singapore has declined during the
past two decades to less than 8 percent a year versus higher growth rates during the previous two decades, in terms of total factor productivity (TFP), Singapore's performance actually remained about the same over the two decades
1980–2000 (around 1.6%), much higher than in the previous decade of 1970–
1980 when it was negative (11.6%). As a share of overall GDP growth rate, Singapore's TFP growth from 1990 to 2000 contributed about 21 percent, just mar-
ginally lower than the previous decade, suggesting that the sources of growth
in Singapore in the 1990s had not changed much from the 1980s and that for
both periods, Singapore had gone beyond growth of input factors alone as as-
serted by Young for the period of the 1970s (1994). Furthermore, Ho, Wong,
and Toh (2003) have recently shown that the TFP growth of Singapore from
1978 to 2001 is significantly correlated with the growth of aggregate R&D expenditure, with a mean time lag of about three to four years.

The negative TFP growth during the period 2001–2002 may have been
anomalous, due largely to adverse shocks in the external environment leading
to temporary underutilization of capacity. In particular, the severe global slowdown in electronics and IT demand (especially the United States) plus the
added adverse impact of September 11 and growing competition from China
and India had significantly affected not only the electronics manufacturing and
IT services cluster in Singapore, but also Taiwan and Silicon Valley itself. However, the poor recent TFP performance does highlight the vulnerabilities of
Singapore's current economic structure to external shocks, and the need to
further diversify its dependence on the electronics/IT cluster.

Dependence of the Overall Economy on Foreign MNCs

Besides maintaining similar TFP performance in the 1990s as compared with
the 1980s, there also appears to have been no major shifts in the structure of
dependency on foreign MNCs in the overall enterprise ecosystem of Singapore, as measured by the share of foreign equity in total share capital of all incorporated companies in Singapore. As indicated in Table 5.9, foreign equity
accounted for over 37 percent of total equity capital in the late 1980s, declined

TABLE 5.9
Foreign Share of Equity Investment in
Singapore-Based Companies, 1984–2000 (%)

Year	Manufacturing	Total Economy	Electronics Industry
1984	65	n.a.	n.a.
1987	70.8	39.6	n.a.
1990	69.4	37.2	n.a.
1993	60.2	33.2	85.3
1994	62.6	32.8	84.8
1995	66.9	31.5	87.2
1996	67.9	32.1	86.4
1997	68.8	33.2	88.1
1998	69.8	35.1	86.9
1999	75.5	36.6	n.a.
2000	75.7	36.8	n.a.

SOURCES: Department of Statistics, *The Extent and Pattern of Foreign Investment Activities in Singapore*, 1995; Department of Statistics, *Foreign Equity Investment in Singapore*, 1997, 2000, 2001; Department of Statistics, *Singapore's Corporate Sector*, 2002.

somewhat to around 32–33 percent in the mid-1990s, but has risen back to around 37 percent since the late 1990s. The pattern for the manufacturing sector alone is also similar, although with higher foreign share (60–70%). (The same U-shaped pattern holds if we measure the split between equity owned by locally controlled firms and foreign-controlled firms.) Thus, at least at the macro level, the dependence of Singapore's private corporate enterprise sector on foreign investment in recent years had not visibly declined as compared with a decade ago. Given that an estimated 13 percent of the corporate enterprise sector (in terms of equity capital) in the late 1990s may have been controlled by the government through its investment holding companies (Singapore Department of Statistics 2002), this suggests that the local private corporate sector of Singapore may account for less than half of the entire corporate enterprise system (not counting sole proprietorships and partnerships).

The share of R&D expenditure by foreign firms in Singapore amounted to 53–58 percent of total private R&D in Singapore during the period 1998–2002 (calculated from ASTAR various years). Although this represents a decline from over 60 percent during the first half of the 1990s, it is still higher than its share of equity investment, implying that foreign firms as a whole have higher R&D propensities than local firms in Singapore, a pattern confirmed by the 1999 survey of manufacturing firms by Wong and He (2003b). Foreign firms also contributed more than half of the total number of U.S. patents granted to organizations in Singapore during 1991–2000 (see Table 5.3a; also Hu 2003). Firm-level studies by Wong and He (2003a, 2003b) also found that foreign firms had higher overall technological innovation intensities as well as international innovation collaboration intensities than local firms.

Dynamism of Key Industrial Clusters

Table 5.10 summarizes the performance of the manufacturing sector of Singapore during the four decades 1960–2000. While the overall growth rate of manufacturing value added (in current prices) slowed down considerably from 22 percent annually in the first two decades to 9.8 percent annually from 1980 to 1990 and 6.1 percent annually from 1990 to 2000, in terms of growth of labor productivity (measured in terms of value added/worker), the decline had been much more gradual; from 1990 to 2000, labor productivity growth (6.3% annually) actually exceeded value-added growth, as there was an absolute reduction in total manufacturing employment. A major factor that influenced the growth in value added per worker in from 1990 to 2000 was the significant structural shift within the manufacturing sector during this period. On the one hand, there was a shift from lower value-adding sectors to higher ones. As can be seen in Table 5.11, using Pavitt's sectoral classification, the share of resource-based and labor-intensive industries has declined significantly over the years, while science-based sectors have grown significantly. On the other hand, there was a shift toward industrial sectors with a higher degree of outsourcing and vertical disintegration, which led to a decline in the aggregate value added to output ratio.

A significant feature in the structural shift of Singapore's manufacturing industry has been the dramatic rise of the electronics industrial cluster, which became the largest industrial cluster in Singapore since the mid-1980s and has since continued to increase its share of total manufacturing value added to more than 44 percent by the end of 2000 (Table 5.12). During the past two decades, not only was the electronics industry growing faster than overall manufacturing, but its labor productivity growth (10.4% annually) had been higher than what was achieved for overall manufacturing, with the result that, by 2000, the electronics cluster had an average labor productivity level 65 percent higher than the overall manufacturing average. Following the rapid rise of electronics manufacturing, the information and communications technology (ICT) services sector also emerged strongly since the mid-1980s to become the largest high-tech services sector in Singapore, with value-added growth performance of 13 percent annually between 1986 and 2001 (Table 5.13). In terms of labor productivity growth, however, the ICT services cluster grew substantially more slowly than the electronics cluster from 1990 to 2000, due to the more labor-intensive nature of many IT services activities.

TABLE 5.10

Manufacturing Growth in Singapore, 1960–2000

Year	Output ($ million)	Number of Workers	Value Added ($ million)	Fixed Asset ($ million)	Value Added/ Labor ($ thousand)	Value Added/ Output (%)	Capital/ Labor ($ thousand)
1960	465.6	27,416	142.1	n.a.	5.2	30.5	n.a.
1970	3,891.0	120,509	1,093.7	1,071.3	9.1	28.1	8.9
1980	31,657.9	285,250	8,521.9	7,461.1	29.9	26.9	26.2
1990	71,333.2	351,674	21,606.8	18,030.6	61.4	30.3	51.3
2000	163,720.8	344,610	38,951.0	42,362.7	113.0	23.8	122.9
			Average per Annum Growth Rate (%)				
1960–1970	23.7	16.0	22.6		5.8		n.a.
1970–1980	23.3	9.0	22.8		12.6		11.4
1980–1990	8.5	2.1	9.8		7.5		7.0
1990–2000	8.7	−0.2	6.1		6.3		9.1

SOURCES: Economic Development Board, *Report on the Census for Industrial Production*, various years; Economic Development Board, *Report on the Census of Manufacturing Activities*, 2000.

TABLE 5.11

Distribution of Singapore Manufacturing Exports by
Technological Categories, 1980–1999

Sector	Percentage		
	1980	1990	1999
Resource-based	44.4	26.9	13.2
Labor-intensive	10.6	10.3	7.6
Scale-intensive	9.3	5.9	5.5
Differentiated	20.5	22.3	21.2
Science-based	15.1	34.6	52.5

SOURCE: He, Z. L., and P. K. Wong (2003). "Host Country Environment and Innovation Intensity of Foreign Subsidiaries: Evidence from Singapore and Thailand." Submitted to *World Development*.

To obtain a clearer picture of the changing structure of dynamism of these two leading high-tech clusters in Singapore in recent years, we examine in more detail the nature of the largest firms that come to dominate the clusters and that contribute the bulk of the growth. In particular, we study the changing composition of the 30 largest firms in each of these two clusters. As can be seen in Table 5.14a, the top 30 firms in the electronics manufacturing sector in terms of revenues were totally dominated by foreign MNCs in 1991. However, by 2001, the degree of foreign dominance has declined somewhat: 25 out of the top 30 firms (83%) and 92.1 percent revenue (Table 5.14b). Of the five indigenous firms that made the list in 2001, only three (Creative, Venture Manufacturing, and GES) were independent entrepreneurial firms, whereas the other two (Chartered Semiconductor Manufacturing and Tech Semi) were government-linked firms. There were actually two other local firms that entered the top-30 list during the late 1990s, but both were acquired by foreign firms by 2000 (Natsteel Electronics, acquired by Solectron, and JIT, acquired by Flextronics).

Notwithstanding the continuing dominance by foreign firms, there has been significant growth of sales by the top 30 firms in the electronics manufacturing clusters between 1991 and 2001 (11.8% annually.). The overall degree of churn among the top 30 firms was also moderately high, with half of the firms in 1991 having dropped out by 2001. This churn was accompanied by significant structural shift in the electronics cluster, with the strong dominance by the consumer electronics and disk-drive subcluster in 1991 diminishing significantly by 2001, while new subclusters (contract manufacturing, IC wafer fabrication, and computer printers and mobile computing devices) grew rapidly. For the overall electronics cluster, the share of semiconductors (mainly in the form of wafer fabrication) increased from 10 percent in 1991 to 38 percent

TABLE 5.12
Electronics Manufacturing Industry Growth in Singapore, 1960–2000

Year	Output ($ million)	Number of Workers	Value Added ($ million)	Fixed Asset ($ million)	Value Added/ Labor ($ thousand)	Value Added/ Output (%)	Capital/ Labor ($ thousand)
1960	17.1	1,252	7.9	n.a.	6.3	46.2	n.a.
1970	212.9	11,251	99.1	n.a.	8.8	46.5	n.a.
1980	5,344.0	71,727	1,668.9	585.1	23.3	31.2	8.2
1990	27,878.1	122,797	7,716.6	3,757.3	62.8	27.7	30.6
2000	83,950.7	102,320	17,228.3	14,885.9	168.4	20.5	145.5
			Average per Annum Growth Rate (%)				
1960–1970	32.4	26.9	32.1		3.4		n.a.
1970–1980	34.2	18.1	29.3		10.2		n.a.
1980–1990	18.0	5.5	16.5		10.4		14.1
1990–2000	11.7	-1.8	8.4		10.4		16.9
			Percentage of Total Manufacturing				
1960	3.7	4.6	5.6	n.a.	121.2		n.a.
1970	5.5	9.3	9.1	n.a.	96.7		n.a.
1980	16.9	25.1	19.6	7.8	77.9		31.3
1990	39.1	34.9	35.7	20.8	102.3		59.6
2000	51.3	29.7	44.2	35.1	165.4		118.4

SOURCES: Economic Development Board, *Report on the Census for Industrial Production*, various years; Economic Development Board, *Report on the Census of Manufacturing Activities*, 2000.

TABLE 5.13

ICT Services Growth in Singapore, 1986–2001

	Number of Establishments	Employment	Turnover ($ million)	Value Added ($ million)	Operating Surplus ($ million)	Value Added/ Labor ($)	Value Added/ Turnover (%)
Telecommunications							
1986	2	12,712	988	805	529	63,299	81.42
1990	4	10,207	1,677	1,433	1,101	140,436	85.48
2000	147	10,743	4,959	3,000	2,327	279,252	60.50
2001	182	11,865	6,153	3,590	2,771	302,571	58.35
			Growth (%)				
1986–1990	18.9	−5.3	14.1	15.5	20.1	22.0	1.2
1990–2000	43.4	0.5	11.5	7.7	7.8	7.1	−3.4
IT Services							
1986	153	2,949	235	89	9	30,200	37.9
1990	356	6,172	616	258	43	41,876	42.0
1991	395	6,970	814	358	79	51,353	44.0
2000	2,397	22,154	4,632	1,719	362	77,593	37.1
2001	2,716	24,241	4,803	1,771	140	73,058	36.9
			Growth (%)				
1986–1990	23.5	20.3	27.2	30.5	47.8	8.5	2.6
1990–2000	21.0	13.6	22.4	20.9	23.7	6.4	−1.2
ICT Services							
1986	155	15,661	1,223	894	539	57,067	73.06
1990	360	16,379	2,293	1,692	1,144	103,296	73.79
2000	2,544	32,897	9,591	4,719	2,689	143,448	49.20
2001	2,898	36,106	10,956	5,361	2,911	148,479	48.93
			Growth (%)				
1986–1990	23.5	1.1	17.0	17.3	20.7	16.0	0.2
1990–2000	21.6	7.2	15.4	10.8	8.9	3.3	−4.0

SOURCES: Department of Statistics, *Economic Survey Series: Real Estate & Business*, various years; Department of Statistics, *Economic Survey Series: Transportation & Communications*, various years; Department of Statistics, *Economic Survey Series: IT and Related Services: Reference Year 2001*; Department of Statistics, *Economic Survey Series: Post & Telecommunications: Reference Year 2001*.

TABLE 5.14A

Top 30 Electronics Manufacturing Companies in Singapore, 1991–1992

Number	Company	Nationality	1991–1992 Sales (S \$ million)	Electronics Manufacturing Sector
1	Asia Matsushita Electric (S) Pte Ltd.	Japan	3,833	Electronic components
2	Seagate	United States	2,677	Disk drives
3	Conner Peripherals	United States	1,936	Disk drives
4	Thomson Consumer Electronics Asia Pte Ltd.	France	1,798	Electronic products
5	Philips (S) Pte Ltd.	Netherlands	1,504	Electronic products
6	Texas Instruments (S) Pte Ltd.	United States	1,298	Electronic components
7	SGS-Thomson MicroElectronics Pte Ltd.[a]	Italy/France	1,295	Electronic components
8	Toshiba Electronics Asia (S) Pte Ltd.	Japan	1,115	Electronic components
9	Western Digital (S) Pte Ltd.	United States	1,030	Disk drives
10	Hewlett-Packard Pte Ltd.	United States	1,015	Computers
11	Motorola Electronics Pte Ltd.	United States	919	Electronic products
12	National Semiconductor Pte Ltd.	United States	847	Electronic components
13	Toshiba (S) Pte Ltd.	Japan	751	Electronic products
14	Maxtor Peripherals (S) Pte Ltd.	United States	732	Disk drives
15	Sankei Pte Ltd.	Japan	728	Electronic products
16	Sanyo Electronics (S) Pte Ltd.	Japan	653	Electronic products

	Company	Country	Revenue	Category
17	Compaq Asia Pte Ltd.	United States	639	Computers
18	Aiwa (S) Pte Ltd.	Japan	625	Electronic products
19	Matsushita Electronics (S) Pte Ltd.	Japan	594	Electronic products
20	Siemens Components Pte Ltd.[a]	Germany	584	Electronic components
21	Hitachi Electronic Devices Pte Ltd.	Japan	570	Electronic components
22	Nissei Sangyo (S) Pte Ltd.	Japan	471	Electronic components
23	Sony (S) Pte Ltd.	Japan	437	Electronic products
24	SCI Mfg (S) Pte Ltd.	United States	434	Electronic components
25	Mitsubishi Electronics Mfg (S) Pte Ltd.	Japan	409	Electronic products
26	Asahi Electronics (S) Pte Ltd.	Japan	360	Electronic products
27	NEC Electronics (S) Pte Ltd.	Japan	337	Electronic components
28	Trio-Kenwood (S) Pte Ltd.	Japan	332	Electronic products
29	Murata Electronics (S) Pte Ltd.	Japan	309	Electronic components
30	AT&T Microelectronics Pte Ltd.[c]	United States	287	Electronic components
	Total revenue for top 30 companies		28,519	

SOURCE: *Singapore 1000 Industrial 1994*, DP Information Network.

[a] Later became STMicroelectronics Pte Ltd.

[b] Later became Infineon Technologies Asia Pacific Pte Ltd.

[c] Later became Agere Systems Pte Ltd.

TABLE 5.14B

Top 30 Electronics Manufacturing Companies in Singapore, 2001

Number	Company	Nationality	2001 Sales (S $ million)	Year of Incorporation	Description
1	Hewlett-Packard Singapore (Pte) Ltd.	United States	11,054.8	1970	Computers and peripherals
2	Seagate Technology International	United States	8,848.3[a]		Hard disk drive assembly
3	Flextronics International Ltd.	United States	7,560.4[b]	1990	Electronics manufacturing services
4	Agere Systems Pte Ltd.	United States	5,087.7	1985	Peripherals
5	Sony Electronics (Singapore) Pte Ltd.	Japan	4,588.6	1990	Components, computer peripherals, and electronic devices
6	Solectron Technology Singapore Pte Ltd.	United States	4,214.7	1981	Electronics manufacturing services
7	Micron Semiconductor Asia Pte Ltd.	United States	4,064.1	1998	Semiconductor components
8	Maxtor Peripherals (S) Pte Ltd.	United States	4,023.4	1990	Hard disk drives
9	Infineon Technologies Asia Pacific Pte Ltd.	Germany	3,048.1	1970	Electronic components
10	STMicroelectronics Pte Ltd.	Italy/France	3,001.5	1969	Integrated circuits and subsystems
11	Philips Electronics Singapore	Netherlands	2,883.5[c]	1997	Electronic devices and telecommunications equipment
12	Matsushita Kotobuki Electronics Industries (S) Pte Ltd.	Japan	2,287.6	1987	Hard disk drives and components
13	Motorola Electronics Pte Ltd.	United States	2,277.0	1983	Telecommunications
14	Creative Technology Ltd.	Singapore	2,236.1	1983	Computers and peripherals
15	Venture Corporation Limited	Singapore	1,430.9	1984	Electronics manufacturing services
16	Celestica Electronics (S) Pte Ltd.	Canada	1,224.6	1987	Electronics manufacturing services

	Company	Country	Revenue	Year	Product
17	Singapore Epson Industrial Pte Ltd.	Japan	945.7	1992	Peripherals
18	Tech Semiconductor Singapore Pte Ltd.	Singapore	940.2	1991	Semiconductors
19	Toshiba Singapore Pte Ltd.	Japan	894.5	1974	Consumer electronics and office equipment
20	Chartered Semiconductor Manufacturing	Singapore	842.0	1987	Semiconductors
21	Nidec Singapore Pte Ltd.	Japan	743.4	1988	Electric and electronic components
22	Murata Electronics (S) Pte Ltd.	Japan	692.9	1972	Electric and electronic components
23	Sanyo Asia Pte Ltd.	Japan	676.7	1972	Electronic components
24	GES (Singapore) Pte Ltd.	Singapore	668.8	1981	Computers and peripherals
25	Hitachi Chemical Asia-Pacific Pte Ltd.	Japan	622.2	1972	Printed circuit boards
26	Elec & Eltek International Co. Ltd.	Hong Kong	596.4	1993	Printed circuit boards
27	SCI Manufacturing (S) Pte Ltd.	United States	575.4	1983	Electronics manufacturing services
28	International Rectifier Southeast Asia Pte Ltd.	United States	561.6	1988	Semiconductors and related products
29	GP Batteries International Ltd.	Hong Kong	554.0	1990	Batteries and related products
30	NEC Semiconductors Singapore Pte Ltd.	Japan	521.7	1976	Electronic devices
	Total revenue for top 30 companies		77,666.8		

SOURCE: *Singapore 1000 Year* (various years), DP Information Network.

[a]1998 figure.

[b]1999 figure.

[c]2000 figure.

156   in 2001, while the share of computer peripherals (including disk drives) declined from 40 percent to 36 percent (calculated from EDB various years).

In summary, our analysis suggests that Singapore's electronics manufacturing cluster, despite being relatively mature, exhibits dynamic growth and healthy churn, within a context of increasingly fierce international competition and dramatic changes in technology and the global market structure. Although foreign global MNCs remain dominant, the overall enterprise ecosystem was vibrant and constantly renewing itself, with the emergence of several local entrepreneurial gazelles to join the league of the largest players, while the declining competitiveness of certain global firms and subsectors has been more than offset by the entrance of new global players in emerging subsectors.

A similar process of dynamic enterprise ecosystem growth, albeit at an earlier stage of formation, appears to be taking shape in the emerging biotech industrial cluster in Singapore (Finegold et al. 2004). While traditionally dominated by large pharmaceutical firms engaging in production activities with very little R&D done in Singapore, a cluster of new, R&D-based life science firms had emerged in recent years as a result of strong government policy support. Although some of these new firms were subsidiaries of established pharmaceutical MNCs, a sizable proportion were independent entrepreneurial start-ups funded by venture capital. By one estimate, close to one-third of the biotech firms founded in Singapore by 2003 were locally controlled, even though none of them have produced any significant revenue so far (Finegold et al. 2004).

On the surface, the picture appears to be even brighter in the case of the ICT services cluster, another high-growth technology cluster in Singapore. First, there has been a very high churn rate among the top 30: Only 7 out of the top 30 firms in 1991 remained in 2001 (Tables 5.15a and 5.15b). Second, local participation has also been at a more significant scale: In 2001, out of the top 30 firms 18 are local-majority owned, up from only 11 in 1991. However, the relatively higher local presence is due primarily to government-linked firms, not independent entrepreneurial firms. While the continuing dominance of local firms in the telecommunications services sector is understandable, given that the sector is subject to regulatory control that has constrained foreign participation, the liberalization of the telecommunications market has at least resulted in the entry of four new local firms, albeit government-linked ones (STT Communications, Starhub, Mobile One, and Keppel Telecoms) in addition to the previous monopoly (Singapore Telecoms). The other new local firms are in non-telecommunications IT subsectors, which in principle are not subject to tariff barriers and DFI restrictions. Nevertheless, it is significant to note that, except for three homegrown entrepreneurial start-ups (Informatics, ECS Holdings, and Frontline Technologies), all the other new local firms are government-

TABLE 5.15A

Top 30 ICT Services Companies in Singapore, 1991–1992

Number	Company	Nationality	Sales (S $ million) 1991–1992
1	Singapore Telecommunications Ltd.[a]	Singapore	2,479.2
2	Hewlett-Packard (F.E.) Pte Ltd.	United States	318.6
3	Singapore Computer Systems	Singapore	127.4
4	Reuters (S) Pte Ltd.	United Kingdom	108.6
5	CSA Holdings	Singapore	105.7
6	AT&T Singapore Pte Ltd.[b]	United States	86.3
7	Matsushita Graphic Communication Systems (S) Pte Ltd.	Japan	70.2
8	Fujitsu (S) Pte Ltd.	Japan	66.7
9	Toshiba Data Dynamics Pte Ltd.	Japan	37.9
10	Folec Communications Pte Ltd.	Singapore	37.8
11	Informatics Holdings Ltd.	Singapore	32.8
12	Telerate Financial Information Services Pte Ltd.	United Kingdom	25.6
13	Transmarco Data Systems (S) Pte Ltd.	Singapore	23.0
14	Singapore Network Services Pte Ltd.	Singapore	20.1
15	B T Services (S) Pte Ltd.	United Kingdom	20.0
16	Teledata (Singapore) Ltd.	Singapore	16.8
17	ABB Nera (S) Pte Ltd.[c]	Norway	16.3
18	Ericsson Network Engrg Pte Ltd.	Sweden	16.1
19	Selex (S) Pte Ltd.	Japan	14.5
20	Siemens Nixdorf Information Systems (RHQ) Pte Ltd.	Germany	14.1
21	Centralab Components (S) Pte Ltd.	Hong Kong	13.1
22	Isolectra Far East Pte Ltd.	Netherlands	11.7
23	Radac Pte Ltd.	Singapore	10.7
24	Nokia Telecommunications (S) Pte Ltd.	Finland	9.3
25	Hellermann Asean Pte Ltd.	Netherlands	9.0
26	Infonet Engineering Pte Ltd.	Singapore	7.9
27	Network for Electronic Transfers (S) Pte Ltd.	Singapore	7.8
28	Associated Technical Services Pte Ltd.	United Kingdom	7.3
29	Jennis & Leblanc Communications Asia Pte Ltd.	Australia	5.7
30	Onkyo (S) Pte Ltd.	Japan	5.5
	Total revenue for top 30 companies		3,725.7

SOURCE: *Singapore 1000 Industrial 1994*, DP Information Network; *Singapore 1000 Service 1994*, DP Information Network.

[a] Includes Singapore Telecom Mobile Pte Ltd. and Telecom Equipment Pte Ltd.

[b] Later became Lucent Technologies Singapore Pte Ltd.

[c] Later became Nera Telecommunications.

TABLE 5.15B

Top 30 ICT Services Companies in Singapore, 2001

Number	Company	Nationality	2001 Sales (S $ million)	Year of Incorporation	Description
1	Singapore Telecommunications Ltd.[a]	Singapore	7,338.2	1992	Telecommunications
2	Hewlett-Packard Far East Pte Ltd.	United States	4,323.7	1987	Computer products and peripherals
3	Microsoft Operations Pte Ltd.	United States	4,038.9	1998	Computer hardware and software
4	Datacraft Asia Ltd.	United Kingdom	997.8	1993	Internet infrastructure, online business solutions, and networking services
5	STT Communications	Singapore	803.7	1992	ICT services
6	Mobileone Ltd.	Singapore	639.1	1992	Telecommunications
7	CSA Holdings Ltd.	United States	624.2	1990	Computer systems
8	ECS Holdings Ltd.	Singapore	552.0	1998	IT products and services
9	Singapore Computer Systems	Singapore	540.7	1980	IT, business consultancy, and systems integration
10	Starhub Pte Ltd.	Singapore	514.0	1998	ICT services
11	Singapore Technologies Electronics Ltd.	Singapore	498.5	1969	Electronic systems
12	Reuters Asia Pte Ltd.	United Kingdom	468.8	1997	Information products
13	National Computer Systems Pte Ltd.	Singapore	414.7	1981	IT and engineering services
14	CPG Corporation Pte Ltd.	Singapore	335.7	1998	Building IT services and enabling technologies and other professional services
15	Autodesk Asia Pte Ltd.	United States	273.4	1992	CAD, engineering, and animation software products
16	Gemplus Technologies Asia Pte Ltd.	France	247.5	1989	Smart card–based solutions and applications

	Company	Country	Year	Revenue	Description
17	Abacus International Pte Ltd.	Singapore	1997	232.4	Computerized reservations systems
18	Nera Telecommunications	Norway	1978	229.5	Telecommunications
19	Infomatics Holdings Ltd.	Singapore	1983	200.2	Education and training
20	Lucent Technologies Singapore Pte Ltd.	United States	1987	193.9	Electrical and electronic components and network and telecom equipment
21	Keppel Communications Pte Ltd.	Singapore	1982	192.2	Telecommunications
22	Nortel Networks Singapore Pte Ltd.	Canada	1993	166.9	Telecommunications
23	Cisco Systems (USA) Pte Ltd.	United States	1995	158.7	Communication networks and systems
24	North 22 Technology Services Group Ltd.	Hong Kong	2000	156.6	IT integration and e-business application services
25	Pacific Internet Ltd.	Singapore	1995	141.1	Internet access solutions
26	Accenture Pte Ltd.	Luxembourg	1975	136.2	Management and IT consulting services
27	Frontline Technologies Corporation Ltd.	Singapore	1998	132.3	Technology infrastructure, consulting, and implementation services
28	CSE Systems & Engineering Ltd.	Singapore	1987	113.9	Systems integration solutions
29	SAP Asia Pte Ltd.	Germany	1989	110.9	Data processing consultancy
30	Singapore Engineering Software Pte Ltd.	Singapore	1986	93.6	Real-time/mission-critical systems
	Total revenue for top 30 companies			24,869.3	

SOURCE: *Singapore 1000 Year 2002/2003,* DP Information Network.

[a] Includes Singapore Telecom Mobile Ltd., Singtel Aeradio Ltd., and Telecom Equipment Pte Ltd.

160   linked firms that derived a substantial proportion of their revenue from public procurement. Thus, despite the healthier churn rate and local share, the picture is one of relatively low independent entrepreneurial success.

The sales by the top 30 firms in the ICT services cluster grew strongly between 1991 and 2001 (20.9% annually), faster than for the electronics manufacturing cluster. The strong growth of the largest players also exceeded the overall ICT services sector sales growth rate of 15.4 percent annually. In addition, various indicators of ICT usage in Singapore suggest that the domestic market had also expanded at healthy rates compared with most countries, thus contributing to part of the growth of the cluster. The lack of successful entrepreneurial firms and the continuing dominance of government-linked firms in what seems to be a fast-growing, dynamically changing cluster is thus worrying. A number of other concerns also emerge from a closer look behind the aggregate cluster growth statistics. First, while mobile phone and Internet penetration in Singapore are among the highest in the world, Singapore had failed to match the growing level of sophistication in mobile usage as found in Japan, Korea, and the Scandinavian countries. Second, Singapore had also fallen behind Korea and Hong Kong in terms of broadband diffusion, while the adoption of e-commerce applications in Singapore also lags behind the more advanced OECD countries. Add to this the much smaller domestic market size, and the apparent dominance of government-linked companies over public-sector contracts, it is clear that all entrepreneurial ICT start-ups in Singapore virtually need to go after international markets from day one, something not easy to execute. Indeed, a number of Singaporean IT entrepreneurs who tried to do this had deliberately chosen to start up in other countries, rather than in Singapore itself. It is thus not surprising that the number of start-ups in the wireless, broadband entertainment and e-commerce market space in Singapore is lower than in Korea, Taiwan, or Japan, probably even on a per capita basis.

Overall Assessment of Singapore's Emerging Environment for Innovation and Entrepreneurship

Overall Assessment of Singapore's Environment for Innovation

In a survey conducted by the author among manufacturing firms in Singapore in 1999, the respondents were asked to rate various dimensions of Singapore's environment affecting the firms' propensity to undertake innovation activities in Singapore. As can be seen in Table 5.16, Singapore's environment for innovation has been moderately well rated by existing companies, with a mean rating statistically significantly above 3 (on a Likert scale of 1 to 5) for 8 out of the 16 dimensions, and around 3 for another 6 dimensions. Particularly well rated

TABLE 5.16

Evaluation of Innovation Environment of Singapore by
Existing Manufacturing Firms, 1999

How Do You Assess the Current Business Environment in Singapore for Innovation Activities? (1 = poor to 5 = good)	Mean Scores		
	Foreign	Local	Average
1. Availability of government incentives for innovation	3.32	3.36	3.35
2. Openness of government departments and regulatory authorities to innovation	3.40	3.32	3.35
3. Availability of suitable manpower in scientific-technical sector	2.84	2.91	2.89
4. Availability of suitable manpower in business sector	3.01	3.05	3.04
5. Consultancy support services	2.94	3.08	3.03
6. Local universities for technical support and R&D collaboration	3.08	3.06	3.06
7. R&D institutions for technical support and R&D collaboration	3.05	3.00	3.02
8. Availability of other technical supporting services	2.94	2.96	2.96
9. Tolerance for failure	2.65	2.71	2.69
10. Attitude of people toward innovation	3.15	3.08	3.11
11. Openness of customers to innovation	3.26	3.22	3.24
12. Openness of suppliers to innovation	3.15	3.14	3.14
13. Intellectual property protection	3.44	3.37	3.40
14. Quality of telecommunications and IT services for enabling innovation	3.93	3.89	3.91
15. Availability of finance for innovation (e.g., venture capital)	2.93	3.00	2.98
16. Listing requirements on local stock exchange	3.27	3.14	3.19

SOURCE: He, Z.L., and P. K. Wong (2003). "Host Country Environment and Innovation Intensity of Foreign Subsidiaries: Evidence from Singapore and Thailand." Submitted to *World Development*.

were the quality of Singapore ICT infrastructure (3.9) and intellectual property protection (3.41). Availability of government incentives for innovation and openness of government/regulatory authorities to innovation (3.35) were also well rated (both 3.35), suggesting that government bureaucracy has not been perceived as a major problem. Only two dimensions — availability of scientific and technical manpower (2.89) and tolerance of failure (2.69) — were significantly below 3.

These findings largely corroborate the various empirical findings cited previously on the development of Singapore's innovation system. In addition, they appear to be broadly consistent with the overall ranking of Singapore's innovation system in a number of international comparative ranking surveys, such as the World Competitive Report (WCR) and the Global Competitiveness Report (GCR). In particular, Table 5.17 highlights the ranking of

TABLE 5.17

Singapore's Relative Ranking in Technological Capability–Related Indicators

	Ranking		
	1996	2000	2002
Overall competitiveness ranking	2	2	5
Overall Technological Development Indicators			
Overall science and technology competitiveness ranking	12	9	n.a.
Technology Using Capability Indicators			
Scientific environment	2[a]	6	9[b]
Science and education are adequately taught in compulsory schools	1	1	1[c]
Science and technology interest the youth of the country	1[a,d]	2	1[e]
Technology management	5	3	3[f]
Technological cooperation is common between companies	9	8	5[g]
Technology transfer between companies and universities is sufficient	4[h]	3	4[i]
Lack of sufficient financial resources does not constrain technological development	10	3	3[i]
Development and application of technology is supported by the legal environment	1[a]	1	2
Relocation of R&D facilities is not a threat to the future of your economy	31[a]	9	33
Qualified engineers are available in your country's labor market	17	9	13
Qualified information technology employees are available in your country's labor market	n.a.	6	9[k]
Employee training is a high priority in companies	n.a.	2	2
Process management is emphasized in your country	n.a.	1	
University education meets the needs of a competitive economy	1[l]	4	6
Technology Creation Capability Indicators			
R&D expenditure	26[a]	15	n.a.
Total expenditure on R&D per capita	n.a.	16[m]	15[n]
Total expenditure on R&D (% of GDP)	24[o]	14[m]	15[n]
Business expenditure on R&D per capita	n.a.	14	15[n]
R&D personnel	38[a]	13	
Total R&D personnel nationwide per capita	n.a.	16[m]	14[n]
Total R&D personnel in business enterprise per capita	n.a.	17[m]	14[n]

Intellectual property	19^a	22	n.a.
Number of patents granted to residents	n.a.^{p}	34^q	41^r
Number of patents secured abroad by country residents	23^s	35^t	n.a.
Patent and copyright protection is enforced in your country	5^u	15	13^v
Number of patents in force per 100,000 inhabitants	n.a.	12^t	13^r
Creation of firms is common in your country	n.a.	15	26
Managers generally have a sense of entrepreneurship	22^w	19	35^x

SOURCE: *World Competitiveness Yearbook* (various years), IMD.

NOTE: Only selected indicators are included.

[a] 1997 ranking.
[b] Scientific infrastructure.
[c] Science in schools is adequately taught in your country.
[d] Science and technology arouse the interest of youth.
[e] Interest in science and technology is strong for the youth of your country.
[f] Technological infrastructure.
[g] Technological cooperation is developed between companies.
[h] Research cooperation between companies and universities is sufficient.
[i] Knowledge transfer between companies and universities is sufficient.
[j] Funding for technological development is generally sufficient.
[k] IT skills are readily available in your country's workforce.
[l] The educational system meets the needs of a competitive economy.
[m] Based on 1998 figures.
[n] Based on 2000 figures.
[o] Based on 1994 figures.
[p] Based on 1993–1994 figures (average annual number).
[q] Based on 1996–1997 figures (average annual number).
[r] Based on 1999 figures.
[s] Based on 1993 figures (per 10,000 residents).
[t] Based on 1997 figures.
[u] Intellectual property is adequately enforced in your country.
[v] Patent and copyright protection is adequately enforced in your country.
[w] Managers generally have a good sense of entrepreneurship and innovation.
[x] Entrepreneurship is common in your country.

164   Singapore on a wide range of indicators on Singapore's innovation system as
derived from the World Competitiveness Report over the period 1996–2002.
As can be seen, despite problems of comparability of indicators over time due
to frequent changes in definitions, two plausible patterns can be observed.
Firstly, Singapore's international ranking in terms of technology-*using* capability indicators is still generally higher than for technology-*creating* capability indicators, confirming the earlier findings of Wong (2003a). Second, there
was a general trend of improvement in Singapore's between 1996 and 2000, although changes between 2000 and 2002 appear to be mixed.

Overall Assessment of Singapore's Environment
for Entrepreneurship

In the GEM survey, 15 dimensions of Singapore's environment for entrepreneurship were rated by a panel of about 40 informants for the three years
2000–2002. As can be seen in Table 5.18, Singapore was highly rated in terms
of such areas as physical and business infrastructure, financial capital availability, and government regulation and tax burden. However, the rating was
below the mean score of three for the following seven dimensions: education,
technology transfer to new enterprises, culture and social norms, barriers to
market entry, market dynamism, perception of business opportunities, and capacity to act on business opportunities. International comparisons of the
mean rating of Singapore's environment versus 36 other countries in 2002
largely confirm that Singapore had been ranked below the mean for the very
same dimensions (except education and technology transfer). In particular,
the low score of Singapore (2.6) for "low barriers to entry" deserves attention,
as it highlights not only the constraints of Singapore's small domestic market
size but also concern about the non-level playing field due to the absence of
anticompetition laws and the considerable presence of large, government-
linked enterprises in the domestic economy. The similarly low score for market dynamism, while somewhat surprising, may reflect a concern with the con-
servatism of large enterprises in Singapore, which has been voiced by many
start-up entrepreneurs as another negative aspect of Singapore's domestic
business environment for entrepreneurship. The relatively low rating of Singapore in terms of technology transfer (2.60) confirms our earlier reported
findings, while that for entrepreneurship education (2.66) appears to be contributed by the subindicator relating to primary and secondary education,
rather than university education. The low rating on "entrepreneurial capacity
to act on opportunities" (2.88), however, suggests the need for training in entrepreneurial skills to be made more widespread among working adults and

TABLE 5.18

Evaluation of Singapore's Entrepreneurial Environment by GEM Expert Informants, 2002

| | Entrepreneurship Environment Ratings by Country Informants (1 = low to 5 = high) | | | |
| | Singapore 2002 | All 37 GEM Countries | | |
Item		Mean	High Score (Country)	Low Score (Country)
Availability of capital	3.27	2.90	3.90 (United States)	1.49 (Argentina)
Importance of risk capital	3.27	2.80	4.29 (United States)	1.73 (Hungary)
Government policy support	3.23	2.67	3.60 (Canada)	1.49 (Argentina)
Low regulation and taxation burden	3.93	2.43	4.27 (Hong Kong)	1.35 (Argentina)
Government program effectiveness	3.41	2.64	3.41 (Singapore)	1.62 (Argentina)
Education and training effectiveness	2.66	2.32	3.13 (United States)	1.62 (Japan)
R&D transfer effectiveness	2.60	2.30	3.38 (Taiwan)	1.75 (Netherlands)
Commercial and professional infrastructure	3.34	3.16	4.20 (Canada)	2.00 (Japan)
Rapidity of change in markets	2.60	2.85	4.01 (Taiwan)	1.83 (Chile)
Low barrier to market entry	2.60	2.75	3.76 (Canada)	2.06 (Hungary)
Ease of access to physical infrastructure	4.42	3.86	4.79 (Canada)	2.98 (Hungary)
Cultural value placed on independence	2.76	2.81	4.51 (United States)	1.89 (Sweden)
Perception of business opportunities	2.88	3.32	3.98 (United States)	2.52 (Argentina)
Capacity to act on business opportunities	2.88	3.10	3.41 (Hong Kong)	1.72 (Japan)
Motivation to act on business opportunities	3.40	3.18	4.44 (Taiwan)	2.62 (Norway)

SOURCE: Wong, P. K., F. Wong, Y. P. Ho, A. Singh, and L. Lee (2002). *Global Entrepreneurship Monitor 2002: Singapore Report.*

university students. Last, but not least, Singapore's poor rating in social and cultural norms (2.76) appears to be consistent with indicators from a number of other sources, including the World Competitiveness Report (see Table 5.17), as well as the low score on tolerance of failure found in the innovation survey by Wong, Kiese et al. (2002) cited previously (Table 5.16).

Another indicator of the influence of social norms on entrepreneurship pertains to the attitude and interest of students of tertiary institutions toward entrepreneurship as a career option. Based on the findings of a large sample survey of more than 15,000 tertiary students in Singapore in 2000, only about 12 percent of the students indicated "strong" interest in starting their own business ventures (score of 5 on a Likert Scale of 1 to 5), with another one-quarter indicating moderate interest (Wong, Singh et al. 2001). The level of interest appears to be significantly lower for females, but higher among noncitizens. The level of interest appears to be constrained by self-efficacy, as a significant correlation is found between interest and the self-rated knowledge about starting a business. Fear of failure was also frequently cited as a deterrent. Similar perceived impediments were found in a recent survey of university graduates within six months of graduation (NUS Consulting 2003). Finally, the GEM

166   2002 survey found tertiary-educated adults to have the lowest entrepreneurial propensities in Singapore. Nevertheless, the picture is not entirely negative, as 2 percent of the students were found to have already started their own businesses even while studying, while 2.2 percent of the recent graduates started their own businesses within six months of graduation. Moreover, participation in a national business plan competition organized annually by the author showed a significant upswing in 2003, after a decline in 2001 and 2002 in the aftermath of the dotcom crash.

Public Policy Changes and Likely Impacts

As chronicled by Wong (2003a), the Singapore government has begun shifting its policy focus since the early 1990s from primarily emphasizing promoting technology adoption to supporting both technology diffusion and technological innovation. More recently, the government has also added the promotion of indigenous entrepreneurship in addition to its traditional emphasis on encouraging and leveraging foreign MNCs, through a Technopreneurship 21 (T21) Initiative announced in 1999, which included a new U.S. $1 billion fund to boost the growth of the venture capital industry, as well as a number of liberalization policies such as allowing entrepreneurs to start up their ventures in their home, relaxation of requirements for being listed on the local stock exchange, and altered bankruptcy regulations.

   In the wake of the dotcom crash, the T21 Initiative appeared to have been scaled back and modified to take on a broader focus on promoting entrepreneurship in general, not just technology start-ups. However, the focus on intensifying investment in R&D received a big boost from a decision to make Singapore into a life science hub in Asia, following the announcement of the breakthroughs of the Human Genome Project (Finegold et al. 2004). With a new U.S. $1 billion fund to boost public investment in several new life science research institutes, to co-fund new R&D projects by global pharmaceutical firms, as well as to initiate the building of a new life science park (Biopolis), major growth in R&D in life science can be expected over the next few years, with the hope that it will help Singapore to diversify away from its current high dependence on electronics and IT.

   Both these two emerging policy shifts have been accorded greater urgency in a recently released report by a high-level Economic Review Committee (ERC) formed by the Singapore government in 2002 to identify the strategic changes needed to make Singapore competitive in the increasingly globalized knowledge economy, in the face of dramatic changes in the global and regional economic landscape, including the rapid rise of China and India as

low-cost yet high-tech production platforms for the world, the regional financial and political volatilities following the 1997 Asian financial crisis, and the
threats of global terrorism.

As part of the ERC Report, the report of the Subcommittee on Entrepreneurship and Internationalization (released in September 2002) in particular
recommended many policy changes to re-make Singapore into a competitive
knowledge-based, entrepreneurially driven economy. Specifically, it identified
six broad areas of policy emphasis to make the Singaporean economy more conducive for entrepreneurial development, as follows:

1. Culture: to influence the cultural values of Singaporeans toward entrepreneurship by providing students and working professionals more opportunities to
   learn about entrepreneurship;
2. Capability building: to attract more entrepreneurial talents from overseas while
   encouraging greater mobility of talents between the public and private sectors;
3. Conditions: to reduce government regulatory red-tape and to review the role of
   GLCs in the domestic economy;
4. Connectivity: to enhance the global connectivity of Singaporeans to the world;
5. Capital: to improve start-up and SME access to capital; and
6. Catalytic role of government: to extend investment and tax incentives
   currently available for large MNCs to smaller enterprises as well (ERC 2002).

Although some of the recommended policy shifts had in fact been initiated
prior to this report, they have been given greater impetus after its release. Table
5.19 summarizes how the various policy initiatives currently in place in Singapore relate to the key elements identified in our framework for a dynamic high-
tech enterprise ecosystem. As can be seen, with some exceptions, the recent policy changes appear to have covered most of the key areas of concerns identified
by the framework. Generally, policies related to boosting the innovation system
appear to have been in place since the early 1990s (with revisions from time to
time), whereas policies related to facilitating entrepreneurial firm formation
appear to be much more recent, and indeed, some are still at the stage of intent
rather than implementation.

While it is beyond the scope of this chapter to provide an assessment of the
impact of public policy changes on the dynamism of Singapore's high-tech enterprise ecosystem, a number of general observations can be made. First, the
policy shifts toward increasing investment in public R&D and providing incentives for private-sector firms to undertake R&D since the early 1990s had
clearly made a significant impact on the intensity of R&D and innovative performance of Singaporean firms in general and the three high-tech clusters in
particular. Wong and He (2003a) had found that manufacturing firms that
received public R&D support achieved higher innovative performance. The

TABLE 5.19

Policy Initiatives Related to Key Elements of High-Tech Enterprise Ecosystem

	Policy Initiatives
	Innovation System
Public R&D	Increase in public funding of R&D over three successive national science and technology 5-year plans (1991–1995, 1996–2000 and 2001–2005)
	Reorganization of public R&D funding system along the lines of U.S. NSF in 2001 (changing the previous NSTB into the new ASTAR with two research councils, one on biomedical, one on (other) research and engineering
Private R&D and technological upgrading	Major public investment in life science R&D and Biopolis since 2001
	Ongoing tax incentives for R&D-intensive DFI by foreign MNCs
	Various ongoing government subsidy schemes (e.g., IDS, Intech) for private-sector firms to invest in innovation projects, train manpower for innovation
	Various ongoing government assistance schemes (e.g., LETAS) to help local SMEs to get financing for investing in technology adoption; new GET-UP program in 2003 to provide technical assistance to SMEs in innovation
Public-private innovation link	New organization (EXPLOIT) within ASTAR to centralize management of IP generated by PRIs for licensing to industry
	Policy on first right of refusal to commercialize IP by universities funded by ASTAR appears to run counter to spirit of Bayh-Dole Act in the United States
	No scheme similar to SBIR or STTR in the United States to bridge gap in seed funding of tech commercialization from PRIs and universities
	Entrepreneurial Firm Formation
Social and cultural norms	Establishment of a public-private consultation forum on entrepreneurship (ACE) in 2003, following ERC report
	ACE activities include monthly forum chaired by minister-in-charge of entrepreneurship, and programs to enlist successful entrepreneurs to give talks at schools, etc.

	Schools encouraged to promote interest in entrepreneurship among students following ERC report
Government regulations and red tape	Various policy liberalizations introduced as part of T21, including allowing business operation from home, relaxation of bankruptcy law, etc.
	Unit within ACE to receive public feedback on government red tape and unnecessary regulations
Barriers to entry	Government reviewing role of GLCs in domestic economy (ongoing)
	Market liberalization (e.g., public procurement, financial services) arising from FTA with the United States
Foreign entrepreneurs	Relaxation of immigration rules to allow foreign entrepreneurs to start up in Singapore more easily

Specialized Resources Development

Attracting foreign technical talent	Continuing foreign talent promotion programs (Singapore Connect, scholarships for foreign students)
Venture Capital	U.S. $1 billion co-investment fund (TIF) to attract local and foreign venture capital funds to establish operations in Singapore established in 1999; second tranche of U.S. $300 million in 2003
	Manpower training subsidies for the VC industry
Angel investors	Co-investing scheme (SEEDS) to promote angel investing in new start-ups
KIBS firms	Incentives to attract DFI in various KIBS industries (media content industry, IP services, etc.)
IP protection and management capability development	Streamlining of IP protection system under new organization (IPOS) and provision of incentives for locals to file patents
	Establishment of a new IP academy to provide training to industry

Dynamism of High-Tech Clusters

Openness to competition	Ministry of Trade and Industry to review possible introduction of anti-competition policy
	Government reviewing role of GLCs in domestic economy (ongoing)

170   rapid growth of Singapore as an emerging biotech hub in Asia over the three to four years would have been impossible without the sizable public sector investment (Finegold et al. 2004).

Second, most of the policies geared toward promoting entrepreneurship are very recent and hence some time must pass before their likely impact can be ascertained; instead, changes in the external environment may have more significant impact in the short run. For example, the dotcom boom in 1998–early 2000 may have accounted for the jump in high-tech start-up rates and the rapid build-up of venture capital funds during that period, even without the T21 Initiative (which in any case was announced only toward the tail end of the dotcom boom). Correspondingly, the subsequent dotcom crash and past global technology market meltdown may have caused technology start-up rates to drop. On the other hand, ironically, the adverse impact of global economic slowdown experienced during 2001 and 2002 may have caused the general entrepreneurial rate to rise, as increasing retrenchment forced more to consider starting their own ventures.

Third, despite the comprehensive scope of policy shifts, some notable gaps can be observed. For example, despite growing public investment in funding R&D, commercialization of technology from public research institutes (PRIs) had not increased at the same rate, due to the lack of mechanisms like the SBIR or STTR schemes in the United States and ITRI in Taiwan to help bridge the gap between R&D and seed investment by venture capitalists or angel investors. Indeed, recent public policy intended to centralize PRI technology commercialization under a commercially driven arm of ASTAR (called EXPLOIT), and giving it the first right of refusal to commercialize university research funded by ASTAR, appears to run counter to the spirit of the Bayh-Dole Act and may have an adverse long-term effect on individual researchers' incentives to commercialize their research by way of starting their own spin-offs. Another area of concerns is the slow pace of withdrawal of GLC dominance over the domestic market. The lack of a base of aggressive lead-users of emerging technology makes it more difficult for Singapore-based technology start-ups to validate their product innovation by having their first customers in Singapore; instead, they need to go international to seek markets, even from day one. The inadequate development of global connectivity, while recognized by ERC, had also not been effectively addressed by any public programs so far. Finally, an effective implementation of the recommendation to change the cultural mindset of Singaporeans toward entrepreneurship may involve more fundamental long-term policy changes related to the educational system, the social security system, and the public sector talent recruitment system, all of which are politically sensitive and hence require significant policy coordination at the highest level. The recent decision by the government to appoint a Minister-in-charge-of Entrepreneurship is a step in the right direction and has certainly hastened the public-private consultation process and increased the pace of incremental policy changes, but the more fundamental policy challenges probably still lie ahead.

CONCLUDING OBSERVATIONS

In this chapter, we have sought to provide empirical evidence on the progress made by Singapore in shifting toward a dynamic high-tech enterprise ecosystem. The following tentative conclusions can be made:

- Contrary to some of the more negative popular media reports, Singapore had actually made significant progress in several major areas, especially in terms of increasing R&D and innovation intensity, the supply of venture capital, and the building of a critical mass for an emerging life science industrial cluster.
- There have also been significant policy changes affecting innovation and entrepreneurship that were introduced in recent years. However, while some of these had already made a recognizable impact, it is likely that many of these policy changes will require longer gestation times to have any significant effect.
- While the dependence on foreign MNCs remains strong in key high-tech clusters, the dynamism of these clusters was moderately high, registering strong export growth performance and exhibiting healthy churn. However, in the domestic ICT market, where the small size is already a major constraint, the dominance of GLCs needs to be further reduced, perhaps through strengthening of anticompetition policy.
- The key challenges to sustaining the development of the innovation system appear to be finding ways to augment the small absolute size of the talent base, increasing investment in basic research capabilities of local universities, and improving policy support for technology commercialization activities through new programs like the SBIR and STTR program in the United States. The need to intensify investment in precompetitive basic research and infrastructures is especially important for the biotech cluster as well as certain ICT subsectors such as wireless and broadband applications.
- The key challenges to accelerating technology entrepreneurship in Singapore appear to be how to overcome the lack of a critical mass in the high-tech start-up ecosystem, and how to change the social and cultural attitudes of the population toward entrepreneurship, acceptance of nonconformity, and tolerance of failure. Educational reform at the primary and secondary educational institution level will play an important role in changing such societal values in the long term, but the emergence of a

greater number of successful technology entrepreneurs will help raise the critical mass in the medium term by serving as viable role models, angel investors, and mentors. In the short run, however, the most likely policy tools that will have visible impact are continuing deregulation of public-sector bureaucracy, increasing teaching of entrepreneurial skills at the tertiary education level and among working technical professionals, attracting foreign entrepreneurial talents to start up in Singapore, and providing incentives and support for universities and public research institutes to commercialize their inventions through spin-offs. There is also a need to build stronger global network links with key high-tech hotspots in the world to expose Singaporeans to the globally emerging opportunities.

REFERENCES

Agency for Science, Technology and Research (ASTAR). (various years). *National Survey of R&D in Singapore*. Singapore: Author.

Amsden, A., and F. T. Tschang. 2003. "A New Approach to Assessing the Technological Complexity of Different Categories of R&D (with Examples from Singapore)." *Research Policy* 32(4):553–572.

Autio, E., P. K. Wong, and P. Reynolds. 2003. "National Factors Influencing the Prevalence of High-Potential Start-ups." Working paper, NUS Entrepreneurship Centre, National University of Singapore.

Birch, D., A. Haggerty et al. 1997. *Who's Creating Jobs?* Cambridge, MA: Cognetics.

Christensen, C. M. 1997. *The Innovator's Dilemma: When New Technologies Cause Great Firms to Fail*. Cambridge, MA: Harvard Business School Press.

DP Information Network Pte Ltd. (various years). *Singapore 1000*. Singapore: Author.

Economic Development Board (EDB). (various years). *EDB Yearbook*. Singapore: Author.

———. (various years). *The Singapore Venture Capital Industry Survey 1999*. Singapore: Author.

———. (various years). *Report on the Census of Industrial Production*. Singapore: Author.

Economic Review Committee (ERC). 2002. *Report of the Entrepreneurship and Internationalization Subcommittee*. September 13, 2002. Singapore: Ministry of Trade and Industry.

Finegold, D., P. K. Wong, and T. C. Cheah. 2004. "Singapore's Emerging Biotech Cluster: Old Strategy Replication or New Approach?" *European Planning Studies*.

He, Z. L., and P. K. Wong. 2003. "Exploration vs. Exploitation: An Empirical Test of the Impact of Innovation Strategy on Firm Performance." Working paper, NUS Entrepreneurship Centre, National University of Singapore.

Heritage Foundation. 2004. *2004 Index of Economic Freedom*. http://www.heritage.org/research/features/index.

Ho, Y. P., M. H. Toh, and P. K. Wong. 2003. "The Impact of R&D on the Singapore Economy: An Empirical Evaluation." Working paper, NUS Entrepreneurship Centre, National University of Singapore.

Hu, A. 2003. "Multinational Corporations, Patenting, and Knowledge Flow: The Case of Singapore." Working paper, Economics Department, National University of Singapore.

International Institute for Management Development (IMD). (various years). *World Competitiveness Yearbook*. Lausanne, Switzerland: Author.

Lee, C.-M., W. Miller, M. G. Hancock, and H. Rowen, eds. 2000. *The Silicon Valley Edge: A Habitat for Innovation and Entrepreneurship*. Stanford, CA: Stanford University Press.

McKendrick, D. G., R. F. Doner, and S. Haggard. 2000. *From Silicon Valley to Singapore: Location and Competitive Advantage in the Hard Disk Drive Industry*. Stanford, CA: Stanford University Press.

Ministry of Labour. (various years). *Singapore Yearbook of Labour Statistics* Singapore: Author.

Ministry of Manpower. (various years). *Singapore Yearbook of Manpower Statistics*. (various years). Singapore: Author.

NUS Consulting. 2003. *NUS 2002 Graduate Employment Survey Report*. Singapore: Author.

Reynolds, P., W. Bygrave, E. Autin, and M. Hayl. 2002. *Global Entrepreneurship Monitor 2002: Summary Report*. Wellesley, MA: Babson College.

Rosenberg, D. 2002. *Cloning Silicon Valley: The Next Generation High Tech Hotspots*. New York: Prentice-Hall.

Saxenian, A. 1999. *Silicon Valley's New Immigrant Entrepreneurs*. San Francisco: Public Policy Institute of California.

Singapore Department of Statistics (DOS). (various years). *Singapore's Corporate Sector*. Singapore: Author.

———. 2001. "Contribution of Government-Linked Companies to Gross Domestic Product." DOS Occasional Paper, March.

Wang, C., P. K. Wong, and Q. Lu. 2002. "Tertiary Education and Entrepreneurial Intentions." In P. Phan, ed. *Technological Entrepreneurship*. Greenwich, CT: IAP Press, pp. 55–82.

Wong, P. K. 1992. "Technological Development through Subcontracting Linkages: Evidence from Singapore." *Scandinavian International Business Review* 1(3): 8–40.

———. 1998. "Leveraging the Global Information Revolution for Economic Development: Singapore's Evolving Information Industry Strategy." *Information Systems Research* 9(4).

———. 1999. "University-Industry Technological Collaboration in Singapore: Emerging Patterns and Industry Concerns." *International Journal of Technology Management* 17(3/4).

———. 2001. "The Role of the State in the Industrial Development of Singapore." In P. K. Wong and C. Y. Ng, eds. *Re-thinking the East Asian Development Paradigm*. Singapore: Singapore University Press, chap. 1.

———. 2002a. "Globalization of American, European and Japanese Production Networks and the Growth of Singapore's Electronics Industry." *International Journal of Technology Management* 24(7/8):843–869.

174   ——. 2002b. "Manpower Development in the Digital Economy: The Case of Singapore." In M. Makishima, ed. *Human Resource Development in the Information Age: The Case of Singapore and Malaysia.* Tokyo: IDE/JETRO, pp. 79–122.

——. 2003a. "From Using to Creating Technology: The Evolution of Singapore's National Innovation System and the Changing Role of Public Policy." In S. Lall and S. Urata, eds. *Competitiveness, FDI and Technological Activity in East Asia.* London: Edward Elgar.

——. 2003b. "The Nexus of Innovation and Entrepreneurship: Towards a Dynamic Model of High Tech Enterprise Ecosystem." Working paper, NUS Entrepreneurship Centre, National University of Singapore.

——. 2004. "Profile of Business Angel Investors in Singapore." Working paper, NUS Entrepreneurship Centre, National University of Singapore.

Wong, P. K., and Z. L. He. 2003a. "The Impact of Public R&D Support on Firm's Innovation Performance: The Moderating Effect of Firm's Innovation Climate." *International Journal of Entrepreneurship and Innovation Management.*

——. 2003b. "Local Embeddedness, Global Networking: The Impact of Innovation Networks on the Innovation Performance of Firms." Working paper, NUS Entrepreneurship Centre, National University of Singapore.

——. 2004. "A Comparative Study of Innovation Behaviour in Singapore's KIBS and Manufacturing Firms." *Service Industries Journal* 25(2).

Wong, P. K., and Y. P. Ho. 2003. *Comparative Analysis of the Pattern and Composition of IP Creation in Singapore vs. Selected Advanced OECD Nations and NIEs.* Research report, NUS Entrepreneurship Centre, National University of Singapore.

Wong, P. K., M. Kiese, A. Singh, and F. Wong. 2003. "The Pattern of Innovation in Singapore's Manufacturing Sector." *Singapore Management Review* 25(1):1–34.

Wong, P. K., L. Lee, and Z. L. He. 2004. "Propensities of Spin-outs from Existing Firms." Working paper, NUS Entrepreneurship Centre, National University of Singapore.

Wong, P. K., and A. Singh. 2004. "The Pattern of Innovation in the Knowledge-Intensive Services Sector of Singapore." *Singapore Management Review* 26(1).

Wong, P. K., A. Singh et al. 2001. *Survey of Attitudes and Interest of Students in Higher Educational Institutions towards Entrepreneurship: Final Report.* Centre for Management of Innovation and Technopreneurship, National University of Singapore.

Wong, P. K., F. Wong, Y. P. Ho, A. Singh, and L. Lee. 2003. *Global Entrepreneurship Monitor 2002: Singapore Country Report.* Singapore: NUS Entrepreneurship Centre.

World Bank. 2002. "GNI per Capita 2002 (Atlas Method and PPP)." *World Development Indicators.* http://www.worldbank.org/data/databytopic/GNIPC.pdf.

Young, A. 1992. "A Tale of Two Cities: Factor Accumulation and Technical Change in Hong Kong and Singapore." *NBER Macroeconomic Annual 1992.* Cambridge, MA: MIT Press.

Zhang, J., P. K. Wong, and P. H. Soh. 2003. "Network Ties, Prior Knowledge, and the Acquisition of Resources in High Tech Entrepreneurship." Academy of Management Best Papers Proceedings, Seattle.

6

The Tale of Two Valleys

Daeduk and Teheran

Zong-Tae Bae, Jun-Woo Bae, Jong-Gie Kim,
Kark Bum Lee, Sang-Mok Suh, and
Sam Ock Park

KOREA'S REMARKABLE RISE IN THE IT INDUSTRY

In information technologies, Korea has concentrated on the semiconductor, mobile telecommunications, broadband Internet, computer, and digital electronics sectors. The ratio of jobs in IT-related industries to total employment is one of the highest among the OECD countries. Total output of this sector in 1997 was $79 billion, of which $58 billion was for equipment (with electronic components being the largest part of this category). In that year, software output came to only $3.7 billion. The IT sector grew from that year to 2002 at an annual rate of 14 percent to $150 billion. All categories grew, with the software sector growing most rapidly to $14 billion.

More than 80 percent of Korean economic growth has been generated by large enterprises, some of which, notably Samsung, LG, Hyundai, and SK, became strong in IT. In spite of being a latecomer, Samsung Electronics has become a leader in memory chips, cellular phones, flat panel displays, and digital consumer electronics. It invested aggressively during the crisis of the late 1990s, has strong finances, and spends heavily on R&D.

With the paradigm shift toward a knowledge-based economy, the greatest concern among Korean leaders has been to enhance the country's competitiveness through greater productivity via the promotion of the IT industry and application of IT throughout the society as a whole (Ministry of Information and Communication 2002).

As a result, Korea is especially strong in mobile telecommunications and broadband; in fact, it pioneered commercial CDMA mobile telecommunications. Currently 32 million subscribers use mobile telecommunications,

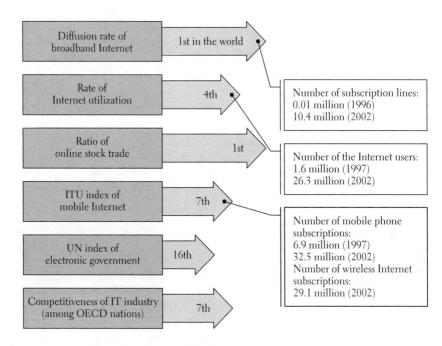

FIGURE 6.1   Status of the Korean IT Industry

amounting to 70 percent of the population. The government has invested U.S. $24 billion in the broadband network backbone that connects all public institutions with an average speed eight times faster than the United States and much cheaper than in other countries. Internet use in 1995 was about 1 percent of the population; the growth rate since then has been the world's highest. This has led to a plethora of online services such as e-shopping, e-banking, e-community, audio/video streaming, and online games. Online gaming is now seen as a Korean cultural phenomenon. More than half of the 10 most popular online games currently offered in China were made by Korean companies. Figure 6.1 shows the status and world ranking of the Korean IT industry.

Small and medium-sized firms also have found roles in this industry through cooperation and competition with these large enterprises. Some entrepreneurial ventures have acquired the world-leading position within the IT industry in such areas as hand-held phones, flat-panel displays, set-top boxes, online games, MP3 players, and so on.

Historically, the Korean system has been unsupportive of the creation of new companies; however, the situation has changed since the late 1990s. The Korean government has strongly promoted the creation of high-tech start-ups, and high-tech regions, notably Teheran Valley and Daeduk Valley,[1] have emerged.

This chapter focuses on the history, status, and weakness of entrepreneurship in Korea, compares two different Korean high-tech habitats, and discusses steps that have been taken and more that should be taken to strengthen entrepreneurship.

BRIEF HISTORY OF HIGH-TECH START-UP FIRMS

Early high-tech start-ups, those that began during the 1980s, were mainly spin-offs from universities and private firms. There were no specific government policies for these ventures, although many benefited indirectly from government R&D programs. Although specialized service providers and venture capital firms emerged during that decade, their services met neither the needs of new firms nor were very different from other institutions for supporting traditional small and medium-sized companies (SMEs) and large firms. Only a few ventures led by visionary leaders grew strongly. For example, Dr. Min-hwa Lee founded Medison Co., a specialist in medical equipment such as ultrasound scanners. It had 50 percent average annual sales growth from inception until it reached U.S. $102 million in 1997.

The financial crisis of 1997 brought about a substantial restructuring of the economic system. Economic output fell. The chaebol (large conglomerate companies) were forced to reduce their financial leverage. Many failed. Many banks had to be reorganized. As a result, some laid-off or resigned employees created small high-tech firms. In addition, business opportunities in information technology fostered the explosive growth of new ventures throughout the late 1990s. Although the government's rapid and effective response soon restored economic growth, the crisis had lasting effects.

One governmental response was to recognize the limits of its large-company-oriented economic system and the potential contribution of new firms, especially knowledge-intensive ones. Nurturing policies were formulated that offered many benefits to start-up companies. However, following the Korean system, the beneficiaries were required to receive government authorization.

Four types of venture (start-up) firms were authorized by the government:

1. Companies with venture capital investment (more than 10% of shares)
2. Companies with high R&D ratios (more than 5% of sales)
3. Companies with major products based on patents, intellectual property, or new technology from government-sponsored projects (more than 50% of sales)
4. Companies evaluated as having excellent technology or good commercial prospects as judged by the evaluating organization.

178   Government's authentication is renewed every three years if the venture firm is small or medium-sized. As a result, many new ventures were created. There was explosive growth of the KOSDAQ market (the Korean equivalent of the NASDAQ). The number of companies authenticated as "venture" increased by an average of 60 percent each year from 2000 in December 1998 to more than 10,000 in 2001.

Also, through spontaneous development and governmental efforts, knowledge-intensive venture clusters such as Teheran Valley and Daeduk Valley appeared, two "valleys" that differ significantly.

The government's actions to put resources directly into venture firms resulted in the creation of many of them, but it could not create high-quality companies. Consequently, these firms ran into serious difficulties with the bursting of the venture bubble in 2000 and the subsequent stagnation of the IT industry. The KOSDAQ fell greatly from its peak (paralleling the NASDAQ's decline). Many new firms collapsed—as they did elsewhere in the world.

There has been much discussion since then about how to create a system that will produce many competitive and profitable ventures. This has led to a belief that regional habitats need to be created that will result in more spontaneous formation of innovative and entrepreneurial companies.

THE STATUS OF VENTURE FIRMS

Table 6.1 shows changes over time in the types and numbers of registered/ authenticated venture firms.

It is notable that about half of these young firms were chosen by subjective evaluation by government officials, not the market, a fact that has generated criticism about the system.

The distribution by industry of these firms is shown in Table 6.2. High-tech manufacturing industry has the most companies, and IT-related services are also prominent.

About half of the ventures in Korea have been established since 1998. Accordingly 50 percent were less than five years old in 2003. About half of the founders were in their 20s or 30s when they started their firms. Few were women, although the proportion has increased over time. The proportion of advanced-degree holders, PhDs or master's, became quite high in software, in IT services, and in high-tech manufacturing areas such as the biotech and optical/precision machinery industries.

Venture firms were, naturally, very small. The average number of employees was 32 in 1999 and 38 in 2001. Capitalization was very small. In 2002, about

TABLE 6.1

Types and Numbers of Registered Venture Firms

Type	1998	1999	2000	2001	2002	2003
VC invested	494	845	1,393	1,545	1,124	718
	(24%)	(17%)	(16%)	(14%)	(13%)	(9%)
High R&D ratio	584	917	830	1,292	1,325	1,483
	(28%)	(18%)	(9%)	(11%)	(15%)	(19%)
IP & government R&D project	766	1,708	1,668	2,402	6,329	5501
	(38%)	(35%)	(19%)	(21%)	(72%)	(71%)
High prospect venture by evaluation	198	1,464	4,907	6,153		
	(9%)	(30%)	(56%)	(54%)		
Total	2,042	4,934	8,798	11,392	8,778	7,702
	(100%)	(100%)	(100%)	(100%)	(100%)	(100%)

SOURCE: Korea SMBA Data.

TABLE 6.2

Venture Firms' Distribution by Industry

Industry	2000	2001	2002	2003
High-tech manufacturing	1,647 (27.9%)	3,193 (40.6%)	2,192 (36.4%)	1,935 (33.9%)
General manufacturing	2,166 (36.6%)	2,002 (25.5%)	1,487 (24.7%)	1,760 (30.8%)
Software/IT services	1,791 (30.3%)	2,074 (26.4%)	1,715 (28.5%)	1,525 (26.7%)
Other	307 (5.2%)	596 (7.5%)	626 (10.5%)	487 (8.5%)
Total	5,911 (100%)	7,865 (100%)	6,020 (100%)	5,707 (100%)

SOURCE: Korea SMBA Survey Data.

30 percent had a capitalization smaller than 1 billion won, and only 15 percent had a capitalization greater than 10 billion won (about U.S. $8 million). However, the invested capital of Korean venture firms increased from about $1 million in 1999 to over $2 million by 2002. Sales had increased slightly, but profits had not.

PROBLEMS AND FUTURE DIRECTIONS OF VENTURE FIRMS

High-tech entrepreneurship is constrained by several obstacles, including the following:

- Entrepreneurs' poor knowledge of markets, management, law, and finance
- A small domestic market
- Poor habitats, networks, and social/financial infrastructure

- Poor understanding of the nature of ventures and entrepreneurship
- Inefficient or heavy-handed government policies

Entrepreneurs' Poor Knowledge of Management

Most founders with backgrounds in technology have emphasized R&D or product development; consequently, they have had difficulty launching their products. Many are trying to acquire market-related knowledge, such as customer contact and access to distribution channels.

Small Domestic Market

The small size of the domestic market forces Korean ventures into looking for opportunities to enter foreign markets. There are obstacles to entry, but certain advantages.

Poor Habitats

Business environments or habitats have been neglected. The collapse of the venture boom revealed that poor physical, financial, and social habitats were an obstacle to success. One thing needed is an attitude that rewards risk taking and does not punish failure. Because Koreans have experienced many successes over the years, they do not accept failures as potentially valuable. It will take time to change this attitude.

Poor Understanding of Entrepreneurship

Although Koreans are perceived as very entrepreneurial in general, some Korean entrepreneurs have understood ventures to be just "high-return" businesses, without proper attention to "high risk" and "business ethics." The rise and fall of many ventures has been teaching them the nature of entrepreneurship, but still there is a long way to go.

Inefficient or Heavy-Handed Government Policies

Active government support for venture firms has led to positive results. Nevertheless, the government needs to change its venture promotion policy. The authentication system, which it considers necessary, encourages inefficiency in resource allocation. In addition, the bureaucracy and the dynamics of entrepreneurship do not always match well.

Although the modern venture capital industry in the United States started with some government help via the Small Business Administration, it soon developed independently. It grew on the basis of a favorable legal system, beneficial tax laws, an abundance of entrepreneurs, and a well-developed stock market.

The Korean supply of risk capital (that is, venture capital) has a different history. The overriding aim of the government for a long time was to create domestic industries that would substitute for imports. This entailed picking firms to support instead of encouraging competition and new entrants. There was little opportunity for venture capital.

Two types of venture capital firms ultimately emerged. The first type is made up of the new technology business financing companies (NTFCs) that support small and medium-sized enterprises with equity investments, loan financing, leasing, and factoring services. The second type, consisting of the small business investment companies (SBICs), focuses on early-stage equity investments. Venture capital firms are now being encouraged to help form new ventures, particularly new technology-based firms.

The first venture capital firm was Korea Technology Advancement Corporation (KTAC), set up in 1974 to help commercialize R&D results from the Korean Institute of Science and Technology (KIST). Afterward, three more NTFCs began under the jurisdiction of the Ministry of Finance. These early NTFCs were neither traditional financial institutions nor current-style venture capital firms. They usually provided diverse financial services with both equity-based investments and non-equity-based financial services. This array was unique and helped compensate for an unfavorable environment for private venture.

In 1981, the Korea Technology Banking Corporation (KTB) was set up under the Ministry of Science and Technology (MOST) with the mandate of promoting technology-intensive industries. Although KTB made loans at the beginning, it later changed to making equity investments in prominent venture firms. KTB was privatized in 1999 and renamed as KTB netwok in 2000.

Furthermore, the Ministry of Trade and Industry (MOTI) enacted the Small and Medium Enterprise Formation Act in 1986, which led to the emergence of SBICs. These companies support venture firms in existence less than 13 years. SBICs assume about 40 percent of total financing. Because of venture capitalists' lack of experience with early-stage firms, there were many losers. Among the NTFCs and SBICs, KTBnetwork maintains a substantial share of the total venture capital sector.

TABLE 6.3

Status of Korean Angels and Venture Capital Firms

		1997	2002 June
Venture capital	Number of venture capital firms	61	136
	Number of total venture funds	79	421
	Number of investment deals	1,327	3,233
	Total investment amount (U.S. $ millions)	1,325	2,577
Angel	Number of angel funds	0	72
	Number of angel investors	105	34,040
	Number of total portfolio firms	7	522
	Total investment amount (U.S. $ millions)	1.2	193

SOURCE: Korea Venture Capital Association (KVCA).

After the mid-1980s, many new venture capital firms were incorporated. Encouraged by the creation of KOSDAQ, 136 venture capital (VC) firms were registered as of 2002, two-thirds of which had started within the prior five years. From $1.3 billion in 1997 to $2.6 billion in 2002 were poured into venture investments.

Other sources of private equity financing are the informal capital market, made up of what are called angel investors. Although reliable statistics are not available, money has been moving into new firms through angel funds since 1999. Estimates of the number of venture capital firms and angels as well as of venture funds are as shown in Table 6.3.

There has also been a qualitative change. The ratio of equity-based investment of the NTFCs grew from 7 percent in 1996 to 32 percent in 2000. More than 80 percent of venture capital firms provided business services, such as strategic consulting and recruiting talented employees to their portfolio firms.

EXIT POSSIBILITIES FOR VENTURE INVESTORS

Because the mergers and acquisition market in Korea is undeveloped, public listing has been the only option for attracting investment. But stringent listing requirements on the Korea Stock Exchange (KSE) kept venture firms from access to it until the mid-1990s. This led in 1996 to the Korean Securities Dealers Automated Quotation System (KOSDAQ) beginning operations. From 1997 to 2002 the number of companies listed on the KOSDAQ doubled from 359 to 810 while their total market value went from U.S. $7.4 billion to U.S. $29.8 billion. The percentage of venture firms increased from 34 percent in 1998 to 45 percent in 2002. The number of firms on the KOSDAQ became 104 percent of those on the KSE. By the end of 2002 the KOSDAQ index had fallen to the level of 1997, the year it started.

PROBLEMS AND FUTURE DIRECTIONS OF VENTURE CAPITAL

Venture capital in Korea is at an early stage and has many challenges, including:

- Lack of experience in investing in risky start-ups and managing and supporting them
- Poor understanding of how to evaluate opportunities
- Missing links in financing of each growth stage
- A poor record in raising money, especially from foreign institutions
- Few harvest options

Lack of experience in risky financing. Korean venture capitalists are not familiar with equity-based investments as a result of the long-standing practice of basing capital operations on loans.

Insufficient industry-specific knowledge. Too few venture capitalists have had experience in specific sectors.

Missing links in growth stage financing. It is hard to find money for the start-up and initial growth stages. Public venture capital should play a leading role here.

Poor performance in fund raising. Korean venture capital firms are corporations (rather than partnerships) and have done poorly in raising money from large companies, financial institutions, and, in particular, foreign institutions.

Limited harvest options. Harvest options for venture capital firms, such as M&As and IPOs, have not been very successful. There were few harvest possibilities in the small M&A and the unstable KOSDAQ markets. This is a reason why these firms avoid risky investments.

The remedies needed follow from these deficiencies. Fund raising targeted for specific industries and stages and promoting M&As claim priority.

REGIONAL CLUSTERS

As shown in Table 6.4, government policy regarding new firms evolved over time. Similarly, regional clusters developed from being pure industrial estates to high-tech science and technology parks and venture clusters.

The first attempt was to build industrial complexes to house heavy and chemical industries in the early 1970s. These parks did not include such functions as education and R&D. The first such park, Daeduk Science Town, was started in the early 1980s by moving existing government-sponsored research institutes from Seoul. At first it had only R&D institutions, but "Daeduk Valley" (by analogy with Silicon Valley) emerged there in the mid-1980s when researchers began to create new companies.

TABLE 6.4

History of Government Policies on Venture Clusters

	Infant	Establishment	Expansion	Enforcement
Time period	–1996	1996–1999	1999–2000	2000–
Critical incidents	No specific policy measures SME programs	Economic crisis Active operation of BIs	A substantial amount of venture creation Dotcom crisis	Selecting sound venture by market mechanism
Government role	Explorer	Initiator	Supporter	Accelerator
Contextual environment for venture	Hesitate to join venture	Venture creation through BIs Service firms to support ventures Willing to join venture	Venture creation through private BI Numerous service firms Willing to create venture	Retreat to create venture M&A acceleration
Producer	Low venture creation	Start to active venture creation	Numerous ventures	Decrease in venture creation
Consumer	Private VC Weak role of VC investment	Appearance of a variety of angels, VCs	Numerous angels and VCs Strong role of VC	Active M&A

The other principal high-tech "valley," Teheran Valley, developed in the southern part of Seoul from the mid-1980s. Although the government helped by building the physical infrastructure, Teheran Valley was essentially a product of autonomous reactions.

TEHERAN VALLEY: HOW IT EVOLVED

In the middle of the deep recession of 1998, new high-tech start-ups began to appear in Seoul, especially along the Teheran Road in the Gangnam District of Seoul. (Teheran Road was named after Seoul's sister city in Iran.) The Gangnam District is the most modern office space in Seoul, and Teheran Road crosses it from east to west. Teheran Valley extends one or two blocks on each side of Teheran Road.

The concentration of firms began when high-tech industrial policy became the leading priority. The World Trade Center was built there in 1988, and trade-related companies established themselves nearby. Since the beginning of the 1990s, financial institutions also proliferated in the area. In the mid-1990s, about 100 IT-related companies located there and dubbed their locality "Teheran Valley."

After that, many IT firms, start-ups, venture capital firms, and corporate headquarters were set up. By 2000 IT, Internet-related, mobile communications, and foreign IT companies had settled there. Additional financial firms, banks, and trading companies moved in. It is becoming established as the center for innovation and incubation in Korea. The representative venture capital companies in Teheran Valley include KTBnetwork, Korea Technology Investment Corp. (KTIC), and Woori Technology Investment Co., Ltd.

There are few manufacturing operations but many software and other kinds of IT companies. About half of all the software and IT ventures in Korea are located in this area. The proportion of venture capital–funded companies is relatively high. This means firms created not only by government — namely, registered or sponsored ones — but firms founded by entrepreneurs who seek opportunities with technology and ideas and money and who have been funded privately. Accordingly, Teheran Valley has the image of a highly innovative and knowledge-generating region and being the center of entrepreneurship in Korea.

The representative examples of high-tech venture firms in Teheran Valley are NCsoft, ReignCom, and Core Logic. NCsoft is the leading Korean on-line game company. It launched the most successful Internet content worldwide, Lineage™, which today has more than 3.5 million subscribers and simultaneous connections in the hundreds of thousands worldwide. Since its establishment in 1997, NCsoft has reached the world market, and today it has

186 over 1,000 employees along with branches in North America, Japan, China, and Taiwan.

ReignCom came up with the world's first Multi-CODEC CD Player in 2000. In six months, ReignCom ranked the top position in the U.S. and domestic markets and fueled into explosive growth. Today, ReignCom has become known as a global leader in the MP3 player market with the world-famous iriver brand.

Core Logic is a mobile multimedia System on a Chip (SoC) specialist established in 1998. Core Logic has grown rapidly and has become a global leader that develops and commercializes Camera Application Processor (CAP) and Multimedia Application Processor (MAP) technology to lead multimedia implementation on mobile phones.

Meanwhile, the rapid growth of Teheran Valley has raised several problems. Above all, its high costs cause venture firms to locate elsewhere. Traffic congestion is another negative factor. An additional one is the low number of academy-industry linkages; because Teheran Valley has no major universities or R&D institutions, interactions among companies, schools, and research organizations are hard to arrange. Furthermore, these small ventures do little R&D (unlike the large, chaebol, technology companies).

Currently, many Teheran Valley companies specialize in culturally related products such as digital content, multimedia, design, fashion, and in service industries such as venture capital, banking, IT services, consulting, and so on.

Although many existing ventures ultimately leave the valley, many new ones are established or move in. It will remain the center of Korean ventures in the future.

SURVEY OF TEHERAN VALLEY: HABITAT FOR INNOVATION AND ENTREPRENEURSHIP

To acquire data on this habitat a questionnaire survey and interviews were carried out. In addition, the data of the SMBA survey on venture firms in Korea were used as reference. Details of the survey are in the Appendix. Here are the main findings.

Collective Learning and Knowledge Creation

Although there are no leading research institutes or universities in Teheran Valley, people actively share knowledge, and provide an environment for collective R&D. Many CEOs meet in seminars, conferences, exhibitions, and through casual encounters. They trade information and coordinate marketing activities.

Production technology and process information sources come mainly from R&D (often from government laboratories), knowledge about talent from personal relationships, market information from customers, and financial and management information from a CEO's personal relationships. Informal networks among agents are also important.

Local Networking

The valley's firms engage in inter-firm collaboration and knowledge exchanges with joint R&D in manufacturing; joint marketing as well as joint product development are also notable. Two-thirds of the venture firms carried out joint activities with outside research centers, customers, suppliers, competitors, or universities during the five years prior to the survey. However, university-industry linkages were weak.

International Networking

Of the venture firms 515 (50%) had international activities. Among them, 264 firms (25%) were exporting products, 141 (14%) had foreign subsidiaries, and 6 (0.6%) had overseas R&D centers. Many foreign companies are located in Teheran Valley. Dell Computer, Yahoo Korea, Sun Microsystems, IBM Korea, Cisco, Sony International Korea, and SAP Korea are examples.

Innovativeness

Teheran Valley is becoming the incubation center of Korea and aspires to become the innovation center. It has better access to information, knowledge, skills, and experience and engages in more rapid exchanges of information than other regions. However, so far its firms lag behind those in Daeduk Valley in size and technology. This is partly because of the absence of major universities and research organizations. Also shorter product life in the software industry makes Teheran Valley firms more applications-oriented than R&D-oriented. But almost half of surveyed firms reported that they had patents and high motivation to innovate.

Table 6.5 addresses the strengths and weakness of Teheran Valley's innovativeness.

From the point of view as a habitat for entrepreneurship, Teheran Valley has 40 percent of Korea's venture capitalists; 526 out of a country total of 1,338 are located in the Gangnam and Seocho districts. Among Teheran Valley's

TABLE 6.5

Strengths and Weaknesses of Teheran Valley's Innovation System

Strengths	Weaknesses
Active exchanges of explicit knowledge based on excellent IT infrastructure	Weak innovation network with universities
Creation and transfer of implicit knowledge through formal and informal meetings	Lack of international network
Collective learning based in face-to-face interactions	Relatively low level of technological capabilities

problems the lack of high-caliber manpower and core technological competence are serious ones, not to mention heavy traffic and high rents.

TEHERAN AND DAEDUK VALLEYS COMPARED

The government provided Teheran Valley with convention centers and exhibition halls and it then developed on its own. Many hotels and convenient housing emerged, and high-tech companies found this a good place in which to locate.

In contrast, Daeduk Valley evolved from Daeduk Science Town (DST), founded in 1971 as a research park in a central region near Daejon City. The main mission of DST was to do scientific research; no company was allowed to produce commercial products before 1997. The total number of researchers and supporting manpower at 67 major research organizations was about 15,000 in 1999; R&D activities were done at 29 industrial research centers, 16 government-sponsored institutes, 8 government agencies, 8 government-invested institutes, and 4 higher educational institutes. DST was criticized for its performance and efficiency and was forced to alter its mission, especially after the IMF crisis of 1997. Most institutes suffered cuts in research budgets and restructuring. Even before that, new technology-based venture firms were recognized as the driving engine. Pioneering young researchers began high-tech spin-offs from research institutes in the early 1990s.

A comparison of Teheran Valley and Daeduk Valley is provided in Table 6.6. It shows the greater number of venture firms and the smaller role of government in Teheran Valley than in Daeduk Valley. Details of the comparison are given in the Appendix.

CONCLUSIONS AND IMPLICATIONS

This chapter overviews entrepreneurship in Korea and explains two different high-tech habitats, Teheran Valley and Daeduk Valley. Although the level of

TABLE 6.6

Comparison of Teheran Valley and Daeduk Valley

Type	Teheran Valley	Daeduk Valley
Regional boundary	Gangnam and Seocho districts in Seoul city	Daejon city
Number of venture companies (2001)	About 2,000	About 500
Origin	Private leading Spontaneous district (e.g., Silicon Valley)	Government leading Planned district (e.g., Taiwan Hsinchu Science-based Industrial Park)
Major type of industry	IT, Internet, S/W	IT, semiconductor, bio, mechanical engineering
University, R&D institutes	Seoul National University and many other universities near the Seoul metropolitan area	KAIST, ETRI, Chungnam National University, KRIBB (Bioscience & Bioengineering)
Merits	Lots of VC, hotels, manpower, and infrastructure	Low office rents, many R&D institutes
Demerits	High office rents	Lack of VC and infrastructure; distance from market

government involvement was different in each region, the Korean government has played key roles in creating critical mass and nurturing the venture community. There are some conclusions and implications to be drawn from the Korean case.

The Role of Government

There is an important role for government in promoting new ventures. This can best be done by creating an appropriate legal environment and fostering certain kinds of institutions such as private venture capital. The government's direct support to new ventures and other supporting organizations should be limited at a certain level of development. Entrepreneurship requires healthy business networks and well-developed infrastructures, which government can foster. In addition, the government's efforts to support close international linkages should be encouraged.

Helping Entrepreneurs and Using Them to Help Others

Korea needs more successful entrepreneurs. Successful entrepreneurs are positive role models and can act as mentors to less experienced people. Through entrepreneurial educational programs and support programs potential founders can be encouraged to commercialize their ideas. Many successful entrepreneurs can become central players in establishing networks among the

190   technical specialists, angel investors, and venture capitalists. Linking governmental R&D policies to those for new ventures should be emphasized. Also, a social atmosphere encouraging entrepreneurship could motivate innovative scientists and engineers to create new firms.

Finance

The financial infrastructure for venture firms remains weak. A combination of public venture capital, private venture capital, corporate capital, and angel investors is needed in which the mix differs for each growth stage. Laws and regulations need changing to improve various harvest methods, such as merger and acquisitions, and to make KOSDAQ more active. Recruiting able venture capitalists in the short term and nurturing Korean venture capitalist overseas in the long term would help.

Internationalization

Recent government policies encourage entrepreneurs to build ventures based on technical innovations, but most venture firms have targeted the domestic market, unlike those in Israel and Taiwan. A common feature in both of those countries is tight links with companies in Silicon Valley. It should try to build stronger links there (beyond the existing incubator, iPark) and nurture domestic venture firms with a presence there. Active use of Korean-Americans in the United States is a good way to connect Korean ventures to the social and financial infrastructure of that country. Also, new business models linking foreign business activities to those of Korea should be developed.

Strategic Partnerships with Local and Foreign Companies

In contrast to large organizations, venture companies with strategic flexibility can make innovative products and services that threaten the products of large companies and force incumbents to leave a competitive market. Established companies have advantages in technology competencies. So there are potential complementarities between small and large firms. Strategic partnerships can help with access to distribution channels and new technology, diversification into new businesses, and legal barriers.

Expanding Social Infrastructures

Networks should be encouraged among research institutes and universities, venture capital firms, law firms, and the government. Research institutes and universities need to improve their basic research and to connect with actors who can commercialize research results. Venture capitalists should supply not only early-stage capital but also expertise on strategy and operations and potential customers. Law firms could be a significant source of key employees, financing, and corporate and intellectual property services. The government should reinforce the general infrastructure with public venture funds, science parks, and business incubators.

Recently, increasing interest has been shown regarding entrepreneurial habitats. We suggest the following as pillars crucial to such habitats. Entrepreneurs are the most important players, and universities and research institutes are important sources of them. Venture capitalists prospect for new ventures and invest in them. Professional service providers, such as lawyers and business consultants, help entrepreneurs develop business opportunities. All interact to create and share their knowledge and expertise.

Government needs to design policies to support innovation and support habitats. The development of the capital market is necessary. Social culture is related to the degree to which the business climate encourages risk taking and tolerates failures in the pursuit of business opportunities created by risky, innovative new technologies.

Although in recent years the Korean government has fostered entrepreneurship, it has paid relatively little attention to building entrepreneurial habitats. It is time that the government's role changes from direct support of players to indirect support of the social infrastructure and systems needed to sustain entrepreneurship.

Appendix

Survey of Teheran Valley

Survey data were collected from 225 venture firms in the Teheran Valley from September to October 2001. The average number of employees of the sample firms was about 50.

Survey results show that the firms' production and process technology came mainly from R&D (33.1%; 31.7%). Regarding networks, the survey revealed that the strongest ties for individuals were from personal relationships (32.6%), market information from customers (19.4%), and financial and management information from the CEO's personal network (30.3%; 38.1%). In addition, informal networks and the codification of tacit knowledge were important.

The cooperation between Teheran Valley venture firms and university or R&D institutes in the Valley was limited.

Of Korea's venture capital funds, 39 percent were invested in Teheran Valley, and, among 1,338 total firms backed by venture capital, 526 were located there.

Table 6A.1 shows the extent to which the Daeduk cluster specializes in manufacturing and Teheran Valley in software and services.

Table 6A.2 shows that corresponding to the differences in type of activity in the two clusters there is also a sharp difference in educational level.

Venture habitats were classified in seven categories as follows: (1) physical infrastructure, (2) financial infrastructure, (3) specialized service sectors, (4) professional consulting services, (5) management support networks, (6) education and training sectors, and (7) basic research sectors. The status of each infrastructure in the two valleys was evaluated. The results are shown in Table 6A.3.

Distribution of Venture Firms by Industry

Industry	Teheran Valley	Daeduk Valley	Korea
High-tech manufacturing	479 (28.6%)	**203 (53.4%)**	3,193 (40.6%)
General manufacturing	97 (5.8%)	**59 (15.5%)**	2,002 (25.5%)
Software/IT services	**937 (56.0%)**	87 (22.9%)	2,074 (26.4%)
Other services	123 (7.4%)	22 (5.8%)	371 (4.7%)
Other	38 (2.2%)	9 (2.4%)	225 (2.8%)
Total	1,674 (100%)	380 (100%)	7,865 (100%)

SOURCE: Korea SMBA Survey Data (2001).

TABLE 6A.2

Distribution of Entrepreneurs by Academic Credentials

Degree	Teheran Valley	Daeduk Valley	Korea
PhD	189 (11.6%)	**121 (40.1%)**	1,038 (13.6%)
Master's	456 (28.0%)	73 (24.2%)	1,543 (20.2%)
Bachelor's	**882 (54.1%)**	81 (26.8%)	3,815 (50.0%)
Other	103 (6.4%)	27 (8.9%)	1,238 (16.2%)
Total	1,630 (100%)	302 (100%)	7,634 (100%)

SOURCE: Korea SMBA Survey Data (2001).

TABLE 6.A3

Habitat Evaluation of the Teheran Valley and Daeduk Valley

Habitat Elements	Teheran Valley	Daeduk Valley
Physical infrastructure	Convention centers, office buildings, business incubators, venture complex, hotels, computer networks	Business incubators, R&D facilities, computer networks, space availability
Financial infrastructure	Venture capital firms, banks, angels	Banks, branches of a few VC firms
Specialized services	Many accounting and law firms (79 law firms)	A few accounting and law firms (not specialized)
Consulting services	Tech-support firms, PR firms	Limited services
Management support networks	Management and strategy consulting	Limited services
Education and training sectors	External training programs on technology and management	Limited training opportunities
Basic research sectors	Limited collaboration with universities, many corporate R&D laboratories	Strong universities and government-supported research institutes

1. Because there is no standard convention for spelling Korean names in English, this chapter uses the spelling of "Daeduk Valley," although recent practice also includes "Daedeok Valley."

REFERENCES

Bae, Z.-T. 1994. "Planning and Principles for the Construction of S&T Industrial Parks: The Korean Approaches." Paper presented at the APEC Seminar on Development Strategies of Science and Technology Industrial Parks in Asia and the Pacific. Beijing.

Bygrave, W. D., and J. A. Timmons. 1992. *Venture Capital at the Crossroads.* Boston: Harvard Business School Press.

Core Logic. http://www.corelogic.co.kr.

Kazanjian, R. K. 1988. "Relation of Dominant Problems to Stages of Growth in Technology-Based New Ventures." *Academy of Management Journal* 31(2):257–279.

Kim, J. G., and SPRIE Team. 2002. *Venture Habitat of Teheran Valley: Analysis and Long-Term Planning* (in Korean). Hoseo University.

Korea Information Strategy Development Institute (KISDI). 2003. *IT Industry Outlook of Korea 2004.*

Korea Technology Investment Corp. http://www.ktic.co.kr/eng/main.asp.

KTBnetwork. http://www.ktb.co.kr.

Lee, C.-M., W. Miller, M. G. Hancock, and H. Rowen, eds. 2000. *The Silicon Valley Edge: A Habitat for Innovation and Entrepreneurship.* Stanford, CA: Stanford University Press.

Lee, J., and Chun, H. K. 2002. "The Venture Habitat to Nurture Technology Transfer from University to Venture in Korea." Paper presented at the Tokyo Technology Transfer Seminar, Tokyo.

Lee, K. B., and SPRIE Team. 2002. *An Analysis of Korea's Venture Nurturing System: Policy Study* (in Korean). Information and Communications University.

Ministry of Information and Communication (MIC). 2002. *IT Korea 2002.*

NCsoft. http://www.ncsoft.com.

ReignCom. http://www.reigncom.com.

Saxenian, A. 1996. *Regional Advantage: Culture and Competition in Silicon Valley and Route 128.* Cambridge, MA: Harvard University Press.

Small and Medium Business Administration (SMBA). 1999–2003. *Annual Survey Report.* Republic of Korea.

Timmons, J. A., and S. Spinelli. 2003. *New Venture Creation: Entrepreneurship for the 21st Century* (6th ed.). Burr Ridge, IL: Irwin.

Woori Technology Investment Co. http://www.wooricapital.co.kr/eng1.htm.

III   THE RECENT ARRIVAL OF TWO GIANTS

7

ZHONGGUANCUN

China's Pioneering High-Tech Cluster

Mulan Zhao

Zhongguancun Science Park in Beijing has the largest concentration of high-tech companies in China. It had 12,000 of them in 2002 with more than 400,000 workers and revenues of $29 billion.[1] Sixty-four percent were in the information technology industry, with the rest in the advanced manufacturing, biomedical, materials, and energy sectors.

HISTORY

In 1979, China began to reform and open up to the outside world, and the region's development began shortly thereafter. Nicknamed "Scientific Town," Zhongguancun (ZGC) has long been the largest center of scientific research and education in China. In 1980, a researcher named Chen Chunxian at the Physics Institute of the Chinese Academy of Sciences (CAS) visited Silicon Valley in the United States. On his return to China he founded the first privately funded scientific research institute in ZGC, as well as in Beijing. His aim was to do scientific consultancy and technology development. The setting up of this organization received much notice in Zhongguancun, at the Chinese Academy of Sciences in Beijing, and more widely throughout China. In accordance with a pattern familiar elsewhere in the world, his venture failed (though he made a comeback later with Chen Chunxian Studio).

Chen was followed by other entrepreneurial scientists and technicians who left their research institutes and state companies. The scientific activities of these organizations were isolated from markets. A striking fact is that from 1950 to 1978 the Chinese Academy of Sciences "which owned all the technology . . . in all that time did not sell one product. Since the reforms, 40,000

198 products have been passed to companies. . . . and have been put on the market." [2] These entrepreneurs slowly helped to build a new economy that differs radically from the old, planned one.

The central government encouraged scientists to solve practical problems of development in a decree issued in 1982. In May 1983, the Academy of Sciences, cooperating with the Beijing Haidian District Government, founded the Kehai Company. In 1987, the Stone Group in Zhongguancun and Mitsubishi of Japan jointly founded Beijing Stone Office Automation Equipment Co. Ltd., the first foreign-funded joint venture in Zhongguancun. By the end of 1987 the Academy had spun out several dozen high-tech enterprises, including the computer companies Legend (now called the Lenovo Group) and China Daheng Information Technology. Sixteen of the top 50 companies in terms of sales came from CAS, all in the information technology (IT) industry. The pioneers began by incorporating advanced foreign technologies into Chinese, such as the Legend Chinese Character Card and the Stone 2400 bilingual typewriter.

Hundreds of companies were crowded along a ten-kilometer long street called Zhongguancun Electronics Street. This was its heroic age with several founders becoming famous, including Liu Chuanzhi of Legend, Wang Xuan of Founder, and Wang Wenjing of UF Soft.

During this period, Tsinghua University and Peking University were also setting up their own high-tech enterprises. There were two main motives: one was to supplement low faculty salaries and enable them to keep the best people; the other was to move technology from laboratories to the market. University-funded enterprises have long played an important role in Zhongguancun through commercializing research findings.

THREE WAVES OF NEW VENTURES

Waves of start-ups in ZGC coincided with, and depended on, the rapid growth of China's IT industry. The domestic market was aided by large government investments in telecommunications. Paralleling this was China's rapidly growing participation in the global IT market. An openness to foreign goods and direct investments was essential to both parts of this strategy.

At the outset of its growth in the early 1980s this region had both important assets and daunting liabilities. The main assets were many scientific and academic institutions, a well-educated and talented group of scientists, and supportive governments, both at the national level and locally, along with a willingness to experiment. The liabilities, also substantial, included poorly defined laws (including those controlling property rights), unclear ownership of companies, an array of state-owned companies, governments with the habit of micromanaging state-owned enterprises, weak managerial skills, isolation from world markets, and an underdeveloped financial system, especially for risk capital.

In 1988, the municipal government set up in Zhongguancun the Beijing Experimental Zone for Development of High and New Technological Industries, with the label *Experimental* giving it the power to try new rules and institutions on a small scale before moving them nationwide. This zone became known as the Zhongguancun Science Park. This marked the official founding of China's first high-tech special zone. Preferences in connection with taxation, personnel, and finances were given. A new organization that had no investments in the enterprises that it administered and served was set up. The 148 certified high-tech companies in what became the Park were all state owned or collectives. (Only in 1995 were the first five private companies certified.)

The Park was small, with only 10,000 workers in 1989, but it was about to take off. Following the first wave of firms founded by local scientists, more coming from other parts of China followed, most recently, by scientists and engineers who had studied and worked overseas. From 1988 to the end of 1991, 300 new technology enterprises were founded in Zhongguancun each year.

The speech given by Deng Xiaoping during his inspection tour in southern China in 1992 gave a big push to creating a market economy. In ZGC, 1992–1993 marked the second big wave of high-tech start-ups, with more than 1,000 of them added each year. This was followed by a slowdown. From 1995 to 1998, an average of 450 new enterprises were set up each year. Then, between 1999 and 2002, the number increased to over 2,000 a year, forming the third start-up wave. Returnees from overseas played a large role in this entrepreneurial push; in those four years, 1,800 enterprises were founded by them. Companies also disappeared. Each year between 1996 and 2002, on the average 12.5 percent of them left. These companies were weaker measured by various criteria: management, technology, marketing, or finance. (However, contrary to the experience in many other high-tech regions, few were dotcoms.) By the end of 2002, 1,500 of the 12,000 high-tech enterprises in the area were foreign, including the multinational giants IBM, Microsoft, and P&G.

SPREADING OUT

These activities produced a land shortage. At the end of 1991, construction of the Shangdi Information Industry Base began, five kilometers north of the Chinese Academy of Sciences. In 1992, the Beijing municipal government decided to develop two pieces of land for high-tech industries, located in Changping District and Fengtai District. In early 1999, the old electronics town in

TABLE 7.1

Revenues, Taxes, and Workers: 1988–2002

Year	Total Income (U.S. $ billion)	Tax Revenues (U.S. $ million)	Workers (thousands)
1988	0.17	6.05	—
1989	0.21	8.46	10
1990	0.30	14.51	15
1991	0.45	18.14	31
1992	0.73	27.81	69
1993	1.21	43.53	108
1994	1.73	58.04	113
1995	2.65	89.48	120
1996	3.60	113.66	125
1997	4.92	143.89	135
1998	8.31	257.56	173
1999	11.41	486.09	243
2000	17.35	672.31	293
2001	24.36	1,081.02	361
2002	29.08	1,204.35	406

SOURCE: Government census and statistics of Zhongguancun Science Park.

NOTE: Data from 1999 to 2002 are for Beijing.

The IT industry is the leading one, as shown in Table 7.2, with around two-thirds of the main economic indicators. In 2002, it had total revenues of U.S. $18.7 billion. Among other industries, advanced manufacturing accounted for 14.6%, new pharmaceuticals and life sciences 4.5%, new materials and energy 6.7%, and others 9.7%.

Chaoyang District, east of Zhongguancun and Yizhuang Science Park in Daxing County and southeast of Beijing, were brought into the Park. In 2000, decisions were made to build Zhongguancun Life Science Park, Zhongguancun Software Park, and Yongfeng Industry Park along Beiqing Road between Shangdi Information Industrial Base and Changping District. Some enterprises located in the core area of ZGC Park began expanding into these new areas, not least because land was cheaper.

THE PARK'S INDUSTRIES

Zhongguancun has a wide range of high-tech industries including IT, biomedicine, and new materials. From 1988 to 2002, the number of enterprises in ZGC grew from 527 to more than 12,000. Table 7.1 shows that the number of employees went from less than 10,000 to 420,000; the total revenue increased from U.S. $169 million to U.S. $29 billion; and total taxes grew from U.S. $6.2 million to U.S. $1.2 billion, a 100-fold increase. Zhongguancun's production

TABLE 7.2

Distribution among Industries, 2002

Statistics	Total 2002	IT	Biomedicine	Advanced Materials	Advanced Manufacturing	New Energy	Environmental	Others
Total income (U.S. $ billion)	29.08	18.74	1.32	1.41	4.23	0.55	0.97	1.85
Gross industrial output value (current price; U.S. $ billion)	17.96	10.58	0.82	1.09	3.86	0.41	0.69	0.51
Export value (U.S. $ billion)	2.88	2.12	0.08	0.16	0.39	0.02	0.01	0.10
Tax revenue (U.S. $ billion)	1.20	0.73	0.07	0.06	0.20	0.03	0.03	0.08
Employees	405,668	206,165	25,755	29,178	85,712	13,241	10,697	34,920
Total profits (U.S. $ billion)	1.35	0.61	0.08	0.10	0.37	0.03	0.05	0.12
Number of enterprises	9,673	5,060	479	664	2,216	313	352	589

SOURCE: Government census and statistics of Zhongguancun Science Park.

accounted for nearly 10 percent of the total of the 53 high-tech parks in mainland China. By the end of 2002, only 7 percent of the companies were state owned and 4 percent were collectively owned.

As shown in Table 7.3, there is a large dispersion in the sizes of companies with a modest number of large and medium-sized ones and many tiny ones. In 2002, 33 of ZGC's 12,000 companies reported over U.S. $121 million in sales, and 307 reported over U.S. $12 million in sales. Fifty-five companies were listed on exchanges, half of Beijing's total. More than 1,000 had between 10 and 100 million yuan in assets (U.S $8–12 million) and had experienced high growth. Known as "Gazelle Enterprises," they represent the future of ZGC. At the other end of the scale, 4,300 companies had sales of less than $120,000. To put these numbers in perspective, the average annual wage at ZGC in 2002 was $3,700 (RMB 30,000); 82 percent of these 4,300 companies lost money that year.

CONDITIONS OF ENTRY AND BENEFITS SUPPLIED

Because the primary purpose of the Park is to promote high-tech innovation and development, entry is regulated. Entrants have to meet several qualifications. First, the applying firm must make "high technology" products or its R&D must be in high technology. High-tech revenues must account for at least 50 percent of the total. Second, R&D expenditure must be no less than 3 percent of total revenues. Finally, at least 20 percent of employees must have college degrees. With these conditions satisfied, the firm will receive a certificate from the ZGC Committee. Such firms then enjoy preferential treatment in taxation, such as a tax waiver for the first three years and subsequent three-year tax reductions. This gives firms a strong incentive to get into the park and try to stay there for at least six years.

THE INFORMATION TECHNOLOGY INDUSTRY IN ZGC

In 2002, Zhongguancun's IT industry generated revenues of U.S. $19 billion, 64 percent of the total; taxes of U.S. $734 million, accounting for 70 percent; and export of goods and services worth U.S. $2 billion, 86 percent of Zhongguancun's total.

- In hardware, the PC manufacturers command about half the domestic market share. Three PC producers—Lenovo, Founder and Tongfang— are the top three in China, and a company named High-tech Wealth is the largest domestic PDA maker.
- Sales of software developed in Zhongguancun account for 40 percent of the national market. The electronic typesetting system developed by

TABLE 7.3
The Distribution of Enterprises by Size

Total Income	Number of Enterprises	Profit (U.S. $ million)	Enterprises in the Black (%)	Percentages						
				Enter-prises	Total Income	Total Industrial Output	Tax Revenues	Export Value	R&D Input	Employ-ment
Over U.S. $ 121 million	33	509.07	90.9	0.3	44.4	48.0	31.3	59.0	19.6	10.5
U.S. $ 12.1 million–121 million	274	776.30	88.7	2.8	32.1	28.9	34.1	33.0	28.7	22.7
U.S. $ 3.6 million–12.1 million	503	284.16	83.1	5.2	10.9	8.0	14.2	4.2	15.7	14.4
U.S. $ 0.6 million–3.6 million	1,858	111.25	74.9	19.2	9.7	13.1	14.0	3.1	19.0	24.7
U.S. $ 0.12 million–0.6 million	2,458	−123.34	55.2	25.4	2.5	1.7	5.7	0.3	8.7	14.2
Below U.S. $ 0.12 million	4,247	−204.35	17.7	47	0.4	0.3	0.7	0.4	8.3	13.6

SOURCE: Government census and statistics of Zhongguancun Science Park.

VIMICRO

VXP Series. In October 2003, Vimicro's leading chip—Starlight 5—was introduced to the market. Starlight 5 has nine core technologies and integrates technologies of Starlight 1 to Starlight 4. The chip has been adopted by Logitech, the largest video product manufacturer in the world. Vimicro has become the world's largest graphic chip supplier and has set the industrial standard for PC graphic input applications. In February 2003, Starlight 4—a mobile phone color message processing chip developed by Vimicro—was adopted by Sprint System, the largest CDMA carrier in the country. This put another chip with proprietary Chinese intellectual property rights into the world market.

ARCA

ARCA is the first supplier of embedded CPUs in China and a leading IC design company. In 2001, the company introduced the ARCA 1 CPU, the first practical 32-bit RISC microprocessor, a milestone in China's IT development history. ARCA's mission is to provide high-performance, low-energy-consumption and high-integration SOC chips for information terminals and the mobile communications industry on the basis of embedded CPUs and DSP. In 2002, it introduced ARCA 2. The product matched the quality of the leading embedded CPU suppliers, ARM and MIPS. Attaining equal status with ARM and MIPS is the target of ARCA, in both technical and market aspects.

Founder Electronics has the largest share of the Chinese character type-setting equipment market at home and abroad. During the past 10 years, UFsoft has led in financial and accounting software.

- In Internet services, Sina, listed on the NASDAQ, is the largest Chinese portal, while Ourgame.com is the leading online game service supplier in China.
- Zhongguancun has an unparalleled position in IC design and R&D in China. Two IC design companies, Vimicro and ARCA, are described in the boxes.

A CENTER FOR HEADQUARTERS, MARKETING, AND R&D

Many firms put their head offices, marketing, and R&D functions in Zhongguancun and their manufacturing arms in lower-cost places elsewhere in Beijing or in coastal areas in southeast China.

Beijing vies with Shanghai as the most desirable location for company headquarters. Beijing has important advantages including the presence of leading universities and research centers and the prestige associated with being the nation's capital, where national economic policies and decisions on government procurement are made. The telecommunications sector is a good example of the last of these.

Zhongguancun is where the agents of China's main IT companies converge, and its products are sold throughout the country. It is the nation's largest electronic products market and a national database service and support center. Several of its universities and institutes are the most important research and development organizations in the country. ZGC enterprises spend an average of 3.2 percent of their revenues on R&D, much higher than the nationwide level of less than 1 percent. Somewhat surprisingly, small companies spend more on R&D than do large ones. Those with annual incomes exceeding 100 million yuan spend 2.5 percent, and those with incomes below 100 million spend 8.6 percent. Money earned from technology sales accounts for over half of the income of more than 2,000 of the region's companies.

ZGC'S MULTINATIONALS

There is a large overlap of interests between the government, including the district government, and foreign firms. The government wants more advanced technology for cutting-edge products and wants to move beyond making products invented overseas. The multinational firms want access to the Chinese market and access not only to cheap labor but, in ZGC especially, to talents that can strengthen their worldwide market positions. Many of them are establishing research centers; by 2002, 24 of the world's top 500 multinational companies had set up R&D centers in ZGC, including Intel, Microsoft, and Novozymes (a Danish enzyme company).

Its research activities notwithstanding, today China gets most of its technology from abroad, with multinational companies as the principal source. There are about 1,500 foreign-funded companies in ZGC. Their importance is shown by their generating 43 percent of the Park's revenues and 78 percent of its exports. Ten of the top 20 taxpayers in 2001 were multinationals. Actually, what is being acquired is not only technology in a narrow sense but also design techniques, know-how, and managerial skills, including knowledge about how to solve problems and how technologies are related to each other. Investments made by multinationals are a kind of "package" that combines money, products, technology, talent, managerial skill, and ideas. Multinationals are also the sources of people who start companies. For example, the founder of the China Electronics Corporation used to be with Motorola.

FOREIGN-FUNDED ENTERPRISES

In 2002, the Park had 1,154 foreign-funded companies, 12 percent of the total. Electronics and information companies had the largest proportion (716, 62%), followed by advanced manufacturing (225, 19.5%) and new materials (58, 5%).The largest number came from Asia (537, 47%), followed by North America (282, 24%) and Europe (132, 12%). Hong Kong had the largest number (293), the United States was second (248), Japan third (97), and Taiwan fourth (60).Foreign firms' exports were 78 percent of the Park's total, with European exports in first place. Their total income accounted for 43 percent of the Park's revenues, with Hong Kong companies in first place. On tax revenues, U.S. firms were in first place. Foreign firms had 22 percent of the Park's employees, with Hong Kong firms in first place.

EXAMPLES OF MULTINATIONALS' R&D ACTIVITIES

1. *Microsoft Research Asia.* Set up in 1998, it has 150 full-time researchers and 200 visiting scholars and trainees. It focuses on basic research: new generation multimedia, digital entertainment, mobile telecommunications and networks, and new-generation user interfaces. Six hundred papers from this source have been published in leading international academic journals, and it holds over 100 patents. Research results have been incorporated in products as Windows XP, Office XP, XBox, and Tablet PC. More than 50 Chinese universities and research institutions are major partners.

2. *Novozymes's China Research and Development Center.* Novozymes in Denmark holds 40 percent of the world's industrial enzyme market. The company is based in Copenhagen. Novozymes (China) was established in 1997 as an investment corporation. Its China Research and Development Center, one of five R&D centers in the world, has 40 staff members and departments for its microbe laboratory, for its enzyme application laboratory, and for application and development.

Multinational companies have become a major source of R&D. In 1994, Nortel and Beijing University of Posts and Telecommunications set up the first multinational R&D center in Beijing. Since then, multinationals have established 24 independent and non-independent R&D organizations. Intel and Microsoft have invested U.S. $50 million and U.S. $80 million, respectively, on technology development.

Some ZGC companies have begun to make R&D investments in the United States, Japan, and Australia. For example, Lenovo has cooperated with National Semiconductor and Texas Instruments (and has recently bought IBM's PC business). Fifty institutions and companies, including Netease, 8848.com, and Lenovo, have joined the Ericsson Multimedia Open Lab.

INSTITUTIONAL INNOVATIONS

Research and development activity is one part of a development strategy, but perhaps more important for ZGC are institutional innovations. Some can be tried on a small scale within the Park, but national policy changes and the developing market at home and abroad will determine the future of the Park. China has high ambitions. It wants not only to become far less dependent on foreign technology but also to develop cutting-edge products. The outcome of this vision will determine whether or not ZGC becomes a globally important center of innovation.

NETWORKS

Within the Region

Essential to the successes of China's enterprises have been networks of relations. These have connected families, new entrepreneurs, the institutes from which they came, universities, local governments, and national ministries. The institutes supported their spun-off entrepreneurs in several ways, including financially; local officials for the most part worked to reduce regulations, arranged for financial support often in the form of loans, and usually did not interfere in the inner workings of enterprises. Universities helped to set up (including funding) enterprises and maintained close ties to their graduates; and national ministries kept research money going to institutes and universities.[3]

Most important, entrepreneurs who came from research institutes and universities retain close relationships with their home institutions in technology, funding, people, and laboratories. These connections are mutually beneficial. For example, Tsinghua Science Park has over 200 enterprises, with most of their founders being graduates or teachers. This Park focuses on high-tech R&D, developing talent, and incubating companies. The University gets money from rents, service and license fees, and (sometimes) returns from its investments.

There is a large flow of financial capital, goods, people, and technology among ZGC and other regions across China, including in Taiwan, and around

208   the world. The importance of foreign multinationals has been noted previously. Furthermore, some ZGC companies have branches abroad in places such as Silicon Valley.

People Flows among Regions

Zhongguancun absorbs the largest number of top-level scientific and technical talents in China. Outstanding people from every part of China come to the universities and research institutes here for learning and study, then return to their hometowns or go overseas for further study, making Zhongguancun the region that has exported the largest number of students overseas. A significant number of these former students are now returning, bringing with them much human capital. Since the emergence of high-tech enterprises, much of this talent finds its way into high-tech industry.

Zhongguancun is a town of immigrants. According to a survey conducted in 2002, 342 of the 795 people surveyed currently living in Beijing came from somewhere else. This has been greatly helped by the lifting of the ban on moving from other parts of China to Beijing for people employed in high-tech companies. Since 1999, about 3,500 highly qualified people have come to ZGC from elsewhere in the country, 97 percent of whom had at least a bachelor's degree and 57 percent of whom are less than 30 years old. In 2001, the park recruited 5,500 college graduates from outside Beijing.

High-tech industry has absorbed a far greater number of returned overseas students than any other sector. They came with experience in technological or managerial work in foreign companies and are entrepreneurs. By June 2003, more than 4,900 returned overseas students and scholars had founded 1,800 ventures in Zhongguancun. Their enterprises have become the most important bridge between industries in ZGC and their overseas counterparts. They track world high-tech developments and are involved in cross-national ventures. Many have investments abroad and use these to develop new products and markets.

ZGC supplies returnees with free funding for their start-ups. As of 2003, RMB 28 million had been given to 340 start-ups. The Park also supplies small collateral loans; 71 returnees had received RMB 52 million to cover interest payments and fees.

Cross-Region Technology Trading

Only a part of the technology that flows in and out of ZGC is recorded. Much of it that moves within companies, foreign and Chinese, is not. However, there is also a recorded trade in technology.

In 2002 estimated technology trade revenues totaled U.S. $1.6 billion in Beijing, up 147.4 percent year-on-year. Eight hundred thirty-seven technology import contracts were recorded, amounting to U.S. $1.1 billion, up 155 percent year-on-year. There were 206 technology export contracts worth U.S. $370 million. Software trade recorded by Beijing Customs came to U.S. $ 93 million, up 34 percent year-on-year.

Zhongguancun's technology transfer contracts account for over half of Beijing's total. It conducts more such transactions than does any other region of China. In 2002, 5,500 contracts transferred technology to regions other than Beijing, accounting for half of the annual total number of signed contracts.

THE SEVERAL ROLES OF GOVERNMENTS

ZGC enjoys certain advantages from being in the capital city, but there are also disadvantages. Among the advantages are being close to large amounts of money from government ministries and the presence of leading institutes and universities, as mentioned previously. However, from the viewpoint of Silicon Valley — or Shanghai or Shenzhen — there are benefits in being far from the emperor, whether he is seen as being in Washington or Beijing.

The Policy and Legal Environment

Legal uncertainties, especially in the 1980s but even today, can be regarded as posing risks that deter investment. In particular, the perceived failure to adequately protect intellectual property limits foreign investments involving advanced technology. There also have been conflicts resulting from ambiguous rules. A notable one is the dispute over the distribution of profits of the Founder enterprise between Beijing University and a series of managers of Founder. Despite difficulties in clarifying property rights, these problems clearly have not prevented great progress. Investors must perceive a social consensus somehow to make things work.

From the beginning, a favorable environment was created by the central and local governments. The central government enacted regulations affecting taxes, company law, development zones, the software industry, the IC industry, and other things. The Beijing government enacted similar ones, in addition to some on attracting talent, equity incentives, and venture capital. Of these regulations, those that seem to have had the greatest impact have been on taxation. Enterprises in the Zone certified as "high-tech" are exempt from income tax for the first three years and their taxes are reduced by 50 percent for the following five years. A notable advantage of ZGC is the rule, "What is not forbidden by

210 the law is not against the law." This permits venture capital organizations in the form of limited partnerships. It also allows the business scope of an enterprise not necessarily to be clearly defined. These are the first cases of their kind in mainland China.

Support for R&D

Zhongguancun has long been one of the top beneficiaries of government R&D funding. In recent years, its universities and research institutes, notably the Chinese Academy of Sciences, Peking University, and Tsinghua University, have received over 300 awards under the 863 Program (State High-tech Research and Development Plan Projects), 30 percent of the national total, and 52 awards under the 973 program (Fundamental Research Plan Projects), 41 percent of the national total. Sixty-five state and municipal laboratories have been established, and 227 projects of the national Torch Plan for the support of science and technology parks have been awarded to ventures. In addition, privately funded institutions are allowed to compete for the government's R&D budget.

Support for Small and Medium-Sized Companies

Because the core assets of high-tech enterprises are embodied as knowledge, generally they have few fixed assets and are risky investments. They do not meet the traditional criteria for bank loans. Therefore, at the end of 1999, a quasi-public service guaranteeing company, Beijing Zhongguancun Sci-Tech Guaranty Company Limited, was founded. By mid-2003, it had provided guarantees covering nearly 3.9 billion yuan worth of loans for 800 enterprises. The guarantee company reports a low failure rate so far.

In 2002, of the 12,000 high-tech companies, more than 1,000 were high-growth operations (the aforementioned "Gazelle Enterprises") with assets between 10 million yuan and 100 million yuan and two consecutive years of high growth. These represent the long-term future of Zhongguancun. Many have annual incomes of less than 20 million yuan, among which the software exporting and IC design enterprises are the main sources of the region's creativity and have huge potential.

Recently, Zhongguancun's government has been cooperating with commercial banks, guaranty companies, and credit rating agencies to create "Green Paths for Guaranteed Loans" to provide better financing to high growth, software exporting, and IC design enterprises. This project, called the "Gazelle Programme," aims to supply them quick financing with interest and guarantee charges on loans being subsidized by the government.

Government Incubators

There are 37 incubators of many types in ZGC with 1,500 enterprises under incubation. Among them, the Beijing High-Tech Incubation Service Center, the Zhongguancun Haidian Returned Overseas Student Business Incubator, the Zhongguancun International Enterprise Incubator, and the Zhongguancun Software Park Incubator are mainly funded by the government. The government also supports international exchanges on managing incubators.

Investing in Enterprises

Although the government no longer invests in high-tech companies that compete in markets, in 2000 ZGC had 879 state companies (including those with over 50% of stock held by the state). These amounted to 14 percent of the total in the Park. Most of these state-owned enterprises were not funded directly by government agencies but rather were funded by universities and public scientific and technological research institutes. In 2002, the numbers were 719 and 7.4 percent, respectively, showing the shrinkage of this category.

Infrastructure

The State Planning Commission has allocated nearly 8 billion yuan for infrastructure construction in ZGC, including transportation and communications, and the State Development Bank has signed a contract for loans worth more than 10 billion yuan. With the investments made by government during the past three years, 30 roads with a total length of 150 kilometers have been built or reconstructed, 300-kms of telecommunication tubes have been laid, and a rail line and infrastructure built in Zhongguancun Software Park, Zhongguancun Life Science Park, and Yongfeng Industry Base.

Changes in the Roles of Government

Although the government will always be of critical importance, its direct role is receding, as shown by the decrease in the number and proportion of state-owned companies. Nonetheless, the role of government will continue to be dominant both through its policies, its procurements, and its funding of basic research.

Increasingly the task of the government is one of indirect support and removing barriers. A "one-stop" service center in ZGC and a green channel for foreign-funded enterprises have simplified procedures. A web site provides

212   policy information while other e-government services include online recognition of high-tech enterprises, tax reporting, and statistics reporting.

HUMAN RESOURCES

ZGC's human resources have impressive credentials. About half its workers have at least bachelor's degrees. As is evident from the growth figures presented above, many are recent arrivals. Worker mobility is high; two-thirds of employees working for less than three years have changed jobs. Although some worker mobility is desirable, a rate this high may be dysfunctional.

In 2002, the high-tech industries in ZGC employed 406,000 people. Among them, 5,800 had doctoral degrees, 29,000 master's, and 155,000 bachelor's.

THE MARKET FOR SKILLED PEOPLE

Since the birth of high-tech enterprises in ZGC, enterprises can hire workers from the labor market and workers have the freedom to choose employers. This decidedly was not the case throughout China at the time; only in 1995 was it permitted nationwide. Just for this reason, the first formal labor exchange in Beijing, or in China, the Haidian District Human Resources Exchange Center was founded in Zhongguancun. Human resources intermediaries (known in the West as "headhunters") in ZGC have become more professional and open to society; they rely increasingly on IT and networks.

Beijing held 702 public personnel recruitment meetings in 2001; these were job fairs, with more than 36,000 institutions and more than 1.3 million individuals participating. In ZGC, 37 percent of the ordinary staff has been hired through these meetings, with many others being recruited through the human resources intermediaries. There are now more than 30 online human resources web sites in Beijing. Their services have evolved from personal documentation safekeeping to talent hunting, consultancy, training, and talent evaluation.

PEOPLE FLOWS

According to a survey, 30 percent of employees work less than one year for an enterprise, 36 percent for one to three years, 12 percent for three to five years, and 22 percent for more than five years. Their experience in their current jobs is typically short, partly because most companies have existed only for short periods of time and partly because people move around. In the enterprises surveyed, new recruits were 31 percent of all employees while 18 percent had left in the preceding period. They left in two ways: voluntary departures were 12.5 percent, and dismissals were 5.5 percent.

As mentioned previously, returned students are a major source of talent. They will go far to meet the demand in ZGC for senior managers and excellent scientists and technicians.

ATTITUDES TOWARD RISK-TAKING AND FAILURE

People face risks in leaving secure positions. This is true for entrepreneurs everywhere, but market systems have developed institutions to help lower risks. So has ZGC. The risks have been mitigated by supportive government policies, the availability to qualified scientists of money on favorable terms, tax advantages, and the aforementioned networks of relations. Many scientists leaving research institutes have been greatly helped through support in securing office space, people, and technology from their home institutes.

People also value recognition. Knowledge, capitalism, and entrepreneurship are honored in China to an extent perhaps not matched anywhere else in the world. Especially in the early days and even now, starting a high-tech venture in China requires a spirit undaunted by risks and able to tolerate the possibility of failure. The pioneer, Chen Chunxian, is widely respected for his pioneering actions.

The development of Zhongguancun is a microcosm of the history of China's IT development, during which many leaders emerged. In China there are now two fashionable and respect-arousing titles: Knowledge Hero and Knowledge Capitalist. Books are written praising them.

In ZGC, the first election of an Excellent Corporate Leader and of an Excellent Entrepreneur has been held, chosen through public voting. More than 100 people applied, and more than 40,000 people from all walks of life voted to elect ten excellent corporate leaders and ten excellent entrepreneurs. The names of the winners have been engraved on a cultural wall. This election will be held once every two years.

THREE GENERATIONS OF ENTREPRENEURS

The first generation of entrepreneurs effectively founded Zhongguancun Science Park, and many of them went on to hold key posts in institutes there. Inspired by the reforms and the successful experiences of Silicon Valley, they left their institutes to start their own ventures. They didn't know what real enterprise was like, and there was no market environment, so their adventures not only

214   involved their own transition from scientists to entrepreneurs, or growing a single enterprise, but the grand transition of China as a whole to a market track. Many have become renowned, including Liu Chuanzhi of Lenovo, Wang Xuan of Founder, and Wang Wenjing of UFSoft. People say, "They are the spiritual leaders of Zhongguancun. Without them, today's Zhongguancun would not exist." Who financed such pioneers as Liu Chuanzhi, Wang Xuan, and Wang Wenjing? Liu and Wang Xuan obtained financing from their former institutes, and Wang Wenjing supported himself.

The second generation of entrepreneurs is developing in an environment in which China's market economy system is taking shape. They understand modern markets, and many have international experience.

The third generation consists largely of Chinese who studied and worked abroad and then have returned and started ventures. During the past two years, on the average there have been two enterprises founded by returnees each working day.

INCENTIVE MECHANISMS IN ZHONGGUANCUN

China's economy is in transition. This affects incentive mechanisms that can be used to motivate the participants. For example, stock grants and stock options have not become the mainstream in ZGC, whereas some short-term and intangible incentives have been quite effective. These include giving scientists and technicians the opportunity to pursue their own careers; such careers, if made successful by one's own actions, are much more attractive than pure materialistic incentives. However, pay is relevant. In 2001, middle managers earned RMB 50,000–80,000 (U.S. $6,000–10,000) and the top ones RMB 100,000–200,000 (U.S. $12,000–24,000).

Since its founding, Zhongguancun has had market managerial systems, including "self fund raising, cooperation at one's own will, independent management, and reaping profits and bearing losses on one's own." The possibility and reality of dismissing incompetents spurs employees to work hard. This measure was very effective in the early stage of Zhongguancun, when other enterprises offered life-long employment.

Business people understand the importance of stock equity in retaining and encouraging talents. Elsewhere in the world many companies use stock option plans in various forms. However, due to obstacles in its basic system, such plans cannot be easily used in China. Changes would be needed in company laws, security market regulations, and tax laws. This situation causes many valuable people to leave and start their own companies in the hope of making more money. It contributes to ZGC's having many small companies.

LINKAGES BETWEEN RESEARCH ORGANIZATIONS AND INDUSTRY

Almost all universities and research institutes in ZGC have established their own enterprises, such as Lenovo Group, PKU Founder, and Tsinghua Tong-fang. The profits generated by those founded by Beijing and Tsinghua Universities alone account for over 60 percent of total profits of university-founded enterprises across the country.

Universities and research institutes in ZGC run their own ventures, frequently holding 100 percent of their equity and being exposed to unlimited liabilities. The peculiar historical background is as follows:

- Because almost all technological and economic resources were controlled by the government in the planned-economy era, no one without a government connection could hardly start or operate a company.
- Therefore, many scientists made deals with their institutions to set up and finance enterprises in return for a share of the profits. This model had its attractions. The government was so short of money that there was too little research and poor compensation for faculty. In those days, there were no donations from society to universities. Universities found it hard to keep superior talents, so setting up and earning money from enterprises became important for faculty members.
- Some universities tried to cooperate with state-owned enterprises, but vast differences in technology and mindsets hindered the successful commercialization of research findings. So the universities chose to set up their own ventures and found this model worked well. For over the past decade, university-funded enterprises have played an important role in ZGC's development.

CHANGING THE UNIVERSITY-BUSINESS CONNECTION

Since the mid-1990s, as the scale of university-founded enterprises grew, problems inherent in this relationship began to surface. (This was dramatically displayed in a long-running dispute between Beijing University and the Founder Group.) Universities tend to interfere too much in the operations of university-founded companies; and because ownership is not clear in law, it has been impossible to sell these companies to other investors. This is also a barrier to the companies' ability to raise money. Moreover, the universities are exposed to the market risks of these companies.

The broad objectives of university-business reforms are (1) clearing up enterprise ownership and restructuring managements so university-founded enterprises can operate independently and (2) setting rules for universities founding high-tech enterprises, so that teaching, research, and operation of

216   university-founded enterprises can be mutually beneficial and not in conflict. Basic to this change is a separation of the teaching and research missions of the university from commercial activities that may be socially useful but that can detract from the core missions.

Under the new model, the university focuses on research and teaching. The main content of the reform includes: managing state assets in universities; regulating current university-founded enterprises, setting up an exit mechanism for university investments, and making appropriate arrangements for the staffs of university enterprises. To help with this last aim, annual compensation packages for senior management, stock options, and employee share-holding are allowed, as are tax breaks.

University Science Parks

In light of the defects described here, both universities and the education authorities are favoring a university incubator model, one used worldwide. In this model, the university focuses on research, and research findings are taken to the science parks for incubation. Once start-ups grow to a certain stage they are moved to other parks. This model makes teachers and students the participants in start-ups rather than the universities.

Overall, university science parks like ZGC are in their early stages. However, some early movers, such as Peking University Science Park and Tsinghua Science Park, have quite a few enterprises under incubation.

Technology Licensing by Universities

The other main way to commercialize research, licensing it to companies, is underdeveloped. Universities have been doing several things to foster commercialization of their research outputs. One is by setting up technology transfer organizations (some are called technology transfer centers, some industry administration offices). Others are engaging in technology trades, developing rules of ownership and the distribution of benefits, making awards to inventors, building science parks, and applying for patents.

The number of research findings made in universities and research institutes is (naturally) far higher than the number commercialized. A survey by the Beijing Education Commission showed that each year there are tens of thousands of research findings produced in universities in Beijing. According to incomplete data, by the end of 2002, 27 universities and colleges filed close to 6,000 patent applications, with about 3,000 patents being granted. However, a relatively small proportion of patents resulted in commercial activities with only 500 technology transfers. Such a small proportion reflects problems within these organizations, problems that restrain the development of ZGC and demand attention there.

THE BUSINESS INFRASTRUCTURE

The ZGC high-tech cluster is attracting professional service providers. Besides traditional intermediaries such as certificate services, legal services, patent and trademark agents, and consulting firms, there are new kinds: electronics product trading markets, headhunters, technology trading centers, information service providers, and professional training houses. By the end of 2000, Beijing had 4,000 professional service organizations, of which 52 percent were consulting firms, 17 percent information service firms, 15 percent other intermediaries, 8 percent supplied fund-raising services, 4 percent human resources services, 3 percent technical services, and 1.5 percent exchange services.

DEVELOPMENT OF THE FINANCIAL SYSTEM

China's financial system, especially that for risk capital, remains problematical. Early firms were financed by their founding or "mother" organizations and by the founders themselves. Lending by banks to them, often directed by local governments, supplied some needed money but was inappropriate for enterprises with few tangible assets; they needed equity investments.

In 1999, the Office of the State Council moved to correct this situation by issuing the *Opinions on the Establishment of Venture Capital System* and removed the "50 percent of net assets" cap for investment companies intending to do equity investment. *Regulations on Zhongguancun Science Park*, approved by the Beijing Municipal People's Congress, was the first local law that allowed limited partnership venture capital firms. These are all experiments intended to promote venture capital development.

Despite these initiatives, the venture capital system is underdeveloped. So far, only two VC firms have adopted the limited partnership format. Investments are small, a multilevel capital market is not yet available (although one with lower listing requirements has just been created at the Shenzhen Stock Exchange — it is too early to know how well it will function), and a mergers and acquisition market has yet to emerge. In 2002, 21 start-ups received RMB 830 million (U.S. $100 million) of venture investments. Twelve local institutions supplied 29 percent of the total, while seven foreign institutions supplied 71 percent.

A common reaction from potential risk capital investors is that without

218 good "exit" opportunities, through public offerings on a stock exchange or acquisitions by established firms, they are reluctant to "enter." They mean by this that they need to be able to quickly generate cash from their winners to compensate for their "losers." It remains to be seen how much the new Shenzhen market will help.

Risk capital investments in ZGC are of three types: foreign venture capital firms represented by IDG, Intel and Softbank; venture capital firms set up by large local companies, such as Lenovo Investment, Tsinghua Unisplendour Investment, and Tsinghua Tongfang; and venture capital supplied by the government, such as Beijing Venture Capital Co., Ltd. and Beijing High-technology Venture Capital Co., Ltd.

The venture capital market in ZGC is changing. Overseas venture capital firms such as Walden International, WI Harper, and Hisun have invested in its companies. The Zhongguancun Venture Capital Foundation, established by 11 international foundations led by Hutchison Whampoa and Sun Hung Kai, is actively seeking investment targets there. Domestic listed companies and non-banking financial institutions are also interested. Tongfang, Zongyi Group and Beijing International Trust and Investment Co., Ltd. have become strategic investors for some ZGC enterprises as have local private capital institutions.

Taking Hisun as an example, its investment managers consist of two groups: (1) senior managers from international and domestic IT companies who have rich operational and management experience in the IT sector and (2) investment professionals in capital operation, law, and finance. Hisun brings modern management into the enterprises in which it puts money to improve their performances.

Zhongguancun is a gathering place for entrepreneurs and investors.

VENTURE CAPITAL IN ZHONGGUANCUN

In 2002, 21 start-ups received a total of RMB 830 million (approximately U.S. $100 million) in venture funding in ZGC. These accounted for 61 percent of the total number of such enterprises and 86 percent of such investments in Beijing during that year. This money came mainly from foreign sources and large domestic institutions. Among them were 12 local investment institutions whose investment was 29 percent of the total, and 7 foreign ones whose investment was 71 percent. The average investment was U.S. $4.8 million in ZGC, 2.5 times the national average. The IT industry received U.S. $97 million, 87 percent of the total. The computer sector had the most venture capital financed start-ups — nine — followed by the Internet sector at four and semiconductors at one.

Through such events as fellowship meetings, project promotion fairs, and entrepreneurial contests, entrepreneurs and investors gather information. Such "multiple choices for both" help venture capitalists to improve their array of opportunities and entrepreneurs to learn how to move investors with their presentations, how to better design their projects, and how to partner with investors.

CONCLUSION

The ZGC system has changed. Tax advantages were reduced in 1993, and the Academy of Sciences ended its support for many successful firms in order to support new ones (in a fashion similar to venture capitalists that need to move money to new ventures). Competition was encouraged among domestic firms, and it has been intensified with the arrival of foreign firms. Corporate forms were adopted, with ownership being expressed through stock issuance and the appointment of general managers and boards of directors. ZGC led the rest of China in doing these things.

Zhongguancun has come a long way in little over 20 years. Its companies are prominent in the domestic market and are preparing themselves to become so in the global market. They face several challenges. Among them are becoming less dependent on foreign technology, which means becoming good at inventing it; growing large companies with an international presence; developing a better system for mobilizing and allocating risk capital; providing better protection for intellectual property; and allowing universities to attend more to their research and teaching missions and less to running businesses.

The achievements of Zhongguancun support the prediction that these challenges will be successfully overcome.

NOTES

I wish to extend my sincere thanks to my colleagues in the Administrative Committee of Zhongguancun Science Park who contributed to this chapter: Mr. Luo Liyuan, Mr. Wang Hongjia, Mr. Xie Qianghua, Mr. Li Liwei, Ms. Luo Ying, Ms. Zhang Yanfeng, Mr.Wang Guangli, Mr. He Jingwei, and Mr. Yan Xiaoxing.

1. The 12,000 companies are those certified by state science and technology authorities. The national criteria are that a company's R&D spending must exceed 5 percent of its total revenue and that its R&D personnel must exceed 30 percent of its total employees. This is similar to the definition of high technologies used by the U.S Department of Commerce—the company's input for R&D must be more than twice the industrial average. The many low-tech companies in ZGC, such as trading or transportation companies or assembling factories are not included.

220   2. Adam Segal, *Digital Dragon; High Technology Enterprises in China*, Cornell University Press, 2002, p. 71.

3. These and some of the following points are emphasized by Segal.

REFERENCE

Segal, A. 2002. *Digital Dragon: High Technology Enterprises in China*, Ithaca, NY: Cornell University Press.

8

Entrepreneurship

The True Story behind Indian IT

Rafiq Dossani

India's software industry is one of the world's most successful information technology (IT) industries. Begun in 1974, in the fiscal year that ended March 2004 it generated $12 billion in revenue, primarily from the export of custom applications software.

India's software industry is 3.3 percent of global IT services and its exports to the United States are 3.5 percent of U.S. IT services spending.[1] As of March 2004, 288,000 people worked in the IT exporting industry,[2] one fourth of the comparable employment in the United States.[3] There are about 3,000 firms in the Indian industry with the 10 largest accounting for 41 percent of total exports.[4] Of the $12 billion of total revenue, $8.6 billion was in exports (see Table 8.1). Among export markets, the United States is the largest, with a 68 percent share,[5] followed by Europe (22%).[6] Exports have grown at an average of 34 percent per year since 1996.

This chapter explains the industry's growth through studying some key aspects of the U.S. industry, the origins of the Indian industry, and supporting factors — labor, the growth of software clusters, infrastructure, and the diaspora.

Origins. From the beginning, the strategy of India's firms was to follow trends in U.S. software service companies. This meant that Indian firms would deal directly with end users rather than becoming subcontractors to U.S. firms. It also meant starting at the bottom of the value chain[7] and the risk chain[8] and graduating to more rewarding work.

The industry grew from private Indian firms, unaided by government or concerted acts by Indian trade bodies.

TABLE 8.1

Software Sales of the Indian IT Industry, 1996–1997 to 2002–2003 (U.S. $ million)

Software and BPO	1996–1997	1997–1998	1998–1999	1999–2000	2000–2001	2001–2002	2002–2003	2003–2004	Average Growth 1996–1997 to 2003–2004 (%)
Domestic	759	1,177	1,411	1,575	2,081	2,311	2,769	3,374	23.8
Exports	1,100	1,759	2,600	3,399	5,287	6,152	7,045	8,600	34.2
Total	1,859	2,936	4,011	4,974	7,368	8,463	9,814	11,974	30.5
Export %	59.2	59.9	64.8	68.3	71.8	72.7	71.8	71.8	

SOURCES: Nasscom (2004), p. 23, provides figures for the Indian software (domestic and exports) and BPO (exports only) industries; p. 63 provides details of BPO exports; and p. 26 provides details of software and BPO exports. The table is derived from these statistics. Prior to 1998–1999, the numbers on p. 23 are assumed to relate to software only.

Three external developments were of great importance. First and unpre-dictably, software outsourcing became a large industry in the United States in the mid-1980s, giving India a crucial first-mover advantage. From 1990, as west-ern IT outsourcing grew and globalized, only India could do the work off-shore. This enabled it to occupy a sustainable niche in the global supply chain. Second, the standardization of Unix and the use of the workstation in the mid-1980s enabled the parsing of a software project into separate compo-nents (modules), some of which could be done remotely. A third enabler was India's 1991 reforms, which enabled new marketing strategies.

This account differs from conventional explanations that center on the labor-cost differential, government policy, or pure chance (although all of these mattered).[9]

Services, not products. Software services are far more important than soft-ware products. This was an unexpected outcome, seen initially from both global and Indian points of view. Globally, software exports have been mostly products, not services. Even in India, some of the earliest and most extensive uses of its programmers, such as by Texas Instruments (TI) and Hewlett-Packard (HP), were in activities related to developing products. Because of the growth of domestic firms and a shortage of product development skills, how-ever, services became more important than products.

Small change in value addition. Even though their work grew more com-plex with time, the position of Indian firms on the value chain did not change much because work at the top of the chain (still done largely in the United States) also became more complex. By contrast, the Taiwanese IC industry has narrowed the gap with the United States, while the security software industry in Israel is on par with the United States.

Government policy. We take issue with explanations that credit the govern-ment.[10] It initially was both a producer of IT services and a policy maker. It failed as a producer while also crowding out the private sector. Its policymak-ing was protectionist and statist until the mid-1980s; this, too, led to failures. Later it removed controls, which obviously helped the industry, especially af-ter aggressive pro-competition reforms in telecommunications and venture capital in the late 1990s. Educational policy, however, remained generally un-favorable for technology development.[11]

Role of a key player. A single firm, TCS, played a leading role: it seeded the industry, developed the "remote project management model" that enabled offshoring in the mid-1980s, and pioneered the shift to applications program-ming in the 1990s. Several start-ups came from former employees of TCS.[12]

Clusters. Bangalore, often held to be as the locus of India's success, was sec-ondary to Mumbai until the mid-1980s. Bangalore's shortage of financial ser-

224   vices skills relative to Mumbai was the reason for the latter's initial prominence (most of the industry's clients were banks). After 1985, two factors changed: TI, the first multinational to locate activities in India, chose Bangalore; and with the modularization of work, domain skills (knowing details about industries) became less important than programming skills. This enabled Bangalore's advantages in skilled programmers, climate, and education to overtake Mumbai. Once Bangalore became the center, it influenced the industry in certain ways. For example, its business environment was unfavorable for start-ups which caused the industry to be dominated by a few large firms. We will argue that Bangalore's importance is likely to grow with time.

The diaspora. Nonresident Indians (NRIs) in the software industry played almost no role until recently, despite their prominence in the United States. The requirements for success did not draw on the skills of the NRIs, reflecting the difference between software services and products. As the Indian industry increases its output of products, the importance of NRIs will grow.

SOFTWARE OFFSHORING

The growth of the Indian IT industry cannot be understood without considering the evolution of certain aspects of the computer industry, particularly the growth in demand for custom applications software — that is, applications software prepared for a particular client's needs as contrasted with product or standard software.

The main points are the following:

- The independent software vendor (ISV) industry began with IBM's decision in 1969 to unbundle its mainframe operating system, applications software, and hardware by creating an open standard. By the end of the 1970s, ISVs had created a new industry, that of developing customer-specific applications software, thus supplementing the product software industry for operating systems and applications. By 1980, custom software revenues in the United States amounted to $4.35 billion. In comparison, product software sales in 1980 totaled $2.85 billion.
- In the 1980s, the invention of the PC created a new mass market for product applications software. Around the same time, the invention of the workstation and the standardization of Unix and C as the operating system and language of programming (collectively, the U-W standard) led small firms to purchase workstations where earlier they had outsourced work to be done on mainframes. U-W also led to the replacement of the mainframe by the workstation as the programmer's primary hardware tool. Both factors led to a large increase in demand for custom applications software, as well as for consultants who could design and integrate increasingly complex software systems — work that had often become too complex to be done in-house.

- In the 1990s, the rising power and use of PCs caused them to replace workstations as the medium for programming, while the development of distributed computing and client-server networks greatly increased the demand for both product and custom applications software, as well as for consultants that could manage software and applications remotely.
- Indian firms were early adopters of the ISV model, beginning soon after the offshoring of software development globally.

THE GROWTH AND FUTURE OF INDIA'S IT INDUSTRY

The Global Outsourcing of Software Services

The moving abroad of software programming by U.S. IT firms began about a decade after they started with the offshoring of manufacturing.[13] Possible reasons for this delay are listed by Siwek and Furchtgott-Roth[14]: "In many other industries, such as most manufacturing, firms can successfully develop a product in one country, manufacture it in a second country and sell it in a third country. The processes of development and manufacture are sufficiently separate from marketing to allow segmenting those operations geographically. It is potentially more difficult for computer software companies to move operations offshore. Product development in software is very closely linked to customer requirements. Although advances in telecommunications are allowing some firms to locate various elements of software development in low-wage countries around the world, these efforts are still primarily coordinated in the U.S. and focused on the U.S. market. Finally, in the competitive race to bring new products and services to market, any cost savings from offshore operations must be weighed against the delay in introducing new products."[15]

Difficulties in coordination might influence a firm to work in-house rather than outsource. Product software is riskier to create than custom software as it usually incorporates higher levels of technology and has higher market risk. Hence, an offshore operation is likely to be a subcontractor to the parent rather than one that independently conceives and develops products. Local firms are likely to start by subcontracting work from multinationals based nearby.

From such beginnings, more sophisticated trajectories might develop. We examine this for India, Ireland, and Israel.

Offshoring to India, Ireland, and Israel

India, Ireland, and Israel were the earliest destinations for offshored work, which began about five years after the independent software vendor (ISV) business began in the United States. The widespread knowledge of English and relatively low costs were the key attractions in all three. However, their

226   small, less sophisticated markets meant that their domain knowledge was low
relative to the United States.

In Ireland, software offshoring began in the 1980s, following hardware offshoring, which had begun in the early 1970s.[16] It was begun by — and continues to be dominated by — U.S. multinational enterprises (MNEs) that use
Ireland as a packaging gateway into Europe for their software products. They
"concentrate their local operations on low value-added, low-skill activities,
such as porting of legacy products on new platforms, disk duplication, assem-
bling/packaging and localization (text translation, changing formats, etc.).
They outsource most of their work and specialize in project management and
administrative or sales back-office activities (including multilingual customer
support). Until recently, the bulk of Irish software exports was accounted for
by multinational corporations that use Ireland as an export platform, where
most of the value is added before the software arrives in Ireland for localization, kitting and distribution."[17]

Exports grew from $2 billion in 1990 to nearly $12 billion in 2003. However,
there were only 23,000 workers in this industry (with revenues per worker at
nearly $500,000, which high number reflects the low value addition in Ireland).

MNEs account for about 90 percent of software exports from Ireland,[18] but
the figure only records the channel for receiving the export revenue and not
who does the work, which is done mainly by local outsourcing firms.

Israel's software exports went from only $90 million in 1990 to $3 billion in
2002. It started out like Ireland but did not follow the expected path of MNE-
led custom software. There, software work began with MNEs entering in the
1970s to access skilled labor and to benefit from government incentives.[19] The
work focused on writing product software. Much of the labor force had earlier
worked in the defense industry.[20] In the 1980s, came domestic software start-
ups, largely funded by government research contracts. At first, they provided
services to the defense industry, but later some developed security software
products for global markets. In the 1990s, domestic start-ups funded by global
VCs[21] developed software products, still security focused, for global markets.
Israel's labor pool during the 1990s was augmented by the emigration of about
a million scientists and engineers from Russia.[22] MNEs currently account for
about 25 percent of total employment in the IT industry[23] and focus on product research and development for in-house use. The software industry's growth
is driven by local firms producing software products for export markets.[24]

Israel's software workforce in 2003 was 15,000, and revenues per worker
were $273,000, a number that reflects their high productivity.

The difference between the Irish and Israeli paths is traceable to domain
skills in defense, with products having a global demand. These skills formed the

TABLE 8.2

Software Offshoring: Predominant Work Types

	United States	India	Ireland	Israel
1970–1980	MNE in-house product support	Body shopping by domestic firms	Not started	MNE in-house product support
Reason for divergence from United States		Foreign firms excluded by law	n.a.	n.a.
1981–1990	Custom software by MNEs; MNE in-house product support	Custom software by domestic firms; MNE in-house product support	MNE in-house product support (conversion work for European markets)	MNE in-house product support; custom software by domestic firms for local market
Reason for divergence from United States		Policy change to allow MNEs	n.a.	Defense industry skills
1991–2003	Software system integration; MNE in-house product support, managed services	Custom software by domestic firms; MNE in-house product support and R&D	MNE conversion work for European markets	Product software by domestic firms for global markets, MNE in-house product support and R&D
Reason for divergence from United States		New R&D skill pool due to new education policy in 1991; lack of domain skills	n.a.	Defense industry skills; new R&D skill pool via immigration; lack of domain skills

core of the early start-ups, initially offering services and later attracting global VC funding for product development, based on creating intellectual property.

A good measure of the difference between these two countries and India is revenues per worker, which amounted to $33,000 in the year 2003. This difference suggests that the Israeli software industry, which relies least on conversion work, has the highest value addition. Ireland relies the most on conversion work and, therefore, has the highest import content. Table 8.2 shows how the types of work done in these three countries, as well as in the United States, changed over time.

The Indian Government as a Producer of IT

In India's highly controlled economy, appropriately described as "statist, protectionist, and regulatory,"[25] and with no domestic market of significance, how did such a nimble business develop? Indeed, the state was keenly interested in IT and followed its favored approach of creating "national champion"

TABLE 8.3

India's National Champions in IT

Company	Year of Establishment	Designated Output	Location
Bharat Electronics Limited (BEL)	1954	Defense electronics equipment	Bangalore
Centre for the Development of Advanced Computing (CDAC)	1988	Supercomputers	Pune
Computer Maintenance Corporation (CMC)	1976	IBM computer maintenance and service	Mumbai
Electronics Corporation of India (ECIL)	1967	Nuclear electronics equipment, minicomputers	Hyderabad
Indian Telephone Industries (ITI)	1948	Telecommunications equipment	Bangalore
Semiconductor Complex Ltd. (SCL)	1984	IC design and fabrication	Chandigarh

SOURCE: Author's compilation from Sridharan (1996).

state-owned enterprises (SOEs)[26] that were granted monopolies, as shown in Table 8.3.

Note the focus on manufacturing, an irony given later developments. The only software firm was CMC,[27] the government's way of capitalizing on IBM's decision to withdraw from India following the imposition of restrictive laws (in the Foreign Exchange Regulation Act of 1973, or FERA-1973).[28]

The creation of national champions resulted, not surprisingly, in championship-scale failures, as described here:

- There was no output of any significance. Me-too products were developed to save foreign exchange, but the amounts produced were small, quality was poor, and the products did not sell (except to other SOEs).[29] For example, though commercially unsuccessful, ECIL produced a line of minicomputers (rumored to be reverse-engineered from DEC's PDP line), BEL produced the TTL 7400 series of logic chips, and C-DAC produced a supercomputer, the Param, capable of parallel processing at a speed of 1 gigaflop (a billion floating-point operations per second).[30]

  Failure was perhaps inevitable given state ownership in a globally dynamic sector. But the lack of R&D is also notable. The money spent on R&D in *all* public sector firms in *all* sectors of the economy during the period 1985–1990 (the seventh five-year plan) was Rs .4,200 million,[31] or less than $300 million. It is remarkable that any output emerged.[32]

- It crowded out the private sector. The SOEs were unwilling to subcontract to the private sector; instead, they stifled them through restrictive licensing.

- The resulting labor force was of low quality. Some writers have argued to the contrary. For example, Balasubramanyam et al. (2000), argue with reference to Bangalore and the IT industry, that "the SOEs' presence has promoted a research and learning culture in the city." However, no evidence supports this, such as patents issued, whereas their commercial failures indicate otherwise.

The Impact of the State Policies and the Growth of Software

Before IBM's unbundling decision in 1969, the only private Indian software firm was Tata Consultancy Services (TCS), founded in 1968 to serve the in-house data-processing needs of the Tata Group. It began offering EDP services to outside clients in 1969 (on a Burroughs mainframe[33]) and became Burroughs's exclusive India sales agent in 1970. The other IT firms were all wholly owned subsidiaries of mainframe manufacturers in the developed countries, such as IBM.

In 1973, the government passed the Foreign Exchange Regulation Act of 1973 (FERA-1973), under which a foreign firm could operate only as a minority partner in a joint venture.[34] While this did not affect the TCS-Burroughs relationship, it led IBM India to shut down in 1978.[35] The government company, CMC, was then issued the sole license to maintain IBM's installed base of mainframes in India.

In 1975, the first IT firm under FERA-1973, Datamatics, was established. It was a joint venture between American minicomputer maker Wang and former employees of TCS. Later, DEC (Digital) and Data General also formed joint ventures. Like TCS, they focused on sales of bundled hardware and software and EDP.

The industry began exporting in 1974 when Burroughs, attracted by the Indian cost advantage,[36] asked TCS to install its system software in the United States.[37] Other domestic firms followed TCS's lead. Thus started "body-shopping,"[38] the export of programmers for assignments typically lasting a few months. The Indian firms did little other than recruiting, while the overseas client decided on the work for the programmers. They initially focused on systems installation and maintenance. Later, they did "conversion" of clients' existing applications software into (primarily) IBM-compatible versions, but still using the body-shopping paradigm.[39] By 1980, the industry had export revenues of $4 million, shared by 21 firms, of which TCS and a sister firm[40] accounted for 63 percent.[41]

Some scholars attribute this early success to IBM's forced departure, noting that India was lucky to be left with a cadre of over more than 1,000 trained programmers as a result (Lateef 1997; Desai 2003). Lateef notes that some started

TABLE 8.4

Founders' Backgrounds of the Leading Firms

Rank	1990	Founder's Name, Education, and Previous Company	2002	Founder's Name, Education, and Previous Company
1	TCS	MIT (Kanodia), Punjab U., Queen's U., Canada, MIT (Kohli), GE Canada (Kohli)	TCS	MIT (Kanodia)
2	Tata Infotech	TCS spinoff	Infosys	U. Mysore, IIT Kanpur (Murthy)
3	Citibank OSL	n.a.	Wipro	Stanford (Premji), Soota (IISc, Bangalore)
4	Datamatics	MIT, TCS (Kanodia)	Satyam	Loyola College, Chennai, Ohio U. (Raju)
5	TI	n.a.	HCL	PSG College, Coimbatore (Nadar)
6	DEIL	U. Washington (Sonawala)	PCS	MIT (Patni)
7	PCS	MIT (Patni)	Mahindra-BT	Harvard (Mahindra)
8	Mahindra-BT	Harvard (Mahindra)	IFlex	BITS Pilani, TCS, Citicorp (Hukku)

SOURCE: Author's compilation from personal interviews and corporation websites.

NOTE: 1990 and 2002 refer to fiscal years ending March 31, 1991 and 2003 respectively. The 10th ranked firm in 2002 was NIIT, co-founded by Rajendra Pawar, who had been educated at IIT Delhi.

software exporting companies, including Prakash Mehra, who left IBM and founded IDM, a software consulting firm.[42] However, this assertion does not do justice to the facts. The first firm, TCS, was founded by J. R. D. Tata, the head of the Tata group, and L. S. Kanodia, a returnee from the United States, in 1974, four years before IBM's exit. By the time IBM had left, there were already 21 firms engaged in the IT business.

Further, apart from the Tata firms and two U.S. firms (Citibank and TI), entrepreneurship in the top eight firms in 1990 (see Table 8.4) came from U.S.-trained returnees rather than former employees of IBM.[43] On balance, IBM's forced exit probably hurt India's software services industry. This was not immediately noticeable, because it happened when the global software services industry was in its infancy and the firms that replaced it kept doing what IBM had been doing. Later on (1985–1990), IBM (had it been allowed to stay) would almost certainly have used India's low-cost workforce as an integral part of its ultimately successful strategy of dominating the global software services business. Instead, it sat out the 1980s, returning to India only after the 1991 reforms. True, Indian firms would have had a lower market share as a result; but the industry's size would probably have been much larger and its development more sophisticated.

If there was a single, dominant force, it was probably TCS and its sister company, Tata Infotech. Their market share was 63 percent in 1980 and had risen to 78 percent by 1986.[44] TCS's CEO, F. C. Kohli, who replaced Kanodia in 1975, continued as CEO until the early 1990s. He is often termed the "father" of the Indian software industry with several key paradigm shifts having been pioneered by TCS. In addition, some TCS graduates went on to found successful companies, including Lakshmi Narayanan of Cognizant, the seventh largest firm in 2000, and Rajesh Hukku of iFlex, the eighth largest firm in 2002.

Another early firm, Wipro, is widely praised for its entrepreneurial culture. Successful IT firms, both in India and the United States, founded by ex-Wipro employees, include Som Mittal of Digital Globalsoft (12th in size in India), K. B. Chandrasekhar of Exodus in Silicon Valley, Ashok Soota of Mindtree, and V. Chandrasekaran of Mascot (11th in size).

Where were the graduates of the oft-praised elite IITs (Indian Institutes of Technology) in this process? Migration took its toll, most leaving India permanently after graduation. For example, from 1986 to 1987, around the time that the industry entered a new growth phase, 58 percent of IIT graduates in computer sciences and engineering left India.[45] As shown in Table 8.4, none of the leading eight firms in 1990 was founded by an IIT graduate. However, the situation had begun to change by 2000 with the IITs and other domestic universities making their mark.

The New Computer Policy of 1984 and the U-W Standard

In 1984, Prime Minister Rajiv Gandhi's new government liberalized imports via the New Computer Policy (NCP-1984). Import duties on hardware were reduced from 135 percent to 60 percent and on software from 100 percent to 60 percent. The software business was recognized as an "industry," thus making it eligible for loans from commercial banks. It was also "delicensed"[46] — that is, permits were no longer needed to enter the business.[47] Wholly owned foreign firms developing software for export were once more allowed, though on a licensed basis. Electronics export processing zones were expanded, the first of which (in Mumbai in 1973) harbored TCS. Rentals at these zones were set below market levels, and procedures to set up business were simplified; power and water were guaranteed. In 1990, the Software Technology Parks system was set

232   up to further simplify procedures and to enable exporters to import equipment against their export dollars without licensing or customs tariffs.[48]

In 1985, all export revenue was exempted from income tax (regardless of the industry). The exemption was later legislated to end in 2007.[49]

These liberalizations were providentially timed because they coincided with the replacement of mainframes by workstations and when Unix and C replaced a variety of operating systems and languages as the programmer's software tools.[50]

As one industry participant noted, "Earlier, firms had been forced to work on the client's site in large part because they could not afford to buy or rent computers locally; they, therefore, needed to offer programming skills that differed with the machines they were working on, be these IBM, Burroughs, Vax, etc. It was not until tariffs were reduced and Unix became an accepted programming standard in the mid-80s that offshore work for clients became feasible."[51]

Having work done in India saved the costs of moving engineers, and less-skilled programmers could be hired. As one industry participant stated, "We were able to better match skills with requirements. Earlier, when we sent programmers overseas, we estimated the skill-sets needed and sent a compact team to the clients' site. That team was necessarily overqualified since it was expensive to replace team members (if found lacking in skills) once they had been dispatched overseas. By doing work in India, we could use our "bench": programmers of different skill levels, depending on the job, and who could switch to different jobs quickly. Thus, we could substantially use lower-skilled programmers at much lower costs than before."[52]

Some MNEs opened wholly owned subsidiaries, beginning with TI in 1985. It entered India to do in-house product development for its parent.[53] TI persuaded the government to supply it with scarce satellite bandwidth and started using programmers in Bangalore. For the first time, work was done in India. Several multinational firms, including HP[54] and Digital, then began doing product development work there, and some global banks with long-established Indian operations, notably Citibank, began developing custom software for in-house use.

Doing the work in India, however, posed problems of control of the work being produced. This was less serious for MNEs doing in-house work, but it raised the question as to whether domestic companies' outsourced work would survive. It did, by their taking responsibility for the clients' projects, thus replacing the personnel-subcontracting model. TCS pioneered this "remote project management model," as it came to be called, which required new management skills. This was an important departure from the in-house model that dominated Irish and Israeli software in the 1980s.

In return, the revenue earned per employee rose, although slowly, in line with the shift to offsite work. By 1988, 10 percent of the work was done offsite, and this had risen to 41 percent by 2000.[55]

An additional benefit of the shift to the U-W standard was that it generated a new source of conversion work—that of converting clients' installed applications into Unix-compatible programs.

Thus, the Indian software industry matured during the second half of the 1980s, at the same time as the industry was maturing globally. This gave India a first-mover advantage in offshoring. The number of firms rose from 35 before the changes to 700 by 1990.[56] Among them, Infosys and Wipro, currently India's largest exporters after TCS, moved to Bangalore around 1985 to take advantage of its superior bandwidth availability.[57] Most of the new entrants were domestic firms offering conversion work and other services.

By 1990, although five of the top eight firms—TI, Digital, Datamatics, Mahindra-BT, and PCS—were subsidiaries or joint ventures with MNEs that focused on product development, the industry was still dominated by custom software developers that made up over 80 percent of exports.[58] This was for several reasons, listed here:

- It was difficult for MNEs to get licenses. For example, they were allowed few branches and were not permitted to sell their products without a license. This may have induced them to keep teams small and not tie-up much capital or develop knowledge in India (at the possible future cost of losing clientele, as had happened to IBM, or proprietary knowledge).
- Domestic firms did not have the skills to do independent product development.[59] This lack came from India's closed economy; it was hard for them to understand customer needs.[60] They also could not get product development contracts from MNEs because of weak enforcement of intellectual property laws and the difficulties of managing intellectual property across borders *and* across firms. (Even in the United States, product development was rarely outsourced, and in Israel product development was done in-house.)
- Product development was hindered by poor telecommunications, which impeded real-time interaction, in contrast to contract programming that requires low interaction.
- Financial infrastructure, particularly venture capital, was almost nonexistent. This led to a focus on projects for which bank loans were obtainable rather than equity. Clearly, banks preferred to finance subcontracts with large multinationals rather than product ideas.

However, we expect that after the reforms, especially in telecommunications and venture capital during the period 1999–2000, both domestic firms and MNEs will be more likely to develop products.

The 1991 Reforms and the Growth of Domestic Firms

Entering the major reform period, which began in 1991, the software industry had several strengths. Although it was small in relation to the global industry, there were 700 firms, including several multinationals. The business was still dominated by the two Tata giants, with 48 percent of total revenue.[61] The next six firms were multinationals or joint ventures.[62] (See Table 8.4.)

Globally, custom software overtook product software after 1990. This helped the Indian IT industry. Had product development overtaken and ultimately replaced custom software, as had been widely expected with the development of the Wintel standard in the mid-1980s, India would likely have remained a small player.[63]

A related consequence is that the Wintel standard did not play a significant role in the development of the Indian industry, unlike its essential role in Silicon Valley and many other parts of the IT world. According to TCS's Ramadorai,[64] "Windows and Intel were never a player in the enterprise space . . . there was no strategic implication of any kind (from the development of the Wintel standard)."

The first feature of the reforms of the 1990s was a reduction in import tariffs. These had risen to 110 percent by 1991 but were reduced to 85 percent in 1993, 20 percent in 1994 for applications software, and 65 percent for systems software and, in 1995, to 10 percent for all software.[65] Hardware duties ranged from 40 percent to 55 percent in 1995, but by 2000 had come down to 15 percent for finished goods, such as computers, and 0 percent for components (microprocessors, storage devices, IC s and subassemblies, display screens and tubes, and the like[66]).

An overseas listing was also permitted from 1992.[67] Several firms were on U.S. stock exchanges during this period. (See Table 8.5.) In the second half of the 1990s, the telecommunications infrastructure was also liberalized and a venture capital industry developed.

A less noticed but significant reform of the early 1990s was that firms were allowed to spend their export dollars on opening offices overseas. Earlier, they learned client needs from their programming staffs on contract overseas, supplemented by senior staff visits and client visits to India. The better interaction with clients had two important outcomes: one was access to mid-sized firms. According to an industry participant, "We moved from marketing to the Fortune 500 to the Fortune 2000 in this period."[68] Another was that large clients who needed proximate support could more easily be serviced. Some later set up dedicated centers at outsourcers' sites, a trend pioneered by TCS.[69] Meanwhile, from 1991 multinational firms could more freely open wholly owned

TABLE 8.5

Top 8 Software Exporters

Rank	1980	1990	2000	Firm's India HQ and Share of Exports (%)
1	TCS	TCS	TCS[a]	Mumbai, 10.1
2	Tata Infotech*	Tata Infotech*	Infosys[b]	Bangalore, 6.6
3	Computronics	Citibank OSL*	Wipro[c]	Bangalore, 6.2
4	Shaw Wallace	Datamatics*	Satyam[d]	Hyderabad, 4.4
5	Hinditron	TI*	HCL[e]	Delhi, 4.0
6	Indicos Systems	DEIL*	Silverline[f]	Mumbai, 2.5
7	ORG	PCS*	Cognizant*	Chennai, 2.5
8	Systime	Mahindra-BT*	NIIT[g]	Delhi, 2.0

SOURCE: Heeks (1996) and Nasscom (2002).

[a] Privately owned by India's largest industrial group, the Tata Group.
[b] Listed on NASDAQ and Indian stock exchanges.
[c] Listed on NYSE and Indian stock exchanges.
[d] Listed on NYSE and Indian stock exchanges.
[e] Listed on Indian stock exchanges.
[f] Listed on NYSE and Indian stock exchanges.
[g] Listed on Indian stock exchanges, affiliate of HCL.
*MNE subsidiary or joint venture with MNE.

subsidiaries.[70] They responded more cautiously than Indian firms, as might be expected (although IBM was an early entrant, starting a joint venture with the Tatas in 1991[71]). EDS came in 1996[72] and Accenture began IT outsourcing operations in 2001.[73] Some MNE product firms also entered after 1991, notably Motorola, Oracle, and Cisco.[74] The top 20 MNE software exporters employed 25,204 persons as of March 2002, or 13 percent of the software exporters' workforce.

Although by 2002 MNEs were growing more rapidly than Indian firms,[75] the latter had become even more dominant in the 1990s. From a peak of seven MNEs subsidiaries or joint ventures out of the leading eight export earners in 1990, there were only two in 1994, Fujitsu and Digital, ranked seventh and eighth (1994 data are not shown in Table 8.5) In the place of MNEs were Wipro, ranked third,[76] and Infosys, ranked fifth.[77] By 2003, there were no wholly owned MNE subsidiaries and one joint venture, Mahindra-BT in the top eight. However, as observed previously, the trend is likely to shift in favor of MNEs.

Product development has remained small. For example, TI had 900 engineers at its facility in Bangalore in 2003.[78] Oracle, currently the largest MNE doing product development in India, employed 3,700 persons (although about half provided software services) in 2003.[79] These numbers might seem substantial, but they were a small part of the industry total. The top 10 product

236   developers had 9,040 workers as of March 2002, or 4 percent of the total IT Indian workforce of 230,000 persons.[80] In all, services accounted for 96 percent
of software export revenue during this period.[81]

Differences among the larger Indian firms appeared during this period. Financial services led, a legacy of the conversion work done for U.S. banks. TCS
offered the widest range of finance-related IT services, from system integration
to the writing of code and the running of the client's systems; Infosys specialized in financial services applications; Wipro, provided applications software
for the IT industry and also offered engineering services.

Impact of Y2K

The Year 2000 problem, also known as the Y2K problem,[82] was an unexpected
factor that helped introduce several new clients. One commentator has noted,
"Y2K allowed us to expand our target client list. Many medium-sized firms
that would not otherwise have considered Indian software firms were forced to
get to know them as a result of the shortage of U.S.-based programmers in the
run up to Y2K. These software firms were later able to get other business from
the medium-sized firms."[83] This may explain why software exports from India
did not drop after Y2K, as had been widely expected (see Table 8.1).

However, Y2K's impact was otherwise small. It came long after the industry
had become well-established. Even the number of service providers was almost the same in 1990 as in 2000. And the Y2K business was unsophisticated
work done on clients' sites.[84] Compared with the offsite work that Indian firms
were already doing it was a step backward. Some large IT providers even rejected it on the grounds that it was not part of their mission of doing more sophisticated work.[85]

Sustainability

Several scholars have argued that India's success cannot continue. Of course,
the record over the past three decades is strong evidence against this view.
Here we consider what sustained that success and how the future might look.

The industry's dependence on exports, shown in Table 8.1, has been criticized by some authors as an indicator of a unsustainability. D'Costa[86] has argued that international outsourcing of software, though commercially lucra-
tive, discourages firms from doing more complex projects at home because
"excessive dependence on outsourcing limits the synergy between vibrant
domestic and foreign markets."[87] A key practitioner, TCS's CEO Ramadorai,
agrees with that, maintaining that a focus on the domestic market will build

up the skills needed to undertake complex projects, thus enabling domestic firms to do similar projects overseas.[88]

Schware[89] has argued the unsustainability view for three reasons. The first is the absence of a domestic market. He notes that, "countries without a relatively active and up-to-date domestic market for software will find it increasingly difficult to develop a software sector which involves absorbing new technologies for software production, monitoring and analyzing trends in the industry, and using software to solve domestic productivity problems. The cost of developing such capabilities increases rapidly over time, making 'catch up' more difficult in terms of an evolving combination of capital outlays, prior experience, labor, skills, multiple levels of intellectual property protection, and the growing importance of organization and management in software production."

Second, Schware quotes Whitman's key factors for software success[90] and argues that India lacks many of them: computerization in industry and schools; university R&D in software and direct interactions with industry; skilled labor; funding sources such as venture capital and government contracts; support services, such as telecommunications infrastructure; social networks among players such as engineers, managers, marketers, and funders; an entrepreneurial culture; an attractive, low-cost work environment; and access to market channels through joint ventures and cooperative arrangements.

Schware finally notes that the "inadequate supply of skilled personnel may well be the major constraint to the expansion of the software sector. All firms experience difficulties recruiting qualified staff . . . the problems are rooted in low capacity . . . (further), faculty are not encouraged to consult."

Correa[91] also considers obstacles to sustaining the industry: "although entry barriers are low, countries seeking to develop software businesses are constrained by the following internal factors: small domestic markets, small firm size, absence of quality standards, weak protection of property rights, low quality labor and infrastructure and poor marketing skills, and relatively low importance of labor cost savings (for packaged software) . . . (as well as the following) external factors: US dominance, monopolies and English language barriers."

Siwek and Furchtgott-Roth also predict stagnation, stating that "the cost advantages that favor Indian-based software development are dwarfed by a problem that undermines growth policies in all developing countries including India: the problem of the brain drain. . . . For 1986–7, 58.5% of IIT graduates in computer science and engineering migrated. . . . We believe that certain programming activities will continue to leave the U.S. to some extent. These activities are more likely to emphasize maintenance rather than basic software design and development."[92]

238   An optimist (from the Indian point of view) has been Yourdon, who declared in 1992 that[93] "The American programmer is about to share the fate of the dodo bird. By the end of the decade, I foresee massive unemployment among the ranks of American programmers, systems analysts and software engineers. Not because fifth generation computers will eliminate the need for programming, or because users will begin writing their own programs. No, the reason will be far simpler: international competition will put American programmers out of work." Yourdon gives the example of India, "A typical Indian programmer with three years' experience might earn $200 (per month) in India—approximately 10 times less than his or her American counterpart in New York, Boston or Silicon Valley."[94]

Arora and Athreye[95] are also optimistic. They respond to Schware's concern on the inadequate supply of programmers by noting that even if costs for programmers rise above competing countries, India may still have a comparative advantage in the production of software due to the sector's relatively high productivity (relative to other sectors in the domestic economy).

Moreover, there are several examples of countries that have succeeded despite lacking several supposedly essential attributes. For example, Israel succeeded without a large domestic market (although it could be argued that it has done best in defense-related software, for which it has a large home market). Similarly, as Bresnahan has shown, Silicon Valley did not have several of these desirable attributes in the 1970s and yet succeeded (Bresnahan and Gambardella 2004).

We hypothesize that these weaknesses were not "killers" but were constraints that took the industry in a particular direction. For example, failure to learn from the domestic market forced the IT industry in India to stay at the low end of an upward-moving value chain, rather than leading to industry failure. As the work overseas became more complex, U.S. firms focused their best people on the high-end work, opening the door for Indian firms to have equally good people do less complex work.

Similarly, the absence of venture capital noted by Schware discouraged start-ups but left unaffected large, well-capitalized firms. Since start-ups are more likely to develop products than large software services or non-IT firms, this discouraged product development. Hence, the absence of venture capital led to a services-oriented industry dominated by large firms.

An unforeseen factor that has greatly helped India is the service industry's becoming increasingly important relative to products. Correa's worry that monopolies might prevent the growth of software production outside the United States implied that product development by large firms would dominate the business. Since services, in which entry barriers are lower, ended up being at least as important as products, this mattered less.[96]

Technology also helped. Unlike the situation in the 1970s, the maintenance of a software system requires little labor as a result of the high reliability of operating systems and software tools. Second, the work of applications programming became simpler and more cost-effective with the development of the U-W standard in the mid-1980s and software tools a few years later.

Table 8.6 matches the weaknesses of and threats to the Indian software services industry (Column A) with the way the software industry responded (Column B) and implications for the future (Column C). We discuss Column D in the following text.

A typical industry activity is custom software programming for the financial services industry done by a large domestic firm. Many factors once believed to make growth unsustainable instead altered the direction of the industry. In the end, it showed that having enough entrepreneurs, low-cost labor, and innovative process management skills made a formidable combination.

The Future

The future might lie in product development done by start-ups and MNEs, as has happened for Israel, but it is too early to say. As Table 8.6 shows, there are still several shortcomings, such as the shortage of R&D in universities and industry. Nonetheless, some signs pointing toward increased product development are visible. In particular, the Indian subsidiaries of MNEs appear to be leading the way in product development. For example, in 2003 Intel's Bangalore subsidiary, with 1,500 workers, filed for 63 patents;[97] GE's Bangalore subsidiary, with 1,800 engineers — a quarter with PhDs — has filed for 95 U.S. patents since the center opened in 2000; and India's oldest IT MNE, TI, with 900 engineers, has 225 patents.[98]

Nevertheless, skeptics abound. Cognizant's CEO Narayanan argues that India does not yet have the capability to develop intellectual property, R&D's contribution to overall growth is minuscule, and MNEs have been upgrading old products, not developing new lines.[99] Sarnoff Corporation's president and CEO, Satyam Cherukuri, argues that India has two of the three requirements for innovation — namely, technical skills and access to capital — but lacks an "indigenous business model."[100] Others assert that the difference in business contexts between India and the United States is too difficult to bridge.[101]

In any case, services will dominate the near future. There are several possible trajectories. Custom projects could become more complex and large as

TABLE 8.6

India's Response to External Challenges

Weaknesses (W) and Threats (T) A	How India Coped B	Current State of Constraints to Service Work C	Prospects for Product Development D
1. Learning from domestic markets (T)	Focus on banking software, the only world-class domain and service delivery skills a priori available in India	Domain and service delivery skills in a wide range of areas being acquired due to domestic reforms post-1991	Same as C
2. Remote project management skills (W)	Developed in mid-1980s	Considered to be of global standards	Same as C
3. IP protection (T)	Not needed for services	Not needed for services	Adequate regulatory environment in place since 1999
4. Firm size (W)	Large firms developed organically over two decades	No longer an issue	Favors a diverse environment of small and large firms, which is already in place
5. Marketing skills (W)	Developed after 1991 reforms	No longer an issue	Remains a challenge
6. Labor costs relatively low for products (T)	Focus on services	Not relevant for services	Remains a challenge
7. Migration of skilled labor (T)	Focus on low-end work	Large increase in labor supply due to privatization of education	Same as C
8. Lack of R&D in universities and industry (T)	Not needed for services	Same as A	Remains a challenge
9. Inadequate telecommunications (T)	Undertook on-site development and, later, developed the remote project management model	Resolved after 1999 reforms	Same as C
10. Inadequate venture capital (T)	Industry dominated by MNEs and subsidiaries of large non-IT domestic firms	Resolved after 1999 reforms	Same as C
11. Lack of global joint ventures (T)	Developed after 1991 reforms	No longer an issue	Same as C
12. Lack of clusters (T)	Service firms relied on MNE linkages for work and learning until 1985, since labor was mostly located overseas at clients' sites	Bangalore developed after 1985	Same as C

SOURCE: Author's compilation based on D'Costa (2002), Schware (1992), Correa (1996), Siwek and Furchgott-Roth (1993), Whitman (1990).
NOTES: Factors attributable to D'Costa, 1; Schware, 1; Correa, 1, 2; Correa, 1, 3, 4, 5, 6; Siwek, Furchgott-Roth, 7; Whitman, 1, 8, 9, 10, 11.

TABLE 8.7

Indian Software Exports' Market Share, 2003

Category	Global Software Services Spending ($ billion)	Indian Software Services Export Revenues ($ billion)	Indian Service Constituents (%)	Indian Global Market Share of Services (%)
Consulting	41.5	0.11	1.9	<1
Applications development	18.4	3.02	54.5	16.4
Managed services	124.9	1.94	35.0	1.6
System integration: hardware and software deployment and support	91.7	0.37	6.7	<1
System integration: applications, tools, and O/S	62.4	0.10	1.8	<1
IT education and training	18.5	0	0	0
Total	357.6	5.54	100	
Product software	200	1.66		<1

SOURCE: Nasscom (2004), pp. 36 and 106. Indian figures are for 12 months ending March 2003. Indian figures do not include product development and design of $0.56 billion and embedded software of $1.1 billion.

DEFINITIONS:

Consulting refers to work on IT strategy, system conceptualization, architecture, and design. It is based on Nasscom numbers for IS consulting and network consulting and integration.

Applications development refers to work on creating the applications programs. It is based on Nasscom numbers for custom applications development.

Systems integration: hardware and software deployment and support refers to the work of making the software and hardware components compatible and interoperable up to the required specifications. It is based on Nasscom numbers for (1) Hardware Deployment and Support and (2) Software Deployment and Support.

Systems integration: Applications, tools, and O/S refers to integration of the software components in a software project.

Managed services refers to services such as managing applications either on site or remotely over the web, managing networks, etc. It is based on Nasscom numbers for applications management, IS outsourcing, network and desktop outsourcing, applications service providers, and system infrastructure service providers.

firms move from programming into systems integration and systems specification and design. The average number of man-years for the typical project has already risen from 5 in 1991 to 20 in 2003.[102] As MNEs become more important, domain skills will develop, so that managed services are likely to become more important; this will match global trends in the outsourcing of applications management and business processes. In recent years, IT-enabled business services have grown in India, led by low-value front-office work such as call centers (led by outsourcers, both domestic and MNE) and higher-value back-office processes such as accounting and finance (mostly done in-house by MNEs).[103] Table 8.7 shows India's share in segments of the software services industry.

India's market share, though still low, exceeds the share of the U.S. market claimed by any other country. Although revenue per employee has risen from $16,000 in 1990 to $33,000 in 2003 (see Table 8.3), it is far behind the U.S.

242   average revenue per employee of $142,000.[104] This differential suggests that India's market share ought to rise, with the pace likely to quicken following upon the reforms in telecommunications and venture capital.

A key issue is the future of applications development in the value chain. Just as system maintenance has lost significance, will applications development go the same way, either due to automation or the development of products that are as good? Applications development has been losing global market share to consulting and is thus slipping down the value chain. However, since information is a source of competitive advantage it is unlikely that customized applications work will disappear. The Indian industry could try to move to more complex activities, taking on larger projects or doing such work as engineering services, integration, and managed services.[105] This seems likely.

How able is this industry to move with the times? Table 8.8 shows that it has done so with a constant lag of nearly a decade as compared with the United States, at least up to 1990. As U.S. firms moved ahead, Indian firms followed. Given the severe infrastructural constraints that were in place up to about 2000, particularly in the field of telecommunications, staying no more than a decade behind the United States was a remarkable achievement.

Table 8.8 shows that, at least until 1990, Indian firms kept their relative position in a rapidly evolving value chain. However, there has been a change since 1991. Consulting and systems integration work was negligible up to 2003, even though it was the principal work of U.S. firms in the 1990s. The difference was probably due to the shortage of domain skills in India, arising from the globally noncompetitive character of its industries until the late 1990s, itself due to state protection until 1991. For example, a competitive insurance industry dates only to the late 1990s. Before then, there were only SOEs, so Indian workers by 2003 lacked consulting and integration skills. Probably only in banking does India have global-quality skills. Outside of programming and remote project management, skills in such processes as automating benefits processing were missing.

However, since the late 1990s, domestic industries with the same level of competence as those in the United States have emerged in a wide range of sectors, such as insurance, telecommunications, financial services, automotive, consumer electronics, and media. The larger Indian software firms have also set up large overseas operations. This should lead to more sophisticated work. Better financial and telecommunications infrastructures will help. We expect that the follower-leader relationship will reestablish itself, probably rapidly.

In conclusion, we have argued that the services business will continue to grow, based on low labor costs and innovative management with a focus still

TABLE 8.8

Comparing Work Done in United States and India During the Same Time Period

Work Type	United States		India	
	More Complex	Less Complex	More Complex	Less Complex
Up to 1970	In-house IT support (mainly conversion work)	O/S, software support for IT firm		EDP
1971–1980	Applications programs and EDP	In-house IT support	In-house IT support (mainly conversion work); EDP	O/S, software support for global IT firms
1981–1990	Systems integration (hardware with systems) and EDP	Applications and O/S programs; Unix conversion work	Off-site conversion work and applications development; in-house product development by MNEs	On-site conversion work and applications development
1991–2003	Consulting, systems integration (software), managed services	Applications programs, web services	Large applications development projects; engineering services; web services; inhouse product development by MNEs	On-site conversion (including Y2K) work, website maintenance

NOTES:

1. The U.S. columns exclude work done by U.S. product developers as this was not significant to India—note that it shows up as the lowest ranked work by dollars spent from 1981 onward.

2. "In-house IT" refers to work given by non-IT firms which had their in-house IT departments. Examples of such work are system maintenance and conversion of client applications software to new operating systems and platforms.

3. O/S (operating system), software support for IT firm refers to work given by software companies to outsourcers.

4. The table's cells in some cases present multiple kinds of work done. These have been ordered by dollars spent. For example, in 1981–1990, in the more complex category for India, off-site conversion work was the largest segment of the business, followed by off-site applications development and in-house product development by MNEs.

244   on developing applications. A shift to higher-end work is underway. The supplies of labor, telecommunications, and venture capital are likely to decide the future of product development.

Telecommunications

Until 1991, the year of general liberalization, the state provided telecommunications services. At the time of NCP-1984, there were 2.95 million telephone lines[106] for a population of 751 million,[107] implying a teledensity of 0.4 lines per 100 persons. In April 1986, the Rajiv Gandhi government had created a national mission to improve telecommunications, called Mission: Better Communications.[108] It sought to bring modern management techniques to the public sector phone company. Furthermore, customer equipment (handsets and office switchboards) could be made by the private sector. These modest liberalizations had a correspondingly modest effect, as the number of telephone lines installed between 1985 and 1990 grew by 55.8 percent to 4.6 million lines compared with a 42.7 percent growth between 1980 and 1985, with teledensity rising to 0.56.

A second round of liberalizations began in 1991, which enabled the private sector to provide cellular services and to make exchange-level equipment. The state kept a monopoly over wireline and international services. This produced little private sector investment[109] because the reforms left in place high upfront fees and a noncompetitive interconnection regime with the wireline service provider and failed to appoint a regulator to manage the incumbent, state-owned monopoly.[110] Private wirelines were licensed in 1994, but with no regulation over the incumbent ones, there was little action. However, the public sector continued to invest. The number of telephone lines grew more strongly to 9.8 million lines by 1995, a growth of 113.5 percent over 1990, raising teledensity to 1.06. By the year 2000, the number of wirelines had grown to 26.6 million, a growth of 271 percent, with teledensity rising to 2.68.

Private wireline services began in earnest only after the New Telecom Policy was instituted in 1999.[111] As of 2002, there were 0.5 million private wirelines, 1.3 percent of the national total of 38.3 million,[112] and the sector was finally well structured and regulated.[113] The private sector's share is likely to increase substantially.[114]

Before the 1999 reforms, Indian telecom costs were high relative to international ones. This forced software firms in India to do less online work, such as remote database maintenance, and more offline work, such as programming applications. It could also have influenced Indian firms to do more work on the clients' site. The greatly improved infrastructure since 2001 has been accompanied by globally competitive costs.

This improvement has been key for the Indian software services industry. Almost all the programming part of applications projects has been done in India since 2002; often work is done from programmers' remote locations using databases located at clients' sites (usually for security reasons). This has cut costs substantially and has opened up new areas of business, such as quality assurance, web services, and database management and maintenance.

Venture Capital

The venture capital industry began in 1988 with World Bank help. Four state-owned funds were set up with an initial capital investment of $45 million.[115] The rules were restrictive. Funds could be promoted by banks, large financial institutions, or private investors, but the last of these could own no more than 20 percent of the fund management company. Investment per firm was limited to Rs. 100 million ($7.7 million). Most restrictive were rules for investments:

- The recipient firm had to have technology that was "new, relatively untried, very closely held or being taken from pilot to commercial stage, or which incorporated some significant improvement over the existing ones in India."
- Its line of work had to belong to a pre-specified list of approved areas.
- Each investment had to be pre-approved by one of two government-sponsored development banks to ensure that it fit the guidelines.
- The Controller of Capital Issues had to approve every line of business that the venture capitalist wished to invest in.

In return, the venture capital fund was accorded some modest advantages, specifically, a tax on capital gains that was set at the individual tax rate on capital gains (the standard corporate rate was higher). However, tax pass-through was not allowed; as a result, a double tax was paid by investors.

No figures are available on the first four firms, but they seem to have done poorly as a group.[116] Their portfolios were usually well diversified with software issues claiming a negligible proportion. These firms were like private equity funds, set up to provide passive investments as part of a diversified portfolio.[117]

In 1992, the government allowed foreign firms to set up shell operations in Mauritius and use them to invest in India, thereby obtaining tax exemptions. Some foreign venture capital firms responded. As tax-exempt investment firms, they did not have to declare their intention to invest venture capital (this was needed only for those wanting tax benefits). Hence, they escaped the restrictions put on domestic venture capital firms. However, the foreign funds

TABLE 8.9

Top 8 Software Firms in India as of 2000 and Source of External Risk Capital

Firm	Sources of External Risk Capital between Founding and Year 2000
TCS	Parent funding
Infosys	Promoters' capital and IPO (1993)
Wipro	Parent funding and IPO (2001)
Satyam	Promoters' capital and U.S. IPO (1992)
HCL	Promoters' capital and IPO (1999)
Silverline	Promoters' capital and IPO
Cognizant	Parent (MNE) funding
NIIT	Parent funding and IPO (1985c)

SOURCE: Nasscom (2002) and corporate websites.

chose not to invest in services outsourcing [118] and looked for software product developers, of which there were few. This probably reflected their experiences at home. For example, the largest fund up to 1995, the Draper India Fund, was founded by a successful venture capitalist in Silicon Valley, Bill Draper, with a record of investing in product companies. Most of its capital ended up not being invested in India, because there were few opportunities. The fund invested mostly in Indian-founded start-ups in Silicon Valley and had a good track record. [119]

The total invested by all venture capital firms between 1988 and 1999 amounted to only $350 million. None of the leading eight firms among India's software exporters, as of 2000, was funded by a venture capital firm, as Table 8.9 shows. The venture capital industry by 1999 was considered to be an unqualified failure.

The government, keen to encourage venture capital investment in technology firms, began reforms in 1999 leading up to legislation in 2000. The new laws sought to globalize the industry. For example, all venture capital firms receive full tax pass-through of returns to final investors and full repatriation of profits overseas; they are unrestricted on their investment portfolios and on timing for divestment. Employees in portfolio companies are allowed to have stock options. These changes put the rules more on par with countries such as the United States. [120]

The changes had an immediate impact. In 2000, $1.16 billion was invested, of which $71 million was invested in computer software firms, $576 million in Internet-related start-ups, $98 million in semiconductors and hardware, and $94 million in communications and media. Thus, the IT industry received $840 million, 72 percent of the total, although software received only 6.2 percent. Due to the Internet bubble, which was happening at the time, firms offering web content dominated IT industry investment. With the bursting of the bubble in 2000, total venture capital invested fell in 2001 to $908 million, of which the IT sector received $703.6 million, or 77 percent of the total, with most in communications networks. The software sector received $45 million, or 5 percent of the total.[121]

In a survey conducted in 2001, software firms reported little dependence on venture capital.[122] Until 1999, this was partly attributable to restrictive rules. Financial backing for such leading firms as Wipro and TCS came from their parent companies. Others raised funds through stock market listings after they became profitable (see Table 8.11).

Fortunately, by 1991 the software industry had a good enough record that profitable firms could raise money through IPOs, the most prominent of these being Infosys, listed in 1993. Had the rules been changed earlier, a larger software industry would likely have developed. Global venture capitalists could have helped with the remote project management model, accessing clients and moving up the value chain.

The role of the venture capital industry is likely to increase, because it is needed for firms to move up the complexity chain of services, especially in engineering services, other consulting, systems integration, and web services and managed services, as well as for product development by start-ups.

Clusters: The Case of Bangalore

In 1998, of the leading 500 software firms in India, 104 were located in Mumbai and 97 in Bangalore.[123] Bangalore's importance had grown while Mumbai's had fallen. Software firms in Bangalore made a quarter of the country's exports as of 2000.[124] As Table 8.7 shows, the top eight exporters in 2000 were located in Bangalore (2), Mumbai (2), Delhi (2), Hyderabad (1), and Chennai (1). In 1980, none of the top eight exporters (see Table 8.7) were located in Bangalore, and only TI was in the top eight in 1990. By contrast, Mumbai firms made up seven of the top eight firms in 1980 and in 1990.

Bangalore's entrepreneurial history may have helped. Although it has ancient roots, its dominant architecture and governance structure is that of a colonial city. It is India's fourth-largest city with a population of 4.3 million.[125] It began as a center for textile production in the 19th century. In the early 20th century, a number of SOEs were set up by the colonial government. Some defense establishments were located in Bangalore by the British, because it was far from theaters of war during WW II. Its relatively cool climate and physical charms (it is called India's Garden City, an appellation it once deserved) helped bring these industries to the city.

248   After independence, the central government put several public-sector research and production facilities there, including those in the defense and
communications industry, such as ITI and BEL (see Table 8.3).[126] As of 1991,
the five largest SOEs employed 81,000 persons. Small-scale textiles and the
public sector, however, have the most jobs.[127]

One scholar has attributed Bangalore's growth as a center for software to the
Indian Institute of Science (IIS), noting that "the Bangalore cluster was seeded
by the establishment, decades earlier, of the elite Indian Institute of Sciences
as well as a number of the largest and most prestigious public sector enterprises
in fields such as electronics, aeronautics and machine tools."[128] The IIS was
established in 1909.[129] Most of its post-independence graduates and research
were directed toward the public sector. Some of this, if indirectly and probably minimally, helped Bangalore's development in IT.[130] The most prominent
success to emerge from IIS was Wipro.[131]

Bangalore's location enabled it to tap into the largest pool of educated engineers in India. The four southern states — Karnataka, Tamil Nadu, Andhra
Pradesh, and Kerala — together have 308 engineering colleges with a capacity
of 82,597 students, or 52 percent of India's total.

Unlike Mumbai and Delhi, with histories of labor militancy, Bangalore
had small companies, including some in textiles that were relatively free of
union troubles. According to Heitzman, this made it attractive to software-
exporting firms, since union troubles might be particularly disastrous to their
operations.[132]

Despite Bangalore's evident advantages, survey results tend to be less positive about it relative to other locations in India. For example, in a recent survey, Akella and Dossani find that Bangalore scores slightly above average for
small firms only in certain advanced labor skills, such as in remote project
management and advanced domain knowledge, but scores poorly on some
other key factors, such as infrastructure and regulatory and tariff barriers.[133]

A more recent Nasscom survey is even more critical of Bangalore.[134] The
Nasscom report noted that elements of Bangalore's infrastructure, especially
power and telecommunications, were not keeping pace with the IT industry's
expansion. While the government promises uninterrupted power supply, the
reality is far removed, and many ITES (IT enabled services) firms have to
maintain their own back-up power systems, thus raising costs. It also noted that
the city's public transport infrastructure is "very weak."

Bangalore's poor infrastructure is linked to its long history of poor public
planning. It took several decades to develop a city plan, during which time the
city grew more or less uncontrollably with, among other things, a severe impact on traffic congestion. Several agencies, such as the Housing Board and

the Electricity Board, had intractable bureaucracies.[135] Meanwhile, political turmoil due to national events led to the state's having three chief ministers between 1994 and 1999, during which time little was done to improve the civic infrastructure. The situation has improved ever since political stability returned to the state in 1999, but it will take years for the infrastructure to reach global levels.[136]

Relative to Mumbai, though, Bangalore fares well. Bangalore scores over Mumbai in climate, real estate costs, and, in the early days, data connectivity. (Mumbai, however, has several advantages such as in financial institutions, an international airport, supply of labor, academic connections,[137] legal and accounting infrastructure, and marketing and sales skills.) What mattered most, though, in 1985, when TI chose Bangalore, was its superior bandwidth. It planned to do in-house work and so did not need Mumbai's accountants and marketers. TI was instead greatly influenced by the government's decision concerning the Software Technology Park (STP) system, started in Bangalore in 1985.[138] STP was set up to offer satellite bandwidth to software exporters, primarily to overcome the deficiencies of the Department of Telecommunications.[139] The next big MNE was ANZ bank, which arrived in 1989 to make software for the bank's internal use. The relatively advanced data communications infrastructure also helped to attract Infosys and Wipro from their original locations in Pune and Mumbai in the mid-1980s.

The importance of TI's decision in 1985 was not only the demonstration of an MNE voting with its feet, it also showed the industry a new and more profitable way of doing business. Its satellite link to the United States allowed programmers to work in India on a real-time basis for the first time.[140] This was quickly copied by Indian firms that set up operations in Bangalore, notably Wipro[141] and Infosys.

TI's establishment in Bangalore also preceded a turning point in the domestic IT industry. Indian firms until then had been body shopping. In the mid-1980s, work shifted to applications programming on a project basis, due to the U-W standard, which made it possible to do programming remotely. Several new firms were set up to provide such services. They, too, preferred Bangalore's availability of general skills and bandwidth and were undeterred by the shortage of domain knowledge. However, the leading firms, notably TCS, which specialized in financial services, continued to find Mumbai more attractive.

It is likely that Bangalore's advantages and disadvantages induced growth in a particular direction. Since it lacked a strong venture capital industry, the firms that entered were large, well-funded ones that mainly needed bandwidth. They could also afford their own power supplies, thus overcoming another key disadvantage of Bangalore. On the other hand, start-ups, which

250   typically need venture capital, lawyers, and other soft infrastructure and also could not afford back-up power, did not go to Bangalore during the early days.

By 2003, the data communications infrastructure was no longer superior in Bangalore. This suggests that other clusters might arise if they have particular strengths. For example, Pune has strengths in biotechnology that might lead to such a cluster. However, Bangalore now has higher earnings per employee than other locations in India, possibly due to agglomeration economies.[142] In a recent survey of 52 software firms in Bangalore, almost 50 percent cited its high-technology professionals and research institutes as the most important reason for their decision to locate there.[143] The emergent managed-services sector, notably back-office processing and call centers, is concentrated in Bangalore, Mumbai, and Delhi. While Delhi and Mumbai have more call centers (neutral accents are often said to be the reason), Bangalore has more back-office work from MNEs. In addition, research work done by MNEs is typically located in Bangalore. For example, GE has its call center business in Delhi and Hyderabad, while its research division is in Bangalore. Intel and IBM have likewise put their research divisions there.

The Supply of Labor

India's growth in software employment is impressive, as shown in Table 8.10.

However, quality may be a problem. Over a third of the IT labor force appears to lack a CS/EE degree.[144] Data from Nasscom show worse numbers, with only 27.12 percent having an undergraduate or graduate degree in computer sciences or electrical engineering.[145]

This limitation seems to stem from India's poor educational policy.[146] The central government is the main financier of tertiary education. While it has greatly expanded the university system, quality is poor, and that appears to have deterred enrollment. According to a government report, "obsolescence of facilities and infrastructure are experienced in many institutions . . . the IT infrastructure and the use of IT in technical institutions is woefully inadequate . . . the barest minimum laboratory facilities are available in many of the institutions and very little research activity is undertaken . . . engineering institutes have not succeeded in developing strong linkages with industry . . . the curriculum offered is outdated and does not meet the needs of the labor market."[147] There were 247 universities and 11,549 colleges in India in 1999. Still, as of 1997, only 7 percent of the eligible population had attended university.[148]

As a result, India has 0.3 scientists and technicians per 1,000 population, ranking 42 out of 62 countries ranked by the World Bank in 1998, below China at 1.3 (ranked 25) and Ireland at 2.0 (ranked 20).[149] Further, the interaction

TABLE 8.10

Employment in the Software Industry in India and the United States

Country	1980	1985	1990	1995	2000	1990s Annual Growth Rate (%)
India	250	2,500	14,500	50,000	182,000	26
United States	304,300	541,500	771,900	1,089,900	2,104,700	13

NOTES:

1. Employment includes exports and domestic work, but excludes IT enabled services.

2. U.S. data source: www.bls.gov, /detailed statistics / national employment hours and earnings for series ID EEU 80737001 (computer and data processing services).

3. Indian data source: Heeks, op. cit., p. 93 for 1980–1995, and Nasscom (2002), op. cit., for 2000 data.

4. The employment of software professionals was 288,000 in 2003, of whom 260,000 were employed in the exporting sector, according to Nasscom estimates. Nasscom (2004), op. cit., p. 186.

between university and industry is minimal. There are few academia-industry research partnerships and few consultancy assignments for faculty from industry. For example, at IIT Delhi, the value of sponsored research and consultancy assignments in 1998 was only $4.5 million.[150]

Very little independent research has been done, partly because until recently, faculty (even at the IITs) have not been expected to do research. According to Nasscom, "Over the years, there has been a general decline in the quality of faculty in Indian universities."[151] The average number of citations over a five-year period for the average faculty member at the Indian Institutes of Technology is less than three. This compares with 45 per faculty member at MIT and 52 per faculty member at Stanford University.[152] The country produces only 300 master's degree graduates and 25 PhDs in computer sciences each year, compared with U.S. numbers of 10,000 and 800, respectively.[153]

Another obstacle to university-industry interaction is restrictive rules. For example, one of India's leading management institute's policy on consulting is that "Consultancy is an academic activity. Projects are taken up only if they have a definite learning value. Faculty members do not solicit consultancy projects. The total time spent on consulting is voluntarily restricted, so that other academic responsibilities are met."[154] Further, faculty is required to share consulting revenue with the university. (The extent to which these rules are obeyed is another matter.)

The central government's initiatives to improve technical education include creating centers of excellence through a focused effort on improving infrastructure and manpower in a few institutions. It hopes that this approach will succeed and will create a "spread effect" through linkages with other institutions.

252   Some states, notably Karnataka, Andhra Pradesh, Tamil Nadu, and Maharashtra allow private colleges. These can get government support provided at least 50 percent of the students pay full fees. Due to excess demand, the first institutions set up under these policies have typically offered undergraduate degree courses; though believed to be of poor quality,[155] they at least offer students better alternatives.

In 1998, the government tried to help the IT sector by setting up Indian Institutes of Information Technology (IIIT) in partnership with industry. For example, IIIT in Hyderabad (recently renamed the International Institute of Information Technology) is sponsored by, among others, IBM, Microsoft, and Oracle.[156] IIIT in Bangalore is sponsored, among others, by Infosys and ICICI.[157] However, given that their graduates have begun to enter the workplace only since 2001, their impact is as yet unknown.

Role of the Diaspora

The global Indian diaspora, consisting of nonresident Indians (NRI), is about 20 million.[158] However, only a very small proportion is in the global IT industry. For example, there are probably no more than 30,000 engineers of Indian origin in Silicon Valley.[159]

The efforts of NRIs in helping India's software industry fall into five categories: Those who returned either (1) as employees of MNEs, or (2) to start a firm or work in a startup; (3) those who stayed overseas and helped their employer's entry by taking responsibility for such a project, or (4) funded domestic firms, including start-ups, or (5) introduced their employer (typically a non-IT firm in the Fortune 2000) to an Indian software supplier. The relative importance of these roles is shown in Table 8.11.

The pattern suggests a modest contribution by NRIs overall. Diaspora members played a role in seeding and staffing MNEs that arrived in the mid-1980s. Although neither TI's decision to enter India nor that of the ANZ Bank seems to have been fostered by the diaspora,[160] the operations of HP, Novell, and IBM were started by NRIs, some of whom temporarily relocated to India for the purpose.[161] Nevertheless, the impact of NRIs has been small, at least up to 1990. Then, as Indian software firms expanded their markets beyond the Fortune 500 to the Fortune 2000 in the 1990s, some had NRIs in sufficiently senior positions to introduce Indian firms to their employers. This was particularly true in the financial sector.[162]

Their investment in India as a group is small, an estimated $160 million annually, or 4 percent of the total annual foreign investment in India.[163]

TABLE 8.11

Role of NRIs in India's Software Industry

Years	Prime Driver of Industry's Growth	Returned as MNE Employees	Facilitated MNE Employer's Establishment in India	Returned to Start Own Firms	Venture Investors into India	Introducers of Indian Firms to Their U.S.-Based Employer
1970–1980	Domestic firms		Negligible			
1981–1990	MNEs	3	1	Negligible		2
1991–1995	Domestic firms	3	2	4	Negligible	1
1996–2003	Domestic firms	3	2	5	4	1

SOURCE: Author's compilation based on interviews.
NOTES: Cells show ranking of the five roles.

TABLE 8.12

Proportions of Engineers from Silicon Valley
Who Have Invested in Start-ups at Home

Response	PRC	Taiwan	India
Yes, more than once	4.7	11.5	9.7
Yes, only once	6.3	4.4	12.5
Never	89.0	84.1	77.7

SOURCE: R. Dossani, "Chinese and Indian Engineers and Their Networks in Silicon Valley," Working Paper, Asia/Pacific Research Center, Stanford University, March 2002.

NOTES: Table based on primary survey of 1,556 engineers born in the PRC, Taiwan, or India and living in Silicon Valley.

Indians—similar to Taiwanese and PRC-born persons—have not invested much in start-ups in their countries of birth as shown in Table 8.12. This might reflect their having better opportunities in Silicon Valley or the difficulty in building up networks overseas.

NRIs also played no significant role in providing venture finance during the mid-1990s[164] because of restrictive rules. After the 1999 reform of the venture capital rules and coincident with their increasing wealth in the United States during the Internet boom, it became more attractive for NRIs to invest in start-ups in India. This is likely to grow in significance.

It is unlikely that the role of NRIs will match that of the overseas Chinese in China, though it may be less needed. Their numbers are smaller,[165] social connections are less relevant in India than in China due to India's stronger rule of law and related institutions, and the regulatory environment in India is more liberal.

India's success in software services is remarkable, real, and sustained. There is a remarkable follower-leader relationship between the United States and India that appears to be unique among services. While India's work is not (yet) innovative, its management has been, for which the credit belongs to the firms that pioneered the remote management of service projects. The role of the state was initially hostile, but this began to change after 1984. However, the impact of the changes was slow, particularly in telecommunications and venture capital. Educational policy has yet to benefit the sector.

Private entrepreneurship has been the key. It enabled the industry to establish itself under adverse state control in the 1970s, it pioneered new ways of managing the business after the modest liberalizations of the 1980s, and it helped it thrive when the shackles were removed in the 1990s. Meanwhile, it managed with a workforce of mediocre (though improving) quality, benefiting from the poor alternative opportunities available for the best talents at home.

Now, the industry has some powerful, sustainable advantages. Outsourcing of customized software remains a growth industry, entering its fourth consecutive decade. Clusters such as Bangalore exist. The telecommunications and venture capital industries are finally taking off. Only poor education puts its growth at some risk because of poor quality. Together, these considerations should lead to more innovative work, led perhaps by MNEs doing R&D and software product start-ups, as in Israel in the 1980s, more likely by moving up the value chain in software services with the follower-leader relationship replaced by one based on being a high-value member of the supply chain.

NOTES

1. Nasscom (2004), pp. 21, 29.
2. Nasscom (2004), p. 186.
3. Nasscom (2004), p. 186. There is no reliable estimate of the number of persons employed in the U.S. IT services industry. Hence, we have used the following: (1) Census data on NAICS industry code 54151. This comprises establishments primarily engaged in providing expertise in the field of information technologies through one or more of the following activities: (a) writing, modifying, testing, and supporting software to meet the needs of a particular customer; (b) planning and designing computer systems that integrate computer hardware, software, and communications technologies; (c) onsite management and operation of clients' computer systems and/or data processing facilities; and (d) other professional and technical computer-related advice and services. The latest available data is for 1997, when the industry employed 764,659

employees and had average revenue per employee of $142,500 (http://www.census.gov/
epcd/ec97brdg/E97B1541.HTM#5415). Current numbers for industry leaders, such as
IBM, EDS, and Accenture, range from $155,000 to $240,000 (Dossani 2003, 1). We
shall use $142,500 as the current average for the entire industry. (2) The U.S. software
services industry generated $163 billion in IT service spending in 2003 (Nasscom 2004,
21). Assuming average revenue per employee of $142,500, the number of employees is
estimated at 1.14 million. (3) Martin and Lowell (2001, 7), estimate that the IT sector
employed between 1.5 million and 2.2 million people in 2000. This includes hardware
and those in software product development, which is smaller than the software services
sector (see Table 8.5.) and probably has a higher revenue per employee. The 1.14 million number may, therefore, be an overestimate, but we shall use this number in the
absence of better information.

4. Nasscom (2003), p. 42. This figure includes business process outsourcing (BPO)
exports due to lack of availability of data on software services only.

5. Nasscom (2004), pp. 29–30. This figure includes BPO exports due to lack of availability of data on software services only.

6. Nasscom (2004), p. 27.

7. We shall use the term value chain to denote activities ordered by firm-specific
value addition per employee — that is, excluding indirect value addition that may occur
outside the firm; the term "supply chain" denotes activities that must occur in a particular sequence. Thus, the supply chain in software services (as shown in Table 8.7.)
consists of consulting, programming, and integration, whereas the value chain is, in de-
scending order, consulting, integration, and programming. Note that the supply chain
is does not change over time, while the value chain may change.

8. The risk chain orders activities by risk of the expected revenue. Subcontracting
labor time (body shopping) is the least risky, followed by hardware and software deployment and support, IT training and education, applications development, system
integration, and consulting and product development (see Table 8.7. for definitions).

9. Some scholars have been puzzled at the origins. For instance, Desai (2003) remarks that "The early stages of the body-shopping market are now lost in obscurity"
(Section III).

10. For example, Arora and Athreye state that, "The initial growth of the software
service industry in India was facilitated by the enlightened 'hands off' policies of the
government of India." "The Software Industry and India's Economics Development,"
Information Economics and Policy, 2002, Section 2.

11. Notwithstanding the establishment of the Indian Institutes of Technology and similar institutes, in 1998 India had 0.3 scientists and technicians per 1,000 population, ranking 42 out of 62 countries ranked by the World Bank, below China at 1.3 (ranked 25) and
Ireland at 2.0 (ranked 20). World Development Indicators, http://wbln0018.worldbank
.org/psd/compete.nsf/f14ea5988b0eec7f852564900068cbfd?OpenView&Start=1.

12. Although no longer dominant, TCS remains India's largest IT firm.

13. We define offshoring as the production of goods and services for export back to
the home country. A multinational may also set up operations in a new country and
sell the products within that country, which is the localization of manufacturing.
India's software business may be described as offshored outsourcing, since the work is

256   typically outsourced to an independent firm located in India. Ireland's software industry is a hybrid case of offshoring and localization: United States–based firms set up software operations in Ireland to create products and services for nearby markets in Europe.

14. Stephen E. Siwek and Harold W. Furchtgott-Roth, *International Trade in Computer Software*, Westport, CT: Quorum Books, 1993, pp. 93–94.

15. Siwek and Furchtgott-Roth focus their explanation on customer requirements and speed to market. Intellectual property protection may also be a factor. Other authors have noted the difficulty in communicating internal information remotely (tacit knowledge). See J. Cantwell and G. D. Santangelo, "The Frontier of International Technology Networks: Sourcing Abroad the Most Highly Tacit Capabilities," *Information Economics and Policy*, 11(1), 1999, pp. 104. Others have commented that offshoring operations might not lead to delays but can reduce them.

16. S. Torrisi, "Software Clusters in Emerging Regions," working paper, October 2002, p. 17.

17. Torrisi, op. cit., p. 18. Also Ashish Arora, Alfonso Gambardella, and Salvatore Torrisi, "In the Footsteps of Silicon Valley: Indian and Irish Software in the International Division of Labor," working paper, Stanford Institute for Economic Policy Research, June 2001.

18. Arora et al., op. cit., p. 7. By contrast, in India, only 15–20 percent of the work is estimated to be done by MNEs, although that situation was different up to 1990 (p. 7). Note that, according to Enterprise Ireland, the official state web site, http://www.nsd .ie/htm/ssii/stat.htm, Irish-owned companies generated about 11 percent of software exports, the rest coming from MNEs in 2002.

19. Torrisi, op. cit., p. 18.

20. However, the IT industry was dominated by hardware manufacturing for the domestic defense industry through the 1970s and the 1980s.

21. Morris Teubal, "The Indian Software Industry from an Israeli Perspective: A Microeconomic and Policy Analysis," *Science, Technology and Society*, New Delhi: Sage, 2002, pp. 151–187.

22. Torrisi, op. cit., p. 3.

23. Torrisi, op. cit., p. 9.

24. Torrisi, op. cit., p. 18. This is consistent with data showing that the number of software patents from Israel has grown rapidly (Rowen 2003).

25. B. R. Rubin, "Economic Liberalization and the Indian State," *Third World Quarterly* 7(4), 1985, pp. 942–957.

26. This section draws on work by Eswaran Sridharan, *The Political Economy of Industrial Promotion: Indian, Brazilian and Korean Electronics in Comparative Perspective, 1969–1994*," Westport, CT: Praeger, 1996. As an aside, Sridharan has a novel explanation for India's obsession with public sector–led development, arguing that it grew out of India's defeat in the Indo-China War in 1962 over land disputes along the Himalayan border. After the war, Indian policy makers were convinced that rapid industrial growth was needed to protect the country against future threats and that only the public sector could mobilize the resources and skills that were needed.

27. Even IC design during that period was primarily a hardware-related activity.

28. The Foreign Exchange Regulation Act of 1973 (FERA-1973) required foreign-owned firms that ran domestic businesses to reduce foreign ownership to 40 percent through divestment or additional capital-raising (privately or through public offerings). After failing to negotiate a compromise with the government, IBM chose, in 1978, to withdraw from India rather than divest. When it withdrew, CMC was awarded the monopoly of servicing IBM's installed base of mainframes in India.

29. There were some successes, such as the rural branch exchange developed by the Center for the Development of Telematics. It is still the mainstay of public sector-provided rural telephone service in India, although exports and sales to private firms within India are believed to be limited, thus raising the question of its real viability.

30. Sridharan, op. cit., p. 140, and http://www.meadev.nic.in/science/elec.htm, December 3, 2002.

31. Sridharan, op. cit., p. 139.

32. From 1991, when India reformed, the idea of public-sector champions began to lose favor among policy makers and no new initiatives have taken place since then.

33. This was, apparently, the only privately owned mainframe in India at the time (Ramadorai 2003).

34. Under FERA-1973, foreign firms could also be publicly listed in Indian markets, but the foreign ownership was not allowed to exceed 40 percent.

35. Another large firm, ICL, a British firm, converted to a joint venture, ICIM, taking a 40 percent stake.

36. S. Ramadorai (2003).

37. TCS CEO F. C. Kohli, often termed the "father of the Indian IT industry," is credited with initiating TCS's exports. This included betting the firm on a mainframe in 1969.

38. A better term might have been "mind shopping" since presumably that was the facility that was being shopped.

39. In an industry first, TCS opened a New York sales office in 1979. According to Ramadorai, obtaining state approval to do so was a major exercise, as the government did not see the logic for such an expense.

40. Interestingly, TCS's parent, the Tatas, later formed another joint venture with Burroughs for doing similar work as TCS, though in a separately incorporated firm, Tata Burroughs Limited. This happened because Burroughs, observing TCS's success in doing work for its own clients, asked TCS in 1978 to join with it to form a joint venture that would provide software services to overseas clients. The Tatas, however, decided not to do so through TCS as it sensed a wider market than doing work for Burroughs only and so wanted TCS to remain "hardware independent." This made good commercial sense because of the rapidly growing market share of IBM in global markets. But an agreement to jointly start an independent competing firm was made. Tata Burroughs Limited (later called Tata Unisys Limited and, still later, Tata Infotech Limited) grew to become the second-largest software services firm after TCS (and retained that position till 1995). It is remarkable that the Tatas created joint ventures in overlapping periods of time with Burroughs/Unisys, IBM, and Honeywell. This was probably as much of a tribute to the reputation of the Tatas as to the shortage of credible joint venture partners in pre-reform India.

41. Richard Heeks, *India's Software Industry*, New Delhi: Sage, 1996, p. 88.

42. R. Naqvi, personal interview, October 1, 2003.

43. Datamatics, a joint venture with Wang, was founded by Kanodia after he left TCS. Kanodia had returned to India after completing his PhD in engineering from MIT. DEIL, a joint venture of Digital and Hinditron, was founded by Hemant Sonawala, who had been educated at the University of Washington and had founded Hinditron in 1966. PCS was founded in 1978 by Narendra Patni after he had completed his graduate studies at MIT (his undergraduate degree was from the Regional Engineering College at Rourkee, India). Finally, Mahindra-BT was a joint venture between a leading industrial family, the Mahindras, and British Telecom. The Mahindra family promoter was Anand Mahindra, a graduate of Harvard College and Harvard Business School.

44. Heeks, p. 88.

45. Siwek and Furchtgott-Roth, op. cit., p. 140.

46. Most other industries required an industrial license that was given based on the state's forecast of demand.

47. Heeks, op. cit., pp. 44–45.

48. Parathasarathy (2000). Parathasarathy gives an example of intrusive behavior prior to the 1990 liberalizations: the Intelligence Bureau posted a person at TI's Bangalore office to check samples of data being sent.

49. This made the domestic market for software development even less attractive.

50. Later, a small set of database management platforms (introduced toward the end of the 1980s and the early 1990s) further simplified the writing of applications software. These were sold by Sybase, Oracle, and IBM in the early days.

51. Suresh Kumar, Head, ADM Practice, TCS, personal communication, November 29, 2002.

52. Phaneesh Murthy, personal interview, November 30, 2001.

53. The initial activity of TI India was the development and support of proprietary electronic design automation (EDA) software systems used for integrated circuit (IC) design by TI's semiconductor design centers worldwide. This activity includes development of applications for creating, simulating, testing, and verifying both logical and physical IC manufacturing processes. http://www.ti.com/asia/docs/india/Company-Profile.htm, downloaded January 2, 2003.

54. HP entered in 1989.

55. Nasscom (1999) and Nasscom (2002), p. 28. The shift to offsite work would probably have been faster if the telecommunications infrastructure had been better. This was not to happen until the late 1990s.

56. The rise in the number of new firms explains the decline in average revenue per firm after NCP-1984. Since revenue per employee is steady, it suggests that the work being done by the different firms was similar.

57. Infosys, established in 1981, moved from Pune to Bangalore, while Wipro, established in 1980, a Mumbai-headquartered firm, shifted its corporate headquarters to Bangalore after its software division had been established there. Wipro Chairman Azim Premji has noted that cheaper real estate and a better civic infrastructure were also important factors, although in a 2003 interview, he bemoaned that the civic infrastructure had weakened considerably to the point where it was becoming a disadvantage for Bangalore.

58. The two Tata firms at the top of the league alone accounted for 45 percent of the industry's revenue (Heeks, p. 88).

59. Heeks, p. 216.

60. With the exception of programming and remote project management skills.

61. However, most firms usually had just one client and so were vulnerable to that client's fortunes and disposition. According to Heeks (p. 84), two-thirds of the typical firm's exports were to a single U.S. client during the period from 1989–1990 to 1994–1995.

62. These were, in order, a subsidiary of Citibank, Datamatics (joint venture with Wang), Texas Instruments, Digital, PCS (joint venture with Data General), and Mahindra-BT (joint venture. with British Telecom). Heeks, ibid., p. 89.

63. It is interesting to speculate who would have done well in such a case. Israel would probably have been more important than it already is. But, most likely, we believe that products would have been developed closer to markets, as is the case with PC-based applications. The product developers might have contracted out parts of the work to Indian software developers. In such a case, the Indian software industry would have taken on a different character. It would have served the U.S. software industry, rather than — as it currently does — serving U.S. banks and other end users of software. In this way, it would have been more like Taiwan's PC components industry, whose end-products mostly serve the needs of U.S. computer firms. Thus, it would have reverted back to its role in the early days when TI set up shop in India.

64. S. Ramadorai, CEO, TCS, personal communication with author, November 19, 2002.

65. Heeks, op. cit., p. 49

66. Finance Minister Yashwant Sinha's Budget Speech, Section 115, March 2000, published by the Ministry of Finance.

67. www.sebi.gov.in

68. Phaneesh Murthy, op. cit.

69. Variously termed overseas development centers or offshore development centers (ODCs). Note that this marked a return to the less sophisticated business model of body shopping, though taking place offsite.

70. Instead of requiring a specific industrial license from the Ministry of Industry, they needed an approval from the Foreign Investment Promotion Board; the former took at least a year to obtain, the latter took typically less than a week. V. Joshi, *India's Economic Reforms 1991–2001*, New Delhi: South Asia Books, 1999.

71. The Tata group later disinvested in 1999.http://www.ibm.com/in/ibm/history.html, downloaded December 6, 2002. As of the end of 2002, IBM employed 4,373 persons in India. http://www.ibm.com/in/ibm/qfacts.html#IN.

72. http://www.eds.com/india/india_profile_history.shtml, downloaded December 9, 2002.

73. http://www.accenture.com/xd/xd.asp?it=enweb&xd=locations\india\delivery _centre.xml, downloaded December 9, 2002.

74. Patibandla and Petersen (2002).

75. Nasscom (2003), pp. 43, 138.

76. Wipro was a late starter. It had begun in 1980 as a hardware firm but entered software in 1985 by linking up with a U.S. marketing firm to sell a packaged software

260   Instaplan project management package in the United States. It apparently sold about 30,000 copies (Heeks 1996, 80). Its move to software services began shortly thereafter as it sought to emulate the TCS model, and it had become the second-largest Indian software firm by 2001 (Nasscom 2002, 35).

77. Infosys, the third-largest firm, began in 1981 by selling domestic software and opened a U.S. office in 1987 (www.infy.com 120402), seeking, like Wipro, to emulate the TCS model.

78. http://www.ti.com/asia/docs/india/about_tii.html, downloaded September 11, 2003.

79. http://www.oracle.com/in/corporate/index.html?content.html, downloaded September 11, 2003.

80. The top 10 product developers ranked by numbers of employees are Oracle, HP, Motorola, ST Microelectronics, TI, Intel, i2, Cisco, Robert Bosch, and Huawei. Nasscom (2003), p. 43.

81. Nasscom (2002), p. 28. Figures are for the period 2001–2002.

82. The Y2K problem was a mainframe computer problem arising from the high cost of computer memory in the 1950s and 1960s. To save memory, databases used two digits rather than four to identify a particular year. This was not a problem until 1999, but it would have been a major concern from 2000 onward, when "00" would be understood as 1900 rather than 2000. Solving the Y2K problem required reprogramming old financial and other date-sensitive software and created employment opportunities for thousands of Unix-skilled programmers worldwide.

83. Phaneesh Murthy , personal interview, 2002.

84. Y2K work was the conversion of old applications and operating systems software that had originally been created with a two-digit year field into a four-digit date field. This was needed since, in the year 2000, the software would otherwise have recognized the year 2000 (entered as "00") as the year 1900. The logic for originally creating a two-digit date field was not due to thoughtlessness but to high memory costs during the times when the old software programs had been first written. According to an industry participant who was part of the original software programming in the late 1970s, "We all knew that there would be a problem come the year 2000; but memory was so costly that we made a conscious decision to create a two-digit field." (Abhay Kale, ex-employee of TCS, personal interview, December 2000).

85. Personal interview with Azim Premji, Chairman, Wipro, June 30, 1999. Wipro was one of the firms that initially rejected such work on the grounds that it was incompatible with their mission. It later regretted this when it became clear that the opportunity was substantial; in Premji's words, "Wipro missed the Y2K bus."

86. Anthony P. D'Costa," Software Outsourcing and Development Policy Implications: An Indian Perspective," *International Journal of Technology Management*, 24(7/8), 2002, pp. 705–723.

87. D'Costa, op. cit., p. 705.

88. S. Ramadorai, personal communication, 2002.

89. Schware, op. cit., p. 144.

90. J. Whitman, "Key Factors for Software Success," unpublished manuscript, Oakland Group, Cambridge, MA, December 26, 1990, quoted in Schware, op. cit., p. 148.

91. Correa, op. cit., p. 174.

92. Siwek and Furchtgott-Roth, op. cit., p. 140.

93. Edward Yourdon, *Decline and Fall of the American Programmer*, Englewood Cliffs, NJ: Yourdon Press, Prentice-Hall, 1992, p. 1.

94. Yourdon, op. cit., p. 299.

95. Arora and Athreye (2003).

96. So, incidentally, did start-ups become important in product development, although this is not relevant for India.

97. According to Intel's India president, Ketan Sampat, its Bangalore R&D staff are engaged in "engineering challenges as complex as any other project on the planet." (*Economist*, April 3, 2004).

98. Kripalani and Engardio (2003).

99. *Economist*, April 3 2004.

100. *Economist*, April 3 2004.

101. Porter (2004).

102. K. Ananth Krishnan (2003).

103. Dossani and Kenney (2004).

104. U.S. Census data, http://www.census.gov/epcd/ec97brdg/E97B1541.HTM #5415.

105. Integration is subject to similar concerns, having lost market share over time.

106. R. Balashankar, *Golden Era of Telecommunications 1947–1997*, Department of Telecommunications, 1998, p. 31. Figures are for 1995.

107. *Statistical Outline of India*, published by Tata Services, Mumbai, 1992–1993, p. 40.

108. Balashankar, op. cit., p. 32.

109. R. Dossani, 2002. *Telecommunications Reforms in India*, Westport, CT: Greenwood Press, p. 3.

110. Due to policy confusions and overly optimistic bids by eager providers, even cellular services were not launched until a shift to a revenue-sharing regime in 1999.

111. These included a revenue-sharing regime that replaced the up-front fees bid earlier.

112. www.trai.gov.in/consultbasicpapertrend.htm December 6, 2002.

113. See *Telecommunications Reform in India*, R. Dossani, ed., Westport, CT: Greenwood Books, 2002.

114. For example, a single company, Reliance Infocomm, planned to offer services to 1.2 million commercial buildings with fiber to the office by December 2003 (notes from meeting with Prakash Bajpai, President, Reliance Infocomm, November 20, 2002). Also, as of mid-2003, India was expected to end the year with about 70 million telephone connections, including wireless connections.

115. R. Dossani and M. Kenney, p. 240.

116. R. Dossani and M. Kenney.

117. R. Dossani and M. Kenney.

118. Infosys, for example, was refused funds by the largest fund at the time, TDICI. R. Dossani and M. Kenney, "Creating an Environment for Venture Capital in India," *World Development*, 30(2), 2002, pp. 227–253.

262   119. Personal interview with Bill Draper, September 13, 2004.

120. There were still some restrictions, such as on the issuance of preference shares and control of the board of the investee company. See R. Dossani and M. Kenney (2002).

121. *Indian Venture Capital Association Yearbook*, 2001, pp. 22–23.

122. R. Akella and R. Dossani, "The Software Value Chain," unpublished manuscript, 2002.

123. http://www.nasscom.org, quoted in P. Ghemawat, "The Indian Software Industry at the Millennium," Harvard Business School, Case 9-700-036, 2000, p. 19.

124. V. N. Balasubramanyam and A. Balasubramanyam, in John H. Dunning, ed., *Regions, Globalization and the Knowledge-Based Economy*, 2000, OUP, p. 350.

125. http://www.censusindia.net/results/millioncities.html

126. According to Balasubramanyam et al., op. cit., p. 351, these high-technology SOEs were located in Bangalore because of its educational and scientific resources and its strategic location away from the borders of India.

127. James Heitzman, "Corporate Strategy and Planning in the Science City: Bangalore as 'Silicon Valley,'" *Economic and Political Weekly of India*, January 30, 1999, pp. 1–2.

128. Ghemawat, op. cit., p. 11.

129. The IIS was started at the initiative of J. N. Tata, the founder of the Tata group. At his request, the Royal Society of London sent Sir William Ramsay, Nobel Laureate, to tour India and suggest a location. Sir William recommended Bangalore. http://www.iisc.ernet.in/about, downloaded December 35, 2002.

130. For example, according to Heitzman, op. cit., p. 5, one of the earliest IT firms in Bangalore was Namtech, started by the son of the CEO of ITI in 1985–1986, KPP Nambiar. The son, P. S. Nambiar, started Namtech in 1984 first for marketing gas discharge tube surge arrestors for telecommunications equipment (sold to DOT) and later for manufacturing the product under license from a French firm, CITEL.

131. Wipro was seeded in IIS by a group of engineers working under Ashok Soota, an academic at IIS (S. Parthasarathy, CEO of Aztec, personal interview, March 2003), and financed by Wipro.

132. Heitzman, op. cit., p. 6.

133. Akella and Dossani, op. cit.

134. http://www.nasscom.org/artdisplay.asp?art_id=1367, downloaded January 7, 2003, report dated August 6, 2002.

135. Heitzman, op. cit., p. 19.

136. Bangalore allows the visitor the odd experience of motoring down nearly unmotorable roads to the campuses of firms such as Infosys and Wipro, and disappearing into a five-star environment once inside. However, there are onsite back-up generators designed to supply twice the amount of power needed — once to back up the regular failure of the municipal power supply and once to back up the first back-up system.

137. Even though Wipro's growth came out of the Indian Institute of Science.

138. www.soft.net, December 25, 2002 and personal communication of the author with B. V. Naidu, Managing Director, STPI Bangalore, August 15, 2003. Naidu related that the Rajiv Gandhi government was able to get TI to come to Bangalore on the

promise that satellite connectivity would be available by a certain date. Because STPI lacked funds, TI even purchased the ground equipment for satellite connectivity at its cost and then leased it to STPI. At several points, TI threatened to leave the project because the promised date was unlikely to be met. It was met, finally, with connectivity being provided to TI on the last day of the contract deadline.

139. Naidu communication, August 15, 2003.

140. Earlier, code was transmitted via hard media (floppies, tape drives).

141. Wipro's shift to Bangalore coincided with its shift to developing software from being a hardware company previously.

142. Akella and Dossani, op. cit.

143. S. Srinivas (1997), "The Information Technology Industry in Bangalore: A Case of Urban Competitiveness in India?" Paper presented at the Fifth Asian Urbanization Conference, London, quoted in Balasubramanyam et al., op. cit., p. 351.

144. Akella and Dossani, op. cit.

145. A. Parthasarathi and K. J. Joseph, "Limits to Innovation in India's ICT Sector," *Science, Technology and Society* 7(1), 2002, p. 20, quoting Nasscom data for 2000.

146. India spent 3.2 percent of GDP on education in 1999, compared with 2.3 percent in China. *Statistical Outline of India*, 2001–2002, p. 243.

147. Ministry of Human Resource Development, "Technical Education Quality Improvement Project of the Government of India," October 29, 2001, Sections 2.1.2–2.1.6.

148. Nasscom, op. cit., p. 78.

149. World Development Indicators. http://wbln0018.worldbank.org/psd/compete.nsf/f14ea5988b0eec7f852564900068cbfd?OpenView&Start=1.

150. A. Parthasarathi and K. J. Joseph, op. cit., p. 32.

151. Nasscom, (2002), op. cit., p. 73.

152. Nasscom, (2002), op. cit., p. 73.

153. Ministry of HRD, op. cit., Section 2.1.12. This is despite excess capacity; only 50 percent of the seats are filled.

154. Indian Institute of Management. http://www.iimahd.ernet.in/acads/acadsmain.htm, downloaded January 8, 2003.

155. Ministry of HRD, op. cit., Section 2.1.19.

156. Nasscom (2002), op. cit., p. 79.

157. http://www.iiitb.ac.in/Management.htm, downloaded January 7, 2003.

158. Indian Express, http://www.indianexpress.com/full_story.php?content_id=16354, downloaded January 9, 2003.

159. The figure of 30,000 is a guesstimate, as there are no reliable numbers. But it is a likely overestimate. Here are two calculations: (1) according to the U.S. Government Census of 2001, there were 66,741 persons of Indian origin resident in Santa Clara Valley, or 3.97 percent of the total population. By comparison, there were 115,781 Chinese, or 6.9 percent of the total population. http://factfinder.census.gov/bf/_lang=en_vt_name=DEC_2000_SF1_U_DP1_geo_id=05000US06085.html, downloaded January 12, 2003. There were 170,113 persons employed in the professional services and information industry in Santa Clara County, which encompasses Silicon Valley (http://censtats.census.gov/data/CA/05006085.pdf#page=3, downloaded January 9, 2003). Therefore, it is unlikely that more than 30,000 (or 45 percent of the Indian population)

Indians work in the software industry. (2) The quoted number of 170,113 might not be a correct estimate of the number of software workers because (1) many manufacturing operations contain a high percentage of workers who develop software and (2) the figure of 170,113 includes all professional services, such as legal and financial services. Assuming that the percentage of software in IT manufacturing is as high as 50 percent, we turn to 2000 data, the census for Santa Clara County http://www.census.gov/epcd/cbp/map/00data/06/06085.txt, downloaded January 9, 2003. The employment recorded under North American Industry Classification System (NAICS) code 5415 (computer systems design and related services, including custom programming and systems design) was 46,836 workers, code 333295 (semiconductor machinery manufacturing) had 7,383 workers, code 334 (computer and electronic product manufacturing) had 125,916 workers, and code 5417 (scientific R&D services) had 13,204 workers, for an adjusted software total of 118,903 workers. Since this is less than the base number of 170,113, the conclusion about the total remains.

160. ANZ Bank's decision to open operations in India was the result of a promise made by Will Bailey, an executive of the bank, to then Prime Minister Rajiv Gandhi that his bank would reimburse India in return for permission to acquire Grindlays Bank's operations in India. Heitzman, op. cit., p. 13.

161. These were Radha Basu (HP), Kanwal Rekhi (Novell), and Kailash Joshi (IBM).

162. S. Ramadorai (2001), op. cit.

163. Indian Express, op. cit. By contrast, the overseas Chinese are believed to estimate much larger sums being returned to China.

164. Bill Draper's India fund commenced operations in 1995 in Bangalore (http://www.draperintl.com/history.htm, downloaded January 13, 2003). It had a number of passive NRI investors, including Exelan founder Kanwal Rekhi.

165. Some NRIs are located near India, such as in the Gulf countries, but these are relatively inactive in the field of software development.

REFERENCES

Akella, R., and R. Dossani. 2001. "A Report on the Software Value Chain: The Indian Suppliers during the Downturn." Working paper, Asia-Pacific Research Center, Stanford University.

Arora, A., and S. Athreye. 2002. "The Software Industry and India's Economic Development." *Information Economics and Policy* 14(2):253–273.

Arora, A., A. Gambardella, and S. Torrisi. 2001. "In the Footsteps of Silicon Valley: Indian and Irish Software in the International Division of Labor." Working paper, Stanford Institute for Economic Policy Research.

Athreye, S. 2002. "The Indian Software Industry." Working paper, Open University.

———. 2003. "The Indian Software Industry and Its Evolving Service Capability." Working paper, Open University.

Balasubramanyam, V., and A. Balasubramanyam. 2000. "The Software Cluster in Bangalore." In J. Dunning, ed. *Regions, Globalization and Knowledge-Based Economy.* Oxford, UK: Oxford University Press, pp. 349–363.

Basant, R. 2002. "Knowledge Flows and Industrial Clusters: An Analytical Review of the Literature." Working paper, Indian Institute of Ahmedabad.

Bresnahan, T., and A. Gambardella, eds. 2004. *Building High-Tech Clusters: Silicon* **265** *Valley and Beyond.* Cambridge, UK: Cambridge University Press.

Bresnahan, T., A. Gambardella, A. Saxenian, and S. Wallsten. 2001. " 'Old Economy' Inputs for 'New Economy' Outcomes: Cluster Formation in the New Silicon Valley." Discussion Paper 00-043, Stanford Institute for Economic Policy Research (SIEPR).

Carr, N. 2003. "IT Doesn't Matter." *Harvard Business Review* (May): 41–49.

Caso, E., and S. Kohler. 1998. "India: The Next Silicon Valley?" BT Alex Brown Research.

Correa, C. 1996. "Strategies for Software Exports from Developing Countries." *World Development* 24(1):171–182.

D'Costa, A. 2000. "Technology Leapfrogging: The Software Challenge in India." In Conceicao et al., eds. *Knowledge for Inclusive Development.* Westport, CT: Quorum Books.

———. 2002. "Export Growth and Path Dependence: The Locking-in of Innovations in the Software Industry." *Science, Technology and Society* 7(1):51–87.

———. 2002. "Software Outsourcing and Development Policy Implications: An Indian Perspective." *International Journal of Technology Management* 24(7/8):705–723.

Dedrick, J., and K. Kraemer. 1993. "Information Technology in India: The Quest for Self-Reliance." *Asian Survey* 33(5).

Desai, A. 2003. "The Dynamics of the Indian Information Technology Industry." Working paper, London Business School.

Dossani, R., ed. 2002. *Telecommunications in India.* Westport, CT: Greenwood Books.

Dossani, R., and M. Kenney. 2002. "Creating an Environment for Venture Capital in India." *World Development* 30(2):227–253.

———. 2003. "Lift and Shift: Moving the Back Office to India." *Information Technology and International Development* 1(2):21–37.

Economist. 2004. "Innovative India." April 3, pp. 65–66.

Gadrey, J., and F. Gallouj. 1998. "The Provider-Customer Interface in Business and Professional Services." *Services Industries Journal* 18(2):1–15.

Ghemawat, P. 2000. "The Indian Software Industry at the Millennium." Case 9-700-036, Harvard Business School.

Handler, M. 2002. "Bust in Bangalore." *San Francisco Chronicle*, April 1.

Heeks, R. 1996. *India's Software Industry.* New Delhi: Sage.

Heitzman, J. 1999. "Corporate Strategy and Planning in the Science City: Bangalore as Silicon Valley." *Economic and Political Weekly* (January 30).

Indian Express. 2003. Retrieved January 9, 2003, from http://www.indianexpress.com/full_story.php?content_id=16354.

Indian Institute of Management. 2003. Retrieved January 8, 2003, from http://www.iimahd.ernet.in/acads/acadsmain.htm.

IT Workforce. 1999. "Assessing the Demand for Information Technology Workers, IT Workforce." Arlington, VA: National Science Foundation.

Kelkar, V., D. Chaturvedi, and M. Dar. 1991. "India's Information Economy: Role, Size and Scope." *Economic and Political Weekly* (September 14): 2153–2160.

Kripalani, M., and P. Engardio. 2003. "The Rise of India." *Business Week* (December 8): 66–76.

266   Lateef, A. 1997. "Linking Up with the Global Economy: A Case Study of Bangalore's Software Industry." Retrieved May 20, 2002, from www.ilo.org.

Ministry of Human Resource Development. 2001. "Technical Education Quality Improvement Project of the Government of India." Sections 2.1.2–2.1.6.

Naidu, B.V. 2002. Personal interview with the author.

Nair, J. 2002. "Singapore Is Not Bangalore's Destiny." *Economic and Political Weekly* (April 29). Retrieved May 30, 2002, from www.epw.org.in.

Nasscom. 2002. *Strategic Review*. New Delhi: Author.

———. 2004. *Strategic Review*. New Delhi: Author.

Parathasarathy, B. 2000. "Globalization and Agglomeration in Newly Industrializing Countries: The State and the Information Technology Industry in Bangalore, India." PhD Thesis, University of California, Berkeley.

Park, A. 2003. "EDS: What Went Wrong." *Business Week* (April 7): 60–63.

Patibandla, M., and B. Petersen. 2002. "Role of Transnational Corporations in the Evolution of a High-Tech Industry: The Case of India's Software Industry." *World Development* 30(9):1561–1577.

Porter, E. 2004. "Indian Techies Lack Creative Ability, Feel US Firms." *New York Times*, April 29.

Porter, M. E. 1998. "Clusters and the New Economics of Competition." *Harvard Business Review* (November–December): 77–90.

Ramadorai, S. 2003. Personal interview with the author.

Rubin, B. R. 1985. "Economic Liberalization and the India State." *Third World Quarterly* 7(4):942–957.

Schware, R. 1992. "Software Industry Entry Strategies for Developing Countries: A 'Walking on Two Legs' Proposition." *World Development* 20(2):143–164.

Siwek, S. E., and H. W. Furchtgott-Roth. 1993. *International Trade in Computer Software*. Westport, CT: Quorum Books.

Srinivas, S. 1997. "The Information Technology Industry in Bangalore: A Case of Urban Competitiveness in India?" Paper presented at the Fifth Asian Urbanization Conference, London.

Teubal, M. 2002. "The Indian Software Industry from an Israeli Perspective: A Microeconomic and Policy Analysis." *Science, Technology and Society*. New Delhi: Sage.

Torrisi, S. 2002. "Software Clusters in Emerging Regions." Working paper, University of Camerino.

Tschang, F., A. Amsden, and S. Sadagopan. 2003. "Measuring Technological Upgrading in the Indian Software Industry: A Framework of R&D Capabilities and Business Models." Working paper, Asian Development Bank Institute.

Viswanathan,V. 2001. "Wipro's Offsprings." *Business World* 12:38–45.

Whitman, J. 1990. "Key Factors for Software Success." Unpublished manuscript, Oakland Group, Cambridge, MA.

World Development Indicators. http://wbln0018.worldbank.org/psd/compete.nsf/f14ea5988b0eec7f852564900068cbfd?OpenView&Start=1.

Yourdon, E. 1992. *Decline and Fall of the American Programmer*. Englewood Cliffs, NJ: Yourdon Press, Prentice-Hall.

IV   SOME COMMON THEMES

9

HOW GOVERNMENTS SHAPED THEIR
IT INDUSTRIES

Henry S. Rowen

Why has Korea become a leader in online games? Why have Taiwan and South Korea become important world leaders in the making of computer chips? Why has Singapore become a leading maker of hard disk drives? Why is Beijing the software center of China and why is Shanghai emerging as the integrated circuit center? What has led to Japan's becoming a major source of advanced information technology products without creating new companies?

The answer to each of these questions is decisions by governments, or more accurately, behavior resulting from interactions among governments and private enterprises — combined with some institutional legacies. These interactions have created competencies that differ among regions. This chapter addresses the different strategies Asian governments have adopted that have strongly influenced such outcomes as these.

THE MANY WAYS GOVERNMENTS INFLUENCE THEIR INDUSTRIES

Governments, inevitably, influence their industrial structures. They do so both indirectly and directly. They do so indirectly through actions that, intentionally or not, foster institutions that affect behavior throughout the economy and directly through policies that favor certain sectors.

Indirect actions include those affecting the rule of law (including protection of intellectual property), investments in general education; macroeconomic policies (taxing and spending, inflation); development of financial institutions (banks, stock markets); state versus private ownership of enterprises; regulation of business (formation of firms, anti-trust policies, bankruptcy

270   laws); labor markets, including labor mobility (laws, pension systems, immigration); degrees of openness to trade and foreign direct investment; corruption; investments in public infrastructure; rules regarding university-industry linkages; and more. In the aggregate this set profoundly affects the ways things work in a given country.

Direct actions regarding an industry, in this case, regarding information technology (IT), include tariff and non-tariff barriers to trade in its products, policies on the ability of foreigners to invest directly in this sector, government spending on research and development, subsidized finance, tax treatment, education in science and engineering, creation of dedicated research institutes, the creation of high tech parks (often with subsidized land), and incentives for skilled expatriates to return. Such actions in support of the IT industry have been taken widely throughout the world, not least in Asia.

Adherence to international agreements, such as membership in the World Trade Organization (WTO), limits the use of some policy instruments. Thus, the Chinese policy of rebating value-added taxes to domestic producers of integrated circuits was dropped out of concern that a WTO suit would be brought. Nonetheless, governments still have an abundant supply of instruments with which to support favorite industries and individual companies.

As a point of reference consider some policies adopted by the U.S. government regarding the IT industry. These include federal government support for basic research in solid-state physics, opto-electronics, and computer sciences (including support for what became the Internet). Specific types of products receiving support have included display technologies, semiconductor manufacturing equipment (via the Sematech consortium), and dynamic random access memory (DRAM). (Supportive actions regarding DRAMs entailed a restriction on trade imposed on Japan during the 1980s.) Not all these actions have succeeded; the display venture failed, and the DRAM restriction was much criticized because it raised costs to users. Support for the sciences and basic technologies is widely seen to be warranted on the grounds that these are public goods undersupplied by the market, whereas products are best decided by the market. (This view leaves open the tricky question of how the pioneering of new industries is to be encouraged.)

With the goal of promoting competition, antitrust actions have been taken *against* U.S. IT companies, notably against IBM, requiring it to license the transistor to anyone who would pay $25,000 and requiring it to allow unbundled sales of hardware and software. More recently, antitrust action was taken against Microsoft. It can be argued that such measures on the whole have strengthened the U.S. IT industry. In any case, similar actions have not been taken by Asian governments.

The economic historian, Alexander Gerschenkron, made a seminal contribution with his thesis that state intervention could enable backward states to catch up with the advanced ones. He pointed to government's role through large banks in France and Germany. Japan's development in the late 19th and early 20th centuries was attributed by Ohkawa and Rosovsky largely to the opening of its economy, technology assimilation from abroad, a high rate of capital formation (promoted by the state), and an elastic supply of labor (Ohkawa and Rosovsky 1973). For the post–World War II period, Chalmers Johnson and Ronald Dore gave much credit for Japan's stellar performance to a single ministry, the Ministry of International Trade and Industry (MITI) (Johnson 1982; Dore 1986). However, claims for the singular importance of MITI have come under criticism (Okimoto 1990).

Similar claims for the role of the state versus the market in the rapid growth of the East Asian "Tigers" (especially Korea and Taiwan) were made by several scholars of whom perhaps the most prominent were Alice Amsden and Robert Wade (Amsden 1989; Wade 1990). Their argument was that government microinterventions in the form of industrial policies were largely responsible for the successes of those countries.

In the early 1990s, the World Bank entered this debate with a report on the East Asian "miracle" (which did not include China) (World Bank 1993). It addressed the sources of the remarkable economic successes of the high-performing Asian economies between 1965 and 1990. It concluded that rapid capital accumulation was a crucial contributor and that this accumulation came largely from making banks more reliable and governments' efforts in encouraging high levels of domestic savings. Another major contributor was universal primary schooling and improved primary and secondary education, which quickly increased their skilled labor forces. There were also productive agricultural programs, low levels of taxation, reduced distortions in prices, and foreign investments that introduced technology and brought cooperation between governments and private companies. In short, although the roles of governments were crucial, the report gave much weight to the operations of the market.

Critics (e.g., Amsden and Wade) argued that the report seriously underestimated the contribution of these governments' microinterventions in the market, those that bore the label "industrial policies." There were no serious disagreements about the facts of such policies, but there was disagreement regarding their contribution to growth.

272   Fuel was added to the fire by Paul Krugman with an article that argued that the high growth rates of several Asian countries, notably Singapore, were largely the result of massive accumulations of capital, not improvements in the efficiency in the use of resources across the economy (Krugman 1994). Krugman wrote,

> The remarkable record of East Asian growth has been matched by input growth so rapid that Asian economic growth, incredibly, ceases to be a mystery. . . . It has become common to assert that East Asian economic success demonstrates the fallacy of our traditional laissez-faire approach to economic policy and that the growth of these economies shows the effectiveness of sophisticated industrial policies and selective protectionism . . . if Asian success reflects the benefits of strategic trade and industrial policies, those benefits should surely be manifested in an unusual and impressive rate of growth in the efficiency of the economy. And there is no sign of such exceptional efficiency growth.

A decade later, more is known about what worked well and what did not. It is fair to say that a large contributor to the rapid growth of many of these countries was (human and physical) factor accumulation rather than skillful industrial policies. In the case of Japan, its performance during the 1990s was so disappointing that questions increasingly were asked about its economic strategy. By the end of the 1990s, its government, long widely held to be the world's most accomplished practitioner of industrial policy, had begun to change course, not by 180 degrees but more than trivially. So, also as the result of the financial crisis of 1997–1998, has that of the Korean government. Overall, it appears that none of the countries/regions under discussion have become more microinterventionist but, instead, have shifted, modestly or more strongly, toward a larger role for markets.

THE ASIAN COUNTRIES' DEVELOPMENT CHALLENGES AND STRATEGIES

Circa 1970, all Asian countries were trying to catch up with the most developed ones. Many of their domestic institutions were distinctive, and they faced varied external conditions. These differences influenced their policies regarding the IT industry.

Their starting points were very different. Japan in 1970 was an industrialized country with a well-functioning economy, an effective bureaucracy, an impressive array of human and physical assets, a record of more than a century of modernization and a quarter-century of high-speed growth. The four Tigers (Korea, Taiwan, Hong Kong, and Singapore) still had low incomes (less so in Singapore) but were growing fast. China was still in the throes of the Cultural Revolution and had almost a decade to go before decisive reforms began. India, even poorer than China, was growing slowly, had a stultifying bureaucracy, a small stock of both human capital (measured by education) and physical assets, and an unpromising outlook. It had to wait 20 years for major economic liberalization to begin.

Another difference was in legacies from the past. It is not easy to draw the line here, but three instances should be mentioned. India had the colonial legacy of the rule of law (one shared by others of these regions to various degrees but not including China) and of English speaking that gave it an edge not only in software but also in learning modern management techniques. Another was the far-flung Chinese diaspora, whose members have a decided advantage in language and family ties in doing business in greater China. A third was the already developed state of Japanese economic institutions.

There were also huge differences in population size. At one end was Singapore with 2 million people in 1970, and at the other were India with 500 million and China with 800 million. These size differences affected the possibilities of coherent, top-down policies. They were easier to implement in tiny Singapore and modest-sized Taiwan and Korea than in mammoth China and India. Size differences also influenced strategies. Small countries have to learn how to compete internationally if they are to succeed. So do large poor ones whose markets initially are also small, but their governments are more easily — and wrongly — tempted to choose autarkic policies.

Key institutions included those of politics, law, and finance. On politics, China was communist and India was socialist (with the difference that private enterprise was illegal in China and disfavored in India). Neither was capable of sustained economic progress, including in the IT industry, until fundamental changes occurred in their economic systems.

Japan. The overarching goal of Japan's postwar leaders was catching up with the United States as quickly as possible. It chose to guide its enterprises "administratively" to this end, preserving in modified form the economic control system introduced during World War II. Finance, labor laws and practices, and foreign trade and investment were all oriented to the support of these firms. What resulted was an internally consistent system of education, finance, labor, trade, foreign investment policy, and tax laws that enabled its established companies to renew themselves. There was little room in this system for foreign firms or for newly formed (at least high-tech) ones. For many years, the Japanese model of government-directed and privately implemented industrial policy was widely seen in East Asia as the model to emulate. However, the economic stagnation of the 1990s caused that model to fall from favor.

South Korea. Many Korean institutions are similar to those of Japan. Its company groups, chaebol, have been likened to prewar Japanese zaibatsu companies, large and powerful. They were protected against foreign competition

274   both from imports and direct investments, and were given preferential access to
imports and to finance. For many years, heavy and chemical industries were favored, with the government giving directions to firms regarding the products
they were allowed to export and import. Korean companies learned much, and
some became world-class and increasingly invested in research. Samsung is the
most successful non-Japanese Asian company to have established an international brand name. There was also little place in the Korean system for new entrepreneurial high-tech companies.

Taiwan. The institutions of the Republic of China were brought to Taiwan
from the mainland in 1949. Until the process of political liberalizing began in
the 1970s, it had authoritarian rule under the Kuomintang Party. Especially
early, but continuing to this day, the government exerts a strong influence over
industry. It initially selected chemicals, consumer goods, and electronics products and later computer components and the assembly of computers. The government adopted the first four-year economic plan in 1953 to develop low-tech
labor-intensive industries, such as textiles, plywood making, and home appliances. In the 1970s, it promoted the making of television sets with selected foreign companies. From 1980, it promoted the IT industry. The state helps industry get technology from abroad, improves it, and spins off companies. In
the past, the companies did little research; their focus was on improving methods of manufacturing rather than on products.

Singapore, like India, inherited from Britain a functioning legal system.
Under effectively single-party rule, it created dominant government financial
institutions along with an economic strategy based largely on private enterprises. As pointed out by Wong, Singapore and Hong Kong were among the
first developing economies to adopt policies of free trade and movement of
capital and of welcoming foreign investment in export-oriented manufacturing. Both provided "business-friendly" environments through emphasizing
the rule of law, relatively clean and efficient government services, and stable
macroeconomic policies. However, the state played a much larger role in
Singapore than in Hong Kong (which remained a colony until 1997). Besides a near monopoly in social and physical infrastructural services, such
as public education and health-care, seaports and airports, telecommunications and public utilities, the Singaporean state was directly involved in many
sectors normally private through government-linked corporations in such
"strategic" industries as airlines, aerospace and defense manufacturing, and
telecommunications, as well as in banking, logistics services, shipbuilding,
construction, and food manufacturing. It also created the Central Provident
Fund, a compulsory wage-savings scheme and uses such policy instruments as
permanent residency and employment control, foreign workers' levy, and a

public scholarship system that draws the best students into public service and government-linked corporations. Furthermore, through its ownership of land and public housing the state influences property markets along with much else.

China. China's case is complex. It has made remarkable economic progress despite a weak rule of law, although it is making some gains on that front. For 25 years its government has progressively been giving a larger role to markets, investing in schooling, engaging actively in international trade, and welcoming direct foreign investment (on certain conditions). It is the destination for a large amount of such direct investment (totaling $60 billion in 2004). It is undergoing far-reaching changes in its economic institutions. With little privatization of state enterprises, the biggest changes have been the emergence of town and village collectives and private companies. In finance, stock markets and venture capital have become accepted institutions — but both are still underdeveloped. A significant step in the legitimization of capitalists was taken in 2000 with the adoption of Party Chairman Jiang Zemin's "Three Represents" formula, one of which enables them to be Party members.

India, in contrast, had the rule of law (albeit often working inefficiently and often corruptly) and the institutions of capitalism all along. Its problem was destructive government policies and stultifying bureaucracies. It underinvested in education and in physical infrastructure (and still does). It blocked trade and nearly kept out foreign direct investment altogether. It made slow economic progress until the mid-1980s and especially after the early 1990s, when it began to liberalize.

Dossani, in Chapter 8, disagrees with explanations that credit the government for its software industry successes.[1] "It initially was both a producer of IT services and a policy maker. It failed as a producer while also crowding out the private sector. Its policymaking was protectionist and statist until the mid-1980s; this, too, led to failures. Later, it removed controls, which obviously helped the industry, especially after aggressive pro-competition reforms in telecommunications and venture capital during the late 1990s. Education policy, however, remained generally negative."[2]

Given the fact that Asian governments acted extensively to shape their industries, how did they avoid the destructive "rent-seeking" (the awarding of privileges to selected private actors in exchange for various considerations) that deforms the economies of most less-developed countries? First, some did not. Such distortions have long been evident, notably in India and China. Second, because these are successful countries, evidently the costs of rent-seeking were more than offset by growth-positive factors. These positives include a sense in several of our societies of external dangers acute enough to make economic

276   success necessary for survival, an attitude that helped inspire social cohesion and discipline (notably in South Korea, Singapore, and Taiwan) (Rowen 1998). Other factors were at work. Japan, Korea, and Taiwan were under the influence of the United States with its liberal economic model for several decades; in any case, Japan was possessed of a national determination to come back after the disaster of World War II. China also had a consensus regarding the urgent necessity of returning to greatness after nearly two centuries of lagging behind the leaders.

All these governments came around to a neodevelopmental state view, one in which the state intervenes in the economy much more than is consistent with the neoclassical model but decidedly less than in a socialist model. Japan and Singapore succeeded in catching up, and the others are making good progress to this end. To continue this process, and especially to forge ahead, the direct role of the state — its microinterventions — will have to be further reduced. In fact, governments have been shifting toward indirect instruments: setting rules, providing infrastructure, and funding research while leaving operations increasingly to the private sector.

In the IT sector, and contrary to some of the literature on economic development that suggests there is one best way, these governments have adopted policies that differed in important ways. The vast disparity in levels of technology in 1970 between the developing Asian countries and the industrial ones implied that much learning was needed — and, sooner or later, much occurred. In the industries encompassing information technologies (IT) learning was not only about technologies but also about markets, modern management, and more.

STRATEGIES ADOPTED FOR THE IT SECTORS

Some industries are seen as very important and strategic, for reasons of national security, or because they are playing a vital role in the domestic economy, or because there are perceived export opportunities. The area of telecommunications has long widely been regarded as strategic, and the computer industry came to be regarded in the same way. (It helped that these technologies converged over time.) More recently, the biotechnology industry is widely seen as strategic as is the nascent nanotechnology industry.

Consumer electronics products such as calculators and digital watches were precursors of computers. They were good fits because they involved labor-intensive manufacturing in which the Asians had a cost advantage and their light weight made them cheap to transport. Computers had similar advantages. Demand was growing rapidly in the advanced countries, transport costs were low, and the modularization of supply chains enabled computer manufacturers to find segments in which to compete.

Strategies for the IT industry naturally fit within those for economic development in general. Although these varied substantially, there were important commonalities. All, except India, attached high importance to creating human capital (i.e., education) and physical capital. All their governments adopted policies that favored some industries over others. The IT industry came to be accorded high priority everywhere.

It made a large difference that the Asians were not trying to blaze paths into the unknown, as were many U.S. and European firms; instead, they were trying to stay current with technologies and types of products that were being defined elsewhere. Governments' roles were to help prepare inputs to the industry (labor, capital, technology), to remove obstacles, to buy some of the products they made, and to foster and protect domestic companies.

Acquiring Technologies

"For most countries, foreign sources of technology account for 90 percent or more of domestic productivity growth. The G-7 countries have carried out 84 percent of world research and development spending" (Keller 2004). Therefore, a crucial task was strengthening capacities to absorb advanced technologies — and in due course, to go beyond them. The emphasis was on industrial applications, although Japan invested in a wide swath of sciences, as have China and India on a smaller scale. Korea and Taiwan also invested substantially in technology development — investments that have recently produced a remarkable rise in patents registered in the United States.

There are many channels for acquiring technologies. Two main ones are trade in goods and foreign direct investment. The evidence is clear that direct investment is efficacious. The literature is less clear regarding trade, but it suggests that importing goods is more effective than exporting them (Keller 2004). Another much employed means was licensing technology from its foreign owners.

Still another mechanism is people with know-how moving from advanced industrial countries to less advanced ones. This has been important for some places, notably Taiwan, as well as other regions. This path recalls the role of the English workman, Samuel Slater, who moved to the United States in the 1790s, bearing the secrets of Arkwright's mechanical weaving frame and thereby helping to launch the nation's industrialization. Slater had to migrate secretly, but his latter-day counterparts move back and forth openly and — on the whole — are welcomed on both sides.

278   Technology cannot flow readily without certain conditions being satisfied. The ability to absorb complex technologies is helped if one is doing research on them; it enables one to understand better what one is seeking. There have to be organizations — research institutes, universities, and, above all, companies — staffed by competent scientists and engineers able to put them to use. There need to be markets on which these goods can be sold. Financial support must be available. All of this requires supportive government policies.

It turned out that governments had a large role in deciding where to do such research: universities, research institutes, or companies? The mix varied. Outside of Japan and then Korea in the 1990s, few Asian companies were capable of doing technically advanced work; in most places separate institutes were preferred rather than universities, because it was easier to focus them on commercially relevant projects. Thus, the Industrial Technology Research Institute (ITRI) in Hsinchu became the major research center of Taiwan, and Korea set up the Korean Institute for Science and Technology (KIST), although in Korea much research came to be done in its big companies, notably Samsung and LG. In China, the Chinese Academy of Sciences is the preeminent institution for scientific and technical research, and major companies have come out of it. Its universities have also assumed significant commercial roles with, for instance, Tsinghua and Beijing Universities each owning more than 200 companies.

Where most research is done in separate institutes, universities focus on teaching. This has been widely true and notably so in India. The Indian Institutes of Technology (IITs), the source of many excellent bachelor's degree engineers, have not been research centers; hence, many IIT graduates have gone to the United States for advanced degrees.

Much learning was also acquired by doing. The process by which firms in the United States, Europe, or Japan contracted for components or assembled products (via original equipment manufacturing) in Taiwan, Korea, and Singapore enabled the newcomers to learn skills not only in manufacturing but also about world markets. A similar process occurred with software in India.

Educating Scientists and Engineers

Even though the proportions in their populations are small, the absolute numbers of people in China and India with science and engineering degrees is large. India has 0.3 scientists and technicians per 1,000 population; it holds position 42 out of 62 countries ranked by the World Bank in 1998, below China at 1.3 (ranked 25), but that small Indian proportion still came to 300,000 people and the Chinese one to 1,600,000. However, it doesn't require having a large population to produce many scientists and engineers; Taiwan, with only 22 million people, graduates 80,000 a year compared with 100,000 in the United States.

The main fields are in electrical engineering and computer science along with chemistry and mechanical engineering, including solid-state physics, integrated circuits, optics, software-related algorithms, robotics, advanced manufacturing, and more.

A pattern that emerged first and strongly in Taiwan was for graduates in science and engineering to go to the United States for advanced degrees, stay to work, and then, for some, to return home.[3] At the Hsinchu Science-based Industrial Park in Taiwan, the number of "returned experts and scholars," many with advanced degrees, rose from 27 in 1983 to 4,300 in 2001, by which time they comprised 4.5 percent of the work force. (Some "returnees" had not originated in Taiwan but in other parts of greater China.) This pattern spread to other countries, notably India and China. In Zhongguancun Science Park in Beijing, in 2002, of 400,000 high-tech workers 5,800 had doctorates, 29,000 had master's, and 155,000 had bachelor's degrees. Only Japan did not participate strongly in this process.

In all of these countries, improvements in their universities are causing more students to stay at home for advanced training. The number of people graduating with PhDs in Korea increased three-fold from 1986 to 1999, in Taiwan it went up four-fold, and in China it increased by forty times (National Science Foundation 2002). The number of students from China, Korea, and Taiwan who have come to the United States for doctoral degrees peaked in the mid-1990s and declined thereafter. Worse, since the disaster of September 11, 2001, the U.S. government's restrictions on issuing visas has discouraged many students and scholars from going there while, at the same time, other countries are vigorously marketing their universities.

Support for "National Champions"

Governments favor not only specific industries, in this case IT, but sometimes specific companies as well. Governments found many ways to do this, including supporting research, favoring local producers in their purchases, erecting tariff and non-tariff barriers against imports, directing banks to lend to designated firms, excluding investments by foreign companies, supplying land at cheap rates, financing companies spun out of government laboratories, and more.

Perhaps the strongest expression of such support among Asian countries was in Korea, whose chaebol system consisted (and to a considerable extent

280   still does) of a set of government-favored companies — although some were recently allowed to go bankrupt by the Kim Dae-Jong government. In return for following government directives these companies received preferential financial support and protection from foreign competition. TSMC in Taiwan is another famous "national champion" company.

Such support is usually held to be justified by the "infant industry" argument that a potentially successful industry will never develop in the face of established competition without help from government. However, the record of governments supporting specific companies — national champions — is unimpressive. These companies have, in effect, soft budget constraints, meaning that they can get funding or protection from competition; hence, they are prone to poor performance. India's national champions have done poorly as have many of China's state-owned companies. Many of Korea's chaebol have folded since the economic crisis of 1997; while, in contrast, Taiwan's smaller-company and competitive structure has been more robust. (That Taiwan's IC foundries, UMC and TSMC, which came out of government laboratories, have done well is evidence that not all favored companies do poorly.)

Trade and Foreign Direct Investment

Engaging in trade and having foreign companies invest are two of the most effective ways to acquire technologies. None of the countries under discussion have adopted a laissez-faire strategy regarding trade and investment while, as we have seen, until the late 1970s China's trade was modest and until the mid-1980s, India was almost economically autarkic. Despite widely pervasive mercantilist attitudes, these countries had to import in order to export because at first (Japan excepted) they could do little more than make low-tech components and assemble finished products. The value added was low during the 1970s and into the 1980s (and still is in China), but these activities were educational and industries grew.

The perceived disadvantage of openness was that foreign competition would prevent local industries from developing and cause loss of control to outsiders of industries deemed strategic. The policy response was sometimes to protect them at the price of forgoing learning advantages by restricting imports and, even more, by restricting direct investment.

Faced with the choice of protecting nonexistent or weak domestic firms versus allowing foreign firms to invest, Singapore made inviting multinational companies (MNCs) central to its strategy. It selected companies that government bodies deemed would not only export but would also bring in advanced technology, which supplier industries would develop. (The computer disk drive industry was welcomed for these reasons.) Taiwan began by encouraging such companies, with some early arrivals from Japan and the United States plus Philips Electronics; then it later favored domestic companies. India was long hostile to all foreign firms and, notably, in the 1960s it drove IBM out of the country. However, Texas Instruments got established in Bangalore in the 1970s and helped seed that high-tech cluster. Japan and Korea remained hostile to MNC investment well into the 1990s; they favored the alternative of licensing foreign technology. During the 1990s, China allowed MNCs in on a large scale, usually on condition that they bring advanced technology. Acquiring technology and business know-how from abroad via direct investment has become a key element of its strategy.[4]

Telecommunications Investments

Decisions by governments to invest heavily in telecommunications along with advances in their technologies greatly helped the diffusion of the IT industry. It is hard to imagine India's software services sector progressing as far as it did without the large decline in international telecommunications prices that has occurred. The adoption of cell phone technology in China, now with 350 million users, along with parallel large investments in fixed lines, is having profound economic and social consequences. Korea is the most broadband "wired" country in the world, and Japan is fast catching up.

This surge in telecommunications puts some Asian countries in a position to lead in new services and technologies. Korea and Japan are ahead in online gaming. China has been trying to establish its own mobile communications standard—a move that has been deferred because of objections by foreign firms and governments—but this story is not over. With growth in their markets and, especially, if they bring new technologies to the table, the influence of Asian countries will grow in the setting of global standards.

Financial Institutions and Industry Structure

Kenney, Han, and Tanaka, in Chapter 10 on venture capital, assert that this institution as known in the United States has barely existed in Asia outside of Taiwan. Asian financial institutions, predominantly banks, favored well-connected and established companies. Thus, Japan created the keiretsu main bank system; Korea the chaebol conglomerates; under government instruction, banks in China supported companies spun out of the Academy of Sciences and leading universities; Taiwanese banks supported companies with links to government research institutes; and government-linked companies in Singapore got preferential treatment.

282 There wasn't much room in several of these systems for young, high-tech firms lacking personal connections. Risk capital of the type needed by such companies — equity — was in short supply. Some companies got started by established firms investing in the new field of computers. Others started in a traditional way, by using entrepreneurs' savings and depending on support by family and friends. Taiwan was an early mover in recognizing the need for organized risk capital, and others followed during the 1990s, but even now the venture capital sector is widely underdeveloped. Its most developed part consists of venture capital arms of established companies that make strategic investments in start-ups.

A key instrument in many governments' IT strategies has been financial subsidies, often bank loans on favorable terms as with Korean government subsidies in the 1980s to Samsung, LG, and Hyundai to enter the DRAM business (Leachman and Leachman 2004). In addition, pioneering companies in the Zhongguancun cluster received financial aid with the support of Beijing's local government.

Different financial policies and institutions were associated with — and reinforced — different industrial structures that were largely financed by banks that were, in turn, responsive to government policies. Japan already had large and medium-sized companies, many of which moved into IT. (Sony was unusual in being a new entrant after World War II.) Korea's path was similar. Samsung began as a grain-trading company in the 1930s, then diversified into construction and many other industries including consumer electronics, before becoming a major IT company. In contrast, Taiwan's IT industry was long dominated by small, agile firms and Singapore's by large foreign ones. With the main exception of Tata Consulting Services (TCS), India's software industry consists mostly of companies created during the past 20 years.

Creating High-Tech Regional Clusters

A policy instrument increasingly chosen was creating science parks or incubators designed to attract and to spawn high-tech companies. A cluster of such companies has workers with the right skills; a supporting infrastructure of suppliers; upstream and downstream companies locate there; specialists in finance and accounting arrive; local governments learn the needs of their companies, create favorable conditions for them, and lobby for support from the central government. Such interactions entail feedback processes in which strength begets more strength, with the result that products are brought to market more quickly and more cheaply than otherwise would happen.[5]

Science parks are especially prominent in Taiwan and mainland China. The inspiration for them came from the United States, notably Stanford University's

Industrial Park (later renamed Research Park) and the high-tech cluster in the Boston area. The fact that these U.S. clusters were not government sponsored was not important; the idea of forming clusters was attractive. In 1980, Taiwan created probably the world's most successful government-created such park, the Hsinchu Science-based Industrial Park. Firms there got favorable loan conditions, tax breaks, reduced charges on utilities, low-priced rentals, established factory and waste management facilities, among other things. The Park attracted many firms, and some have become world-class such as TSMC and UMC. This led to Taiwan's creating two more such parks in the south and central regions.

Science parks are a major feature of China's high-tech scene. The Ministry of Science and Technology has 53 in its nationwide Torch Program. The most prominent, Zhongguancun Science Park in Beijing, is discussed in Chapter 7.

Sometimes universities or major research institutes are foci for a cluster and help create and sustain it, as MIT and Harvard have done in Boston, Stanford, University of California–Berkeley, and University of California–San Francisco have in Silicon Valley, KAIST in Daeduk in Korea, ITRI in Hsinchu, and the Academy of Sciences and major universities in Zhonggcuancun in Beijing. Universities benefit from the clusters they foster by placing graduates in local companies and getting feedback of technology and gifts from them.

Not all of the Asian clusters have been government formed. The Teheran Valley software cluster in Seoul (a district named after a sister city) was created through market forces. So was the pop culture media cluster in Tokyo. The main Indian regions—Bangalore, Mumbai, Hyderabad, New Delhi, and Chennai, all major cities where educated workers were in supply—were also basically formed by the market, not government. (However, as pointed out by Dossani in Chapter 8, only after the Indian government created the first software park with satellite communications did Bangalore take off.) With the exception of a group of integrated circuit companies in Kyushu and media companies in Tokyo, high-tech clusters are not prominent features of the Japanese landscape. This is probably a consequence of there being few young companies.

Why should governments create such parks? They are not without cost; the tax and other benefits to firms in them are not free. Moreover, there are reasons to doubt the ability of politicians and bureaucrats to make such decisions in the broader national interest. Many science parks seem to have more to do with developing real estate than with developing technology. In any case, there are market incentives for companies in similar lines of work to cluster, because they can gain spillover benefits from each other. Nevertheless, there are two broader national reasons for governments to create them. One is that to the extent they are net economically beneficial, governments can speed their formation. The

284   other is to create local environments favorable to forming new high-tech firms when the broader environment is unfavorable. China is a case in point. Zhong-guancun Science Park was originally named the "Beijing Experimental Zone for Development of High and New Technological Industries." New rules could be tried there that, if successful, might be applied nationwide.

Clusters can last a long time, but there is no good reason to assume that they are eternal. Growth eventually slows as empty space is filled, land prices increase, congestion worsens, and — sometimes — changes in technology and markets disfavor a region's companies. (The fate of Detroit in the auto indus-try is such a case.) New clusters can then arise. Dossani reports that infra-structure limitations are holding back — but clearly not yet stopping — the fur-ther growth of Bangalore. Shih et al. report that a shortage of land is limiting the further growth of Hsinchu; as a result, the Taiwanese government is developing science parks elsewhere. Silicon Valley faces these constraints — notably expressed in high housing prices — as well as competition from in-creasingly skilled companies is Asia.

One might reasonably ask whether the arrival of low-cost, digitized infor-mation is making clusters obsolete. Is the future likely to see companies spread out more geographically? Activities that do not have to be in high-cost locali-ties, such as Silicon Valley, have been moving elsewhere for a long time, and no doubt this is aided by low-cost telecommunications. Perhaps the arrival of technology that virtually erases distance will change this pattern, but there is reason to doubt that clustering will soon end at the high end of value chains where the creation of ideas entails much personal interaction.

THE UNDIRECTED AND THE DIRECTED: INDIA AND SINGAPORE

India and Singapore differ not only in size but also in the role of their govern-ments in shaping their IT industries.

India

In India, the sectors that have received most outside attention, software and business processing services, had long been ignored by government. Given the record of government performance, that is perhaps just as well. India still is do-ing a poor job in education, its labor market is heavily regulated, and it still has sizable trade barriers. But the vector is positive in all of these areas.

Its early aim in the IT industry, as in others, was autarky, which meant substituting domestic production for imports. (In that respect it was not very different from Japan and Korea, but it lacked their human assets and it adopted less successful means.) Ironically in light of later software successes, the early strategy was focused on building a manufacturing industry with each state-owned company given a monopoly in its line of work. The results were dismal. As Dossani reports in Chapter 8, India's national champion companies did not produce output of even national, much less global, significance; quantities were small, quality was poor, little research was done, the private sector was stifled, and state-owned companies created work cultures hostile to research and learning. Among other blunders, the government forced IBM to leave while the government did not have enough money to support research. However, it can be credited with having created the Indian Institutes of Technology, which produced many stellar graduates. Still, many computer scientists and engineers then left the country.

The government began to end its destructive policies in 1984 by reducing tariffs, ending the need for a permit to enter the software industry, making firms in this industry eligible for bank loans, and loosening limits on the entry of foreign firms. During the 1990s, import tariffs were cut further, IT firms could spend export earnings on offices abroad, and overseas stock listings were allowed. A major step was taken in 1991 with reform of the telecommunications system.

At least it can be said for the government's IT strategy that it did not strangle the software industry at birth, although for some years it did little to help it. Dossani reports that Tata Consulting Services (TCS) was the pioneer. It developed the remote project management model and led the shift to software applications in the 1990s. In short, this success was not due to a government initiative, nor to a concerted industry push. It stemmed from U.S. firms deciding to outsource some software services work and India being well situated to take advantage of the opportunity with its advantages of a low-cost, English-speaking, technically educated workforce plus the presence of entrepreneurs. The work sent to India at first supported in-house product work by such firms as Texas Instruments and Hewlett-Packard, but the main activity shifted after the mid-1980s from making products for sale to supplying services.

A new era for the Indian software services industry began in 1984 when Prime Minister Rajiv Gandhi's new government liberalized imports. Import duties on hardware were reduced from 135 percent to 60 percent and on software from 100 percent to 60 percent. The domestic software business was recognized as an "industry," thus making it eligible for loans from commercial banks. It was also "delicensed," so that no permits were needed to enter the business.[6] Wholly owned foreign firms developing software for export were once more allowed in, though they had to be licensed. Another policy change was economy-wide: the exempting of all export revenues from income tax (regardless of the industry) from 1985 onward.

286   The government deserves credit for improvements in telecommunications and venture capital—albeit with long delays. It has done markedly less well with education, a deficiency that is likely to hurt India over the longer run.

Singapore

The importance of the IT industry to the Singaporean economy is shown by the fact that the electronics industry became its largest cluster after the mid-1980s with its share of total manufacturing value added rising to more than 44 percent by the end of 2000.

Consistent with its overall decision to rely on direct investment by foreign firms, Singapore attracted early some major IT MNCs such as Hewlett-Packard and Seagate. The success of Singapore in key ICT industrial clusters—for example, hard disk drives (McKendrick et al. 2000), semiconductor wafer fabrication (Mathews and Cho 2000), and contract manufacturing (Wong 2002)—would not have been possible without such a proactive industry promotion strategy.

The government did many things. One was to invest in the education of graduates in science and engineering. As Wong reports in Chapter 5, the number graduating in technology fields increased from 2,200 per year in the 1970s to over 17,000 by the early 2000s. It also made itself attractive to foreigners by relaxing immigration rules. Wong (2002) found over one-third of Singapore's IT workers in recent years to be foreigners.

From the early 1990s, the government began to emphasize technology innovation and entrepreneurship. As part of this effort it undertook to attract the venture capital industry. One means to this end was government holding companies (Temasek Holdings, TIF Ventures) investing in venture funds; another was government agencies or government-linked companies directly managing VC funds. These initiatives led to Singapore's becoming something of a VC hub but not a place for heavy VC investment; during the 1999–2002 period, 90 percent of Singapore-based funds were invested overseas. It also increased public spending on research and development, especially on the life sciences, increased tax incentives for MNCs to do R&D in Singapore, reduced government red tape, and set up a public-private forum on entrepreneurship.

There are several indicators of results from the government's efforts to increase R&D. Its ratio to GDP went from 0.2 percent in 1978 to 2.2 percent in 2002, a ratio higher than those of the UK and the Netherlands. The number of research scientists and engineers per 10,000 workers went from under 30 in 1990 to 74 in 2002. Its publications per capita in 1998 exceeded those of Japan and came close to those of France and Germany. In patenting, by 2001, Singapore's level of patents per capita was higher than those of France and the UK although behind Taiwan, Germany, Japan, and the United States. Although foreign firms received more than half of Singapore-origin patents during the 1990s, the share of those held by individuals and domestic firms had grown.

An important aspect of the move to create technology was the decision to make Singapore a center of research in the life sciences, a move that implies reduced dependence on the IT industry, in part because of the rise of China and India in that sector.

Wong reports on proposed policy changes to remake Singapore into "a competitive, entrepreneurially knowledge-driven economy." These entail exposing professional people to entrepreneurship, attracting more talent from abroad and encouraging worker mobility at home, reducing red-tape, increasing international connectivity, improving access of start-ups to capital, and extending tax benefits from large MNCs to small firms.

As Wong states in Chapter 5,

> In the domestic ICT market . . . the dominance of GLCs [government-linked corporations] needs to be further reduced, perhaps through strengthening of anti-competition policy. The key challenges to sustaining the development of the innovation system appear to be finding ways to augment the small absolute size of the talent base, increasing investment in basic research capabilities of local universities, and improving policy support for technology commercialization activities through new programs like the SBIR and STTR program in the United States. The need to intensify investment in precompetitive basic research and infrastructures is especially important for the biotech cluster as well as certain ICT subsectors such as wireless and broadband applications.

Wong emphasizes the importance of changing "the social and cultural attitudes of the population toward entrepreneurship, acceptance of nonconformity and tolerance of failure." He also mentions "continuing deregulation of public sector bureaucracy, increasing teaching of entrepreneurial skills . . . attracting foreign entrepreneurial talents to start up in Singapore, and providing incentives and support for universities and public research institutes to commercialize their inventions through spin-offs. There is also a need to build stronger global network links with key high-tech hotspots in the world to expose Singaporeans to the globally emerging opportunities."

CONCLUSIONS

The governments of these Asian countries greatly influenced their IT sectors both directly and indirectly. With the exception of India, their influences were overall positive. There were some common elements in educating scientists

288   and engineers and, in one way or another, becoming connected to global markets. However, there was much diversity in the means chosen to accomplish these ends. This diversity is perhaps even more striking than the commonalities among them.

NOTES

1. For example, Arora and Athreye state, "The initial growth of the software service industry in India was facilitated by the enlightened 'hands off' policies of the government of India." "The Software Industry and India's Economic Development," *Information Economics and Policy*, 2001, Section 2.

2. Notwithstanding the establishment of the Indian Institutes of Technology and similar institutes, India had 0.3 scientists and technicians per 1,000 population, ranking 42 out of 62 countries ranked by the World Bank in 1998, below China at 1.3 (ranked 25) and Ireland at 2.0 (ranked 20). Source: World Development Indicators.

3. This flow diminished during the 1990s as better job-related and educational opportunities emerged in Taiwan. The Taiwanese government is now undertaking a scholarship program to reinvigorate the flow of students to the United States.

4. Yasheng Huang argues that China's discrimination against domestic private companies in favor of foreign ones has been a second-best strategy, albeit a successful one (Huang 2003).

5. Not all of a region's growth should be attributed to internal processes. Some of its firms would have succeeded if located elsewhere. To the extent this is so, some cluster growth is a diversion from other locations.

6. Most other industries required an industrial license that was given based on the state's forecast of demand.

REFERENCES

Amsden, A. 1989. *Asia's Next Giant: South Korea and Late Industrialization.* New York: Oxford University Press.

Aoki, M., H.-K. Kim, and M. Okuno-Fujiwara. 1997. *The Role of Government in East Asian Economic Development: Comparative Institutional Analysis.* Oxford, UK: Clarendon Press.

Arora, A., and S. Athreye. 2002. "The Software Industry and India's Economic Development." *Information Economics and Policy* 14(2):253–273.

Dore, R. 1986. *Flexible Rigidities: Industrial Policy and Structural Adjustment in the Japanese Economy 1970–1980.* Stanford, CA: Stanford University Press.

Gerschenkron, A. 1962. *Economic Backwardness in Historical Perspective.* Cambridge, MA: Harvard University Press.

Huang, Y. 2003. *Selling China.* Cambridge, UK: Cambridge University Press.

Johnson, C. 1982. *MITI and the Japanese Miracle: The Growth of Industrial Policy, 1925–1975.* Stanford, CA: Stanford University Press.

Keller, W. 2204. "International Technology Diffusion." *Journal of Economic Literature* 42(3):752.

Krugman, P. 1994. "The Myth of Asia's Miracle." *Foreign Affairs* (November).

Leachman, R. C., and C. H. Leachman. 2004. In M. Kenney and R. Florida, eds. *Locating Global Advantage*. Stanford, CA: Stanford University Press.

Mathews, J. A., and D.-S. Cho. 2000. *Tiger Technology: The Creation of a Semiconductor Technology in East Asia*. Cambridge. UK: Cambridge University Press.

McKendrick, D. G., R. F. Doner, and S. Haggard. 2000. *From Silicon Valley to Singapore: Location and Competitive Advantage in the Hard Disk Drive Industry*. Stanford, CA: Stanford University Press.

Miwa, Y., and J. M. Ramseyer. 2002. "Socialist Bureaucrats? Legends of Government Planning from Japan." Discussion Paper 385, John M. Olin Center for Law, Economics and Business, Harvard University.

National Science Foundation. 2002. S&E Indicators. Appendix Table 2-41.

Ohkawa, K., and H. Rosovsky. 1973. *Japanese Economic Growth: Trend Acceleration in the Twentieth Century*. Stanford, CA: Stanford University Press.

Okimoto, Daniel. 1990. *Between MITI and the Market: Japanese Industrial Policy for High Technology*. Palo Alto, CA: Stanford University Press.

Rowen, H., ed. 1998. *Behind East Asian Growth*. London: Routledge.

Wade, R. 1990. *Governing the Market: Economic Theory and the Role of Government in East Asian Industrialization*. Princeton, NJ: Princeton University Press.

Wong, P. K. 2002. "Manpower Development in the Digital Economy: The Case of Singapore." In M. Makishima, ed. *Human Resource Development in the Information Age: The Case of Singapore and Malaysia*. Tokyo: IDE/JETRO, pp. 79–122.

World Bank. 1993. "The East Asian Miracle: Economic Growth and Public Policy." Washington, DC: Author.

World Development Indicators. http://wbln0018.worldbank.org/psd/compete.nsf/f14ea5988b0eec7f852564900068cbfd?OpenView&Start=1.

10

Venture Capital in Asia

Martin Kenney, Kyonghee Han, and
Shoko Tanaka

Venture capital is broadly acknowledged as being an important constituent of
a mature habitat for high-technology entrepreneurship as practiced in Silicon
Valley (Lee et al. 2000). Each chapter in this book has examined the significance of venture capital in the economies of the regions under discussion and
its particular place in the regional habitats for innovation that have appeared.
As with other institutions, in each habitat the venture capital industries have
differing operational characteristics, different relative mixes of national and
international venture capital participation, and different investment patterns
and targets. When considering and comparing these nations, it is useful to
have one ideal-typical case to use as a standard of comparison. For this reason
and because reproducing the Silicon Valley experience is the goal of many
economic planners in Asia and around the world, this chapter uses Silicon
Valley as the template for comparing the other venture capital industries.

The venture capital industries of six nations examined in this book—
China, India, Japan, Korea, Singapore, and Taiwan—share certain resem-
blances and significant differences. As we shall show, the national industries
differ on a number of dimensions, one of which, the direct relationships to
Silicon Valley, we shall highlight in our discussion of Transpacific connections. The development of venture capital in each nation was evolutionary
and had path-dependent characteristics.[1] Further, this chapter argues that,
though venture capital can provide a catalytic function for the growth of a high-
technology habitat, this catalysis is not automatic. As with any transplanted institution, venture capital can contribute to transforming its environment, but,
conversely, it can be transformed by the environment to the point at which it
no longer resembles the institution in its original environment. In Asia, both

outcomes have occurred. This diversity of outcomes is a fascinating result for those interested in the transfer and diffusion of institutions and institutional practices (Guillen 2001).

The general belief is that the awareness and interest by businesspersons and policy makers in Asian nations in venture capital is rather new or, at least, has only occurred since 1980. This belief is erroneous. As early as 1951, only six years after the first U.S. venture capital firm—American Research and Development—was formed, a director of Nomura Securities visiting New York was quoted by the *Wall Street Journal* ("Japan's Recovery" 1951) as saying that Japan suffered from a scarcity of venture capital. Fifty years later, each Asian nation studied in this book has a venture capital community, although a great disparity exists in the level of development, practices, and sophistication of venture capitalists.

To orient the chapter, we begin by describing venture capital as a practice in Silicon Valley and sketching the birth and development of venture capital in the Silicon Valley habitat. The examination of the evolution of venture capital in Asia follows. For ease in understanding the differences between these nations, the venture capital industries are separated into four groups: (1) Japan and the Republic of Korea; (2) China; (3) Taiwan; (4) Singapore; and (5) India. In the penultimate section, we discuss the international linkages that these Asian venture capital industries have. The conclusion reflects upon the effect that the Silicon Valley experience has had on the growth of venture capital in these Asian nations and the future evolution of the venture capital industry and its relationship to these habitats.

VENTURE CAPITAL DESCRIBED

The common operational definition of venture capital is the distillation of a practice that was pioneered in Boston in the 1950s, developed in Silicon Valley beginning in the 1960s, and became routinized in the 1980s. The U.S. practice is relatively easy to define because venture capital and private equity are considered distinctly different—a distinction that does not hold true in some parts of the world. For example, both the European Venture Capital Association (EVCA) and the *Asian Venture Capital Journal* combine venture capital and private equity investing. As a professional investment activity, venture capital is an older practice than private equity (although it is possible to argue that today's private equity resembles the traditional role of Wall Street financiers or English merchant banks—that is, using capital to organize and reorganize firms and industrial sectors). In practice it also differs inasmuch as venture capitalists support fledging firms, whereas private equity investors

292   practice financial engineering. For much of the world, however, private equity and venture capital are combined both statistically and in the minds of policy-makers, though we shall see that in India, Singapore, Taiwan, and, increasingly, China, venture capital is the dominant practice.

Classic venture capital investing requires business opportunities that have the potential for annualized capital gains of greater than 30 to 40 percent, because investments in seed or early-stage firms experience significant failure rates (that is, bankruptcy or negligible growth) of at least 50 percent. The successful investments must compensate for the failures and return a higher rate than less risky investments. When such opportunities do not exist, venture capital organizations are difficult to sustain. Venture capitalists cannot survive by funding firms that do not appreciate rapidly. For this reason, venture capitalists cannot evaluate investments on the basis of social goals such as reducing unemployment, increasing research and development (R&D), or building a community's technological or tax base. The sole relevant criterion is the potential for large capital gains. The only industries that have consistently offered such levels of return are the information technologies (IT) and the medical fields.

In return for investing, venture capitalists demand a significant equity stake in the firm and seats on the board of directors from which they monitor the firm. Each investment is staged, and the entrepreneurs are given milestones to be achieved prior to receiving another tranche of funds. Experienced venture capitalists provide more than just money, which is a salient difference between venture capitalists and passive investors. They actively monitor, assist, and even intervene in their portfolio firms. Given this intimate involvement, a venture capitalist's experience, connections, and ability should contribute to their portfolio firm's growth. The objective is to leverage this involvement to increase the recipient firm's probability of success. This involvement extends to ad hoc assistance in a variety of functions, including recruiting key persons; providing advice; and introducing the firm's officers to potential customers, strategic partners, later-stage financiers, investment bankers, and various other contacts (Bygrave and Timmons 1992; Florida and Kenney 1988a, 1988b; Gompers 1995). It is this involvement that differentiates venture capitalists from other funding sources.

Since the venture capitalist is investing to secure capital gains, investments are liquidated through bankruptcy, merger, or an initial public stock offering (IPO). For this reason, venture capitalists are temporary investors and, in most cases, are members of the firm's board of directors only until the investment is liquidated.[2] For the venture capitalist, the firm is a product to be sold, not retained. Nations that erect impediments to any exit paths (including bankruptcy) handicap the development of venture capital. This does not mean that such nations cannot have venture capital, only that it is less likely to thrive.

In the United States, the predominant institutional format is the venture capital firm operating a series of partnerships called *funds* that raise money from wealthy individuals, corporations, pension funds, foundations, endowments, and various other institutional sources. The general or managing partners are the professional venture capitalists, whereas the investors are passive limited partners. The typical fund operates for a set number of years (usually 10) and then is terminated. Normally, each firm manages more than one fund; one fund is usually fully invested, another one is being invested, and a third is in the process of being raised. The limited partnership form is common in most of Asia (except Taiwan), but many other forms, such as bank-based and corporate venture capital firms, are also extant.

A successful venture capital industry is not easy to create. Of the 36 nations with a national venture capital association, fewer than 15 have industries of any significance. As an institution, venture capital is quite fragile and requires a number of preconditions for emergence and growth (Avnimelech et al. 2005). In contrast to much of the financial literature, we believe that the most important single factor for explaining the development of a vibrant venture capital industry is the availability of investments capable of providing sufficiently large returns to justify the high risk. In other words, there must be a sufficient supply of opportunities capable of supporting a community of venture capitalists. If the number and quality of venture capitalists is insufficient, a downturn in the economy and the failure of a few venture capital firms could lead to the collapse of the industry. In other words, without a sufficient number of deals, it might be possible to establish a venture capital industry, but the industry would not be sustainable.

Context is also important. There should be a relatively transparent and predictable legal system that offers some protection to investors. If foreign investors are to be encouraged, then currency convertibility is important. It is also necessary that a portion of the labor force be well educated and capable of managing start-up firms, and willing to leave existing employment for a start-up. Some of these conditions appear to be missing or incomplete in a number of East Asian countries. Finally, there are cultural attributes of the local habitat that are required. For example, entrepreneurs must be willing to sell significant amounts of equity to the venture capitalists and be prepared to share control. A vibrant venture capital industry cannot be created in the absence of the appropriate context, though as we have argued elsewhere that these conditions also can co-evolve with a fledgling venture capital industry (Avnimelech et al. 1995).

The first professional venture capital firms were established in Boston and New York in the immediate aftermath of World War II (Florida and Kenney 1988b). Prior to 1957, in the San Francisco Bay Area there were informal investors willing to invest in small firms, though there is no evidence to indicate that there were a greater number of these investors in the Bay Area than in other regions with relatively sophisticated financial markets. The first professional venture capital firm in the Bay Area was a limited partnership—Draper, Gaither, & Anderson—which was formed in 1958. In the prior year, Arthur Rock, then based in New York, had assisted in the funding of Fairchild Semiconductor. Also, in San Francisco, there were a number of young men who were actively investing personal funds in technology start-ups.

In 1958 the U.S. federal government passed the Small Business Investment Corporation (SBIC) Act, providing matching federal funds on a two-to-one basis for anyone willing to invest $150,000 or more in an SBIC. This offer convinced a number of the informal investors to form SBICs, thereby formalizing their angel investment activities. The SBIC program increased the number of venture investors nationally and had a significant impact in the Silicon Valley region. In 1962, a number of local SBIC participants formed the Western Association of Small Business Investment Corporations (WASBIC). WASBIC was, for the most part, an organization that hosted social functions where the members and guests presented and discussed possible deals. In 1969, the WASBIC officially changed its name to the Western Association of Venture Capitalists, which was the first organized venture capital association in the world.

The non-SBIC venture capital industry also was expanding along with an increasing number of start-ups. For example, in 1961 Arthur Rock moved from New York to the Bay Area to join Thomas Davis, who left the Kern County Land Company to form the second Bay Area limited partnership, Davis & Rock (D&R). D&R was important in two ways: First, it was very successful, and during the next six years it returned to investors $100 million on their initial investment of $3 million (Kenney and Florida 2000). This had a powerful demonstration effect, and, quite naturally, attracted more venture capitalists and investors. Second, D&R's investors included Gordon Moore, Eugene Kleiner, Robert Noyce, and other entrepreneurs. This created a commonality of interest between the financiers and successful entrepreneurs that exists to this day. In addition, a number of entrepreneurs and corporate managers who had become wealthy from their start-ups decided to become venture capitalists. They brought with them technical and managerial expertise that the finance-oriented East Coast venture capitalists often did not have.

The 1970s were difficult for macroeconomic reasons and for reasons specific to venture capital. The early 1970s were plagued by social unrest related to the Vietnam War and an oil crisis–induced recession. These and other troubles depressed the stock market. More directly troubling was the passage by the U.S. Congress of the Employment Retirement Income Security Act (ERISA) in 1974, which mandated criminal penalties for pension fund managers who lost money in high-risk investments. Legal experts interpreted ERISA to include venture capital as a high-risk investment. The response was a cessation of institutional investment and the onset of the most difficult period in the history of U.S. venture capital. However, only slightly more than two years later, thanks to a major lobbying effort, the stringent ERISA interpretation began to be loosened to permit investment in venture capital limited partnerships. Gradually, institutional investors came to consider venture capital an asset class worthy of including in their portfolio, and the U.S. government began to see venture capital as an important institution.

Despite the economic difficulties of the 1970s, technological investment opportunities centered in Silicon Valley continued to emerge; some of which would, in retrospect, reshape the economy and create enormous wealth. For example, Intel introduced the microprocessor, making personal computers possible; the Xerox Palo Alto Research Center pioneered workstations and Ethernet; and Bay Area universities were leaders in pioneering the new recombinant DNA techniques. These formed the basis of new investment opportunities for Silicon Valley venture capitalists. For example, in 1976, Genentech and Apple Computers were established. Genentech is particularly interesting, because the initial investment by venture capitalists financed the demonstration and validation that molecular biology could have commercial applications (Kenney 1986). Apple Computer secured its first angel funding in 1977 and received its first venture capital investment in 1978. The computer networking business also began in Silicon Valley with the creation and funding of Ungermann-Bass and 3Com in 1979 (Burg 2001). On October 14, 1980, Genentech went public at $35 per share and soared to $89 per share, and on December 12, 1980, Apple Computer went public at $22 and closed at $29 per share. The difficult IPO market had vanished, and the difficulties of the 1970s were past.

In the 1980s, the Silicon Valley venture capital industry matured, and its practice became increasingly routinized. From this point forward, Silicon Valley would invariably receive between 30 and 35 percent of total venture capital investment in the United States. This routinization occurred in other ways. For example, Mark Suchman (2000), found that by the middle of the 1980s investment contracts between entrepreneurs and venture capitalists had become more standardized, indicating a routinization in the relationship between

296   venture capitalism and entrepreneurs. One key law firm advocating this standardization was the Palo Alto–based firm Wilson, Sonsini, Goodrich &
Rosati. In organizational terms, an ideal-typical Silicon Valley venture capital
firm was a limited partnership whose limited partners were institutional investors and the venture capital funds were invested overwhelmingly in electronics, with smaller sums devoted to the biomedical and biotechnology fields.
Further, non–Bay Area firms wanting to invest in Silicon Valley deals could
no longer wait to be approached for later-stage investments. The success of the
Silicon Valley venture capitalists and their use of the limited partnership for
fund raising meant they could raise sufficient capital to support their portfolio
firms. To participate in good Bay Area deals it was necessary to have a branch
office in the region, and East Coast firms established branches in the region.
Naturally, this reinforced the Bay Area venture capital industry.

   The habitat also evolved. Beginning in the early 1980s with the opening of
the 3000 Sand Hill Road office complex dedicated to venture capital offices,
there was an exodus of venture capitalists from San Francisco to the Palo Alto
area. Proximity to the firms and entrepreneurs was increasingly vital. By the
late 1980s, the Silicon Valley venture capital industry had, in terms of organizational form and practice, matured. However, the size and the number of
venture capitalists in Silicon Valley continued to grow. Informal codes of behavior also emerged as entrepreneurs learned how to prepare and present their
business plans and what to expect in the venture capitalist-entrepreneur relationship. By the end of the 1980s, venture capital as a mature institution dedicated to the support of high-technology entrepreneurship and functioning as
a central actor in the Silicon Valley habitat was firmly established. It had become a model that policy makers and advocates of entrepreneurship in the
United States and around the world were keen to emulate.

INTERNATIONAL COMPARISONS

The venture capital industries in these East Asian nations have different evolutionary trajectories, and in each nation government agencies have played a
significant role.[3] As an institution, venture capital differs substantially in each
of these environments because it is shaped by the political, social, and economic institutions within which it is embedded. Each political economy thus
has a venture capital industry that is shaped by the local economy and that differs significantly from the venture capital industry in other economies.

   Given the dramatic differences in the stage of development and the size of
these economies, it is not surprising that the size of the venture capital industries should also differ. These national differences are substantial, as Table 10.1

TABLE 10.1

National Venture Capital Pools — Selected Nations in Asia and the United States (nominal U.S. $ millions)

Year	United States	China	India	Japan	Korea	Singapore	Taiwan
1991	30,100	n.a.	93	15,352	1,547	868	412
1992	30,300	878	113	16,028	1,629	896	470
1993	31,600	1,422	149	17,750	1,687	1,013	508
1994	35,300	2,384	243	17,750	1,902	1,833	562
1995	40,200	3,458	281	14,851	2,567	3,164	696
1996	48,900	3,612	784	11,254	3,224	3,981	1,336
1997	65,100	3,500	1,016	7,722	1,857	4,468	1,913
1998	90,900	3,112	1,053	12,513	2,995	5,258	3,598
1999	142,900	3,735	1,826	21,729	4,986	7,791	4,447
2000	209,800	5,201	2,891	21,138	6,020	9,286	5,852
2001	256,900	6,044	2,442	21,515	6,251	9,754	6,261
2002	258,500						4,337
2003	257,500						5,038

SOURCE: NVCA, *National Venture Capital Association Yearbook,* various years; AVCJ, *Guide to Venture Capital in Asia,* various years; Taiwanese Venture Capital Association, various years.

NOTE: All Asian statistics combine venture capital and private equity.

indicates. From the time series we present, it is clear that during the last decade there has been significant growth in the venture capital industries of every country studied with the exception of Japan.

In keeping with the great differences between these nations, not surprisingly, the sources of funds vary, and there are some striking differences between the United States and all of the Asian economies. The first difference is that in the United States a large number of nonprofit institutional funding sources, such as university endowments, foundations, and pension funds, have long-term capital appreciation goals and will commit up to 5 percent of their capital to alternative investments. The second difference is that a number of the Asian governments are willing to invest directly in venture capital, whereas the U.S. government has not recently done so,[4] as evidenced in the aggregate statistics on sources of funds committed to venture capital (see Table 10.2).

In all the Asian nations, industrial corporations are the largest source of funds, whereas in the United States, industrial corporations have committed little to the private venture capital funds (though some such as Intel do have significant venture capital subsidiaries). The differences are great. For example, in Taiwan industrial commitments constituted 53 percent of the total commitments to venture capital, an achievement no doubt fueled by a 20 percent tax rebate. In the case of Japan, and perhaps China, the total contribution by pension funds is partially attributable to U.S. pension funds' investing in Asia. Endowments and foundations were negligible sources of funds in Asia. In contrast,

TABLE 10.2

Sources of Venture Capital Commitments in Asia and the United States, 2000 (%)

Economy	Corporations	Individuals	Banks	Insurance Firms	Pension Funds	Government	Other
China	41	3	18	18	12	7	1
India	48	7	21	8	10	5	1
Japan	48	2	25	13	9	2	1
Korea, Republic of	45	2	23	12	6	10	2
Singapore	37	5	16	12	9	20	1
Taiwan	58	9	14	10	4	4	1

	Corporations	Individuals	Financial and Insurance Firms	Pension Funds	Endowments and Foundations	Other
United States	3	11	22	37	20	7

SOURCE: For Asian economies, Asia Venture Capital Journal (AVCJ 2002); for the United States, NVCA (2001).

they provided 20 percent of the U.S. total. In all of the Asian economies, the government had some role in providing capital to the venture capital industry, and in Singapore, the government was the second-largest investor.

Japan and Korea

Japan and Korea share somewhat similar insertions into the global economy and have somewhat similar industrial structures.[5] And yet, in contrast to Korea, Japan had a much more vibrant small-firm manufacturing sector, whose genesis can be traced to the Tokugawa Shogunate (Amsden 1992; Nishiguchi 1994). Korea, until the 1980s, was a harsh military dictatorship in which the government actively determined the direction of the economy through direct intervention and massive subsidization. Only in the 1980s did this dirigiste style of economic planning gradually loosen and give way to a market-driven economy. However, the chaebol-centered nature of the economy (which revolves around conglomerates of many companies clustered around one parent company) continues to this day. The massive government involvement in all parts of the Korean economy and the national venture capital industry means that although the economies are similar on many dimensions, Japan experiences less government involvement.

Japan was the first Asian nation to take an interest in venture capital. In 1963, the Japanese government authorized the use of public funds to create firms like the U.S. SBICs, establishing one firm in each of three cities Tokyo, Nagoya, and Osaka. Through March 1996, these three firms cumulatively invested 69.2 billion yen[6] in 2,500 companies, of which 78 had had public stock offerings. These firms supported some existing small and medium-sized enterprises (SMEs) by providing stable, long-term capital, but they funded few start-ups (Niimi and Okina 1995) and never catalyzed the creation of an entrepreneurial habitat.

The first fully private venture capital firms were created in the early 1970s. In 1972, Kyoto Enterprise Development (KED), whose express model was American Research and Development, the first U.S. non-family-funded venture capital firm, was established through investments by 43 prominent Kyoto companies. However, KED failed and was liquidated only four years later (Ono 1995). Contemporaneously, in Tokyo the Nippon Enterprise Development was formed by a group of 39 firms. In 1973, Nomura Securities and 15 other shareholders established Japan Godo Finance, which was the precursor to the present JAFCO. Between 1972 and 1974, other important financial institutions, including major banks (such as Sumitomo, Mitsubishi, and Daiichi Kangyo) and major security firms (such as Yamaichi and Nikko), formed venture capital subsidiaries. This first wave ended following the 1973 oil crisis, when the number of investments declined and the industry stagnated. Of the eight firms formed during this period, six have survived.

In the 1980s, new initiatives to spark the venture capital industry were launched. From 1982 to 1984, the city banks, securities firms, and regional banks formed 37 new venture capital subsidiaries. Whereas the goal of Silicon Valley venture capitalists is to fund new firms, the Japanese venture capitalists meant to use their "venture investments" to build relationships with small and medium-sized firms in an effort to sell them other services. Furthermore, the Japanese venture capitalists did not seek capital gains; rather they wanted to develop long-term banking relationships with their portfolios firms. Given these goals, due diligence did not have to be overly rigorous. Although organizationally the Japanese venture capital firms operated as subsidiaries, in 1982, JAFCO introduced the limited partnership format (Hamada 1999, pp. 38–41). This created a superficial resemblance to Silicon Valley practice, but it did not change the modus operandi. The venture capital boom soon subsided due to a recession in 1986 and 1987, and activity declined substantially.

Beginning in the mid-1990s, interest in the role of venture capital returned due to the technology boom in the United States. This time, however, the renewed interest coincided with heightened concern on the part of Japanese industrial and government leaders about the continuing stagnation of the economy. So to facilitate new business creation and start-ups in knowledge-intensive and high-technology industries, the Japanese government created new incentives. For example, in 1995 SMEs were made eligible to receive

300   financial as well as informational support from the government. New laws
        simplified the process for forming venture capital firms, and another wave of
        regional banks and corporations established venture capital affiliates. This
        time a number of independent venture capital firms were formed as well.

        The emergence in the mid-1990s of Softbank and other Japanese firms as
        funders of new firms was a significant change in the availability of funding for
        start-ups. Softbank originally was a Japanese software distribution firm owned
        by Masayoshi Son, who had made early investments in U.S. Internet start-ups,
        including Yahoo!, Geocities, and E*Trade. When those firms went public,
        Softbank reaped enormous capital gains, some of which was recycled into
        hundreds of Japanese Internet start-ups, as well as into other start-ups around
        the world. By January 2001, Softbank had invested $8.8 billion in more than
        600 start-ups (Softbank Investment 2001). Softbank was not alone; a number
        of other Japanese firms such as Hikari Tsushin plunged into venture investing
        in Internet firms. Moreover, the existing venture capital firms switched from
        providing loans to established firms to investing in equity in start-ups. The ac-
        companying stock market bubble made it easy to undertake public stock of-
        ferings, and many firms went public on two new Japanese markets, which
        were created to ease the listing of SMEs. In the collapse of the tech bubble,
        Japanese venture capitalists such as Softbank experienced enormous losses.
        Since then, there has been little investment in start-ups.

        It is fair to say that there was a moment in 1999 and early 2000 when it ap-
        peared that a habitat for entrepreneurship similar to Silicon Valley might
        emerge in Japan, particularly in the Shibuya district of Tokyo (then called "Bit
        Valley"). Unfortunately, the bursting of the Internet bubble took most of those
        start-ups with it. But there are a few larger points to be recognized. First, as a
        generalization this start-up boom did not include firms with deep technical
        expertise or attract the best young engineers from Japanese university engi-
        neering departments or from the established electronics firms. Second, few of
        the Japanese venture capitalists were technically savvy former entrepreneurs
        or experienced managers. Third, the other constituents of the habitat such as
        experienced lawyers and accountants along with the myriad of other support
        network constituents never existed in Japan. As a result, when the downturn
        came, few start-ups were able to survive; like the New York phenomenon of
        "Silicon Alley," the "Bit Valley" habitat simply disbanded.

        Korean interest in venture capital is more recent than that of Japan. The
        first Korean experiment in developing venture capital was in the 1970s. As dis-
        cussed in Chapter 6, in 1974, the Korean government created what it termed
        a "venture capital firm," Korea Technology Advancement Corporation
        (KTAC). KTAC's funding came from government research institutions, and its

objective was to be an intermediary financial institution that assisted in the transfer of research results from government-supported research institutes to technically competent SMEs. By U.S. standards, KTAC could not be considered a venture capital firm, but rather some type of technology transfer organization. In contrast to what took place in Japan and Korea, the early efforts were direct government initiatives.

In 1981, the Korean government returned to the goal of creating venture capital, with the incorporation of the Korea Technology Development Corporation (KTDC) under a special law aimed at funding industrial R&D and its commercialization (KTB 2001).[7] Once again, this "venture capital" firm KTDC did not operate like a Silicon Valley venture capital firm; rather it was yet another technology commercialization intermediary (Choi 1987, 352). Then in 1982, following a Japanese model, the Korean Development Investment Corporation (KDIC) was formed as a joint venture between seven Seoul-based short-term financing companies, a number of international development institutions, Westinghouse, and JAFCO (KDIC 1986).[8] KDIC was organized as a limited liability venture capital firm, with the purpose of fostering and strengthening Korean technology-oriented SMEs through equity investment or equity-type investments. In 1984, yet another venture capital firm, Korean Technology Finance Corporation, was established by the Korea Development Bank.[9] Of these, only KDIC emphasized equity investments and was not an arm of a government agency. Put simply, KDIC was the beginning of Korean private venture capital.

Despite the previously organized firms, there still was little true venture capital investing. To address this problem, in 1986, the government enacted the Small and Medium-Size Enterprise Start-up Support (SMESS) Act to support the establishment and growth of small enterprises. Also in 1986, the New Technology Enterprise Financial Support (NTEFS) Act was promulgated to support the four earlier venture capital organizations (AVCJ 1992). With these two laws, the Korean venture capital firms were divided into two types, each having different roles and characteristics. The first four venture capital companies were now called "new technology enterprise financial companies" (NTEFC). Though NTEFCs were permitted to invest their funds with less government oversight, they were required to provide consulting services to the government, especially with respect to directing government funds to SMEs.

As creations of the government bureaucracy, the venture capital firms were burdened with restrictions. The firms covered by the SMESS Act were required to invest in start-up and early-stage enterprises that were fewer than five years old. This reflected the interests of the Ministry of Trade and Industry (MTI), which administered the SMESS Act, and the Ministry of Finance (MOF), which administered the NTEFS Act. Because of the restrictions, the SMESS

302   Act venture capital companies under MTI administration were in a disadvantageous position. Han-Seop Kim (2001), who was a director in KTB at that time, said, "SMESS Act venture capital companies were so restricted, because they were at the boundary of the financial industry that traditionally had been under MOF administration." This situation would be further complicated in 1992, when KTDC, the largest NTEFC, was transferred to the control of the Ministry of Science and Technology and changed its name to Korea Technology Banking Corporation (KTB).[10] The predictable result of these bureaucratic machinations was confusion, overlap, and ineffectiveness.

To increase Korea's technological capabilities the government rapidly increased the amount of targeted funds, which the NTEFCs helped direct. The result was that the NTEFCs expanded rapidly. However, these targeted funds were in the form of loans because the government was not interested in equity. The passage of the SMESS Act sparked the formation of many new venture capital firms, and in 1990 there were 54 new venture capital firms. Though meant to operate like Western venture capital firms, most investments were loans. In the early 1990s, the inexperienced professionals in these firms, characterized by their lack of ability to conduct serious due diligence and assist their portfolio firms, contributed to the failure of the portfolio firms and of the venture capital firms themselves. In response to the difficulties, the venture capital firms tightened their investment criteria.

In August 1993, to counteract this investment slowdown, the government loosened regulations and expanded the range of the industries permissible for investment, extended the age limit for investment-eligible firms from under five years old to under seven years old, and removed the investment ceilings for fund investors. With the 1994 economic recovery and the reduction of regulations, investment once again increased, although it remained subdued until the tech boom arrived.

Venture capitalists continued to agitate for change, and the problems with the industry became apparent. Therefore, the Korean government created yet more incentives for the venture capital industry by changing a number of laws to promote innovative small firms. Also, in 1997, the government launched its own venture capital funds and established a program to provide matching funds for venture capital limited partnerships. In August 1997, the government permitted pension funds to invest up to 10 percent of their capital in venture capital partnerships. In May 1998, the restrictions on foreign investment in Korean venture capital partnerships were lifted, and tax benefits for venture capital were increased. In addition, measures were adopted to increase tax benefits for venture capital partnerships. Those efforts catalyzed the establishment of a number of limited partnerships.

As noted in Chapter 6, two habitats were created roughly simultaneously, "Teheran Valley" and "Daeduk Valley." Daeduk, the government-created science and technology center, has attracted little venture capital investment and is unlikely to do so in the future. Teheran Valley, a cluster that emerged spontaneously, appears to have experienced greater success in moving toward the creation of a habitat replete with local venture capital investors. However, the collapse of the high-technology boom has had a severe impact on both habitats.

In both Japan and Korea, the development of a Silicon Valley–type venture capital industry appears elusive. The entrepreneurship that was sparked by the tech boom may be forgotten in the aftermath of the collapse. In both nations, policy makers have found it difficult to create a policy mix conducive to creating an entrepreneurial habitat. Some of the problems are social. For example, potential entrepreneurs in large organizations are unwilling to bear the risk of resigning to establish smaller firms. As Chapters 2 and 6 indicate, the local venture capitalists are, for the most part, relatively inexperienced in the process of forming new firms and are more comfortable investing in or providing loans to established firms. Moreover, given the recent downturn, it seems likely that the venture capitalists' skills and experience may not improve in the future. The difficulties venture capital has had in taking root in both Korea and, especially, Japan seems to be intimately linked to the overall configuration of those societies and their political economies.

Taiwan

The inception of the venture capital industry in Taiwan can be traced to a concerted government effort to create a Silicon Valley–like habitat. The strategy adopted by Taiwanese government officials was quite different from that adopted in Korea. In 1983, after officials and businesspeople from Taiwan made a study trip to the United States and Japan, the government passed legislation providing attractive tax incentives to individuals who were willing to invest in professional venture capital firms. The core of the 1983 legislation was a tax rebate of up to 20 percent for individuals who maintained an approved venture capital investment for at least two years. To qualify, the investment had to be made by a venture capital fund approved by the Ministry of Finance (Asian Technology Information Program 1998; Republic of China Ministry of Finance 1996, pp. 9–10). In a prescient move, the law allowed investment abroad in firms that might benefit Taiwan. In the vast majority of these cases, the investment was in the United States, where a number of Taiwanese expatriates worked in Silicon Valley. In 1991, the statute was revised to allow corporate investors the same 20 percent tax rebate, dramatically increasing the amount of capital

304   available for venture capital when corporations rushed to secure the rebate
(Liu 2001).

The tax rebate was by far the most important incentive, but there were others including making 80 percent of the venture capital firms' investment income tax exempt in the current fiscal year, thereby providing a grace period of one year. In addition, those choosing to reinvest the earnings garnered from a venture capital investment were allowed to deduct the venture capital income from their tax return in that year. This provision encouraged the investors to reinvest their earnings, thereby expanding the capital pool.

The first venture capital firm in Taiwan was an Acer subsidiary — Multi-venture Investment. Inc. That firm was formed in November 1984 and made its first investment in a Silicon Valley start-up that year (Shih 1996, 35). However, the firm of the greatest significance was formed by the Silicon Valley investment bank Hambrecht and Quist (H&Q). H&Q launched its fund with investments from major industrial groups in Taiwan and from government-controlled banks and agencies (Kaufman 1986; Sussner 2001). H&Q's first investment was in the Taiwanese subsidiary of Data Corporation, a Santa Clara manufacturer of disk drive controllers and floppy disks (Kaufman 1986, 7D). This fund was the beginning of what would become H&Q Asia Pacific, which now operates throughout Asia. In 1987, the Walden Group — a San Francisco–based venture capital firm that was owned by Asian Americans — established a fund called International Venture Capital Investment Corporation with investments from various private and government entities and citizens of Taiwan. This fund evolved into the Walden International Investment Group. Its first two investments were in Northern California (Besher 1988, C9). The venture capital firms in Taiwan learned-by-doing in Silicon Valley.

The 1990s were a period of rapid growth for the Taiwanese venture capital industry. There were benefits for Taiwan. Wang (1995) found that on venture capital investments from 1990 to 1992, the Taiwanese government collected 10 or more times the tax dollars it expended in industry support. Despite this apparently strongly positive cost-benefit ratio, the Taiwanese government eliminated the tax benefit in 2000. This was especially untimely, because the Taiwanese venture capital industry, like those in other nations, was hard hit by the collapse of the tech bubble and has found fundraising particularly difficult. The environment in Taiwan has become particularly severe, because China's emergence as the manufacturing center of the world is undercutting Taiwan's economy. Whereas Taiwanese venture capitalists previously invested in manufacturing operations in Taiwan, now, though in principle it is illegal, they are investing in China. The upshot is that they are investing less in Taiwan.

The last five years have been difficult for the Taiwanese VC industry as there are fewer domestic investment opportunities and VC firms continue to face internal political obstacles to investing in China. In policy terms, there has been a revision of the statute that originally provided tax rebates only for individuals so that corporations could also benefit (Liu 2001). Of course, the most significant factor was the success of the high-technology electronics industry in Taiwan, which became the world's largest producer of many components used in personal computers, peripherals, and electronic devices; the leading center for outsourcing personal computer assembly; and the location of the two largest semiconductor foundries in the world. These industries were the source of many spin-offs. Despite the current difficulties the venture capital industry in Taiwan has experienced, there is little question that it will survive the current downturn.

Singapore

Venture capital emerged later in Singapore than in Hong Kong. In 1983, South East Asia Venture Investment Fund, which was administered by Boston's Advent International, was established in Singapore with investment from the International Finance Corporation (Wang 2002). In 1983 and 1984, Singapore Technologies, a former government-owned industrial conglomerate, began informal investment in start-ups. In 1988, the venture investment activities of Singapore Technologies were spun off into a firm called Vertex Management, and it began investing globally, especially in Silicon Valley (Hock 2001).

In the mid-1990s, the government recognized that, because of rising labor costs, manufacturing could no longer be the driver for Singapore's economy. Its response was to launch an initiative to transform Singapore into a knowledge-based entrepreneurial economy. Policy makers believed that venture capital could assist in this transformation, and so the government used tax and various other incentives to attract venture capital firms from around the world, such as JAFCO, H&Q Asia Pacific, and 3i (Wang 2002). For this reason, the 1990s were a period of extremely rapid growth for Singapore's venture capital industry, and assets under management increased from U.S. $830 million in 1991 to U.S. $9.286 billion in 2000 (AVCJ 2001, 2002, 2003). The growth of venture capital in Singapore was encouraged by massive subsidies, such as capital investments in venture capital funds along with other incentives. The Technopreneurship Fund alone has invested approximately U.S. $1 billion from 1998 to 2003. Singapore's venture capital industry was heavily dependent on these subsidies, the majority of which were made in 1999, and it is almost

306   certain that Singapore has experienced enormous losses during the bursting of the Internet bubble.

Singapore's small size is a significant obstacle to the creation of a strong venture capital industry, because internally it can generate only a small deal flow. To overcome the lack of deal flow, the country established numerous programs to increase entrepreneurship. Singapore also is enhancing its role as a service center for entrepreneurs in the rest of the Southeast Asian region; however, these nations also have only limited deal flows. Moreover, Singapore-based venture capitalists must compete with the indigenous venture capitalists in those other nations. Singapore is striving to enhance its role as an offshore service center for venture capital investors in India and also China.

The government has fashioned a comprehensive strategy aimed at establishing a venture capital industry. Despite this effort, success is not guaranteed, because of the lack of local deals. Singapore's strategy of becoming a service center for India seems precarious because the Indian government will likely also wish to attract foreign firms. However, the Singaporean government has made a well thought out and deliberate plan to create a habitat capable of supporting a venture capital industry. It has judiciously invested resources in creating opportunities for learning the craft of venture investing from regions such as Silicon Valley. The continued maturation of Singapore as a venture capital center is by no means guaranteed.

China

From the early 1990s onward, China has hosted an enigmatic venture capital industry.[11] Roughly speaking, the growth of the Chinese venture capital industry tracked the process of economic liberalization. The impetus for the development of the Chinese venture capital industry was government policy. In 1984, the National Research Center of Science and Technology for Development suggested that China establish a venture capital system to promote high technology (White, Gao, and Zhang 2002). Many of the earliest technology start-ups received capital from local government, universities in the case of spin-offs, and other organizational entities that anticipated the possibility of significant capital gains (Lazonick 2004). It was only in the late 1980s that the Chinese government allowed the formation of the first venture capital firm, which was a government-foreign joint venture. It was followed in the early 1990s by a proliferation of venture capital operations backed by state and local government. Because of the lack of experience, not only among the government officials but also among the entrepreneurs, nearly all of these early efforts failed (Oster 2001). In keeping with the general decentralization of decision-making, there are three major centers of Chinese venture capital investment: Beijing, Shanghai, and Shenzhen. Each of these cities/regions has its own venture capital industry association. It was only in 2002 the Chinese Venture Capital Association was established.

Four distinct types of venture capital firms operate in China: local government firms, corporate firms, university firms, and foreign firms (White, Gao, and Zhang 2002). Of course, those are ideal types, and in practice there are permutations in each category. This proliferation of forms and formats can be understood in two ways. First, it can be understood as a large-scale experiment in which there is a search for the format or formats that will be most effective in the Chinese environment. The second possibility is that this experimentation indicates that the markets remain too difficult for any stable form to arise. At this time, only a few foreign venture capitalists have achieved sustained success.

Until 2001, monies from the government actors (most often the local and provincial governments) made up anywhere from 12 to 80 percent of the total venture capital invested (AVCJ 2001; *UltraChina.com* 2000). Apparently, the venture capital firms operated by the local and provincial governments have lackluster track records, though there is no English-language confirmation of this perception. The national government had abstained from venture capital investing until late 1999, when the Chinese Ministry of Foreign Trade and Economic Cooperation announced that it was establishing a venture capital fund (*ChinaOnline* 1999). It is very difficult to ascertain the success of the Chinese venture capital firms because reporting is not standardized.

With a rise in the number of successful listings and trade sales of venture capital-backed Chinese firms and the growth of firms like Huawai and Shanda, there has been a significant increase in foreign venture capital investing. Since 2003, the most significant growth in activity has been among the foreign venture capital firms. For example, as Table 10.3 indicates, foreign firms were the most active investors in China in 2004. Of course, they have some important advantages over domestic firms in that it is easier for them to organize an offshore IPO. This is important because at this moment there are not yet any exit mechanisms in China.

As indicated in Chapter 7, investments in China are widely scattered among industries and locations, but since 2003 investment appears to be increasingly concentrated in Beijing, Shanghai, and Shenzhen and in technology sectors. Still, it is fair to say that a consensus does not yet appear to have formed as to what are attractive opportunities or what regions will yield an ongoing flow of successful deal exits. During the Internet bubble, the NASDAQ and the Hong Kong stock market opened to a number of Chinese start-ups. Western venture

TABLE 10.3

Import and Export of Venture Capital for Various Asian Nations, 2000 (%)

Economy	Source			Destination		
	Home	Asia	Non-Asian	Home	Asia	Non-Asian
China	56	17	27	81	17	2
India	10	21	69	92	5	3
Japan	76	20	4	82	7	11
Korea, Republic of	68	8	24	94	3	3
Singapore	30	31	39	16	67	17
Taiwan	82	6	12	78	9	13

SOURCE: AVCJ (2002).

capitalists that were attracted to the Chinese market had some important successes, such as Sina and Sohu. There were also successes such as the 2001 acquisition of Newave, a Shanghai semiconductor design house by IDT. This growth was temporarily blocked with the end of the tech bubble and was complicated by the disastrous performance of the Hong Kong Growth Enterprise Market. After 2003, the situation shifted again as Chinese firms such as Shanghai Manufacturing Industrial Corporation, Shanda, Tom Online, and Techfaith Wireless successfully listed on the NASDAQ in 2004 and 2005. In addition, some of the earlier Internet firms such as Sina and Sohu have done well, and there have been trade sales of firms to Chinese and foreign firms such as Lei Wei Jing to Tom Online. Sohu.com purchased Go2Map and CNET purchased the Chinese firm PCHome, to name only a few. Not only have these exits been successful, but they have encouraged further exits. Recently, a number of Chinese semiconductor fabless design firms were funded, and they plan to list on the NASDAQ in 2006. According to the Chinese venture capital consulting firm, Zero-2-IPO in 2004, total venture capital investments in China reached $1 billion.

After years of procrastination, it is possible that the government will approve the opening of a NASDAQ-like second board in Shenzhen. If the Shenzhen board is successful, it will provide a new vehicle for small firms to raise capital and provide an exit vehicle for early investors. Of course, alternatively, it might be that the Shenzhen board will adopt the casino-like characteristics currently on display in Hong Kong and that have led the Chinese main board stock exchange to its disappointing performance. There are many positive signs that China's economy and technological abilities will continue to increase. Exit opportunities internally continue to be unpredictable, but exiting on stock markets in other nations is feasible if the firm has global appeal.

Despite the government's desire to see greater technological development   309
and notwithstanding its efforts to make the environment favorable to foreign
investment in high-technology start-ups, investors continue to be subject to
the vagaries of the Chinese legal and political system. And yet, during this first
phase, the firms that made profits were those that did Internet deals and were
able to quickly list their investments on the NASDAQ. A more stable environment is necessary for the creation of an innovation hotbed.

In 2005, venture capital investment in China continues to expand; however,
its ultimate long-term profitability has not been proven. For this reason, the ultimate fate of the Chinese venture capital industry is not yet certain. Given the
growing market, the support by the government, and the likelihood that Chinese technology will continue to improve, there is reason to believe that China
will become a successful hotbed for venture capital-financed innovation.

In terms of habitat creation, at this moment there are three important centers of venture capital activity—Beijing, Shanghai, and Shenzhen. Each of
these has a different character and even differences in technological competency. In general terms, Beijing has been the technological center of China
because of the numerous top-quality universities and research institutes. The
earliest Chinese high-technology start-ups including Legend, Stone, and
Founder, were established in the Zhonggcuancun area of Beijing. Even today,
Beijing attracts venture capital funding in the software, Internet-related, and
other technological fields. Shanghai has developed a specialization in semiconductors and is the location of many foreign venture capital firms, particularly those from Taiwan. Shenzhen is the first significant free trade zone and
recently has begun a concerted effort to upgrade its technological base. Very
important is the fact that a number of China's largest telecommunications
equipment makers, particularly Huawei and ZTE, were established there. Interestingly enough, the Beijing, Shenzhen, and Shanghai venture capital associations were formed prior to the formation of the China Venture Capital
Association. It is probably fair to say that all three regions now have formed
habitats for new firm formation.

The linkages between Silicon Valley and China that run through Taiwan
are fascinating. Taiwanese venture capitalists have the relationships, knowledge, and capital to perform this intermediary function. However, continued
maturation of China and the instability of the Taiwanese political environment could result in the demise of this set of relations and a more direct relationship with Silicon Valley venture capital firms that have recently begun
more active forays into China. In mid-2004, an enormous $1.8 billion IPO of
Shanghai Manufacturing Industrial Corporation (SMIC) took place. SMIC,

310   which has not been profitable, was backed by venture capitalists from around the world. The success of this and other public offerings in 2004 promises to be very important for the future of the Chinese venture capital industry.

A summary of the state of the Chinese venture capital industry is difficult because there are so many different aspects, firms, and levels of government involved. Moreover, China is evolving so rapidly that any summary is immediately dated. Though not discussed to any extent in this chapter or in Chapter 7, there is the role of Hong Kong, which traditionally has been a "window" opening on China, where large institutional venture capitalists can operate in a developing-nation environment with legal transparency, There are the various indigenous venture capital organizations, public and private. Finally, there is the Silicon Valley, Taiwan, and China connection. This reinforces the fact that the Chinese venture capital industry is still in formation. The plethora of organizational forms described in the chapter and the large variety of investments in one sense can be seen as a strength in that there is much experimentation underway. China has enormous potential both in terms of the internal market and the use of the linkages through Taiwan to the United States, but success is not guaranteed.

India

The Indian venture capital industry is, like China's, a relatively recent phenomenon.[12] As in the case of China, in the early 1980s the idea that venture capital might be established in India would have seemed unrealistic. Until the late 1980s, the government had a strong grip on the economy, and large portions of the financial system were nationalized. Despite these obstacles, Indians were oriented toward technical and managerial education. The important changes began in the early 1980s under Rajiv Gandhi, when a process of liberalization began. An important aspect of this liberalization was the willingness by the Indian government to permit export-oriented investment by multinational firms in the Indian economy. Much of this early investment came from U.S. information technology firms seeking access to low-cost Indian engineering talent. This was contemporaneous with a movement by a number of Indians who had received an education in the United States and then worked in U.S. high-technology firms to found their own firms, particularly in Silicon Valley. These developments prepared the ground for the emergence of an Indian venture capital industry.

The earliest discussion of venture capital in India came in 1973, when the government appointed a commission to examine strategies for fostering small and medium-sized enterprises, but it was not until the 1980s when concrete

efforts were made to encourage venture capital. Prior to 1988, the Indian government had no policy toward and little interest in venture capital. The government's awakening to the potential of venture capital occurred in conjunc-
tion with the World Bank's effort to encourage financial liberalization in India.
In November 1988, the Indian government announced an institutional structure for venture capital (Indian Ministry of Finance 1988). This structure had
received substantial input from the World Bank, which found that the focus on
lending rather than equity investment had led to institutional finance becoming "increasingly inadequate for small and new Indian companies focusing on
growth" (World Bank 1989, 6). A 1989 World Bank (1989, 2) report on India
noted that "Bank involvement . . . has already had an impact on the plans and
strategies of selected research and standards institutes and, with support from
the IFC, on the institutional structure of venture capital." With the financial
support of the IFC, four new venture capital funds were created: two of which
were established by two well-managed state-level financial organizations
(Andhra Pradesh and Gujarat), one by a large nationalized bank (Canara Bank)
and one by a development finance organization (ICICI). This was an innovative initiative for both India and the World Bank (Dossani and Kenney 2002).

The World Bank also was meant to play an important monitoring role.
The first venture capital organization formed—TDICI, which was an ICICI
division—was prevented from taking equity in its portfolio firms so it adopted
an instrument used in Korea, the "conditional loan." However, since it was a
loan, TDICI could not receive capital gains (Pandey 1998, 256). Consequently,
the venture capital firm was still prohibited from receiving the compensation
that rewarded the risk of investing in a new firm. TDICI opened its operations
in Bangalore. The reason for this was that by 1988, when TDICI was prepared
to begin serious investing, interest in technology had increased due to the
success of multinationals such as Texas Instruments and Hewlett-Packard that
were operating in Bangalore, which would provide an aspect of a prime high-
technology habitat. TDICI chose Bangalore because the Indian software firms
such as Infosys, PSI Data, and Wipro were based in Bangalore (Dossani and
Kenney 2002). In addition, Bangalore was the beneficiary of an earlier decision
by the Indian government to establish it as the national center for high technology. The research activities of state-owned firms such as Indian Telephone
Industries, Hindustan Aeronautics Limited, the Indian Space Research Organization (ISRO), and the Defense Research Development Organization, along
with the Indian Institute of Science (India's best research university), were
centralized there.

Despite its difficulties, TDICI was the most successful of the early govern-
ment-related venture capital operations. Moreover, TDICI personnel played

312   an important role in the formalization of the Indian venture capital industry. Kiran Nadkarni established the Indian Venture Capital Association. Also, a number of TDICI alumni became managers in Indian technology firms or joined other venture capital firms. Therefore, the legacy of TDICI not only includes evidence that venture capital could be successful in India, despite all of the constraints, but it also provided a cadre of experienced personnel that would move into the private sector.

This first stage had difficulties as management needed to develop experience,[13] and there were handicaps such as regulations regarding which sectors were eligible for investment, a deficient legal system, successive scandals in the capital market, economic recession, and the general difficulties in operating in the Indian regulatory environment. However, the success of Indian entrepreneurs in Silicon Valley became quite visible in the 1990s, and foreign venture capitalists began eyeing India as a possible location for investment. During the mid-1990s, the role of the multilateral development agencies and the Indian government's financial institutions declined, and the overseas private sector investors became a dominant force in the Indian venture capital industry.

The involvement of the overseas private sector in the Indian venture capital industry was an evolving process. Of critical importance was the 1993 decision by Bill Draper to form Draper International to invest in India; the Indian office was headed by Kiran Nadkarni, formerly of TDICI. Only in 1996 did overseas and truly private domestic venture capitalists begin investing. In late 1996, Walden-Nikko India Venture Co., a joint venture between WIIG and Nikko Capital of Japan, began investing in early- and late-stage companies. Other foreign firms soon followed, especially as the tech bubble accelerated. Quite naturally, the collapse of the bubble had a severe effect on a number of the local Indian venture capitalists. However, the rise of the service offshoring phenomenon provided new impetus for venture capital investing in India.

The increase in investment was accelerated by SEBI's announcement of the first guidelines for registration and investment by venture capital firms. Though these changes had a salutary effect, the development of venture capital continued to be inhibited because the overall regulatory regime remained cumbersome. The inhibition was partly responsible for the fact that as of December 1999 nearly 50 percent of the offshore pool of funds had not yet been invested (Dossani and Kenney 2002). Despite the successes of the 1990s, the regulatory environment continued to be difficult.

In the late 1990s, the Indian government came to appreciate the potential benefits of venture capital in improving and upgrading the economy. In 1999, new regulations were promulgated to liberalize participation by financial institutions in venture capital. However, there still were bureaucratic obstacles and a confusing array of new statutes limiting the freedom of operation to venture capitalists. The result of these various restrictions was micromanagement of investment by multiple government agencies, complicating the activities of the venture capital firms without either increasing effectiveness or reducing risk to any appreciable extent. Like China, India has cumbersome foreign currency regulations, and the most difficult of these is a lack of unfettered convertibility of the rupee.

It is very difficult for Indian venture capitalists to invest overseas. This is illustrated in Table 10.4 by the lack of top Indian VCs in China. This is in marked contrast to Taiwan, where Taiwanese venture capitalists were encouraged to invest overseas in firms that might assist in the development of the national economy. India cut off this type of learning for its venture capitalists. In the current environment Indian firms seeking to build their markets for business process outsourcing cannot receive funding from their venture capitalists to purchase a foreign firm. This limits the flexibility of Indian venture capitalists and their ability to assist fledgling Indian firms and thus provides an important advantage to the foreign venture capital firm.

If there are obstacles to Indian venture capitalists in globalizing, there are also obstacles for overseas venture capitalists. Currently, foreign venture capitalists require permission from the government for all investments and liquidations. Regulations also restrict the ability of Indian firms to trade their stock for that of an overseas firm, and it was difficult to sell an Indian firm to a foreign firm — an important restriction on venture capitalists for whom acquisition is an exit strategy.

The Indian venture capital industry has grown and experienced some maturation. The recent growth in business process offshoring to India has provided the venture capitalists with a number of successes such as the acquisition by Wipro of venture capital–funded Spectramind in 2002 for roughly $100 million and, in 2004, venture capital–financed Daksh was acquired by IBM for approximately $170 million. However, identifying the business areas that will generate the next generation of portfolio firms still remains a problem. An important consideration for the continued health of the Indian venture capital industry is whether a sufficient number of attractive deals can be discovered in the habitat to justify a vibrant venture capital industry. This is particularly true, because, unlike their counterparts in Japan, Korea, Singapore, and Taiwan, indigenous Indian venture capitalists cannot invest overseas.

Though Bangalore is the closest approximation to a Silicon Valley–like habitat, it has not yet become the dominant location for Indian venture capital investing. The Indian industry continues to be a mix of indigenous and

314   foreign firms, and though there have been some successful investments, it is not entirely certain that a sufficient number of attractive deals are available to create a robust industry.

THE GLOBAL CONNECTIONS

The venture capital industry is experiencing a dramatic globalization as opportunities proliferate in many nations. A number of venture capitalists have internationalized their investment practices. And yet, despite this globalization, the United States and, more particularly, Silicon Valley, remain the center of both venture capitalism and global high-technology industry. In terms of business models and economic development, Silicon Valley has near iconic status for Asian policy makers, entrepreneurs, and venture capitalists. The reasons include Silicon Valley's location on the Pacific Rim, the massive numbers of Asian nationals trained in U.S. universities, and the seemingly inexorable movement of Silicon Valley manufacturing functions to Asia that began in the 1960s (McKendrick, Doner, and Haggard 2000; Saxenian 1999).

Three links between Silicon Valley and Asia have been especially important. The first link is the human linkage provided by Asian students who remained in the United States and were employed by Silicon Valley firms. They were rapidly assimilated into the Silicon Valley business structure and soon began launching their own start-ups. Not surprisingly, they maintained close relationships with their friends and family in Asia. The second link was the Asian students and seasoned managers who returned to their various nations, either joining the Asian operations of Silicon Valley firms or establishing firms that subcontracted with Silicon Valley firms. The third link was the Asians who were trained in their home country and then joined the overseas operations of Silicon Valley firms. Each link was a conduit for information transfer and virtuous circles of learning. The repeated interactions that occurred on various levels created an awareness of what was occurring in Silicon Valley, not only in terms of the technical and managerial skills that blossomed there but also of the Silicon Valley entrepreneurial perspective.

The Taiwanese high-technology industries are the ones with the most explicit business ties to Silicon Valley. These ties can be traced to the efforts Taiwanese firms made to become subcontractors to the U.S. personal computer industry and then to establish semiconductor foundries that did chip fabrication for Silicon Valley firms. Venture capitalists in Taiwan use their ethnic connections and, more significant, their connections with Taiwanese contract manufacturers as leverage for participating in U.S. deals (Saxenian and Li 2003). For example, they would offer to assist U.S. fabless semiconductor start-

TABLE 10.4

Top Venture Capital Investors in China, 2004

Rank	Firm	Nationality
1	SoftBank Asia Infrastructure Fund	Japan
2	IDG Technology Venture Investment	United States
3	Doll Capital Management	United States/Silicon Valley
4	CDH Investments	United States
5	NewMargin Ventures	China
6	Carlyle Group	United States
7	Warburg Pincus	United States
8	Legend Capital	China
9	Acer Technology Ventures Asia Pacific	Taiwan
10	Shandong High Technology Investment	China
11	Walden International	United States/Silicon Valley
12	Draper Fisher Jurvetson ePlanet	United States/Silicon Valley
13	JAFCO Asia	Japan
14	Intel Capital	United States/Silicon Valley
15	Shenzhen Capital Group Co.	China
16	Vertex China Investment	Singapore
17	China Science & Merchants Venture Capital	China
18	J.P. Morgan Partners Asia Pte.	United States
19	New Enterprise Associates	United States/Silicon Valley
20	3i	United Kingdom

SOURCE: Zero-2-IPO (2005).

ups in negotiating production contracts with the silicon foundries in Taiwan. In this way, they offered more than money, thus creating value added for the start-up firm.

Singapore operates far more as a financial center, importing and then re-exporting capital as VC investments (see Table 10.4). One difference is that the government in Singapore has invested much of its own capital in a conscious effort to build international links. The central program was the Technopreneurship Investment Fund (TIF), which was established in 1999. TIF has invested U.S. $1 billion in venture capital and in related areas. As of 2001, TIF had announced 45 different investments in venture capital firms headquartered in Canada, France, Germany, India, Israel, Sweden, Taiwan, the United Kingdom, and the United States. In addition to diversifying risks, this investment helped Singapore's government to collect information about venture capital practices globally. In return for the investment, these firms often agreed to open offices in Singapore. Singapore also boasted one of the most far-reaching venture capital firms, Vertex Management, which has offices abroad and invests globally.

Japanese and Korean venture capital firms also have operations abroad, and a number of the large U.S. and European private equity firms have operations

316   in Korea and Japan, though the latter are almost entirely devoted to private equity buyouts (Kenney, Han, and Tanaka 2002). Both India and China are almost entirely importers of capital, and their connections to Silicon Valley are as capital importers.

Venture capital in Asia is now globalized. One dimension of this globalization takes the form of trans-Pacific flows of capital. There is also a significant intra-Asian investment network. For example, the larger Japanese venture capitalists have operations throughout Asia. Another network is the informal Silicon Valley–Taiwan–China network. This fascinating network combines U.S. design capabilities and Taiwanese manufacturing prowess and venture capital with Chinese manufacturing costs. It may become one of the most significant global high-technology connections. One other possible international network could connect developed-nation venture capital firms in Singapore with start-ups in India, though the ultimate fate of this Singaporean initiative is still unknown. An often unnoticed aspect of the growth of the Asian venture capital industries was the effort by the International Finance Corporation (IFC) to establish a venture capital industry by investing in a number of pioneering firms in Singapore, Korea, China, and India. As vital as the provision of capital was, the efforts by the IFC to liberalize the markets in those various Asian nations to improve the condition for venture investing were probably even more significant. The IFC also invested in international venture capital funds that committed to investing in Asia in an effort to encourage capability transfer, within which Singapore also participates.

CONCLUSION

The venture capital industries in Asia have differing levels of development and quite different institutional characteristics. If one adopts a strict Silicon Valley definition of venture capital, then probably Taiwan, China, India, and, possibly, Singapore would qualify as having a venture capital industry. In terms of funding high-technology firms, Taiwan is clearly the Asian leader. However, if we accept local definitions of venture capital, then we can conclude that a sustainable venture capital industry exists in each Asian nation studied in the book. Venture capital in China continues to appear promising, though the industry remains immature.

Despite the existence of venture capital in Asia, to date no Asian venture capital firm has entered the first rank of global venture capital firms (which includes, but is not limited to, firms such as Accel Partners, Greylock, Kleiner Perkins Caufield & Byers, New Enterprises Associate, Sequoia Capital, Warburg Pincus, and Venrock). Leading Asian venture capitalists have attributed this gap to factors ranging from an endemic lack of experienced management to excessive regulation, problems in educational systems (especially at the postgraduate level), a need for better funding of research, and an unwillingness of entrepreneurs to cooperate and build firms (Hsu 1999). These and other reasons have prevented Asia from creating venture capital firms that are leaders on the global stage. Neither has Asia, with the exception of Taiwan, given rise to a sufficient number of start-ups that would provide the extremely large returns necessary to justify the growth of vibrant, self-sustaining venture capital industries.

All Asian governments have played an important role in both creating the macroeconomic environment and providing support for the emergence of a venture capital industry. Taiwan is a textbook case for the ways in which the government can alter the risk-reward calculation. The 20 percent tax rebate created a powerful incentive, but it did not eliminate risk. Moreover, the government created relatively simple and transparent rules that aligned the incentives for the fledgling venture capitalists with the government's objectives. In marked contrast, the Korean efforts created a system that encouraged micromanagement by government bureaucrats and aimed at encouraging the venture capitalists to undertake financial activities for purposes other than maximizing their capital gains from equity investments. These rules and regulations led to the development of risk-averse venture capitalists who concentrated on extending loans rather than investing in equity.

More general issues concern every Asian economy. These include upgrading the research functions of their universities, ensuring a stable political and social environment, and providing for a functioning legal system. It may also be necessary to create strictly regulated "exit" paths for high-quality firms to encourage venture capital investing. This may not be easy, as many Asian and European nations created a new stock market or sections with loosened listing requirements during the Internet bubble. However, nearly all either began with low liquidity or, after the bursting of the bubble, dropped so precipitously that they now suffer from low liquidity. With such low liquidity, these new markets do not offer viable exit paths. Addressing the entire question of how to create a well-functioning stock market will be important to creating exits. This is not a question of "opening it and then they will come."

There can be no doubt that the U.S. venture capital model has been successfully transferred to certain nations, particularly Israel and Taiwan. Whether it is an appropriate model for all nations can be determined only after examination of a given nation's initial conditions and consideration of whether an appropriate habitat might evolve. Unfortunately, few other models have proven to be viable without an entrepreneurial environment based on high technology.

318   Thus far, there have not been many successful hybrid models—venture capital seems to be a fragile institution that does not hybridize well. The Asian economies that have been most successful in creating a venture capital industry are those with the closest human ties to the United States—namely Taiwan and Singapore. Also, these nations have largely adopted the U.S. model with specific changes to suit their environments. In each case, the governments developed policies that singled out venture capital as an important aspect of their efforts to mobilize entrepreneurship. India and China also have strong ties to the United States, and it is possible and, perhaps, likely that a viable Silicon Valley–like venture capital industry will evolve in these two enormous nations.

Despite the many obstacles to creating a vibrant venture capital community, during the past two decades the industry has taken root in each of these countries. There are ample reasons to be optimistic about the prospects for venture capital in China. The current downturn is a major test for the industry in all of these economies, and it is likely that more firms will fail. Unfortunately, there may be little governments can and, indeed, should do to protect venture capital from failure. However, the venture capitalists and national venture capitalist communities able to survive without becoming wards of the government should be poised for substantial growth during the next recovery.

NOTES

The authors would like to thank the Alfred P. Sloan Foundation and the World Bank for providing the funding for this research. This chapter draws upon material from a Berkeley Roundtable on the International Economy, working paper BRIE 156, and a report completed for the World Bank. The authors are solely responsible for the research and conclusions.

1. Nelson and Winter (1982); David (1986); Arthur (1994).

2. Exceptions do exist. For example, Arthur Rock, the lead venture capitalist in funding Intel, remained on the Intel board of directors for two decades. Donald Valentine, the lead venture capitalist in funding Cisco, continues on the board 15 years after the firm went public.

3. Some parts of this section are drawn from Kenney et al. (2004).

4. The Small Business Investment Research grants do provide monies for start-up research projects and thus perform a function superficially similar to that of venture capital.

5. For a discussion of Japanese venture capital using roughly the same sources, see Kuemmerle (n.d.).

6. At an average conversion rate of 150 yen to the U.S. dollar over this period, this amount would be in excess of U.S. $400 million.

7. In July 1992, KTDC was renamed the Korea Technology and Banking Network Corporation.

8. In 1996, KDIC changed its name to Trigem Ventures after it was acquired by Trigem Computer Inc., Korea's largest PC manufacturer. See http://www.tgventures .co.kr.

9. The Korean Technology Finance Corporation was renamed KDB Capital after it merged with the Korea Development Lease Corporation in 1999. At present, KDB Capital is a subsidiary of Korea Development Bank. See http://www.kdbcapital.co.kr.

10. For further discussion, see Kenney, Han, and Tanaka (2002).

11. This section draws heavily upon White, Gao, and Zhang (2002).

12. This section draws heavily on Dossani and Kenney (2002).

13. There is a saying in the U.S. venture capital industry that it takes $20 million in losses as part of the process of training a new venture capitalist.

REFERENCES

Amsden, A. 1992. *Asia's Next Giant: South Korea and Late Industrialization.* New York: Oxford University Press.

Arthur, W. B. 1994. *Increasing Returns and Path Dependence in the Economy.* Ann Arbor: University of Michigan Press.

Asian Technology Information Program. 1998. "Venture Capital in Taiwan." Report ATIP98.009, Asian Technology Information Program (ATIP).

Asian Venture Capital Journal (AVCJ). 1992. *The 1992/1993 Guide to Venture Capital in Asia.* Hong Kong: Author.

———. 2001. *The 2001 Guide to Venture Capital in Asia.* Hong Kong: Author.

———. 2002. *The 2002 Guide to Venture Capital in Asia.* Hong Kong: Author.

———. 2003. *The 2003 Guide to Venture Capital in Asia.* Hong Kong: Author.

Avnimelech, G., M. Kenney, and M. Teubal. 2005. "A Life Cycle Model for the Creation of National Venture Capital Industries: Comparing the U.S. and Israeli Experiences." In E. Giuliani, R. Rabellotti, M. P. van Dijk, eds. *Clusters Facing Competition: The Role of External Linkages.* London: Ashgate Publishers.

Besher, A. 1988. "Taiwan, U.S. Firms Team Up on Venture Capital Fund." *San Francisco Chronicle,* June 13, p. C9.

Burg, U. Von. 2001. *The Triumph of Ethernet: Technological Communities and the Battle for the Lan Standard.* Stanford, CA: Stanford University Press.

Bygrave, W. D., and J. A. Timmons. 1992. *Venture Capital at the Crossroads.* Boston: Harvard Business School Press.

ChinaOnline. 1999. "China Launches New High Tech Venture Capital Fund." (October 5).

Choi, H. 1987. "Mobilization of Financial Resources for Technology Development." *Technological Forecasting and Social Change* 31:347–358.

Dossani, R., and M. Kenney. 2002. "Creating an Environment for Venture Capital in India." *World Development* 30(2):227–253.

Florida, R., and M. Kenney. 1988a. "Venture Capital–Financed Innovation and Technological Change in the U.S." *Research Policy.* 17(3):119–137.

———. 1988b. "Venture Capital, High Technology and Regional Development." *Regional Studies* 22(1):33–48.

320 Gompers, P. 1995. "Optimal Investment, Monitoring, and the Staging of Venture Capital." *Journal of Finance* 50:1461–1489.

Guillen, M. F. 2001. *The Limits of Convergence: Globalization and Organizational Change in Argentina, South Korea, and Spain.* Princeton, NJ: Princeton University Press.

Hamada, Y. 1999. *Nihon no Bencha Kyapitaru.* Tokyo: Nihon Keizai Shimbun.

Hock, C. J. 2001. Telephone interview of senior vice president, Vertex Management Inc., by Martin Kenney, Redwood City, California, March 29.

Hsu, T.-L. 1999. Interview with Ta-Lin Hsu. *Asian Venture Capital Journal* (December): 26.

Indian Ministry of Finance. 1988. Venture Capital Guidelines. Press Release S.11(86)-CCI(11)/87, Department of Economic Affairs, Office of the Controller of Capital Issues, November 25.

Kaufman, S. 1986. "H&Q's Open Door Policy into Far East Venture Capital." *San Jose Mercury News,* November 17, p. 7D.

Kenney, M. 1986. *Biotechnology: The University-Industrial Complex.* New Haven, CT: Yale University Press.

Kenney, M., and R. Florida. 2000. "Venture Capital in Silicon Valley: Fueling New Firm Formation." In M. Kenney, ed. *Understanding Silicon Valley: Anatomy of an Entrepreneurial Region.* Stanford, CA: Stanford University Press, pp. 98–123.

Kenney, M., K. Han, and S. Tanaka. 2002. "Scattering Geese: The Venture Capital Industries of East Asia." Report to the World Bank, Washington, DC.

———. 2004. "The Venture Capital Industries." In S. Yusuf, M. A. Altaf, and K. Nabeshima, eds. *Global Change and East Asian Policy Initiatives.* New York: Oxford University Press.

Kim, H.-S. 2001. Telephone personal interview with the director, Korea Technology & Banking (KTB) Network Corporation, by Kyonghee Han, Seoul, Korea, May 16.

Kleiner Perkins Caufield & Byers (KPCB). 2001. Retrieved from http://www.kpcb.com.

Korean Development Investment Corporation (KDIC). 1986. *Annual Report.* Seoul: Author.

Korean Technology and Banking Network Corporation (KTB). 2001. Retrieved from http://www.ktb.co.kr.

Kortum, S., and J. Lerner. 2000. "Assessing the Contribution of Venture Capital to Innovation." *RAND Journal of Economics* 31(4):674–692.

Kuemmerle, W. 2001. "Comparing Catalysts of Change: Evolution and Institutional Differences in the Venture Capital Industries in the U.S., Japan and Germany." In R. A. Burgelman and H. Chesbrough, eds. *Research on Technological Innovation, Management and Policy.* Greenwich, CT: JAI Press, pp. 227–261.

Lazonick, W. 2004. "Indigenous Innovation and Economic Development: Lessons from China's Leap into the Information Age." *Industry and Innovation* 11(4): 273–297.

Lee, C.-M., W. Miller, M. G. Hancock, and H. Rowen. eds. 2000. *The Silicon Valley Edge: A Habitat for Innovation and Entrepreneurship.* Stanford, CA: Stanford University Press.

Liu, B.-H. D. 2001. Personal interview with director, Business Department, Development Fund, Executive Yuan, by Martin Kenney, Taipei, Taiwan, May 3.

McKendrick, D. G, R. Doner, and S. Haggard. 2000. *From Silicon Valley to Singapore:*   **321**
Location and Competitive Advantage in the Hard Disk Drive Industry. Stanford, CA:
Stanford University Press.

National Venture Capital Association (NVCA). 2001. *National Venture Capital Association Yearbook.* Arlington, VA: Author.

———. 2002. *National Venture Capital Association Yearbook.* Arlington, VA: Author.

Nelson, R. R., and S. G. Winter. 1982. *An Evolutionary Theory of Economic Change.*
Cambridge, MA: Harvard University Press.

Niimi, K., and Y. Okina. 1995. "Bencha Bijinesu no Seicho o Habamumono ha
Nanika." *Japan Research Review* (May). Retrieved from http://www.jri.co.jp/jrr/
1995/199505.

Nishiguchi, T. 1994. *Strategic Industrial Sourcing: The Japanese Advantage.* New York:
Oxford University Press.

Ono, M. 1995. "Venture Capital in Japan: Current Overview." Retrieved August 24,
2000, from http://www.asahi-net.or.jp/~sh3m-on/venturecapitalommune/javc/
jvcs.htm.

Oster, S. 2001. "Nothing Ventured." *AsiaWeek.com,* July 27–August 3.

Pandey, I. M. 1998. "The Process of Developing Venture Capital in India." *Technovation* 18(4):253–261.

Republic of China, Ministry of Finance. 1996. "The Venture Capital Industry in the
Republic of China" (May).

Saxenian, A. 1999. *Silicon Valley's New Immigrant Entrepreneurs.* San Francisco: Public Policy Institute of California.

Saxenian, A., and C.-Y. Li. 2003. "Bay-to-Bay Strategic Alliances: The Network Linkages between Taiwan and the US Venture Capital Industries." *International Journal
of Technology Management* 25(1/2):136–150.

Shih, S. 1996. *Me-Too Is Not My Style.* Taipei: Acer Foundation.

Softbank Investment. 2001. "Kaisha Gaiyo." Retrieved from http://www.sbinvestment
.co.jp.

Suchman, M. C. 2000. "Dealmakers and Counselors: Law Firms as Intermediaries in
the Development of Silicon Valley." In M. Kenney, ed. *Understanding Silicon Valley.* Stanford, CA: Stanford University Press, pp. 71–97.

Sussner, H. 2001. Telephone interview with senior managing director, H&Q Asia
Pacific, by Martin Kenney, San Francisco, March 30.

UltraChina.com. 2000. "Hidden Risks in China's Venture Capital Investment."
(June 2).

Wall Street Journal. 1951. "Japan's Recovery Seen Dependent on Inflow of Venture
Capital." November 16, p. 16.

Wang, C. 2002. "Differences in the Governance Structure of Venture Capital: The Singaporean Venture Capital Industry." Paper presented at the European Union/
United Nations University International Conference on Financial Systems, Corporate Investment in Innovation and Venture Capital, Brussels, November 7–8.

Wang, L.-R. 1995. "Taiwan's Venture Capital: Policies and Impacts." *Journal of Industry Studies* 2(1):83–94.

White, S., J. Gao, and W. Zhang. 2002. "China's Venture Capital Industry: Institutional
Trajectories and System Structure." Paper presented at the European Union/United

322   Nations University International Conference on Financial Systems, Corporate
Investment in Innovation and Venture Capital, Brussels, November 7–8.

World Bank. 1989. "India Industrial Technology Development Project Staff Appraisal
Report." Washington, DC: Author.

Zero-2-IPO. 2005. "Top 50 Venture Capitalists of the Year." Retrieved July 6, 2005, from
http://www.zero2ipo.com.cn/en/China%20VC%20Ranking/China%20Venture%
20Capital%20Annual%20Ranking%202004-list.pdf.

11

UNIVERSITIES AND INDUSTRIES EXCHANGE
TECHNOLOGIES IN AMERICA AND ASIA

Jon Sandelin

Transfers of knowledge and technology occur in many ways. Graduating students entering the workforce or people returning to their homeland after working in another country represent two means. Collaborative research, in which researchers from industry work with researchers in public research institutes, is another. Researchers in public institutes disclosing inventions and participating in the transfer of new technology to industry, through licensing to an existing company or by forming a start-up company, is yet another. Each region described in this book uses a different mixture of transfer techniques, in many cases responding to government policies.

PRACTICES IN THE REGIONS COMPARED

Japan

Chapters 2 and 3 make a strong case that the environment in Japan for creating high-tech clusters and for forming start-up companies is improving. A major impediment, the reluctance of professionals in large companies or ministries to leave and become involved in start-ups, is starting to change. As successful role models become more prevalent, this trend could accelerate. Maeda presents evidence that most of the successful spin-offs are from the corporate community, not the academic community. The technology transfer process is the passing of company-owned intellectual property (IP) and know-how to the spin-off company.

Imai provides one example of reverse technology transfer, a process that Stanford University has also greatly benefited from. Stanford obtained important knowledge in solid-state physics and semiconductor technology by re-

324   cruiting researchers from industry. An example is William Shockley, who won the Nobel Prize as co-inventor of the transistor at ATT, who was recruited to the Stanford faculty. He also formed a company to commercialize the transistor, and this led in due course to the formation of Fairchild Semiconductor and dozens of other semiconductor companies (including Intel) in Silicon Valley. Other Stanford faculty members, notably James Gibbon, later to become the Dean of the School of Engineering, gained valuable knowledge and experience when working in or interacting with these semiconductor companies. In Japan, Fujio Masuoka, while working for Toshiba, pioneered flash memory, which is now widely used in mobile and digital phones. Toshiba chose not to pursue it and subsequently licensed the technology to Intel. Masuoka then left Toshiba to join the faculty of Tohoku University to conduct research on more advanced forms of flash memory.

Imai, Maeda, and Yamaguchi discuss several possible candidates for emerging clusters. One would combine the business expertise in Sendai with research at Tohoku University. The focus would be NBI Converging Technologies, the convergence of nanotechnology, infotechnology, and biotechnology to create new products in emerging new fields of use. Accomplishing this will require strong networking and technology transfer systems. At Tohoku, the New Industry Creation Hatchery Center (NICHe) was created in April 1998, and its related Technology Licensing Office (TLO), named Tohoku Technoarch Co., Ltd., became an approved TLO in December of the same year. Tohoku was among the first Japanese national universities to receive approval status for its TLO.

The university-to-industry technology transfer system in Japan, especially for the National Universities, is in a state of transition. The status of the National Universities changed on April 1, 2004, when they became National University Corporations (Kneller 2004a, 2004b). University employees, including professors, are no longer civil servants, and the universities may now take direct ownership of inventions created by their faculties. However, the law only says they may take ownership, so each university must determine its own policies regarding ownership. This is different from the U.S. Bayh-Dole law, where first right to ownership by the university is guaranteed for inventions developed under government funding.

The Japanese government since 1998 has enacted several laws and programs to encourage university-to-industry transfers, both through licensing to existing companies and through assisting start-up companies (Tanaka 2003; Hashimoto 2003). The laws are listed as follows:

- 1998. Law Promoting Technology Transfer from Universities to Industry. This law provided funding for approved Technology Licensing Offices (TLOs).

- 1999. Law on Special Measures for Industrial Revitalization. This law reduced patent fees for approved TLOs by 50 percent. Another was the Small and Medium-Sized Business Innovation Research System, often referred to as the Japanese SBIR system or the Japanese Bayh-Dole law, because it contains many of the U.S. Bayh-Dole provisions. These provisions were optional until a directive from MEXT in 2003 made them mandatory as of April 1, 2004.
- 2000. Law to Strengthen Industrial Technology. This law permitted professors to be paid as consultants under certain conditions and allowed them to also hold management positions in companies when commercializing their inventions. It also allowed approved TLOs to use National University facilities free of charge.
- 2002. Revisions to existing laws allowed university-based venture companies to use National University facilities and encouraged the start-up activities of approved TLOs.
- 2003. Basic Law on Intellectual Property.

In 2003, the Prime Minister's Council on Intellectual Property Strategy (an advisory group to the Prime Minister) recommended establishing Intellectual Property Offices (IPOs) within universities that would work with TLOs (Nishizawa 2003). The intent was to prepare the universities for ownership of all of their IP after April 1, 2004, by having an internal organization that would focus on commercializing their inventions. The Ministry of Education (MEXT) provided 2.4 billion yen per year for five years. From the 83 applications, 34 IPOs were selected, consisting of 25 national universities, four private universities, three consortia of private universities, and one consortium of eight laboratories from various universities. Each will receive an annual subsidy for five years that averages about $640,000 annually. Their challenge is creating effective working relationships (1) with inventors so that they will disclose and assign inventions to the university (inventors can claim their invention is not work related and thus seek to retain ownership for themselves) and (2) with their affiliated TLO, which has experience in evaluating and marketing of inventions.

The first four TLOs were approved on December 4, 1998, and 38 of them had been approved as of January 2005. Each receives an average of about $180,000 annually (for five years) in subsidies from the government. However, approved TLOs receive a 50 percent discount on patent application fees and they may use state-owned facilities (i.e., university facilities) free of charge. TLOs affiliated with National Universities have been organized as separate for-profit corporations. If they had been established internally before the change in status on April 1, 2004, the employees would be MEXT civil servants (subject to rotation every two years), the TLO could not accept outside funds, and the TLO could not distribute royalties back to the university (which can be done by the external organization as a gift).

TABLE 11.1

Key Statistics for Japanese Approved TLOs

Statistic	1999	2000	2001	2002
National patent filings	280	618	1,145	1,335
Foreign patent filings	37	73	208	284
Royalty income	$182,000	$1.2 million	$2.7 million	$3.7 million

SOURCE: "Guide to Technology Licensing Organizations (TLOs) in Japan," Industry-University Cooperation Division, Ministry of Economy, Trade and Industry, 2003.

TABLE 11.2

Key Statistics for All Reporting TLOs of North American Universities

Statistic	1999	2000	2001	2002
Patents filed	5,545	6,375	6,812	7,741
Royalty income	$862 million	$1.26 billion	$1.07 billion	$1.27 billion

SOURCE: Association of Technology Managers in Taiwan (AUTM).

The performance of the Japanese approved TLOs (as shown in Tables 11.1 and 11.2) when compared to the performance of U.S. TLOs appears weak, but this is not surprising given that they have existed for only a few years. Studies of U.S. TLOs reveal that those with large numbers of invention disclosures, patent filings, and royalty income have almost all been in existence for 20 years or more. Stanford University is a good example. It was started in 1969, with $55,000 in royalties in its first year. For the period 1969–1980 total cumulative royalties were $4 million. For 1981–1990 it was $40 million, and for 1991–2000 cumulative royalties were $400 million. Moreover, and most important, most of the $400 million can be traced to a small number of inventions disclosed in the 1970s. For example, $255 million came from a single invention disclosed in 1974 with most of the royalties from it coming in the late 1980s and the 1990s.

The TLOs for universities in the United States that report many patent filings and substantial royalty income have been in existence for 15 to 20 years or more. A large part of the royalty income is from inventions in the life sciences, where regulatory approvals can take many years before products can be sold. The upward growth in disclosure of inventions, patent filings, and royalty income for the Japanese TLOs has just started, and with time and under the new transfer policies for the National Universities, they should accelerate greatly in future years.

Japan adopted as a national goal in May 2001 the creation of 1,000 university-based venture companies during the fiscal years 2002–2004 (Hashimoto 2003). This is called the "Hiranuma Plan," taking the name of the Minister of

METI when it was announced. METI's programs to help this process include the following:

- An industrial technology research grant program: Under it, companies submit research themes. The company provides one-third of the budget and the government two-thirds. The minimum research investment for the company is $45,000, and the maximum term of the research project is three years. The government allocated $22 million to this program in FY 2003.
- Small and Medium Enterprise (SME)-supporting R&D by the National Institute of Advanced Industrial Science and Technology (AIST). Grants are made for feasibility studies of the commercial potential of university technologies by SMEs. Again, the government funds two-thirds and the company one-third.
- A support program for technology development aimed at practical use: This provides support for the further development of technologies by university spin-out companies and venture businesses.
- A program to support management of university-based venture business: This provides management, financial, and legal advisors for university-based start-up companies. It recognizes that professors have high technical skills, but may lack the business, financial, or legal skills important in the formation and growth of new ventures.
- A program to develop business incubators: This provides funding for incubators in selected locations.
- Tax credits: R&D expenses incurred by a private company in a university/industry joint research project get tax credits.

There are also METI supported programs to build networks of university, industry, and government collaborators for new venture formation.

A nongovernmental group also focused on university-based new ventures is the Japan Association for University Intellectual Property and Technology Management (JAUIPTM) (METI 2003). Originally formed in September 2000 as the Japan TLO Association, the initial members came from each of the approved TLOs and from METI and MEXT. With the introduction of the MEXT-subsidized IPOs in 2003, membership was opened to representatives from the IPOs. It has now been expanded to include (1) legal entities and organizations engaged in technology transfer from universities that intend to contribute to the Association and (2) individuals in universities engaged in technology transfers and who intend to contribute to the activities of the Association.

The announced plans for JAUIPTM in FY2003 were as follows:

- To promote coordination, exchanges, and cooperation among TLOs and universities.
- To promote international partnerships by building closer ties with the AUTM and establishing networks within the Asian region.

- To create a program to develop human resources for technology transfer.
- To become a legal entity and thereby strengthen the administrative system.

There are also a few private universities with significant research programs, and these have relatively successful technology transfer programs. They have been able to own the inventions of their faculties, and their technology transfer offices can be an integral part of the university.

Some ways in which the TLO process in Japan differs from that in the United States are the following (Kneller 2003):

1. Inventors in Japanese universities, in most cases, retain more influence over the disposition of their inventions than is typically the case in the United States. Inventors can declare that their inventions have no commercial value and thus have them pass into the public domain, or they may declare that the invention was not work-related and that they should retain ownership rights.
2. For most universities in Japan, there are only four weeks from the disclosure of an invention to the decision on claiming ownership. In the United States, under the Bayh-Dole provisions, for government-sponsored inventions the period for claiming ownership is the earlier of two years from disclosure or 60 days prior to a patent bar date. This extended time is important, because many university inventions are not developed to the stage where effective evaluations can be made when first disclosed. The ability to "table" inventions to obtain confirming research results or to create a prototype that shows the invention actually works before committing to the costs of patenting appears not to be available to many Japanese universities.
3. The MEXT policies appear to apply only to faculty and not to graduate students and post-docs. In the United States, any person getting financial support in connection with research projects (including students and post-docs) is normally required to sign an agreement to assign invention ownership rights to the university. This is important as most inventions include a professor and one or more graduate students or post-docs as co-inventors, and most have outside sponsorship that requires the delivery of certain rights to the sponsor. Without an obligation to assign, the university might not be able to comply with its contractual obligations. However, Japanese universities can require that any student who uses university facilities in making an invention must assign ownership rights to the university, and most if not all are likely to require this.
4. Many National Universities still retain a contractual relationship with a separate for-profit TLO organization that handles licensing and the return of royalty income to the source university, normally as a "gift." This is quite different from the vast majority of technology licensing offices in the United States.

In summary, just as Bayh-Dole removed barriers and allowed for an efficient and effective technology transfer process in U.S. universities, the recent laws and policy changes in Japan have also removed most of such barriers. And just as it took many years in the United States following the 1980 Bayh-Dole law to build the infrastructure of experienced technology transfer professionals, so it will take many years in Japan. The key to success will now be the successful integration of the IPOs and TLOs to create an efficient and effective technology transfer process.

Korea

The Teheran Valley, located within the Gangnam District of Seoul, is home to about half of all the software and IT ventures in Korea. It has the services, such as venture investment organizations, important in the incubation and growth of new companies. However no major universities or research organizations are located in "the valley," and there is little industry or public research organization collaboration or interaction. Technology transfer occurs instead through knowledge sharing via personal networks and inter-firm collaborations. It should be noted that such sharing of knowledge and cooperation between individuals and firms has been cited as a major factor in the success of the Silicon Valley.

Daeduk Valley evolved from Daeduk Science Town (DST), founded in 1971. DST has more than 60 government-operated and privately operated research institutes, four universities, and many venture firms. It's best known resident is the Korean Advanced Institute for Science and Technology (KAIST), with close ties to other major educational organizations such as Stanford University, MIT, and Tsinghua University in China. KAIST had a research volume of $87 million in 2002, which included collaborative R&D projects with industry. It encourages the formation of venture firms. There is a New Technology Venture Business Committee that oversees the Technology Innovation Center and also the Latest Technology Venture Business Alimentation Center. The claim is that at least 580 venture firms have been started by KAIST graduates since 1981. An Internship Program at Venture Companies for KAIST undergraduate students was started in the year 2000.

In 2001, an OECD survey of the patenting and licensing practices at public research organizations in a number of countries, including Korea (OECD 2003), reported that (1) Korea has recently changed funding regulations, giving universities more control over the intellectual property generated by their researchers (2) that Korea recently eliminated fiscal rules that would prevent public research organizations from receiving and keeping royalty income from licenses; and (3) that Korea is experimenting with Technology Transfer Offices that are regional or sector based and that manage technology transfer activities for several public research organizations.

330   The OECD report provided some comparative statistics in which Korea did quite well. For total active patents managed by both university and non-university public research organizations in 2001, Korea reported 9,391, compared to 5,404 for Germany, 991 for the Netherlands, and 682 for Japan. For patent applications, the United States led with 8,294; Korea was next with 1,692, followed by Germany with 1,058, Australia with 834, and Japan with 567. In licenses issued, Korea did not fare as well, claiming 247. The United States reported 7,056, Germany issued 555, Switzerland issued 475, Australia issued 417, the Netherlands issued 368, and Japan reported only 89. And for gross royalty income received, Korea had only a total of $4.75 million. The United States reported $1.23 billion, Australia was next with $124 million, followed by Germany with $58 million. At the low end, both Japan and Russia reported $1.75 million.

These statistics suggest that Korea has been proficient in acquiring patents, but not in converting them into licenses and royalty income. As with other Asian countries, it appears that new venture formation, not licensing to existing firms, is the focus in Korea. There is a private company primarily funded by the Korean government that provides technology transfer services. Named the Korea Technology Transfer Center, it was established to implement the aims of the "Technology Transfer Promotion Act 2000." It has its headquarters in Seoul, Korea and information about it and its activities can be found at the web site www.kttc.or.kr.

Singapore

In the 1980s and early 1990s, technology transfer activities by research institutes and agencies and universities in Singapore were minimal. There were weak incentives for researchers to do this. In 1992, the National University of Singapore (NUS) formed its technology transfer office (Sandelin 2004) and Nanyang Technological University (NTU) formed its office in 2000. The Agency for Science, Technology and Research (A*STAR), which oversees a large number of public research institutes, formed its technology transfer office (named Exploit Technologies Pte Ltd) in 2002. Both NUS and NTU operate incubators and encourage university start-ups. The NUS teaches courses in entrepreneurship and has cooperative internship programs in overseas locations such as Stanford University, where NUS students take entrepreneurship courses and work as interns in start-up companies.

For the same reasons given in the section on Japan (i.e., the extended length of time from disclosure of invention to significant royalty income, and that most earned royalty income is from life science–related inventions), the amount of royalty income collected by NUS, NTU, and A*STAR so far is small. The total amount for the three in their most recent fiscal year was less than $1 million

(Sandelin 2004). However, the recent commitment to the life sciences of $1 billion, for (1) investment in life science research institutes; (2) co-funded R&D projects with pharmaceutical companies; and (3) building a new life science park (Biopolis), will likely result in life science technologies with significant commercial value. Furthermore, the trend at NUS is upward, with 69 invention disclosures and 11 license agreements in FY 01 and 121 invention disclosures and 18 license agreements in its most recent FY. Exploit Technologies has similarly experienced an upward trend in invention disclosures and license agreements in FY 03 as compared with FY 02.

In terms of volume (invention disclosures, patents filed, license agreements, and royalty income) A*STAR is the leader. It has first right to commercialize any invention arising from extramural grants provided by A*STAR for projects undertaken by public-sector institutes, which include NUS, NTU, hospitals, and specialty centers. Ownership of inventions resides with the creating institution. When A*STAR elects to commercialize an invention, A*STAR bears the full risk of patent and commercialization costs, and revenues are shared equally with the creating institution. For research organizations without an internal technology transfer/licensing capability, this policy ensures that the inventions are effectively commercialized for the benefit of the Singaporean economy while the inventors and institutions are compensated. Stanford's experience is that the active involvement of the inventor in the technology transfer/licensing process is essential for success. This is difficult if the transfer/licensing organization is remote from the inventor. Exploit Technologies, NUS, and NTU appear to have well-organized and well-managed technology transfer/licensing offices with policies and incentives for inventors to work with them. The proximity of the technology transfer offices to the inventors, coupled with Singapore's size, makes the interactions between the inventors and technology transfer offices relatively easy.

As Poh Kam Wong points out in Chapter 5, Singapore is moving toward less reliance on technology provided by outside corporations and toward exploiting its own innovation through technology creation and entrepreneurship. These changes are of fairly recent origin and it will take time and perhaps some refinement of policy before the effects can be seen.

Taiwan

Under several influences the universities of Taiwan are undergoing change. One was a detailed study of the Taiwan university system completed in 2003 (Liu 2004). The findings included the following recommendations:

- To classify about 150 universities in Taiwan into four categories and to provide different funding levels based on need and merit. Funding had been based on the head count of students at the universities. The four categories are (1) research universities, (2) teaching universities, (3) special-purpose universities, and (4) community colleges. The hope is that this classification system, with a reapportionment of funding, will lead to a small number of world-class research universities within a decade.

- To change existing rules so that professors' compensation is based on quality of work; to award research grants for high-risk, leading research areas; and to give universities greater autonomy.
- To improve university-industry relationships, which have historically been weak or nonexistent.

Industry in Taiwan has relied much more on interactions with the many research institutes than with universities. Professors are government employees on salaries with few incentives to seek out relationships with industry. Industry has found that working with university faculties has not been rewarding on the whole. The National Science Council (NSC) has initiated an Industry-University Collaboration Program, but so far it has met with little success. Under this program, companies can form collaborations with university faculty to work on R&D areas of interest, with approved projects receiving up to 75 percent of the funding from the NSC.

Recommendations to improve matters include (1) changing regulations; (2) allowing the hiring of qualified people from industry as adjunct professors; (3) including patents, technology transfer efforts, and consulting work in promotion decisions; and (4) creating summer internship programs or work co-op programs to give students real-life work experiences.

Among recent changes are the following. The NSC has provided guidelines on IP rights for the research it sponsors in the universities; the Small Business Administration of the Ministry of Economic Affairs has funded incubation centers at some universities; and the question of whether professors should be involved in start-up companies and universities should be more active in encouraging entrepreneurship is now being discussed.

Also recently formed is the Association of Technology Managers in Taiwan (ATMT). This organization is patterned after the Association of University Technology Managers (AUTM) in the United States. The first listed objective of ATMT is "Transfer AUTM experience in the United States as our role model." AUTM has played a pivotal role in the growth and success of university-industry technology transfer in the United States, and it is hoped that ATMT will play a similar role for universities in Taiwan. Assuming that the recommendations of the university review committee will be implemented over the next few years, this will create a much more conducive environment for industry-university relations and technology transfer.

Government supported research institutes have played a more important role in technology sourcing and transfer in Taiwan than its universities; of these institutes the most important has been the Industrial Technology Research Institute (ITRI) (Wang 2004). There are reasons why this may change, but so far the creation of R&D results by these institutes and the transfer of these results to industry have made vital contributions to Taiwan's high-tech industries.

Most of the major manufacturers in the electronics industry are located in the corridor between Taipei and the Science-based Industrial Park in Hsinchu. And just as Stanford University provided a pipeline of technology and trained graduates to build the Silicon Valley in California, the "Silicon Valley Corridor" in Taiwan has relied on ITRI in a similar way. Since 1973, over 15,000 graduates from ITRI have fueled the growth of the electronics industry in Taiwan. ITRI has also welcomed back returning Taiwanese people from overseas, many from California's Silicon Valley, who bring important knowledge and skills to ITRI programs.

For Taiwan to move up the value chain and become more innovative, it needs to improve its universities and to build stronger relationships between them and companies (Tsay 2004). An analysis done by Professors C. Y. Tsay and Yun-Peng Chu reports that 79 percent of people with PhD degrees are in universities, 9 percent are in research institutes, and only 12 percent are in industry (Tsay and Chu 2004). They assert that due to the lack of effective collaborations, universities are producing academic papers with little industry relevance and industry is primarily creating improvement patents for defensive purposes. They believe this must change if Taiwan is to create the innovation important in remaining competitive in the future.

The government has recently taken measures to encourage university-industry links (Tsay and Chu 2004). Starting in 2002, the NSC has funded grants in which it contributes from 50 percent to 75 percent of approved project cost. The NSC also has created an "Outstanding Awards for Industry-University Collaboration" to recognize professors who are involved in successful collaborations. And the NSC is encouraging universities to start technology transfer programs, with 20 of them having been established by 2002.

The Ministry of Education is also changing the rules. It has also established six "University-Industry Collaboration Centers" at six Science and Technology Universities. And the Ministry of Economic Affairs (MOEA) has, since 1996, helped universities form incubation centers, with 60 in place by 2002. It also established three Science and Technology Special Programs for universities, industry, and research institutes for development of key technologies; in 2001 it put forth the National Science and Technology Development Plan. The projects fall into three categories with funding in 2002 of national

334   projects at $2 million, main projects at $19 million, and general projects at $81 million.

Although the government has been encouraging collaborations between universities and industry, the university culture so far has not changed much; industry continues to look to the research institutes for interaction and collaboration because their researchers strongly value industry collaborations.

China

In China, especially since 1985, faculty members in engineering and other applied disciplines have been encouraged to seek closer ties to industry (Lan 2004). "The Resolution of the Central Committee of the Communist Party of China on the structural reform of the educational system" issued in 1985, directed educational institutions to engage in economic and social development to improve society. Its purpose was similar to that of the 1980 Bayh-Dole legislation in the United States: to inform senior officers of universities that they have a part to play through proactive transfer of university expertise and research results to industry.

This has occurred in several ways, some more successful than others. They include (1) consulting by faculty, (2) patenting and licensing, (3) technical service contracts and joint research projects with companies, (4) collaborative R&D with multinational companies, (5) university-based science parks, and (6) university-affiliated enterprises. Universities have become dependent on the income generated from these interactions with industry.

The government share of operating funds for universities declined from about 75 percent in 1985 to less than 50 percent by the mid-1990s as universities aggressively sought support from industry. Less than 20 percent of all R&D spending by Chinese universities is for basic research, a characteristic government responsibility (Xue 2004). Most of the more than 80 percent spent on applied research and development is from technical service contracts and joint research programs with industry. Because state-owned enterprises (SOEs) in China have historically invested very little in R&D (less than 0.5% of sales income), they have little infrastructure for doing R&D. Thus, contracting with universities for such work is an attractive alternative for them, and the universities need the money.

The government in 1993 issued the "Law on Progress of Science and Technology of P.R.C.," which encouraged R&D collaborations with foreign entities, and some of the best universities, such as Tsinghua University, have established collaborative R&D projects with multinational companies (Ma 2004). In 2003, Tsinghua received $18 million from foreign partners representing 21 different regions and countries with $15 million coming from the top five countries or regions (the United States, Japan, the UK, Hong Kong, and France). Regarding ownership of the IP created, an analysis of 303 projects found 14 percent was with Tsinghua, 11 percent with the partner company, and 75 percent was jointly owned.

Patenting and licensing to generate royalty income is not yet important for the universities. It has not yet received senior-level support; there is a wide lack of expertise in the complex processes involved; and the lack of enforcement of patent rights weakens the value of patents as a licensing base (Sandelin 2002). This will likely change as some universities establish technology transfer and licensing offices and place greater emphasis on protecting intellectual property. There is also a growing concern about the financial risk associated with university-affiliated companies. And there is concern about the impact on the quality of teaching and research resulting from the involvement of professors and administrators in university-connected businesses. The government is now shifting away from its 1991 decree that encouraged universities to form university-owned enterprises.

In China, the National Association of Chinese Universities has a subgroup for intellectual property and technology transfer, and there have been discussions within this group on establishing an independent association for university technology transfer people. These discussions led to the formation of the Association of Chinese University Intellectual Property Offices in October 2004. At the initial three-day conference in October, Yongping Zheng, Director of the Tsinghua University Intellectual Property Office, was elected president of the newly formed Association.

University-affiliated enterprises (UAEs) have existed for a long time (Lan 2004). Since the 1950s, universities have had small-scale factories for training students and have operated service facilities such as printing shops and hotels. After the 1985 decree on structural reform, service facilities expanded as a source of income, and universities created joint commercial entities with outside organizations. A few also began to create university-owned companies, with university faculty members often serving as the chief operating officer or chief technology officer. In 1991, based on a review of over 30 universities by a government-commissioned investigative team, China's State Council endorsed university-affiliated enterprises. The creation of UAEs then accelerated, with their sales growing from $211 million in 1991 to $5.8 billion in 2000. In 2000, according to statistics of the Science and Technology Development Center of the Ministry of Education, there were 5,451 UAEs, with 2,097 identified as Science and Technology enterprises. Although less than 40 percent of the total, they generated over 90 percent of the business-related income to universities, with most of that income coming from a very few enterprises affiliated with the top universities. For example, in 2000 sales from companies

336   affiliated with Beijing and Tsinghua universities were $2.1 billion of the $5.8 billion for all universities.

As of 2003, Tsinghua's portfolio, which is managed by Tsinghua Holdings Co, Ltd., included 38 companies with a controlling equity position (over 50%) and 48 companies with a participating equity position (less than 50%) (Song 2004). Total sales were $1.8 billion, more than double the $755 million in 2000. Although most start-up companies from universities used faculty as initial management, it is more widely perceived that professors typically lack skills in management, marketing, and other business operations. Zhao Mulan (Zhao 2004) lists this problem of professors as managers as a reason why "university-owned firms perform quite poorly compared to other firms in Zhongguancun Science Park." Other reasons include ill-defined property rights and inter-ventions by university owners in the management of these businesses.

To address this problem, Tsinghua Holdings is recruiting outside manage-ment talent, primarily from the large alumni base of Tsinghua University. Currently about 30 percent of the Tsinghua-affiliated companies have CEOs recruited from the outside. The Tsinghua Science Park has a special section (Returned Overseas Students Start-Ups Incubator) devoted to companies formed and managed by returning alumni.

Another important aspect of the technology transfer process is university-owned science parks (Mei 2004). The first was created in 1989 by Northeast University. In 2001 and 2002, the Ministry of Science and Technology identi-fied 44 university science parks as the "National University Science Parks." As of October 2002, these parks had over 5,500 companies in residence. Of the 5,500, 2,300 are start-up companies in incubation facilities. To date, 920 com-panies have "graduated" from the incubation facilities. An official from this Ministry reported in 2004 that 30 percent of the National University Science Parks are doing well, 50 percent are at least breaking even, and 20 percent are doing poorly.

Tenants include a wide variety of enterprises: start-up companies, university-owned companies, R&D facilities or sales offices of large multinational com-panies, government research institutes, and many kinds of service providers including recreational facilities, cafes and restaurants, and hotel services. Some make university resources available to tenant companies, such as access to libraries. It is not clear what percentage of the companies in the University Research Parks are directly associated with the host university.

There are large differences between policies and practices in the United States and China, listed as follows:

   1. *Basic research versus applied research and development.* According to Professor Xue Lan of Tsinghua University, more than 80 percent of R&D spending by

Chinese universities is for applied research and development, mostly funded by industry (Xue 2004) whereas, according to the AUTM Annual Surveys, less than 10 percent of R&D funding at U.S. universities is by industry. Stanford professors are granted release time (one day per week) to serve as paid consultants when they can work on applied research and development projects. Much research within Stanford is done by graduate students and the research must be basic in nature for them to obtain doctorates.

2. *Central government involvement in university oversight, administration, and policies.* In China, there is a strong Ministry of Education and Ministry of Science and Technology that play active roles in setting the agenda and operating policies for universities. The central government also directly funds some of the operations of the universities. In the United States, there are no such ministries. It has a mixed system of private and state universities (in each of the 50 states) that operate with considerable autonomy. The U.S. federal government provides most of the research funding for research universities, but it does not exercise any direct control over the operations of U.S. universities.

3. *University-owned or -affiliated companies.* Although there appears to be a growing concern about some of the risks involved with such companies in China, their numbers, as reported previously, are large. In the United States, almost no universities directly form companies or own a controlling interest in them. The prevailing model is to grant a limited-term exclusive license to start-up companies for the university-owned intellectual property and to take a small amount of founding equity (normally under 5%) as partial compensation for the license. One reason for this model in the United States is its strict and punitive product liability laws. For universities such as Stanford with large endowments, the concern is very real. Thus, when Stanford professors are acting as paid consultants and doing work related to applied development, they are serving not as university employees but as independent contractors. This shields the university from any product liability claims that might result from such applied work.

4. *University-owned or -controlled science parks.* Although such parks exist in the United States (usually referred to as research parks), they are not part of a planned effort by the federal government. In China, the size and scope of the 44 "National University Science Parks" are much greater than that of their U.S. counterparts.

5. *Conflict of interest and conflict of commitment.* These topics, which are of great concern at most U.S. universities, are starting to draw attention in China. A conflict of interest occurs when potential financial gain may cause an individual or an institution to act in ways that may damage or embarrass either or both of them. A conflict of commitment occurs when outside interests cause an individual not to fulfill teaching or research commitments. U.S. research universities have expended much time and effort in developing comprehensive policies and protocols for identifying and trying to resolve such conflicts (but by no means to the satisfaction of all concerned). It appears that this topic is not yet of comparable priority at research universities in China.

6. *Ownership of IP.* In the United States, the general policy is that any IP created within the university by university employees or students is owned by the

338   university. Sponsors of research normally receive a nonexclusive right to practice the IP, and if such a sponsor is a company it normally would have first
right to a royalty-bearing exclusive license. Only with a collaborative research
project where both a university person and a company person are named as
co-inventors would there be joint ownership, and this is rare. Even rarer is the
situation when in a research collaboration an invention is made solely by a
company person, in which case ownership would be vested with the company.
At Stanford, less than 5 percent of inventions have joint or company ownership.
In any case, most research work is government funded (about 85% at Stanford)
and is basic. It appears that universities in China instead negotiate ownership
rights on a case-by-case basis.

In summary, policies of the Ministries of Education and of Science
and Technology have strongly influenced the paths taken by universities. A
Bayh-Dole-like directive in 1985 encouraged universities to create closer ties
to industry, and in 1991 a directive provided support and encouragement for
university-owned companies. A 1993 directive encouraged universities to seek
relationships with foreign entities. And in 2001, there came National University
Science Parks. The results have been (1) to make applied research and development contracts and joint research projects with companies a major source of
funding; (2) to create many university-owned or -affiliated companies and incubators; (3) to encourage collaborative relationships with foreign multinational companies; and (4) to build large, multipurpose university-owned or
-controlled science parks, with incubators for start-up companies linked to university faculty and alumni.

India

To protect the software industry in India, the country has implemented some
of the strongest copyright legislation in the world. The original Indian Copyright Act of 1957 underwent major changes that went into effect in 1995 (Briggs
and Watt 2001). However, as Dossani points out in Chapter 8, the vast majority of software creation is for custom services and not for creating software
products. This fact bears on the small amount of interaction between the universities and public research organizations and industry. At universities, few
faculty members do research, and policies and rules frequently discourage
professors from providing consulting services.

One concern is the brain drain, with the brightest graduates from the leading academic institutions emigrating in large numbers. Thus, many of the
graduated students, a primary source of technology transfer, are choosing to
work for foreign companies (with possible assignments overseas) or to apply for
work visas in developed countries that offer considerably higher wages. These

people, who obtain valuable work experience in places like California's Silicon Valley, could become a major resource for India's future economic development.

India has, of course, high-quality research organizations. The Council on Scientific and Industrial Research (CSIR) includes a chain of about 130 national laboratories in the sciences, engineering, and medicine, and there are others sponsored by other government agencies. However, there is criticism that most of these public research organizations do not have effective linkages with the private sector and thus little commercialization has occurred. ICAR, the agricultural research council, has about 50 laboratories throughout India and about 20,000 scientists. At its New Delhi laboratory, it has established an IPR Cell that is responsible for reviewing any intellectual property created by ICAR scientists (Maredia 2004). Each of the 50 laboratories within ICAR has an assigned liaison person who forwards IP-based invention disclosures to the IPR Cell for review and possible patenting.

The Tata Institute of Fundamental Research (TIFR) is widely recognized for its research programs. TIFR's newest center is the National Center for Biological Sciences (NCBS), located in Bangalore. With an 80,000-square-foot academic building filled with lab space, its mandate is to conduct basic research at the frontiers of biology. It is also actively seeking collaborative research projects with the private sector.

The Indian Institute of Science (IIS) in Bangalore is also well known for the quality of its research programs. In 1975, it established the Center for Scientific and Industrial Consultancy (CSIC). The CSIC now has a range of consulting arrangements with industry, from retainer relationships to the total development of processes, products, or software. And in recent years, the Indian Institutes of Technology (IIT), with mostly private sector support, have increased their R&D activities. IBM has established an R&D lab at the ITT in Delhi.

Assisting small and medium-sized enterprises (SMEs) is the Small Industries Development Organization (SIDO) (WIPO 2004). In 2001, SIDO began offering workshops for SMEs on intellectual property rights (IPR). The purpose is to educate SMEs about the role of IPR in business planning and success in the marketplace. The workshops provide an overview of the IP system from a business perspective, covering patents, trademarks, designs, and copyrights. SIDO has formed a collaboration with the World Intellectual Property Organization (WIPO) that is providing training for SIDO employees, and WIPO's training materials on IPR have been adopted for use in India.

Although there are industry associations, such as the National Association of Software and Service Companies (NASSCOM) that have been effective in

340   influencing policy reforms and in the professional development of its members, there currently is no association for technology transfer professionals in India. A few individuals contributed 5,000 rupees each to attempt to start such an association in 2004, with headquarters at the University of Pune Science and Technology Park in Bangalore (Maredia 2004).

It appears that the best description of public sector to private sector technology transfer in India is that of laissez faire. The government has not enacted any laws to stimulate this activity such as the Bayh-Dole Act. There have been few proactive attempts to encourage collaboration between the public sector research organizations and industry, and there has not (yet) been a call, as in Singapore, to move from using technology to creating it.

However India does have strong copyright laws, and it has recently enacted a new plant protection law and a law to protect pharmaceutical compounds. These new patent-related laws reflect India's becoming compliant with the Trade Related Intellectual Property Standards under the WTO standards. India has trained scientists and engineers with good English-speaking skills, many with work experience in various high-tech regions in the world and some with experience in starting companies in these high-tech regions. And it has many public-sector R&D organizations whose research results may have future commercial value.

COMPARISON WITH U.S. PRACTICES

Central Government Involvement

In the United States, the federal government has played an indirect role by encouraging universities and government laboratories receiving federal funds for research to actively engage in technology transfer activities. The 1980 Bayh-Dole Act and similar legislation for the federal labs enacted in 1986 provided first right of ownership of intellectual property rights (IPR) to the institution and required a sharing of royalty income with inventors; this was to encourage inventors to disclose inventions and to participate in the technology transfer process. The U.S. government also provides funding for research, both directly to the institutions and also in the form of joint research programs with industry such as the Advanced Technology Program. It also provides public venture funds, such as the SBIR and STTR programs (Etzkowitz, Gulbrandsen, and Levitt 2001, 420). The United States does not have a "Ministry of Education" or similar government agency that exerts direct control over the policies and activities of universities. Thus, U.S. universities have a great deal of independence in determining teaching, research, and public service agendas.

Ownership of Intellectual Property Rights

Most invention disclosures at U.S. universities identify the government as at least a partial sponsor, and thus IPR ownership falls under the Bayh-Dole Act (first right of ownership goes to the institution). For invention disclosures that are not government sponsored, the institution can make its own policy, but almost all U.S. universities require assignment to the university if the invention is made as part of its employment responsibilities or if university resources have been used in creating the invention.

Relative Emphasis on New Venture Formation versus Licensing to Existing Companies

Until recently, as documented in the AUTM Surveys, the Licensing Model (licensing to existing companies) has been by far the dominant model in the United States. The reasons for this include the following:

- Concerns by senior university officers about individual and institutional conflicts of interest that could have potential damaging effects on the institution's reputation resulting from involvement with start-up companies
- Potential product liability claims if the university is closely involved with a start-up company
- Professors failing to fulfill university responsibilities due to involvement with a start-up company
- Tax laws that exempt royalties from unrelated business income taxes
- The acceptance of licensing by the life sciences industries (especially biotechnology) that have provided good sources of royalty income.

However universities are learning how to effectively manage potential conflict situations, and some universities such as MIT, CalTech, and Stanford are building large portfolios of equity from the licensing of start-up companies. The growing interest in this area led AUTM to first offer a course in this area four years ago, and the course has been well attended every year since then.

Funding Sources for Technology Transfer Organizations (TTOs)

The U.S. federal government does not and has not provided any funding for TTOs in the United States. Operating costs for TTOs must be funded from royalty income, and if this is not sufficient, then the institution must cover the deficit. Under the Bayh-Dole provisions, a recipient of federal funding must have a technology transfer program. However, use of an agent, such as Research

342   Corporation Technologies (RCT), does fulfill this requirement. There are a
number of such agents, and most of them can be found at the "networking
fair" at the AUTM's annual meeting.

Use of Incubators, Science Parks, and Economic or High-Tech Zones

There are no "economic zones" in the United States, but some universities
have affiliated research/science parks. There are 123 university members of the
Association of University Research Parks (www.aurp.net), and a recent survey
revealed 62 percent of the parks have incubation facilities. In addition, some
universities have incubator facilities onsite, although this is not nearly as prevalent in the United States as in the six Asian regions covered in this book.

Status of Technology Transfer Associations

The existence of well-developed and well-supported professional associations
for technology transfer people in the United States is an important contributor to the country's relative success in this area. The Association of University
Technology Managers (www.autm.net) has more than 3,000 members (about
10% from overseas) and provides a wide spectrum of services, including conferences, courses, publications, and surveys. Over 1,700 people attended the
2004 AUTM Annual Meeting in San Antonio, Texas. Other associations related to technology transfer are the Licensing Executives Society, the Federal
Laboratories Consortium, and the Technology Transfer Society.

Appendix

SUCCESS FACTORS IN UNIVERSITY TO INDUSTRY
TECHNOLOGY TRANSFER BASED ON THE
STANFORD UNIVERSITY MODEL

Successful licensing of research results (sometimes referred to as undeveloped technology) created in universities or federal laboratories is difficult. The "product" to be licensed is not developed in response to commercial market need, the technology is very embryonic with uncertainty as to whether it will work reliably outside of the laboratory environment, and the financial risk to the licensee in bringing such embryonic technology to market is typically very significant. The licensee must anticipate what competing products will exist some years in the future (when the licensed product finally reaches the market) and have faith that the product can gain sufficient market share to justify the development, manufacturing, and marketing investments. The up-front and advanced royalty payments are typically inconsequential when compared with the other required investments to bring a new product to market.

A key attribute of organizations or licensing offices that are successful is that they view the process from a marketing perspective. They recognize the key role of the inventor, and develop policies and operating procedures that provide incentives to the key participants in the process. The key participants include (1) the inventor, (2) the licensing associate employed by the university or federal lab, and (3) a person employed by the potential licensee who believes the invention is important to his or her company's future. The latter person we will refer to as the Invention Advocate within the Company ("IAC").

THE INVENTOR'S ROLE

The inventor's participation and cooperation in the licensing process is normally required for there to be a successful outcome. The inventor (1) creates and discloses the invention to be licensed, (2) identifies people within the

344   industry who should be interested in the invention (such contacts are extremely valuable), (3) participates in obtaining patent protection, (4) responds to technical questions about the invention, and (5) hosts laboratory visits of potential IACs, where future research may lead to important discoveries of value to the licensee. The inventor may also, via a separate consulting agreement, provide know-how and show-how that may be critical to the commercialization of the invention.

It should be noted that for university researchers, involvement in the licensing process is normally not required and is seldom, if ever, included in their job description. Thus, policies must create incentives to encourage inventor participation in the process. Potential benefits to inventors may include some or all of the following: (1) a share of net royalties from the licensing of their invention (at Stanford, the share is one-third); (2) research funding by the licensee directly to the lab of the inventor; (3) paid consulting agreements between inventors and the licensee; (4) employment of the inventor by the licensee (this is common when students are inventors/co-inventors); and (5) payment (cash or equity or both) to serve on scientific advisory boards (this is relatively common when the licensee is a start-up company).

THE ROLE OF THE LICENSING ASSOCIATE

The licensing associate first evaluates invention disclosures and selects those to be patented and marketed (at Stanford, from 30% to 40% of the invention disclosures received are selected and of those selected, about 65% are eventually licensed). Selection factors include (1) prior success in licensing the inventions of this inventor, (2) the inventor's reputation in the field of the invention and his or her willingness to participate in the licensing process, (3) the expectation of future new discoveries related to the invention, (4) the application areas of the invention and whether they are in growing markets, and (5) responses from industry contacts asked to review the invention.

The key to licensing success lies in identifying a person within a company, gaining the attention of that person, and then converting interest into a conviction that a particular invention is needed by the company. The inventor is an important source of names of people in companies that may be interested in his or her invention. By referring to the inventor when contacting such people, there is a good chance of creating initial interest in the invention. Without such a referral, gaining the attention of people in industry is usually very difficult. The initial contact document should be a brief one-page invention summary that can be read in a few seconds, providing an abstract of the invention, its advantages over currently available technology, and applications for its use. Once initial interest has been aroused, more detailed information can be provided, such as invention disclosure material, journal articles describing the invention, and issued or pending patents. At this stage, it is normally a good practice for the licensing associate to coordinate a meeting between the potential IAC and the inventor.

The next stage is the negotiation of the License Agreement. This requires a realistic assessment of the value of the licensing arrangement to the company as well as an understanding as to what the company is seeking from the licensing arrangement. The Licensing Associate should have full authority to negotiate the final terms of the License Agreement, although the licensing associate may wish to consult with others (e.g., the inventors, other licensing associates, or the licensing office director) if unusual or difficult requests are made by the other party. Once this process has been completed, the licensing associate monitors the progress of licensed product development by the licensee to ensure that diligence terms are followed. Because the licensed invention is typically far from market and much can happen as a product is prepared for market, amending license agreements is a very common practice.

THE ROLE OF THE INVENTION ADVOCATE WITHIN THE COMPANY

The IAC convinces the management of his or her company that the licensed invention is important to the future of the company. The IAC therefore must be fully aware of both the present and future value of the licensed invention and the potential value of the relationship between the company and the university. For example, in 1974, an engineer based at his company's headquarters in Japan was visiting his company's office in Los Angeles. By chance, he happened to sit in on a presentation of a computer-based sound synthesis technique given by a professor at Stanford. Although this invention had been shown to many others, only this engineer recognized its potential. He became an invention advocate and convinced his company to become licensed. Ten years later, licensed products were introduced. These products were highly profitable for the company, and Stanford received many millions of dollars in royalties. In 1989, Stanford developed a follow-on technology, and an alliance was created between Stanford and this company. That young engineer subsequently became president of this multi-billion-dollar company.

POLICIES, PROCEDURES, AND RESOURCES

Policies to be followed are listed here.

- Inventors must be stakeholders in the financial success of licensing. They should receive a meaningful share of royalty income. This creates a justification for inventors to disclose inventions and to participate in various aspects of the licensing process. At Stanford University, inventors receive one-third of net royalties earned by their invention.

- The licensing office should receive a share of royalties, to offset the costs of the office and to further the objective of total self funding. This motivates the licensing office people, as they create the funding for their salaries and office operations from their success in bringing in licensing income.
- The licensing associate should be empowered to make all decisions concerning an invention assigned to him or her. Decisions include (1) if an invention should be accepted and a patent filed, (2) who files the patent; (3) what companies to contact; (4) how to market the invention; (5) the type of license appropriate for the situation (option agreement, exclusive or nonexclusive license); (6) financial terms of the license; (7) diligence provisions of the license; and (8) issues that arise after the license has been signed.
- Patent investments should be treated as inventory (an asset), and expensed only when it is clear that they cannot be licensed.

Procedures to be followed are listed here.

- Have a very simple invention disclosure form. Detailed information can be obtained at the first interview with the inventor. The barrier to disclosure should be minimal.
- Maintain a contacts file, indexed both by company name and by the person's name. Contacts are essential in this business.
- Be responsive to inquiries from inventors and companies. Always return telephone calls promptly.
- Maintain a simple docketing and filing system, with an effective tickler system for follow-up as needed.
- Keep the inventor(s) fully informed about actions taken on their invention.
- Always be on the lookout for a better way to do things.

Resources to be acknowledged are listed here.

- *Licensing associates.* Effective people in licensing usually have some experience in industry — in marketing, sales, or business development. Good communication skills (both oral and written) are essential. The emphasis and related allocation of time by associates should be focused on finding potential licensees and on structuring effective license agreements. Effective license agreements should be written in easy-to-understand plain language and should contain terms that both sides view as fair. The licensing associate only needs to know in very general terms what the invention is or does, why it is useful, and where it can be applied.
- *Clerical support.* Licensing generates lots of telephone calls and lots of correspondence. Most marketing materials are paper based. Keeping track of multiple deals in progress requires efficient filing and tracking

systems. An efficient support infrastructure frees licensing associates to focus on marketing.

- *Communication and computer tools.* Telephone, facsimile, and elec- tronic mail have become essential tools in the licensing office. The use of regular mail has declined dramatically, given the explosive growth of e-mail and facsimile machine use. Access to computer tools and services is essential, and investments in hardware, software, and training are required.

Important guiding principles are listed here.

- Focus attention on marketing and finding the IAC.
- Target efforts toward likely buyers and give them personal attention.
- The inventor must be a willing participant in the licensing process. Keep inventors fully informed about what you are doing to license their invention.
- Make it as easy as possible for people to join and/or participate in the licensing process. License agreements should be written in easy-to- understand plain language. It should be a simple straightforward process to obtain a license.
- Universities and industry are motivated to be good friends, and many benefits flow from industry to the university outside of licensing. Main- tain a university view, not a licensing office view, when looking at issues.
- Attorneys can provide good advice, but they should not be in control of the license negotiation. Also, decisions should be made by individuals, not committees.
- Negotiation is a mutual problem-solving process. Seek creative solutions to the concerns of the other party. Understanding what is important to the other side is necessary for reaching a strong lasting agreement.

REFERENCES

Association of Technology Managers in Taiwan (ATMT). Brochure.
Branscomb, M. L., F. Kodma, and R. Florida. 1999. *Industrializing Knowledge: University-Industry Linkages in Japan and the United States.* Cambridge, MA: MIT Press, p. 630.
Briggs, A. T., and S. Watt. 2001. "Impacts of National Information Technology Envi- ronments on Business." American University, Washington, DC.
Division of University Corporate Relations (DUCR). 2004. "The University of Tokyo Organization and Objectives." Power-Point presentation.
Dossani, R. Private Interview, November 23, 2004.
Etzkowitz, H., M. Gulbrandsen, and J. Levitt. 2001. *Public Venture Capital: Sources of Government Funding for Technology Entrepreneurs.* New York: Aspen, p. 420.
Forbes, N.. 2003. "Higher Education, Scientific Research and Industrial Competitive- ness: Reflections on Priorities for India." Conference on India's Economic Reforms

348   Center for Research on Economic Development and Policy Reform, Stanford University, June 5–7.

Hashimoto, M. 2003. "New Industrial Policy to Enhance the Cooperation between University and Industry by METI." Presentation, Status of Japanese Technology Transfer Workshop, AUTM Annual Meeting, February.

Ito, T. 2003. "Expectation and New Strategy for New University Collaboration." Presentation, Status of Japanese Technology Transfer Workshop, AUTM Annual Meeting, February.

Jun, M. 2004. "Collaborative R&D between Tsinghua University and Multinational Companies." Paper submitted to SPRIE Research Workshop: University-Research Institute-Industry Relations in the U.S., Taiwan and Mainland China, Stanford University, September 7–8.

Kneller, R. 2003. "University-Industry Cooperation and Technology Transfer in Japan Compared with the US: Another Reason for Japan's Economic Malaise?" *University of Pennsylvania Journal of International Law* 24(2).

———. 2004a. "Transformation of Japan's National Universities into Administratively Independent Corporations." *Les Novelles* (March): 1–5.

———. 2004b. "The New Japanese System of Technology Transfer: Concerns Related to the Role of University IP Centers." *Les Novelles* (June): 69–72.

Kodato, S. 2003. "New Management Policy for IP and Technology Transfer." Presentation, Status of Japanese Technology Transfer Workshop, AUTM Annual Meeting, February.

Korea Times. 2004. "More High-Tech Research Centers Flock Here." (October 22).

Liu, C. H. 2004. "Taiwan's Higher Education Reform towards Building a Knowledge-Based Economy." Paper submitted to SPRIE Research Workshop: University-Research Institute-Industry Relations in the U.S., Taiwan and Mainland China, Stanford University, September 7–8.

Maredia, K. Private Interview, November 24, 2004.

Meng, M. 2004. "Innovation Feedback: Interactive Development in Research Universities and Their Science Parks." Paper submitted to SPRIE Research Workshop: University-Research Institute-Industry Relations in the U.S., Taiwan and Mainland China, Stanford University, September 7–8.

Ministry of Economy, Trade and Industry (METI). 2003. "Guide to Technology Licensing Organizations (TLOs) in Japan." Industry-University Cooperation Division.

Nishizawa, A. 2003. "The New Management System of Intellectual Property Rights in Japanese National Universities." *Innovation Matters* 1(6).

Organization for Economic Co-operation and Development (OECD). 2003. "Turning Science into Business: Patenting and Licensing at Public Research Organizations."

Sandelin, J. 2002. Report from the Higher Education Policymakers Exchange on Technology Transfer and IPR Protection, October 26–November 8, People's Republic of China.

———. 2004. Survey Results from National University of Singapore, Nanyang Technical University, and Agency for Science, Technology and Research (A*STAR); and materials obtained during August 2002 visit with NUS and A*STAR.

Saxenian, A. 2000, "Bangalore: The Silicon Valley of Asia?" Conference on Indian Economic Prospects: Advancing Policy Reform, Center for Research on Economic Development and Policy Reform, Stanford University.

Shanghai Jiao Tong University Science Park. 2004. Presentation, International Forum of University Science Park, October 20–21.

Shimizu, K. 2003. "Management and Tech-Transfer Activities at a Private University — Keio University's Experience." Presentation, Status of Japanese Technology Transfer Workshop, AUTM Annual Meeting, February.

Song, J. 2004. "How Tsinghua Manages Its Companies." Paper submitted to SPRIE Research Workshop: University-Research Institute-Industry Relations in the U.S., Taiwan and Mainland China, Stanford University, September 7–8.

Tanaka, S. 2003. "New System of IP Management and Technology Transfer of the Japanese University." Presentation, Status of Japanese Technology Transfer Workshop, AUTM Annual Meeting, February.

Tsay, C. Y., and Chu, Y.-P. 2004. "Building Bridges among Universities, Research Institutes, and Industry in Taiwan." Paper submitted to SPRIE Research Workshop: University-Research Institute-Industry Relations in the U.S., Taiwan and Mainland China, Stanford University, September 7–8.

Wang, K. 2004. "The ITRI Experience: Innovative Engine of Taiwan's High Tech Industry." Paper submitted to SPRIE Research Workshop: University-Research Institute-Industry. Relations in the U.S., Taiwan and Mainland China, Stanford University, September 7–8.

"The Window to the World Technology." Publication of Tsinghua Science Park.

WIPO: Small and Medium-Sized Enterprises. 2004. "Outreach Activities on Intellectual Property of the Small Industries Development Organization (SIDO) of India."

Xue, L. 2004. "University-Market Linkages in China: The Case of University-Affiliated Enterprises." Paper submitted to SPRIE Research Workshop: University-Research Institute-Industry Relations in the U.S., Taiwan and Mainland China, Stanford University, September 7–8.

Young, T. 2004. "Financing University Technology Transfer Offices." *Innovation Matters* 2(10).

Zhao, M. 2004. "A Research Report on the Performance and Problems of University-Owned Firms in the Zhongguancun Science Park." Paper submitted to SPRIE Research Workshop: University-Research Institute-Industry Relations in the U.S., Taiwan and Mainland China, Stanford University, September 7–8.

12

CONCLUDING REMARKS

Moving from Making IT to Creating IT

Henry S. Rowen, William F. Miller, and
Marguerite Gong Hancock

By 2006, the information technology industry was showing signs of maturing after more than 50 years of rapid growth. This does not mean that there are no breakthroughs yet to come or that its economic and social effects are fully developed. However, some technology paths have become well trodden and the way ahead for some industry sectors appears fairly clear — at least for several years ahead.

Although the technology might not leap ahead as fast in the future as in the past, rapid growth in the demand for the products of this industry will continue from an already large base — and it will shift to Asia. This will be for the simple reason that world economic growth will increasingly occur in that region and a significant portion of the growing incomes will be spent on products containing information technologies. Already, China has the world's largest market for cell phones and this will soon be true of mobile communications devices in general, PCs, online services, and much more. And India is coming along behind.

In hindsight, it might seem inevitable that Asia would rise to a prominent position in the technologies of information, perhaps in time to a dominant one, but it did not look that way to most observers from the vantage point of 1970. Then, only Japan was developed and had strong scientific and commercial competencies. The four "Tigers" — South Korea, Taiwan, Hong Kong and Singapore — were growing rapidly, but they were small and technically backward. China was still in the throes of the Cultural Revolution that had disrupted its scientific community and was almost a decade away from beginning to liberalize its economy, while India was two decades from making its decisive move away from socialism. This book shows for the IT industry how six

regions transformed themselves. Their achievements were not only in this industry; indeed, what they did in the IT industry would not have been feasible
without their adopting effective overall economic policies. It is easy to forget
how poor most were, excepting Japan and to some extent Singapore. But they
all clearly have "made IT," or are "making IT." It is no coincidence that only
when governments made major changes in their overall economic policies
did their IT sectors take off. This happened, notably, not long after China began to liberalize its economy in 1978 and after India expanded reforms in 1991.

This book shows that major Asian players pursued several paths to developing a significant place in the global IT industry. By the 1990s, the governments of all six countries or regions had adopted a portfolio of strategies or exhibited patterns of behavior that were similar in many ways, even though they
differed markedly in others.

SIMILARITIES

Eventually all adopted growth-positive development policies. This book does
not focus on a random sample of regions. We do not have chapters on Vietnam, Indonesia, Malaysia, or Myanmar, countries that have not played a significant role in IT. No country that failed to adopt at least a minimum set of
policies to promote development—including substantial reliance on the private sector, some kinds of openness to the outside world, encouragement of
capital formation, and investment in education—has succeeded in the IT
industry. India and China were late, but by the 1990s they had both done so.

All these regions invested in educating enough scientists and engineers to be
able to participate significantly in this sector. This does not mean that all had
good general educational policies. India's educational policies have been notoriously weak, and the distribution of education in China was uneven,
though it is improving. Because the pool of talent is large in these two countries, when even a small proportion become well educated a very able set of
people can rise to prominence.

All had to acquire these information technologies. At the beginning of the
period examined in this book (circa 1970), only Japan among the six had a substantial technological base and in the following decades even it had to acquire
many technologies from abroad (while also advancing them). Dependence on
foreign technology was much greater for the others. This pattern is changing.
Various indicators, discussed subsequently, show a rise in scientific competencies and technical innovation.

All these governments actively promoted their IT industries. Central and local government leaders all identified IT as a key set of industries. Telecom-

352   munications has widely been seen as "strategic" throughout the world, and computers came to be seen as a leading-edge sector in which they could establish market positions. The products were light and hence cheap to move, the adoption of (nearly) universal standards enabled new firms to enter, demand for products was growing rapidly, and the largest market, the United States, was relatively open.

All regions exercised strategic openness to the outside world. No successful country/region can be isolated. These six—eventually—were engaged with the world, not only through trade but also through other mechanisms as well. These mechanisms—licensing, investments by MNCs, flows of people to and from other countries—enabled them to acquire foreign technology and know-how.

In particular, all had linkages with the United States. These were of several kinds and the mix of them varied among countries. They included students coming to the United States for advanced degrees (notably ethnic Chinese from all over the region, as well as Indians), often staying to work and, for some, then returning home. This flow peaked for several countries in the mid-1990s and then declined. (Restrictions on visas after the attack on September 11, 2001, have further reduced the numbers coming to study.) Other linkages have included extensive trade in goods and services, direct investments, and payments for technology.

Universities were rarely sources of technology. Their role was to produce trained people; for most of this period this was especially the case at the undergraduate level. An exception to this general pattern is the role of some leading universities in China, notably Tsinghua and Beijing Universities, each of which has been the source of many companies.

The financial systems of all these countries changed. These changes affected their IT industries. The role of banks diminished and that of stock markets increased. All sought to develop venture capital industries, although the results were mixed.

DIFFERENCES

Legal rules were either inherited or established and were reasonably effective in all regions, except for mainland China. Because such rules limit the ability of those with political power to extort resources from private parties and provide predictable processes for making and enforcing contracts, they encourage investment. Why, then has China done so well? Part of the answer is that some assurance is given to investors by the support of local governments that want their localities to prosper; another part is that China was at first so backward in this

respect that a modicum of good government has gone a long way toward fostering investment.

Competition among localities (towns and provinces) helped to accelerate commercial development. It was pointed out by Rosenberg and Birdzell that Europe's early development was helped by competition among its various independent political entities.[1]

Openness was expressed in many different ways:

- Japan, Korea, and India long held off foreign direct investment whereas Singapore, Taiwan, and mainland China welcomed it — but selectively.
- Japan, Korea, and Taiwan became major acquirers of technology through licensing.
- Flows abroad of students, many of whom stayed to work, and the in-migration of people skilled in technology and management were important for Taiwan, India, Singapore, and mainland China, but much less so for Japan and Korea.

Government promotion of IT industries. This was done in different ways, some effectively and some less so. A wide array of instruments was used: the training of computer scientists and engineers; trade protection; inviting MNCs, or, on the contrary, preferring other instruments, such as licensing; government spending on research; tax incentives for private R&D; the creation of dedicated research institutes; recruiting of experts with foreign experience; supplying cheap real estate to favored companies, targeted tax breaks; and more. A method that China, especially, is using is trying to establish standards for products sold in its market with the aim of collecting the royalties and license fees now being paid to foreign owners of intellectual property. This campaign so far has not succeeded, but the game is just beginning.

Linkages with the United States. Although all had strong links with the United States, the mixture of ways differed in the areas of trade, foreign direct investment, licensing, and movements of people. There were also widespread connections between Japan and East Asia. Dense business connections have been established between Taiwan and mainland China.

Entrepreneurship. Some regions had active entrepreneurship expressed through the formation of new firms (Taiwan, India, mainland China) while there was little in others. Singapore, Japan, and Korea have been making legal and policy changes to encourage it, so far with modest results.

Innovation. Only Japan among the six countries displayed technical innovativeness throughout the period. Taiwan, Korea, and Singapore, especially, began to develop it during the 1990s (measured, for instance, by the number U.S. patents granted). There are good reasons to expect an increase in innovations throughout Asia in the years ahead.

354   *Regional clusters* became prominent in all these countries except Japan. These were mostly government-created, except for Teheran Valley in Korea, the Indian clusters, and the nascent IC cluster in Fukuoka, Japan, where market forces have dominated.

Mobility of labor. All six countries had mobile labor markets except Japan and Korea (whose governments recently have taken actions to encourage mobility). A question that has arisen is whether mobility of professionals is too high in places like Shanghai and Beijing, where "job-hopping" is alleged to be a problem. If it is, the market will sort it out.

Financial systems evolved during this period, but only Taiwan had a well-developed venture capital system by 2000. A recent phenomenon is a marked rise of interest on the part of U.S. venture capitalists in investing in China and India, and such investments might become substantial in the years ahead.

Research institutes specializing in IT became ubiquitous, but their significance varied. In particular, they were significant sources of new companies in Taiwan and mainland China, but not in the others.

A LOOK AHEAD

Three topics are flagged here: (1) the growing importance of Asian demand for IT products; (2) the further development of venture capital; and (3) the prospect of Asia's becoming a creator of technology. These are discussed in the following subsections.

Asia's Growing Market for IT Products

Asia's role as a supplier has long been prominent, and it is clear now that it will be a huge consumer. Japan, with total economic output one-half that of the United States, is already a consumer, but the economic development of China and India will transform the world market for these goods. With — not assured but plausible — projections that China's economic output (in purchasing parity) will overtake that of the United States by around 2030 and that of India perhaps 20 year later, an enormous demand for products is in store. Nor will large markets be limited to these countries. Indonesia, for example, has the potential to become a large consumer.

The rise on the demand side in Asia is having a feedback effect on the supply side. Even in an age in which telecommunications costs have plummeted, distance can matter. Producers of many products want to be close to their customers and, increasingly, these customers will be in Asia. To cite a recent case, the Wyse Corporation, a maker of computer terminals, is broadening into the mobile telecommunications market and, at the same time, is moving 60 percent of its jobs from Silicon Valley to India and China. Those remaining will perform headquarters and research functions. It is making this move to be closer to customers and because engineers work cheaper there than in Silicon Valley. Wyse's management forecasts a five-fold expansion in sales by 2010.[2] Because this is not necessarily a zero-sum game, if Wyse succeeds, by 2010 it might have more—and higher-level—workers in Silicon Valley than it does today. This is the history of the disk drive industry in Silicon Valley and its general story line is being repeated in other industries.

The Further Development of Venture Capital

Venture capital as it has developed in the United States is a very productive but complex system that turns out not to be easily transferred to other economic systems. It depends not only on having favorable financial rules and institutions but also on having a cadre of experienced participants, and it takes time to produce them. As Kenney et al. report in Chapter 10, it has been transferred to some nations, particularly Israel and Taiwan. They point out that the Asian economies most successful in creating a venture capital industry are those with the closest human ties to the United States, Taiwan and Singapore. And their governments have adopted policies to encourage it. Because India and China also have strong ties to the United States, Kenney et al. suggest that a Silicon Valley–like venture capital industry will evolve in them and that China will become a "successful hotbed for venture capital innovation." But they also point out that investors are subject to the vagaries of the Chinese legal and political system, that the long-term profitability of investment in China is not yet proven, and that a more stable system is needed.

Advances in Higher Education, Science, and Technology

There is a growing belief in scientific and technical circles that Asia is not only a place for making things but also a place where important technologies will be created—perhaps soon. All of our regions that have not already done so are establishing the requisites for this. They have able, well-trained people, have or are developing needed institutions, and have researchers with personal experience and connections in productive research establishments around the world.

The American experience supports the view that the core need for having innovative science-based industries is having excellent universities, and these are in short supply in much of Asia. Dr. Morris Chang, Chairman of Taiwan

356   Semiconductor Manufacturing Company, is quoted to this effect: "I wish Taiwan had a world-class university."[3] Taiwan is not alone. According to a recent survey of the world's top 500 universities by Shanghai's Jiao Tong University, Asia has none in the top 100 outside of Japan.[4] The *New York Times Higher Education Supplement* rates Asian universities rather higher, with eight in its top 100 outside of Japan: Beijing University (17), National University of Singapore (18), Hong Kong University (39), Indian Institute(s) of Technology (41), Hong Kong University of Science and Technology (42), Nanyang University (50), Tsinghua University in Beijing (62), and the Chinese University of Hong Kong (84).[5] This is not very many for a region with 40 percent of the world's people.

The problem is not with the quality of the students; rather, it is with the organization of their university systems and the research support provided for universities. On the whole, they are over-regulated. In some, faculty members are civil servants; there is too little peer review for promotions and research grants (using foreign as well as domestic peers); and there is too little competition for faculty and students among them. As a result, many talented students have gone abroad for graduate studies and stayed there; many first-rate academics from Asia are found in U.S. and European universities; others have moved to careers in business; and governments have tended to allocate research funds preferentially to research institutes rather than universities. Given the importance of graduate students in advancing science, this is a dubious allocation of resources. The U.S. experience has been that linking advanced research with graduate education helps both teaching and research.

There is currently a strong interest in all the Asian countries we have studied in having more collaboration between academic institutions and industry. At the same time, there is strong interest in moving the technology base of the countries to higher value-added products. These two objectives are somewhat in conflict. Too strong faculty-industry ties can lead faculty and graduate students away from the creation of new, cutting-edge technologies. In top U.S. universities, the criteria for promotion of faculty are based solely on teaching and contributions to leading-edge research. Collaborations with industry and commercial work are not included.

One indicator of change is the large and growing numbers of scientists and engineers with advanced degrees. The number of PhDs granted in Korea from 1986 to 1999 increased by four times, in Taiwan by five times and in China by about 50 times (from 100 to 200 to more than 7,000).[6] There is increased spending on research and development as well as growth in the number of scientific publications and in their quality, as measured by citations.

On the commercial side, there is a high and rising level of patents in Japan,

Korea, and Taiwan; the beginning of international patenting from China; and a shift toward net zero in the balance of royalty and license payments with the United States. Taiwan subsidizes firms nominally up to 50 percent (actually closer to 20%), and the number of Taiwanese firms with R&D centers had risen to 39 by 2003.[7] Singapore has recruited a stellar group of biologists from around the world, and many foreign firms have set up R&D centers in China — supposedly over 600 in number. There is a question about what activities are actually taking place in these centers; many seem currently to be designing products for the domestic market rather than doing research or leap-ahead development but this is likely to change.

China has great ambitions in science and technology, and given its accomplishments, they are likely to be realized — although the timing is uncertain. Between 1995 and 2000, its spending on R&D more than doubled. It still was only 1 percent of GDP but was growing at 10 percent a year, and the government says it wants to increase that share.[8] In the year 2000, China ranked eighth in the world in scientific papers contributed by Chinese authors (3% of the world total) compared with its rank as 15th in the world five years earlier. This is not to assert that China's capacities are up to those of the industrialized countries. This will not likely happen soon, but China is on the move.[9]

Its advance in nanoscale science is one indicator of progress. From publishing no articles in this field in the period 1984–1987, in 2003, Chinese scholars produced about 12 percent of the articles published in the world, nearly half of those produced in the leading country, the United States. This was more than was published by scientists in Japan.[10] However, China was still short with high-impact articles (judging by citations), with about 15 percent as many as the United States (2001–2003).

A creative Asia will have mixed impacts. The generation of new ideas can benefit everyone. It also gives their creator an industrial advantage — as Silicon Valley has demonstrated — in being a pioneer. What should not be in doubt is that the United States and every other nation will face new opportunities for collaboration as well as significant challenges in competition with the rise of an innovative Asia.

NOTES

1. Nathan Rosenberg and L. E. Birdzell, Jr., *How the West Grew Rich*, Basic Books, 1986, pp. 136–137.
2. *San Jose Mercury News*, July 8, 2005.
3. *Financial Times*, July 8, 2005.
4. http://ed.sjtu.edu.cn/rank/2004/top500list.htm.

358   5. *The Times Higher Education Supplement*, November 5, 2004.

6. Diana Hicks, "Benchmarking Growth: Are We Looking in the Wrong Direction?" Presentation, Tokyo, September 2004. Also, National Science Foundation, S&E Indicators, 2002, Appendix Table 2-41.

7. Douglas B. Fuller, "The Changing Limits and the Limits of Change: The State, Private Firms, China and Global Industry in the Evolution of Taiwan's Electronics Industry." *Journal of Contemporary China* 14(45).

8. Kathleen Walsh, "Foreign High-Tech R&D in China: Risks, Rewards and Implications for U.S.-China Relations." Henry L. Stimson Center, 2003.

9. Kathleen Walsh, op. cit.

10. Lynne Zucker and Michael Darby, "Socio-Economic Impact of Nanoscale Science: Initial Results and Nanobank," National Bureau of Economic Research Working Paper 11181, March 2005.

References

Abernathy, F. H., J. T. Dunlop, J. H. Hammond, and D. Weil. 2004. "Globalization in the Apparel and Textile Industries: What Is New and What Is Not?" In M. Kenney and R. Florida, eds. *Locating Global Advantage: Industry Dynamics in the International Economy*. Stanford, CA: Stanford University Press.

Acs, Z. J., ed. 2000. *Regional Innovation, Knowledge, and Global Change*. London: Pinter.

——. 2002. *Innovation and the Growth of Cities*. London: Edward Elgar.

Acs, Z. J., and D. B. Audretsch, eds. 2003. *Handbook of Entrepreneurship Research: An Interdisciplinary Survey and Introduction*. Dordrecht: Kluwer Academic Publishers.

Acs, Z. J., H. L. F. de Groot, and P. Nijkamp, eds. 2002. *The Emergence of the Knowledge Economy: A Regional Perspective*. New York: Springer.

Agency for Science, Technology and Research (ASTAR). (various years). *National Survey of R&D in Singapore*. Singapore: Author.

Akella, R., and R. Dossani. 2001. "A Report on the Software Value Chain: The Indian Suppliers during the Downturn." Working paper, Asia-Pacific Research Center, Stanford University.

Amsden, A. 1989. *Asia's Next Giant: South Korea and Late Industrialization*. New York: Oxford University Press.

——. 1992. *Asia's Next Giant: South Korea and Late Industrialization*. New York: Oxford University Press.

Amsden, A., and F. T. Tschang. 2003. "A New Approach to Assessing the Technological Complexity of Different Categories of R&D (with Examples from Singapore)." *Research Policy* 32(4):553–572.

Amsden, A. H., and W. Chu. 2003. *Beyond Late Development: Taiwan's Upgrading Policies*. Cambridge, MA: MIT Press.

Aoki, M., and A. Haruhiko, eds. 2002. *Modularity* (in Japanese). Toyokeizaishinposha.

Aoki, M., H.-K. Kim, and M. Okuno-Fujiwara. 1997. *The Role of Government in East Asian Economic Development: Comparative Institutional Analysis*. Oxford, UK: Clarendon Press.

360   Arora, A., and S. Athreye. 2002. "The Software Industry and India's Economic Development." *Information Economics and Policy* 14(2):253–273.

Arora, A., A. Gambardella, and S. Torrisi. 2001. "In the Footsteps of Silicon Valley? Indian and Irish Software in the International Division of Labour." Discussion Paper 00-041, Stanford Institute for Economic Policy Research (SIEPR).

Arthur, W. B. 1994. *Increasing Returns and Path Dependence in the Economy*. Ann Arbor: University of Michigan Press.

Asian Technology Information Program. 1998. "Venture Capital in Taiwan." Report ATIP98.009, Asian Technology Information Program.

Asian Venture Capital Journal (AVCJ). 1992. *The 1992/1993 Guide to Venture Capital in Asia*. Hong Kong: Author.

——. 2001. *The 2001 Guide to Venture Capital in Asia*. Hong Kong: Author.

——. 2002. *The 2002 Guide to Venture Capital in Asia*. Hong Kong: Author.

——. 2003. *The 2003 Guide to Venture Capital in Asia*. Hong Kong: Author.

——. 2004. *The 2004 Guide to Venture Capital in Asia*. Hong Kong: Author.

Association of Technology Managers in Taiwan (ATMT). Brochure.

Athreye, S. 2002. "The Indian Software Industry." Working paper, Open University.

——. 2003. "The Indian Software Industry and Its Evolving Service Capability." Working paper, Open University.

Autio, E., P. K. Wong, and P. Reynolds. 2003. "National Factors Influencing the Prevalence of High-Potential Start-ups." Working paper, NUS Entrepreneurship Centre, National University of Singapore.

Avnimelech, G., M. Kenney, and M. Teubal. 2005. "A Life Cycle Model for the Creation of National Venture Capital Industries: Comparing the U.S. and Israeli Experiences." In E. Giuliani, R. Rabellotti, and M. P. van Dijk, eds. *Clusters Facing Competition: The Role of External Linkages*. London: Ashgate Publishers.

Bae, Z.-T. 1994. "Planning and Principles for the Construction of S&T Industrial Parks: The Korean Approaches." Paper presented at the APEC Seminar on Development Strategies of Science and Technology Industrial Parks in Asia and the Pacific, Beijing.

Bahrml, H., and S. Evans. 1995. "Flexible Recycle and High-Technology Entrepreneurship." *California Management Review*.

Balasubramanyam, V., and A. Balasubramanyam. 2000. "The Software Cluster in Bangalore." In J. Dunning, ed. *Regions, Globalization and Knowledge-Based Economy*. Oxford, UK: Oxford University Press, pp. 349–363.

Barabasi, A.-L. 2002. *Linked: The New Science of Networks*. Japan Broadcast Publishing Co.

Basant, R. 2002. "Knowledge Flows and Industrial Clusters: An Analytical Review of the Literature." Working paper, Indian Institute of Ahmedabad.

Besher, A. 1988. "Taiwan, U.S. Firms Team Up on Venture Capital Fund." *San Francisco Chronicle*, June 13, p. C9.

Birch, D., A. Haggerty et al. 1997. *Who's Creating Jobs?* Cambridge, MA: Cognetics.

Branscomb, M. L., F. Kodma, and R. Florida. 1999. *Industrializing Knowledge: University-Industry Linkages in Japan and the United States*. Cambridge, MA: MIT Press, p. 630.

Bresnahan, T., and A. Gambardella, eds. 2004. *Building High-Tech Clusters: Silicon Valley and Beyond*. New York: Cambridge University Press. **361**

Bresnahan, T., A. Gambardella, A. Saxenian, and S. Wallsten. 2001. "'Old Economy' Inputs for 'New Economy' Outcomes: Cluster Formation in the New Silicon Valley." Discussion Paper 00-043, Stanford Institute for Economic Policy Research (SIEPR).

Briggs, A. T., and S. Watt. 2001. "Impacts of National Information Technology Environments on Business." American University, Washington, DC.

Brown, J. S., and P. Duguid. 2000. In C. M. Lee, W. F. Miller, M. G. Hancock, and H. Rowen, eds. *The Silicon Valley Edge: A Habitat for Innovation and Entrepreneurship*. Stanford, CA: Stanford University Press.

Bureau of Statistics. http://140.111.1.192/statistics/service/sts4-5.htm.

Burg, U. Von. 2001. *The Triumph of Ethernet: Technological Communities and the Battle for the Lan Standard*. Stanford, CA: Stanford University Press.

Bygrave, W. D., and J. A. Timmons. 1992. *Venture Capital at the Crossroads*. Boston: Harvard Business School Press.

Cabral, R. 1998. "The Cabral-Dahab Science Park Management Paradigm: An Introduction." *International Journal of Technology Management* 16(8):721–722.

Carr, N. 2003. "IT Doesn't Matter." *Harvard Business Review* (May): 41–49.

Caso, E., and S. Kohler. 1998. "India: The Next Silicon Valley?" BT Alex Brown Research.

Castells, M. 1989. *The Informational City: Information Technology, Economic Restructuring, and the Urban-Regional Process*. London: Blackwell Publishers.

Chabbal, R., and N. Maeda. 2000. "The Development of Research Related Start-ups — A France-Japan Comparison." National Institute of Science and Technology Policy (NISTEP) Discussion Paper 16.

Chang, B. L., and C. W. Hsu. 2002. "Government Policy's Influences on Science-Based Industrial Park Development in Taiwan." *Made in Taiwan: Booming in the Technology Era*. Singapore: World Scientific Publishing.

Chen, T.-J., and Y.-H. Ku. 2002. "The Development of Taiwan's Personal Computer Industry." International Centre for the Study of East Asian Development (ICSEAD), Kitakyushu.

Chen, X., L. K. Cheng, K. C. Fung, and L. J. Lau. 2003. "The Estimation of Domestic Value-Added and Employment Induced by Exports: An Application to Chinese Exports to the United States." Unpublished manuscript.

ChinaOnline. 1999. "China Launches New High Tech Venture Capital Fund." (October 5).

Choi, H. 1987. "Mobilization of Financial Resources for Technology Development." *Technological Forecasting and Social Change* 31:347–358.

Christensen, C. M. 1997. *The Innovator's Dilemma: When New Technologies Cause Great Firms to Fail*. Boston: Harvard Business School Press.

Core Logic. http://www.corelogic.co.kr.

Correa, C. 1996. "Strategies for Software Exports from Developing Countries." *World Development* 24(1):171–182.

362 Curry, J., and M. Kenney. 2004. "The Organization and Geographic Configuration of the Personal Computer Value Chain." In M. Kenney and R. Florida, eds. *Locating Global Advantage*. Stanford, CA: Stanford University Press.

Davenport, S., A. Carr, and D. Bibby. 2002. "Leveraging Talent: Spin-off Strategy at Industrial Research." *R&D Management* 32:241–254.

D'Costa, A. 2000. "Technology Leapfrogging: The Software Challenge in India." In Conceicao et al., eds. *Knowledge for Inclusive Development*. Westport, CT: Quorum Books.

——. 2002. "Export Growth and Path Dependence: The Locking-in of Innovations in the Software Industry." *Science, Technology and Society* 7(1):51–87.

——. 2002. "Software Outsourcing and Development Policy Implications: An Indian Perspective." *International Journal of Technology Management* 24(7/8):705–723.

Dedrick, J., and K. Kraemer. 1993. "Information Technology in India: The Quest for Self-Reliance." *Asian Survey* 33(5).

Desai, A. 2003. "The Dynamics of the Indian Information Technology Industry." Working paper, London Business School.

Division of University Corporate Relations (DUCR). 2004. "The University of Tokyo Organization and Objectives." Power-Point presentation.

Dore, R. 1986. *Flexible Rigidities: Industrial Policy and Structural Adjustment in the Japanese Economy 1970–80*. Stanford, CA: Stanford University Press.

Dossani, R., ed. 2002. *Telecommunications in India*. Westport, CT: Greenwood Books.

Dossani, R., and M. Kenney. 2002. "Creating an Environment for Venture Capital in India." *World Development* 30(2):227–253.

——. 2003. "Lift and Shift: Moving the Back Office to India." *Information Technology and International Development* 1(2):21–37.

DP Information Network Pte Ltd. (various years). *Singapore 1000*. Singapore: Author.

Economic Development Board (EDB). (various years). *EDB Yearbook*. Singapore: Author.

——. (various years). *The Singapore Venture Capital Industry Survey 1999*. Singapore: Author.

——. (various years). *Report on the Census of Industrial Production*. Singapore: Author.

Economic Review Committee (ERC). 2002. *Report of the Entrepreneurship and Internationalization Subcommittee*. 13 September 2002. Singapore: Ministry of Trade and Industry.

Economist. 2004. "Innovative India." April 3, pp. 65–66.

Etzkowitz, H., M. Gulbrandsen, and J. Levitt. 2001. *Public Venture Capital: Sources of Government Funding for Technology Entrepreneurs*. New York: Aspen, p. 420.

Feigenbaum, E. 2002. *The Japanese Entrepreneur: Making the Desert Bloom*. Nikkei.

Feldman, P. M. 1994. *The Geography of Innovation*. Dordrecht: Kluwer Academic Publishers.

Financial Times. July 8, 2005.

Finegold, D., P. K. Wong, and T. C. Cheah. 2004. "Singapore's Emerging Biotech Cluster: Old Strategy Replication or New Approach?" *European Planning Studies*.

Fischer, M. M. 2001. *Knowledge, Complexity and Innovation Systems.* New York: 363
Springer.

Florida, R. 2002. *The Rise of the Creative Class.* New York: Basic Books.

Florida, R., and M. Kenney. 1988. "Venture Capital–Financed Innovation and Technological Change in the U.S." *Research Policy* 17(3):119–137.

——. 1988. "Venture Capital, High Technology and Regional Development." *Regional Studies* 22(1):33–48.

Forbes, N. 2003. "Higher Education, Scientific Research and Industrial Competitiveness: Reflections on Priorities for India." Conference on India's Economic Reforms, Center for Research on Economic Development and Policy Reform, Stanford University, June 5–7.

Fujimoto, T. 2003. *Competition in Creating Core Competence* (in Japanese). Chuokoron-sha.

Fujimoto, T., A. Takeishi, and Y. Aoshima, eds. 2001. *Business Architecture: Strategic Design of Products, Organizations, and Processes* (in Japanese). Yuhikaku.

Fuller, D. B. 2005. "The Changing Limits and the Limits of Change: The State, Private Firms, China and Global Industry in the Evolution of Taiwan's Electronics Industry." *Journal of Contemporary China* 14(45).

Gadrey, J., and F. Gallouj. 1998. "The Provider-Customer Interface in Business and Professional Services." *Services Industries Journal* 18(2):1–15.

Gerschenkron, A. 1962. *Economic Backwardness in Historical Perspective.* Cambridge, MA: Harvard University Press.

Ghemawat, P. 2000. "The Indian Software Industry at the Millennium." Case 9-700-036, Harvard Business School.

Gibson, D., G. Kozmetsky, and R. Smilor. 1992. *The Technopolis Phenomenon.* Lanham, MD: Rowman & Littlefield.

Gompers, P. 1995. "Optimal Investment, Monitoring, and the Staging of Venture Capital." *Journal of Finance* 50:1461–1489.

Goto, A. 2000. *Innovation and Japanese Economy.* Iwanami Shinsho.

Granovetter, M., and R. Swedberg, eds. 2001. *The Sociology of Economic Life.* Boulder, CO: Westview Press.

Grove, A. S. 1999. *Only the Paranoid Survive: How to Exploit the Crisis Points That Challenge Every Company.* New York: Doubleday.

Guillen, M. F. 2001. *The Limits of Convergence: Globalization and Organizational Change in Argentina, South Korea, and Spain.* Princeton, NJ: Princeton University Press.

Hamada, Y. 1999. *Nihon no Bencha Kyapitaru.* Tokyo: Nihon Keizai Shimbun.

Handler, M. 2002. "Bust in Bangalore." *San Francisco Chronicle,* April 1.

Hashimoto, M. 2003. "New Industrial Policy to Enhance the Cooperation between University and Industry by METI." Presentation, Status of Japanese Technology Transfer Workshop, AUTM Annual Meeting, February.

Hayashi, T., and T. Bunno. 2003. "Venture Business Growth and the Cluster Factors" (in Japanese). SJC Discussion Paper DP-2003-004-J. http://www.stanford-jc.or.jp/research/publication/DP/DP_e.html.

364   He, Z. L., and P. K. Wong. 2003. "Exploration vs. Exploitation: An Empirical Test of the Impact of Innovation Strategy on Firm Performance." Working paper, NUS Entrepreneurship Centre, National University of Singapore.

Heeks, R. 1996. *India's Software Industry.* New Delhi: Sage.

Heitzman, J. 1999. "Corporate Strategy and Planning in the Science City: Bangalore as Silicon Valley." *Economic and Political Weekly* (January 30).

Heritage Foundation. 2004. *2004 Index of Economic Freedom.* http://www.heritage .org/research/features/index.

Hicks, D. 2004. "Benchmarking Growth: Are We Looking in the Wrong Direction?" Presentation, Tokyo.

High Tech Austin Annual LLC. 2002. "High Tech Austin: The Ultimate Who's Who of the Austin High-Tech Community." 4th ed.

High Tech Austin Annual OECD. 1999. "Boosting Innovation: The Cluster Approach."

———. 2001. "Innovative Clusters: Drivers of National Innovation System."

Ho, Y. P., M. H. Toh, and P. K. Wong. 2003. "The Impact of R&D on the Singapore Economy: An Empirical Evaluation." Working paper, NUS Entrepreneurship Centre, National University of Singapore.

Hock, C. J. 2001. Telephone interview of senior vice president, Vertex Management Inc., by Martin Kenney, March 29. Redwood City, California.

Hokkaido History of IT Industry. 2000. "The Birth of Sapporo Valley." Yellow Page.

Hong, C. Y. 2001. "Capital Investment and Industrial Takeoff." *Energy: How to Create Miracles for Semiconductor and PC Industries.* Chinatimes.

Hong, Y. E. 2003. "Innovation Engine—ITRI: The Hand That Rocks the Success of Industry in Taiwan." Common Wealth.

Hsinchu Science-based Industrial Park. http://www.sipa.gov.tw/index_apis.php.

Hsu, C. W., and H. C. Chiang. 2001. "The Government Strategy for the Upgrading of Industrial Technology in Taiwan." *Technovation* 21:123–132.

Hsu, J. Y. 1997. "Development of Semiconductor Technology in Taiwan—Government Intervention, Cross-Boundary Social Network and High-Tech Development." *Geography Journal* 23. Department of Geography, College of Natural Sciences, National Taiwan University.

———. 1999. "A Flowing Mount: Labor Market and High-Tech Development in HSIP." *Taiwan: A Radical Quarterly in Social Studies* 35.

———. 2001. "Time Strategy and Dynamic Learning of Enterprises: An Example of IC Industry in HSIP." *Cities and Design* (11/12):67–96.

Hsu, T.-L. 1999. Interview with Ta-Lin Hsu. *Asian Venture Capital Journal* (December): 26.

Hsu, T. S., C. Y. Tong, and M. H. Chuang. 1998. "National Innovation System and Innovation Policy Analysis—Empirical Study on IC Industry in Taiwan." *Science and Technology Management Journal* 3(2):127–154.

Hu, A. 2003. "Multinational Corporations, Patenting, and Knowledge Flow: The Case of Singapore." Working paper, Economics Department, National University of Singapore.

Hu, A. G. Z., and A. Jaffe. 2001. "Patent Citations and International Knowledge Flow:

The Cases of Korea and Taiwan." Working Paper 8528, National Bureau of Economic Research.

Huang, C. C., and R. I. Wu. 2003. "Entrepreneurship in Taiwan: Turning Point to Restart." CELCEE Publications, c20031276.

Huang, T. H. 2001. "The Legend of Notebook Computer." *Energy: How to Create Miracles for Semiconductor and PC Industries.* Chinatimes.

Huang, W. C. 1998. "Make the Dreams Come True: The Incubator." *ST-Pioneer* 4.

Huang, Y. 2003. *Selling China.* Cambridge, UK: Cambridge University Press.

Iizuka, T. 2003. "Challenge of Spin-off Start-up." PHP.

Imai, K. 1992. "Japan's Corporate Networks." In S. Kumon and H. Rosovsky, eds. *The Political Economy of Japan: Cultural and Social Dynamics.* Stanford, CA: Stanford University Press.

Imai, K., and I. Kaneko. 1988. *Network Organization Theory* (in Japanese). Iwanami Shoten.

Indian Express. 2003. Retrieved January 9, 2003, from http://www.indianexpress.com/full_story.php?content_id=16354.

Indian Institute of Management. 2003. Retrieved January 8, 2003, from http://www.iimahd.ernet.in/acads/acadsmain.htm.

Indian Ministry of Finance. 1988. Venture Capital Guidelines. Press Release S.11(86)-CCI(11)/87, Department of Economic Affairs, Office of the Controller of Capital Issues, November 25.

Industrial Technology Research Institute (ITRI). 2003. "Industrial Technology and ITRI—The Seeing Brain." Industrial Technology Research Institute, Hsinchu, Taiwan.

International Institute for Management Development (IMD). (various years). *World Competitiveness Yearbook.* Lausanne, Switzerland: Author.

Ishihara, Y., N. Maeda et al. 2003. *Strategy for Cluster Initiatives in Japan.* Yuhikaku.

IT Workforce. 1999. "Assessing the Demand for Information Technology Workers, IT Workforce." Arlington, VA: National Science Foundation.

Itami, H., S. Matsushima, and T. Kikkawa. 1998. *Sangyo Shuseki no Honshitsu* [*The Nature of Industrial Agglomeration*]. Tokyo: Yuhikaku.

Ito, T. 2003. "Expectation and New Strategy for New University Collaboration." Presentation, Status of Japanese Technology Transfer Workshop, AUTM Annual Meeting, February.

Jacobs, J. 1961. *The Death and Life of Great American Cities.* Kajima Institute Publishing.

Johnson, C. 1982. *MITI and the Japanese Miracle: The Growth of Industrial Policy, 1925–1975.* Stanford, CA: Stanford University Press.

Johnson, S. 2001. *Emergence: The Connected Lives of Ants, Brains, Cities, and Software.* New York: Scribner.

Jun, M. 2004. "Collaborative R&D between Tsinghua University and Multinational Companies." Paper submitted to SPRIE Research Workshop: University-Research Institute-Industry Relations in the U.S., Taiwan and Mainland China, Stanford University, September 7–8.

366   Kaufman, S. 1986. "H&Q's Open Door Policy into Far East Venture Capital." *San Jose Mercury News*, November 17, p. 7D.

Kazanjian, R. K. 1988. "Relation of Dominant Problems to Stages of Growth in Technology-Based New Ventures." *Academy of Management Journal* 31(2):257–279.

Kelkar, V., D. Chaturvedi, and M. Dar. 1991. "India's Information Economy: Role, Size and Scope." *Economic and Political Weekly* (September 14): 2153–2160.

Keller, W. 2004. "International Technology Diffusion." *Journal of Economic Literature* 42(3):752.

Kenney, M. 1986. *Biotechnology: The University-Industrial Complex*. New Haven, CT: Yale University Press.

Kenney, M., and R. Florida. 2000. "Venture Capital in Silicon Valley: Fueling New Firm Formation." In M. Kenney, ed. *Understanding Silicon Valley: Anatomy of an Entrepreneurial Region*. Stanford, CA: Stanford University Press, pp. 98–123.

———. 2004. *Locating Global Advantage*. Stanford, CA: Stanford University Press.

Kenney, M., K. Han, and S. Tanaka. 2002. "Scattering Geese: The Venture Capital Industries of East Asia." Report to the World Bank, Washington, DC.

———. 2004. "The Venture Capital Industries." In S. Yusuf, M. A. Altaf, and K. Nabeshima, eds. *Global Change and East Asian Policy Initiatives*. New York: Oxford University Press.

Kim, J. G., and SPRIE Team. 2002. *Venture Habitat of Teheran Valley: Analysis and Long-Term Planning* (in Korean). Hoseo University.

Kleiner Perkins Caufield & Byers (KPCB). 2001. Retrieved from http://www.kpcb.com.

Kneller, R. 2003. "University-Industry Cooperation and Technology Transfer in Japan Compared with the US: Another Reason for Japan's Economic Malaise?" *University of Pennsylvania Journal of International Law* 24(2).

———. 2004. "Transformation of Japan's National Universities into Administratively Independent Corporations." *Les Novelles* (March): 1–5.

———. 2004. "The New Japanese System of Technology Transfer: Concerns Related to the Role of University IP Centers." *Les Novelles* (June): 69–72.

Kodama, T. 2003. "TAMA Initiative as a Leading Example of Cluster Formation in Japan" (in Japanese). Unpublished manuscript.

Kodato, S. 2003. "New Management Policy for IP and Technology Transfer." Presentation, Status of Japanese Technology Transfer Workshop, AUTM Annual Meeting, February.

Kondo, M., and N. Maeda. 2002. "A Study of European Start-up Supporting Policies." Unpublished manuscript, Economic Research Center/Kochi University of Technology.

Korea Information Strategy Development Institute (KISDI). 2003. *IT Industry Outlook of Korea 2004*.

Korea Technology Investment Corp. http://www.ktic.co.kr/eng/main.asp.

Korea Times. 2004. "More High-Tech Research Centers Flock Here." (October 22).

Korean Development Investment Corporation (KDIC). 1986. *Annual Report*. Seoul: Author.

Korean Technology and Banking Network Corporation (KTB). 2001. http://www.ktb.co.kr.

Kortum, S., and J. Lerner. 2000. "Assessing the Contribution of Venture Capital to 367 Innovation." *RAND Journal of Economics* 31(4):674–692.

Kripalani, M., and P. Engardio. 2003. "The Rise of India." *Business Week* (December 8): 66–76.

Krugman, P. 1991. *Geography and Trade.* Cambridge, MA: MIT Press.

———. 1994. "The Myth of Asia's Miracle." *Foreign Affairs* (November).

Kuemmerle, W. 2001. "Comparing Catalysts of Change: Evolution and Institutional Differences in the Venture Capital Industries in the U.S., Japan and Germany." In R. A. Burgelman and H. Chesbrough, eds. *Research on Technological Innovation, Management and Policy.* Greenwich, CT: JAI Press, pp. 227–261.

Kyushu Industrial Advancement Center. 2000. *An Approach to the Strategic Industries in Kyushu Area* (in Japanese).

Lateef, A. 1997. "Linking Up with the Global Economy: A Case Study of Bangalore's Software Industry." Retrieved May 20, 2002, from www.ilo.org.

Lazonick, W. 2004. "Indigenous Innovation and Economic Development: Lessons from China's Leap into the Information Age." *Industry and Innovation* 11(4): 273–297.

Leachman, R. C., and C. H. Leachman. 2004. In M. Kenney and R. Florida, eds. *Locating Global Advantage.* Stanford, CA: Stanford University Press.

Lee, C.-M., W. Miller, M. G. Hancock, and H. Rowen, eds. 2000. *The Silicon Valley Edge: A Habitat for Innovation and Entrepreneurship.* Stanford, CA: Stanford University Press.

Lee, J., and Chun, H. K. 2002. "The Venture Habitat to Nurture Technology Transfer from University to Venture in Korea." Paper presented at the Tokyo Technology Transfer Seminar, Tokyo.

Lee, K. B., and SPRIE Team. 2002. *An Analysis of Korea's Venture Nurturing System: Policy Study* (in Korean). Information and Communications University.

Lin, H.-Y., and Y. Lin. 1990. "Industrial R&D Trends and Related Policy in Taiwan." Industrial Technology Research Institute, Hsinchu, Taiwan.

Lin, T. I., and Y. Lin. 1990. "The Study of Industrial R&D Development and Policy in Taiwan." Industrial Technology Research Institute, Hsinchu, Taiwan.

Liu, C. H. 2004. "Taiwan's Higher Education Reform towards Building a Knowledge-Based Economy." Paper submitted to SPRIE Research Workshop: University-Research Institute-Industry Relations in the U.S., Taiwan and Mainland China, Stanford University, September 7–8.

Maeda, N. 1999. "Japanese New Business Model." NISTEP Policy Study 3.

———. 1999. *The Transnational Strategy by Autonomous New Combination* (in Japanese). Tokyo: Doyukan.

———. 2000. "From Collaboration to Combination of University, Industry and Government." *Organizational Science* 34(1).

———. 2002. *Spin-off Revolution.* Toyo Keizai Publishing.

———. 2003. "Restructuring of Japanese Innovation System with High-Tech Start-ups: Creative Destruction of Catch-up Model, in Micro, Macro and Regional Levels" (in Japanese). SJC Discussion Paper DP-2003-003-J. http://www.stanford-jc.or.jp/research/publication/DP/DP_e.html.

368   Maeda, N., et al. 2003. "Success Factors and Policy of Regional Cluster." NISTEP Discussion Paper 29.

MAP2003 Organization Committee. 2003. Database of Semiconductor Companies in Kyushu and Asian Countries. Kyushu Economic Research Center.

Mathews, J. A., and D.-S. Cho. 2000. *Tiger Technology: The Creation of a Semiconductor Technology in East Asia.* Cambridge, UK: Cambridge University Press.

McKendrick, D. 2004. "Leveraging Locations: Hard Disk Drive Producers in International Competition." In M. Kenney and R. Florida, eds. *Locating Global Advantage.* Stanford, CA: Stanford University Press, pp. 142–174.

McKendrick, D. G., R. F. Doner, and S. Haggard. 2000. *From Silicon Valley to Singapore: Location and Competitive Advantage in the Hard Disk Drive Industry.* Stanford, CA: Stanford University Press.

Meng, M. 2004. "Innovation Feedback: Interactive Development in Research Universities and Their Science Parks." Paper submitted to SPRIE Research Workshop: University-Research Institute-Industry Relations in the U.S., Taiwan and Mainland China, Stanford University, September 7–8.

Meyer-Krahmer, F. 1997. "Science-Based Technologies and Interdisciplinarity: Challenges for Firms and Policy." In C. Edquist, ed. *Systems of Innovation: Technologies, Institutions, and Organizations.* London: Pinter, pp. 298–317.

Ministry of Economy, Trade and Industry (METI). 2001. *The Creative Transformation of Japanese Organizations* (in Japanese). Marui Press.

———. 2003. "Guide to Technology Licensing Organizations (TLOs) in Japan." Industry-University Cooperation Division.

Ministry of Human Resource Development. 2001. "Technical Education Quality Improvement Project of the Government of India." Sections 2.1.2–2.1.6.

Ministry of Information and Communication (MIC). 1991. "Review on PC Industry in Taiwan."

———. 2002. *IT Korea 2002.* Republic of Korea.

Ministry of Labour. (various years). *Singapore Yearbook of Labour Statistics.* Singapore: Author.

Ministry of Manpower. (various years). *Singapore Yearbook of Manpower Statistics.* Singapore: Author.

Miwa, Y., and J. M. Ramseyer. 2002. "Socialist Bureaucrats? Legends of Government Planning from Japan." Discussion Paper 385, John M. Olin Center for Law, Economics and Business, Harvard University.

Murtha, T. P., S. A. Lenway, and J. Hart. 2001. *Managing New Industry Creation: Global Knowledge Formation and Entrepreneurship in High Technology.* Stanford, CA: Stanford University Press.

Nair, J. 2002. "Singapore Is Not Bangalore's Destiny." *Economic and Political Weekly* (April 29). Retrieved May 30, 2002, from www.epw.org.in.

Narin, F. 2003. Presentation, CHI Research, NAS Sackler Colloquium, Irvine, CA, May 11.

Nasscom. 2002. *Strategic Review.* New Delhi: Author.

———. 2004. *Strategic Review.* New Delhi: Author.

National Science Foundation. 2002. S&E Indicators. Appendix Tables 2-29, 2-36, 2-41.
——. 2004. S&E Indicators. Appendix Tables 2-36, 5-52.

National Venture Capital Association (NVCA). 2001. *National Venture Capital Association Yearbook*. Arlington, VA: Author.

——. 2002. *National Venture Capital Association Yearbook*. Arlington, VA: Author.

NCsoft. http://www.ncsoft.com.

Nelson, R., and N. Rosenberg. 1993. "Technical Innovation and National Systems." In R. Nelson, ed. *National Innovation Systems*. New York: Oxford University Press.

Nelson, R. R., and S. G. Winter. 1982. *An Evolutionary Theory of Economic Change*. Cambridge, MA: Harvard University Press.

Niimi, K., and Y. Okina. 1995. "Bencha Bijinesu no Seicho o Habamumono ha Nanika." *Japan Research Review* (May). Retrieved from http://www.jri.co.jp/jrr/1995/199505.

Nishiguchi, T. 1994. *Strategic Industrial Sourcing: The Japanese Advantage*. New York: Oxford University Press.

Nishizawa, A. 2003. "The New Management System of Intellectual Property Rights in Japanese National Universities." *Innovation Matters* 1(6).

NUS Consulting. 2003. *NUS 2002 Graduate Employment Survey Report*. Singapore: Author.

Oakey, R., and S. Cooper. 1989. "High Technology Industry, Agglomeration, and the Potential for Peripherally Sited Small Firms." *Regional Studies* 23:347–360.

Ohkawa, K., and H. Rosovsky. 1973. *Japanese Economic Growth: Trend Acceleration in the Twentieth Century*. Stanford, CA: Stanford University Press.

Okimoto, D. 1990. *Between MITI and the Market: Japanese Industrial Policy for High Technology*. Palo Alto, CA: Stanford University Press.

Ono, M. 1995. "Venture Capital in Japan: Current Overview." Retrieved August 24, 2000, from http://www.asahi-net.or.jp/~sh3m-on/venturecapitalommune/javc/jvcs.htm.

Organization for Economic Co-operation and Development (OECD). 2003. "Turning Science into Business: Patenting and Licensing at Public Research Organizations."

Oster, S. 2001. "Nothing Ventured." *AsiaWeek.com*, July 27–August 3.

Pandey, I. M. 1998. "The Process of Developing Venture Capital in India." *Technovation* 18(4):253–261.

Pandey, I. M., and A. Jang. 1996. "Venture Capital for Financing Technology in Taiwan." *Technovation* 16(9):499–514.

Parathasarathy, B. 2000. "Globalization and Agglomeration in Newly Industrializing Countries: The State and the Information Technology Industry in Bangalore, India." PhD Thesis, University of California, Berkeley.

Park, A. 2003. "EDS: What Went Wrong." *Business Week* (April 7): 60–63.

Patibandla, M., and B. Petersen. 2002. "Role of Transnational Corporations in the Evolution of a High-Tech Industry: The Case of India's Software Industry." *World Development* 30(9):1561–1577.

Porter, E. 2004. "Indian Techies Lack Creative Ability, Feel US Firms." *New York Times*, April 29.

Porter, M. E. 1990. *The Competitive Advantage of Nations*. New York: Free Press.

370 ———. 1998. "Clusters and the New Economics of Competition." *Harvard Business Review* (November–December): 77–90.

———. 1998. *On Competition.* Boston: Harvard Business School Press.

———. 2000. "Location, Competition, and Economic Development: Local Clusters in a Global Economy." *Economic Development Quarterly* 14(1):15–34.

———. 2001. "Cluster of Innovation." Regional Foundations of U.S. Competitiveness, Council on Competitiveness.

Porter, M., and H. Takeuchi. 2000. *Can Japan Compete?* Diamond.

ReignCom. http://www.reigncom.com.

Republic of China, Ministry of Finance. 1996. "The Venture Capital Industry in the Republic of China" (May).

Reynolds, P., W. Bygrave, E. Autin, and M. Hayl. 2002. *Global Entrepreneurship Monitor Global 2002 Summary Report.* Wellesley, MA: Babson College.

Rosenberg, D. 2002. *Cloning Silicon Valley: The Next Generation High Tech Hotspots.* New York: Prentice-Hall.

Rosenberg, N., and L. E. Birdzell, Jr. 1986. *How the West Grew Rich.* New York: Basic Books.

Rowen, H., ed. 1998. *Behind East Asian Growth.* London: Routledge.

Rowen, H. S., and A. M. Toyoda. 2003. "Japan Has Few High-Tech Startups: Can It Be Changed? Does It Matter?" Asia/Pacific Research Center, Stanford University.

Rubin, B. R. 1985. "Economic Liberalization and the India State." *Third World Quarterly* 7(4):942–957.

Sagari, S. B., and G. Guidotti. 1991. "Venture Capital: Lessons from the Developed World for the Developing Markets." Discussion Paper 13, International Finance Corporation.

Sakakibara, K. 1999. "Entrepreneur Business—Japanese Issue." NISTEP Policy Study 2.

San, G. 2001. "The Returnee's Influence to High-Tech Industry—The Case of HSIP." *Human Resource and High-Tech Industrial Development in Taiwan.* Research Center for Taiwan Economic Development, National Central University.

San Jose Mercury News. July 8, 2005.

Sandelin, J. 2002. Report from the Higher Education Policymakers Exchange on Technology Transfer and IPR Protection, October 26–November 8, People's Republic of China.

———. 2004. Survey Results from National University of Singapore, Nanyang Technical University, and Agency for Science, Technology and Research (A*STAR); and materials obtained during August 2002 visit with NUS and A*STAR.

Saperstein, J., and D. Rouach. 2002. *Creating Regional Wealth in the Innovation Economy: Models, Perspectives, and Best Practices.* Upper Saddle River, NJ: Pearson Education, p. 235.

Sapporo Valley. 2002. "Spirits of Sapporo Valley." Sapporo Industry Development.

Saxenian, A. 1994. *Regional Advantage: Culture and Competition in Silicon Valley and Route 128.* Cambridge, MA: Harvard University Press.

———. 1999. *Silicon Valley's New Immigrant Entrepreneurs.* San Francisco: Public Policy Institute of California.

———. 2000. "Bangalore: The Silicon Valley of Asia?" Conference on Indian Economic Prospects: Advancing Policy Reform, Center for Research on Economic Development and Policy Reform, Stanford University.

———. 2004. "Taiwan's Hsinchu Region: Imitator and Partner for Silicon Valley." In *Building High-Tech Clusters: Silicon Valley and Beyond.* Cambridge, UK: Cambridge University Press, pp. 190–228.

Saxenian, A., and C.-Y. Li. 2003. "Bay-to-Bay Strategic Alliances: The Network Linkages between Taiwan and the US Venture Capital Industries." *International Journal of Technology Management* 25(1/2):136–150.

Schumpeter, J. A. 1926. *Theorie der Wirtschaftlichen Entwicklung.* Iwanami Shoten.

———. 1934. *The Theory of Economic Development.* Cambridge, MA: Harvard Business Press.

———. 1939. *Business Cycles.* New York: McGraw-Hill.

Schware, R. 1992. "Software Industry Entry Strategies for Developing Countries: A 'Walking on Two Legs' Proposition." *World Development* 20(2):143–164.

Segal, A. 2002. *Digital Dragon: High Technology Enterprises in China.* Ithaca, NY: Cornell University Press.

Shanghai Jiao Tong University Science Park. 2004. Presentation, International Forum of University Science Park, October 20–21.

Shih, C. T. 2001. "History and Prospects of IC Industry Development in Taiwan."

———. 2001. "Innovation and Entrepreneurship—High Technology Development in Taiwan." SPRIE Research Workshop.

———. "R&D and Innovation Trends of Industry-Research Institution Cooperation." Science and Technology Policy Development Report SR9001.

Shih, S. 1996. *Me-Too Is Not My Style.* Taipei: Acer Foundation.

Shimizu, K. 2003. "Management and Tech-Transfer Activities at a Private University— Keio University's Experience." Presentation, Status of Japanese Technology Transfer Workshop, AUTM Annual Meeting, February.

Singapore Department of Statistics (DOS). (various years). "Singapore's Corporate Sector." Singapore: Author.

———. 2001. "Contribution of Government-Linked Companies to Gross Domestic Product." DOS Occasional Paper, March.

Siwek, S. E., and H. W. Furchgott-Roth. 1993. *International Trade in Computer Software.* Westport, CT: Quorum Books.

Small and Medium Business Administration (SMBA). 1999–2003. *Annual Survey Report.* Republic of Korea.

SME White Book. 2002.

Smilor, R. W., G. Kozmetsky, and D. V. Gibson. 1988. *Creating the Technopolis: Linking Technology Commercialization and Economic Development.* New York: Ballinger.

Softbank Investment. 2001. "Kaisha Gaiyo." Retrieved from http://www.sbinvestment .co.jp.

Song, J. 2004. "How Tsinghua Manages Its Companies." Paper submitted to SPRIE Research Workshop: University-Research Institute-Industry Relations in the U.S., Taiwan and Mainland China, Stanford University, September 7–8.

372 Srinivas, S. 1997. "The Information Technology Industry in Bangalore: A Case of Urban Competitiveness in India?" Paper presented at the Fifth Asian Urbanization Conference, London.

STAG. http://www.stag.gov.tw/content/application/stag/about/index-english.php?ico=1&selname=about.

Suchman, M. C. 2000. "Dealmakers and Counselors: Law Firms as Intermediaries in the Development of Silicon Valley." In M. Kenney, ed. *Understanding Silicon Valley*. Stanford, CA: Stanford University Press, pp. 71–97.

Taiwan Stock Exchange Corporation. http://www.tse.com.tw/home.htm.

Taiwan Venture Capital Association (TVCA). 2003. *Taiwan Venture Capital Association Yearbook*.

Tanaka, S. 2003. "New System of IP Management and Technology Transfer of the Japanese University." Presentation, Status of Japanese Technology Transfer Workshop, AUTM Annual Meeting, February.

Teubal, M. 2002. "The Indian Software Industry from an Israeli Perspective: A Microeconomic and Policy Analysis." *Science, Technology and Society*. New Delhi: Sage.

The Times Higher Education Supplement. November 5, 2004.

Timmons, J. A., and S. Spinelli. 2003. *New Venture Creation: Entrepreneurship for the 21st Century* (6th ed.). Burr Ridge, IL: Irwin.

Tomokage, H., ed. 2003. *Innovation: Spirits of Technology* (in Japanese). Kyushu Semiconductor Industries Technology Innovation Association.

Torrisi, S. 2002. "Software Clusters in Emerging Regions." Working paper, University of Camerino.

Tsai, C. L., and B. F. Dai. 2001. "Trends and Impacts of Returned Talents in Taiwan: An Example of High-Tech Industry."

Tsay, C. Y., and Chu, Y.-P. 2004. "Building Bridges among Universities, Research Institutes, and Industry in Taiwan." Paper submitted to SPRIE Research Workshop: University-Research Institute-Industry Relations in the U.S., Taiwan and Mainland China, Stanford University, September 7–8.

Tschang, F., A. Amsden, and S. Sadagopan. 2003. "Measuring Technological Upgrading in the Indian Software Industry: A Framework of R&D Capabilities and Business Models." Working paper, Asian Development Bank Institute.

UltraChina.com. 2000. "Hidden Risks in China's Venture Capital Investment." June 2.

Viswanathan, V. 2001. "Wipro's Offsprings." *Business World* 12:38–45.

Wade, R. 1990. *Governing the Market: Economic Theory and the Role of Government in East Asian Industrialization*. Princeton, NJ: Princeton University Press.

Wall Street Journal. 1951. "Japan's Recovery Seen Dependent on Inflow of Venture Capital." November 16, p. 16.

Walsh, K. 2003. "Foreign High-Tech R&D in China: Risks, Rewards and Implications for U.S.-China Relations." Monograph, Henry L. Stimson Center.

Wang, C. 2002. "Differences in the Governance Structure of Venture Capital: The Singaporean Venture Capital Industry." Paper presented at the European Union/United Nations University International Conference on Financial Systems, Corporate Investment in Innovation and Venture Capital, Brussels, November 7–8.

Wang, C., P. K. Wong, and Q. Lu. 2002. "Tertiary Education and Entrepreneurial Intentions." In P. Phan, ed. *Technological Entrepreneurship*. Greenwich, CT: IAP Press, pp. 55–82.

Wang, E. C. 2002. "Public Infrastructure and Economic Growth: A New Approach Applied to East Asian Economics." *Journal of Policy Modeling* 24(5):411–435.

Wang, K. 2001. "The Comparison of Innovation Strategy to IC Industrial Clusters of Taiwan and China." The Technological Policy Forum of Taiwan and China in 2001, Kuo Ding Li's Technological Development Fund.

———. 2002. "Report of Technology Talent Requirement Survey." ITRI-IEK.

———. 2004. "The ITRI Experience: Innovative Engine of Taiwan's High Tech Industry." Paper submitted to SPRIE Research Workshop: University-Research Institute-Industry Relations in the U.S., Taiwan and Mainland China, Stanford University, September 7–8.

Wang, K., et al. 2003. "Hsinchu Science-based Industrial Park: Past, Present and Future." Anthology of papers presented at the First ITRI Symposium on Science Cluster Development—Silicon Valley, Hsinchu and Shanghai.

Wang, L.-R. 1995. "Taiwan's Venture Capital: Policies and Impacts." *Journal of Industry Studies* 2(1):83–94.

Wang, W. C. 2002. "Analysis on Development of Advanced Level Science and Technology Labor in HSIP." *Guidepost for Science and Technology Development Quarterly* 2(2).

White, S., J. Gao, and W. Zhang. 2002. "China's Venture Capital Industry: Institutional Trajectories and System Structure." Paper presented at the European Union/United Nations University International Conference on Financial Systems, Corporate Investment in Innovation and Venture Capital, Brussels, November 7–8.

Whitman, J. 1990. "Key Factors for Software Success." Unpublished manuscript, Oakland Group, Cambridge, MA.

"The Window to the World Technology." Publication of Tsinghua Science Park.

WIPO: Small and Medium-Sized Enterprises. 2004. "Outreach Activities on Intellectual Property of the Small Industries Development Organization (SIDO) of India."

Wong, P. K. 1992. "Technological Development through Subcontracting Linkages: Evidence from Singapore." *Scandinavian International Business Review* 1(3):8–40.

———. 1998. "Leveraging the Global Information Revolution for Economic Development: Singapore's Evolving Information Industry Strategy." *Information Systems Research* 9(4).

———. 1999. "University-Industry Technological Collaboration in Singapore: Emerging Patterns and Industry Concerns." *International Journal of Technology Management* 17(3/4).

———. 2000. In D. G. McKendrick, R. F. Doner, and S. Haggard, eds. *From Silicon Valley to Singapore: Location and Competitive Advantage in the Hard Disk Drive Industry*. Stanford, CA: Stanford University Press.

———. 2002. "Benchmarking the Regional Nexus of Innovation and Entrepreneurship." SPRIE Research Workshop, February 25–27.

374 ———. 2002. "Globalization of American, European and Japanese Production Networks and the Growth of Singapore's Electronics Industry." *International Journal of Technology Management* 24(7/8):843–869.

———. 2002. "Manpower Development in the Digital Economy: The Case of Singapore." In M. Makishima, ed. *Human Resource Development in the Information Age: The Case of Singapore and Malaysia.* Tokyo: IDE/JETRO, pp. 79–122.

———. 2003. "From Using to Creating Technology: The Evolution of Singapore's National Innovation System and the Changing Role of Public Policy." In S. Lall and S. Urata, eds. *Competitiveness, FDI and Technological Activity in East Asia.* London: Edward Elgar.

———. 2003. "The Nexus of Innovation and Entrepreneurship: Towards a Dynamic Model of High Tech Enterprise Ecosystem." Working paper, NUS Entrepreneurship Centre, National University of Singapore.

———. 2004. "Profile of Business Angel Investors in Singapore." Working paper, NUS Entrepreneurship Centre, National University of Singapore.

Wong, P. K., and Z. L. He. 2003. "Local Embeddedness, Global Networking: The Impact of Innovation Networks on the Innovation Performance of Firms." Working paper, NUS Entrepreneurship Centre, National University of Singapore.

———. 2003. "The Impact of Public R&D Support on Firm's Innovation Performance: The Moderating Effect of Firm's Innovation Climate." *International Journal of Entrepreneurship and Innovation Management.*

———. 2004. "A Comparative Study of Innovation Behaviour in Singapore's KIBS and Manufacturing Firms." *Service Industries Journal* 25(2).

Wong, P. K., and Y. P. Ho. 2003. *Comparative Analysis of the Pattern and Composition of IP Creation in Singapore vs. Selected Advanced OECD Nations and NIEs.* Research report, NUS Entrepreneurship Centre, National University of Singapore.

Wong, P. K., M. Kiese, A. Singh, and F. Wong. 2003. "The Pattern of Innovation in Singapore's Manufacturing Sector." *Singapore Management Review* 25(1):1–34.

Wong, P. K., L. Lee, and Z. L. He. 2004. "Propensities of Spin-outs from Existing Firms." Working paper, NUS Entrepreneurship Centre, National University of Singapore.

Wong, P. K., and A. Singh. 2004. "The Pattern of Innovation in the Knowledge-Intensive Services Sector of Singapore." *Singapore Management Review* 26(1).

Wong, P. K., A. Singh et al. 2001. *Survey of Attitudes and Interest of Students in Higher Educational Institutions towards Entrepreneurship: Final Report.* Centre for Management of Innovation and Technopreneurship, National University of Singapore.

Wong, P. K., F. Wong, Y. P. Ho, A. Singh, and L. Lee. 2003. *Global Entrepreneurship Monitor 2002: Singapore Country Report.* Singapore: NUS Entrepreneurship Centre.

Woori Technology Investment Co. http://www.wooricapital.co.kr/eng1.htm.

World Bank. 1989. "India Industrial Technology Development Project Staff Appraisal Report." Washington, DC: Author.

———. 1993. "The East Asian Miracle: Economic Growth and Public Policy." Washington, DC: Author.

———. 2002. "GNI per Capita 2002 (Atlas Method and PPP)." *World Development Indicators.* Retrieved from http://www.worldbank.org/data/databytopic/GNIPC.pdf.

World Development Indicators. http://wbln0018.worldbank.org/psd/compete.nsf/f14ea5988boeec7f852564900068cbfd?OpenView&Start=1.

Wu, S. H., and R. C. Shen. 1999. "Formation and Development of IC Industry in Taiwan." *Taiwan Industry Studies* 1:57–150.

Wu, T. Y., et al. 1980. "How the Foreign Investment Influences Taiwan's Economy." Unpublished manuscript, Central Research Institute.

Xue, L. 2004. "University-Market Linkages in China: The Case of University-Affiliated Enterprises." Paper submitted to SPRIE Research Workshop: University-Research Institute-Industry Relations in the U.S., Taiwan and Mainland China, Stanford University, September 7–8.

Yamazaki, A. 2002. *Cluster Strategy.* Yuhikaku.

Yamazaki, A., and H. Tomokage, eds. 2001. *A Scenario for Creating Semiconductor Cluster* (in Japanese). Nishinihon-shinbunsha.

Yasunobe, S. 2003. "Social and Economic Stickiness Surrounding Entrepreneurs and Evolving Changes in Japan" (in Japanese). Unpublished manuscript.

Young, A. 1992. "A Tale of Two Cities: Factor Accumulation and Technical Change in Hong Kong and Singapore." *NBER Macroeconomic Annual 1992.* Cambridge, MA: MIT Press.

Young, T. 2004. "Financing University Technology Transfer Offices." *Innovation Matters* 2(10).

Yourdon, E. 1992. *Decline and Fall of the American Programmer.* Englewood Cliffs, NJ: Yourdon Press, Prentice-Hall.

Zero-2-IPO. 2005. "Top 50 Venture Capitalists of the Year." Retrieved July 6, 2005, from http://www.zero2ipo.com.cn/en/China%20VC%20Ranking/China%20Venture%20Capital%20Annual%20Ranking%202004-list.pdf.

Zhang, J., P. K. Wong, and P. H. Soh. 2003. "Network Ties, Prior Knowledge, and the Acquisition of Resources in High Tech Entrepreneurship." Academy of Management Best Papers Proceedings, Seattle.

Zhao, M. 2004. "A Research Report on the Performance and Problems of University-Owned Firms in the Zhongguancun Science Park." Paper submitted to SPRIE Research Workshop: University-Research Institute-Industry Relations in the U.S., Taiwan and Mainland China, Stanford University, September 7–8.

Zucker, L. G., and M. R. Darby. 1995. "Virtuous Circles of Productivity: Star Bioscientists and the Institutional Transformation of Industry." Working Paper 5342, National Bureau of Economic Research.

———. 2005. "Socio-Economic Impact of Nanoscale Science: Initial Results and Nanobank." Working Paper 11181, National Bureau of Economic Research.

Index

Note: Page numbers in *italics* refer to figures and tables; those followed by *n* indicate endnotes.

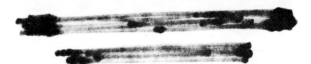

322

Nations University International Conference on Financial Systems, Corporate Investment in Innovation and Venture Capital, Brussels, November 7–8.

World Bank. 1989. "India Industrial Technology Development Project Staff Appraisal Report." Washington, DC: Author.

Zero-2-IPO. 2005. "Top 50 Venture Capitalists of the Year." Retrieved July 6, 2005, from http://www.zero2ipo.com.cn/en/China%20VC%20Ranking/China%20Venture%20Capital%20Annual%20Ranking%202004-list.pdf.

McKendrick, D. G, R. Doner, and S. Haggard. 2000. *From Silicon Valley to Singapore: Location and Competitive Advantage in the Hard Disk Drive Industry.* Stanford, CA: Stanford University Press.

National Venture Capital Association (NVCA). 2001. *National Venture Capital Association Yearbook.* Arlington, VA: Author.

———. 2002. *National Venture Capital Association Yearbook.* Arlington, VA: Author.

Nelson, R. R., and S. G. Winter. 1982. *An Evolutionary Theory of Economic Change.* Cambridge, MA: Harvard University Press.

Niimi, K., and Y. Okina. 1995. "Bencha Bijinesu no Seicho o Habamumono ha Nanika." *Japan Research Review* (May). Retrieved from http://www.jri.co.jp/jrr/1995/199505.

Nishiguchi, T. 1994. *Strategic Industrial Sourcing: The Japanese Advantage.* New York: Oxford University Press.

Ono, M. 1995. "Venture Capital in Japan: Current Overview." Retrieved August 24, 2000, from http://www.asahi-net.or.jp/~sh3m-on/venturecapitalommune/javc/jvcs.htm.

Oster, S. 2001. "Nothing Ventured." *AsiaWeek.com,* July 27–August 3.

Pandey, I. M. 1998. "The Process of Developing Venture Capital in India." *Technovation* 18(4):253–261.

Republic of China, Ministry of Finance. 1996. "The Venture Capital Industry in the Republic of China" (May).

Saxenian, A. 1999. *Silicon Valley's New Immigrant Entrepreneurs.* San Francisco: Public Policy Institute of California.

Saxenian, A., and C.-Y. Li. 2003. "Bay-to-Bay Strategic Alliances: The Network Linkages between Taiwan and the US Venture Capital Industries." *International Journal of Technology Management* 25(1/2):136–150.

Shih, S. 1996. *Me-Too Is Not My Style.* Taipei: Acer Foundation.

Softbank Investment. 2001. "Kaisha Gaiyo." Retrieved from http://www.sbinvestment.co.jp.

Suchman, M. C. 2000. "Dealmakers and Counselors: Law Firms as Intermediaries in the Development of Silicon Valley." In M. Kenney, ed. *Understanding Silicon Valley.* Stanford, CA: Stanford University Press, pp. 71–97.

Sussner, H. 2001. Telephone interview with senior managing director, H&Q Asia Pacific, by Martin Kenney, San Francisco, March 30.

UltraChina.com. 2000. "Hidden Risks in China's Venture Capital Investment." (June 2).

Wall Street Journal. 1951. "Japan's Recovery Seen Dependent on Inflow of Venture Capital." November 16, p. 16.

Wang, C. 2002. "Differences in the Governance Structure of Venture Capital: The Singaporean Venture Capital Industry." Paper presented at the European Union/United Nations University International Conference on Financial Systems, Corporate Investment in Innovation and Venture Capital, Brussels, November 7–8.

Wang, L.-R. 1995. "Taiwan's Venture Capital: Policies and Impacts." *Journal of Industry Studies* 2(1):83–94.

White, S., J. Gao, and W. Zhang. 2002. "China's Venture Capital Industry: Institutional Trajectories and System Structure." Paper presented at the European Union/United